Celebrating the Freedom of Literacy

**The Twenty-Fifth Yearbook
A Peer Reviewed Publication of
The College Reading Association
2003**

Co-Editors
**Mary Beth Sampson
Patricia E. Linder**
Texas A&M University-Commerce

Jo Ann R. Dugan
Ohio University

Barrie Brancato
Clarion University of Pennsylvania

Editorial Assistants
**Naga V. R. K. Burugapalli
Kimberly Klakamp
Sujith K. Chithamur**
Texas A&M University-Commerce

ISBN 1-883604-31-1

Printed at Texas A&M University-Commerce
Cover Design by Jonathan Sampson
Cover Photograph by Michael Sampson

Committee and Commission Chairpersons
Conference/Research Focus
Conference Coordinator, Barbara Reinken, Grand Valley State University
Program, Wayne M. Linek, Texas A&M University-Commerce
Elections, Maria Valeri-Gold, Georgia State University
Awards, Jane Brady Matanzo, Florida Atlantic University
Research, Julie K. Kidd, George Mason University; Charlene E. Fleener, Old
    Dominion University
Publications, Timothy G. Morrison, Brigham Young University

Organization Focus
Membership, Angela M. Ferree, Western Illinois University; Linda Thistle-
    thwaite, Western Illinois University
Public Information, Marie F. Holbein, State University of West Georgia; Donna
    M. Harkins, State University of West Georgia
Media, Patricia Douville, University of North Carolina at Charlotte
Historian, Gary L. Shaffer, Middle Tennessee State University
Photographer, Frederick J. Fedorko, East Stroudsburg University (Emerita)
Resolutions & Rules, William Dee Nichols, Virginia Tech; John P. Helfeldt, Texas
    A&M University
Legislative & Social Issues, Barbara J. Fox, North Carolina State University

Ad Hoc Committee
Technology, Marino Alvarez, Tennessee State University

CRA Editorial Advisory Board 2002-2003

Ruth A. Oswald, University of Akron
Gary M. Padak, Kent State University
Nancy Padak, Kent State University
Jackie Peck, Kent State University
Monica Gordon Pershey, Cleveland State University
Michael J. Pickle, St. Cloud State University
Diana J. Quatroche, Indiana State University
Taher Rahim, University of Toronto
Joanne Ratliff, University of Georgia
Mary Rearick, Eastern Michigan University
Ray D. Reutzel, Utah State University
Mary F. Roe, Washington State University
Lynn Romeo, Monmouth University
Leslie S. Rush, University of Wyoming
Barbara Kane Schneider, Grand Valley State University
Jonaid Sharif, Paine College
Roger Stewart, Boise State University
Mary W. Strong, Widener University
Agnes Stryker, Texas A&M University-Commerce
Denise H. Stuart, University of Akron
Mary E. Styslinger, University of South Carolina
Margaret-Mary Sulentic, East Baton Rouge Parish School System
Allison Swan, West Virginia University
Carol Wickstrom, University of North Texas
Katherine Wiesendanger, Alfred University
Linda S. Wold, Purdue University-Calumet
Yuanzhong Zhang, Miami-Dade Community College-North Campus

TABLE OF CONTENTS

ACKNOWLEDGEMENTS

We are grateful to so many who committed both time and expertise to make this yearbook possible. Obviously, this volume would not exist without the authors who devoted much energy and thought toward writing the articles presented here. We are especially grateful to the Editorial Review Board members who make possible the review/selection of manuscripts. They made a significant contribution to the selection and revision processes and we gratefully acknowledge the expertise they brought to the task. In addition, we express our gratitude to the CRA Publications Committee, which is chaired by Timothy G. Morrison of Brigham Young University. Furthermore, we are thankful for the unwavering commitment of the CRA Board of Directors who have supported the editorial team and the publication of the *CRA Yearbook* year after year.

This has been a year of transition of many of the people whose daily work make this yearbook a reality. We have been fortunate to have had three outstanding editorial assistants who attended to fine details and tracking of the manuscripts. We began this yearbook with Sujith K. Chithamur as our graduate assistant at Texas A&M University-Commerce. When he graduated and became a full time employee in New Jersey in June 2003, we were fortunate to complete the process with Texas A&M University-Commerce graduate assistants Kimberly Klakamp and Naga Burugapalli. Their dedication, enthusiasm, commitment and intellect made a smooth transition possible. We commend all three for their hard work and the long hours they spent reading manuscripts, communicating with reviewers, and communicating with authors.

We are extremely grateful for the extensive support provided by our universities. At Texas A&M University-Commerce, we thank President Keith McFarland, both former Provost and Academic Vice President Finnie Murray and current Provost and Academic Vice President Joyce Scott, and former Dean of the College of Education Jerry Hutton and current dean, Ed Siefert, for ongoing financial assistance, time and encouragement. We also extend a warm thanks to faculty in the Department of Elementary Education for their ongoing advocacy of the publication. At Clarion University of Pennsylvania, we thank President Diane L. Reinhard and Dean Gail Grejda, for supporting the Yearbook. In addition, at Ohio University we thank Dr. James L. Heap, Dean of the College of Education.

We are also grateful for the clerical assistance provided by our secretarial staff, Frances Norman and Jan Hazelip at Texas A&M University-Commerce. We both thank and recognize the dedication and expertise of Vivian Freeman at Texas A&M University-Commerce, who was in charge of the printing and production of the Yearbook. In addition, we wish to extend our appreciation to Jonathan Sampson for the cover design and Michael Sampson for the cover photo.

Finally, we extend a heartfelt thanks to our families, colleagues, friends, and readers. They have provided continual support of our professional efforts with their encouragement, acknowledgement, and genuine interest.

MBS, PEL, JRD, & BAB
November, 2003

INTRODUCTION
CELEBRATING THE FREEDOM OF LITERACY

At the conclusion of the 2002 Philadelphia conference, it seemed appropriate to continue the conference theme of "Celebrating the Freedom that Literacy Brings" to the title of this twenty-fifth volume—*Celebrating the Freedom of Literacy*. The title is intended to reflect the affirmation of the value and impact of literacy that we observed both in sessions at the conference and the manuscripts submitted to the *Yearbook*.

If you still have the Philadelphia program (and can find it!), we urge you to peruse the sessions and keynotes for the conference. Then, skim and scan the articles in this Yearbook. Every presentation and article focus in some way on examining and ensuring that all learners have access to literacy—for learning, communicating and personal use.

Our professional work indicates a belief that access to literacy does enhance the freedom that an individual and society has—the freedom to learn—to grow—to explore—to question—to communicate—to contrast and compare—to make informed decisions—the list goes on and on. Our presentations and manuscripts also indicate that we believe that as we engage in literacy research, teaching, and service it is critical for us to examine the impact of our actions on the people we work with—whether they be teachers, children, families, adult learners, community members, politicians, or colleagues. The title of this yearbook attempts to reflect these beliefs while the articles address them from many perspectives.

In Jane Mantanzo's Presidential Address, "Going Beyond: The Possibilities of Thinking and Literacy" we are challenged to both "think outside the box" and explore the differences between characteristics that promote innovation and those that maintain the status quo. It provides an opportunity to reflect on the lives of people such as Mary Bethune whose belief in the freedom of literacy motivated her to devote her life to providing increased access to literacy learning for young African American women who had previously been denied educational opportunities.

Cathleen Doheny and Sabiha Aydelott explore the impact of literacy "mentorship." They elaborate on how Dr. J. Estill Alexander challenged them to explore and extend both their own literacy and ways to enhance the literacy of teachers and students. You will read how he continually modeled this process of ongoing growth and learning by exploration, refinement and extension of his own literacy.

Our award winners explore ways to enhance literacy instruction. One examines how preservice strategy instruction impacted the beliefs and practices of a literacy teacher and the resulting influence on the instruction of children. The other describes a vocabulary learning process that positively impacted the literacy of college freshmen.

Perhaps the strongest message or theme from this year's *CRA Yearbook* is that it is how we use our literacy that determines if we are truly "celebrating the freedom of literacy." To "celebrate" the "freedom" we must assume the responsibility of using our "literacy" to both extend and refine our own understandings, knowledge and expertise and positively impact the lives of others. You will see this through the various sections of the *Yearbook* containing articles addressing elementary and secondary classrooms, diversity, preservice and inservice teacher education, technology, and programs that have undergone change.

The content of *Celebrating the Freedom of Literacy* reminds us that as educators we serve a pivotal role in ensuring that all learners value and understand the power of literacy and are proficient users of it. As you read the articles, you will observe that as educators we are dedicated to the literate—and personal growth of our students. It is our challenge—and opportunity—to remain dedicated so our future students will have access to the "freedom of literacy."

As educators, we should all remember the words of George Bernard Shaw:

> Life is not a brief candle to me.
> It is a sort of splendid torch which I have got
> Hold of for the moment,
> And I want to make it burn
> As brightly as possible before handing it on
> To future generations.

(Shaw, 1903, p. 31)

With the above words in mind, we dedicate the twenty-fifth volume of this yearbook to our colleagues—the educators who are dedicated to "handing on" the "torch" of literacy to present and future generations. We honor and are grateful for all you do to ensure that every learner has access to the *freedom* of literacy.

MBS, PEL, JRD, & BAB
November, 2003

Reference

Shaw, G. B. (1903). *Man and Superman: A comedy and a philosophy.* Cambridge, MA: The University Press.

PRESIDENTIAL
ADDRESS

GOING BEYOND: THE POSSIBILITIES OF THINKING AND LITERACY

PRESIDENTIAL ADDRESS

Jane Brady Matanzo

Florida Atlantic University

Jane Brady Matanzo has been very active in CRA for 30 years. She has served as President, President-Elect, an elected member of the CRA Board of Directors, Chair of the Public Information Committee for six years, Editor of Reading News for eight years, and a member of the Publications Committee. She has been a professor at various colleges and universities in Maryland, Washington, DC, Pennsylvania, and Ohio. She also has been an administrator in two school systems in Maryland. She currently is an Associate Professor at Florida Atlantic University where she has been honored as the University-wide Distinguished Teacher of the Year.

Abstract

This Presidential Speech focused on encouraging members to think "outside the box" and to ascertain areas of thinking and literacy development that should be stressed outside of what the National Reading Panel and others are saying, concerning scientifically based research and an emphasis on phonemic awareness and phonics instruction. Various CRA members were polled and their ideas about directions for the future are among the content presented. Tongue in cheek humor was given; however, it must be noted that efforts by the National Reading Panel and others are respected.

November 2, 2002

I am a collector of stories. As I travel and visit classrooms, I often leave with stories to share. My first story has its origins in India with another more familiar tale but has been retold here with different characters having a similar dilemma. As I paraphrase this story, consider which original story it reminds you of and how it might relate to the possibilities of literacy and thinking.

The title of this story is *Seven Blind Mice* (Young, 1992). It features six blind mice who are investigating a strange "something" that has landed near the pond where they live. They each make guesses which none of the other mice believe. Their guesses are it's "a pillar," "a snake," "a spear," "a great cliff," "a fan," and "a rope." The mice didn't agree with each other and began to argue. When the seventh mouse appeared, she inspected ALL parts of this strange "something." She ran top to bottom, side-to-side, and end-to-end. She exclaimed that they all were right but, when it was put all together, it was an elephant. The other mice then joined her and they, too, inspected ALL parts of this thing Mouse Seven was calling an elephant until they all agreed. The moral of the tale in Young's words is "Knowing in part may make a fine tale, but wisdom comes from seeing the whole" (Young, 1992, p. 36).

In this tale, each part was important! Without those sturdy pillars, the elephant would have no foundation. Without being as supple as a snake or as stringy as a rope, it would be missing a beginning and an end! Without seeing how each of those parts would build to form a workable whole, there would be NO elephant!

I have a high respect and admiration for people—and mice—who can see and think beyond given parts and envision possibilities not yet fathomed. One such person is Mary McLeod Bethune (McKissick & McKissick, 1992). Although I read a section of the book at the conference, I will paraphrase that section here for copyright purposes.

Mary Bethune heard that living conditions for Black people were a disgrace in Daytona, Florida and that they did not even have a school. She felt she needed to go there and build a school. Upon arriving, she announced that she was going to build a school for Black girls. She got a loan and rented a cottage for eleven dollars where she and her husband lived upstairs. The three rooms on the first floor were the school. She immediately tried to get support from the Black community and winter residents such as Thomas Proctor, Henry Kaiser, and John D. Rockefeller. In 1904, Mary opened the Daytona Normal and Industrial Institute for Girls. Boxes served as desks with trashed paper and charcoal used for the school materials. Five students arrived the first day who were each charged a tuition of fifty cents. The students made and sold food to railroad workers to meet expenses. As word traveled, the students in her school soon numbered more than 100! She needed a bigger school, so she bought a trash dump.

As she was looking at her trash dump unaware of the broken bottles, furniture, and ugly trash, someone passing by asked her why she was looking at all that junk. Her reply was that she was looking at her school!

If Mary had only seen parts when she saw that trash pile, it might still be a trash heap today piled with more broken furniture, bottles, and useless junk. Without Mary's belief, it may not have developed into a workable whole. IT DID! The school became a reality and later merged with Cookman Institute to become Bethune-Cookman College as it is known today.

Mary MacLeod Bethune summed up her life and beliefs in her will:

My worldly possessions are few. Yet, my experiences have been rich. From them I distilled principles and policies in which I firmly believe . . . and, finally, a responsibility to our young people. (McKissick & McKissick, 1992, p. 31).

As I considered more people of vision, I thought of our own CRA members and suddenly an idea struck me! Why not e-mail members? Hence, I combed through the CRA Directory "randomly" for this most scientific research "tongue in cheek" adventure, and selected e-mails that were, of course, representative even though a number of servers and addresses were returned or sent who knows where! My query to given members was:

I would appreciate your input for the CRA President's Address I am preparing. My title is "Going Beyond: The Possibilities of Thinking and Literacy." The description is "Examples and encouragement will be given for 'stepping outside traditional and mandated boxes' in terms of thinking and literacy practices." Please entertain some interesting ideas as to possibilities and innovations we might consider that relate to any aspect(s) of literacy, thinking, and/or CRA.

Sixty-three members responded. As the responses were examined, five predominant categories emerged:

1. Definitions of literacy and instruction,
2. Adolescent literacy,
3. Collaboration instead of "Discollaboration!,"
4. Critical thinking is critical!, and
5. Technology and media.

The five categories are not arranged in any scientific research order but sequenced according to the Matanzo Right Brain Organization Method! It would be my pleasure to share all 63 responses . . . but there are other things scheduled on the program today! I have selected several responses representative of each category and will share those with you with hopes to pique your thinking as you listen.

Definitions of literacy and instruction

Cindi Hasit, Rowan University, replied as follows:

I'm thinking of the expanded definition of literacy, which includes visualizing and viewing. Art, photography, and other media can be integrated into our literacy instruction. We should capitalize on the expertise of the specialists in our schools (or outsiders, of course) in those areas to create lessons that address these areas. I think in most schools we use the arts as an add-on or a response to a piece of literature. We should rethink to include these specialists as part of the "literacy team." Using multiple intelligences is probably not that novel, but we should think about providing students with opportunities to use areas of strength or intelligence (linguistic, logical-mathematical, spatial, musical, bodily kinesthetic, interpersonal, and intrapersonal) to enhance and demonstrate comprehension. That would include various school personnel on the "literacy team."

Jackie Peck and Steve Snyder, Kent State University, observed faculty who successfully bring innovations into their practice and faculty who resist innovative practice. They found that the innovators and the resistors used very different language when talking about teaching and learning. They concluded that uncertainty and higher-level thinking resulted with the language used by the innovators. They gave me permission to share their list with you in Table 1.

Table 1. Innovative and Status Quo Language Differences About Teaching and Learning

INNOVATIVE	STATUS QUO
Chaos	Order
Designing	Performing
Inquiring	Telling
Organic	Mechanistic
Social networks	Organizations
Stories	Data
Isearch	Research
Customization	One size fits all; Mandated testing
Insight	Evaluation
Risk taking	Security
Divergence	Convergence
Ambiguity	Clarity

Adolescent Literacy

Yesterday, Jack and Drew Cassidy, Texas A&M, Corpus Christi, presented their "What's Hot-2003 Survey Results." Adolescent Literacy received one check on their list of "What's Hot" but responders to their survey recommended with three checks that it should be hot and, indeed, two times hotter than what is now perceived. Peggy Daisey, Eastern Michigan University, agrees with the "what should be" as she stated:

> As a secondary content area literacy professor, who teaches a required course to students from every subject area, and who come with every attitude toward the course under the sun, my life revolves around getting future teachers to think outside the box; to not teach the way they were taught, to expand their ideas about reading and writing, and reading materials. How sad that these adults come to me in need of having their interest in reading and writing revitalized, due to chronic experiences in middle/high school and college that have beat their interest in reading and writing out of them.

Joan Elliott, Indiana University of Pennsylvania, espouses using interactive strategies with adolescents and to consider the findings of brain research. She advocates that strategies such as having Reflective Practice Groups be implemented. Wayne Linek, Texas A & M University-Commerce, also thinks the new focus on adolescent literacy is a possibility as it looks at literate behavior in all contexts and not just traditional context, such as the contextual dependence of literacy. Examples he gives are the use of cell phones, instant messaging, interactive TV, and computer games that indicate literate behavior among adolescents and their impact on what is culturally and socially accepted and expected. In other words, text that once was rigid or sequential has now become open to new avenues and interactions with much more flexibility. This should be reflected in the way we teach and motivate adolescents.

Donna Alvermann, University of Georgia, further comments on the need to focus on adolescent literacy:

> We know *something* needs to be done to help underachieving adolescent struggling readers but we're not sure just what, and further, we have little data on which to base our understanding of *how* these readers approach learning in other than formal school contexts (Hull & Schultz, 2001). Why this is the case, I'm not sure. Perhaps as researchers we feel more at home studying the pedagogies of scientific literacy in the classroom rather than in other less formal learning environments. Maybe it's a sense of having easier access to and more control over what we study when we observe in familiar and safe places. Yet I would contend that it's in out-of-school contexts such as after-school clubs,

community organizations, workplaces, public libraries with free Internet access, and mall video arcades where we're more likely to observe young people using their everyday literacies in ways that foster informal, but powerful and complex learning. Ways, in fact that could inform science content teaching and learning in schools.

Collaboration instead of "Discollaboration!"

Working together to encourage literacy and to solve related problems seems to be high on the list of the next three responders. Karen Bromley, SUNY at Binghamton, writes:

How about thinking about concrete, substantive collaboration between our teacher education programs and area schools? I am co-teaching a literacy assessment course in a local middle school that has one of our most difficult populations. My co-teacher is a reading specialist in the building. We teach our course there in the library and our graduate students tutor struggling readers for part of the class. They have the opportunity to do the assessments and instruction one-on-one as well as an in-depth case study, and we provide a needed service to the local school. We called it Partner Power last year and the district loved it.

Mary Roe, Washington State University, also encourages collaboration through partnerships. She comments:

Instead of simply thinking outside of the "traditional and mandated boxes," I think literacy professionals also must closely consider how their thinking relates to those boxes and, especially when differences appear, ponder how their research agendas and public actions might nudge the people behind the traditional and mandated in a broader-perhaps more enlightened-direction. Especially in these highly charged times, I find it imperative to have the communicative competence to move forward in partnerships rather than embrace thinking that is too far afield or too dismissive of the "boxes" to nurture these alliances.

Linda Rogers, East Stroudsburg University, also believes that collaboration is a very significant aspect in providing students with good instruction. She tells how her university offers a block of courses that are taught by a team of five professors representing three different departments. This collaboration has made a rigorous semester exciting for her as well as for the host teachers and the faculty team. She claims the bonus is that the preservice teachers witness the collaboration of their instructors as they see the team make decisions about planning, instruction, and assessment. It also has resulted in respect for another's discipline and work. In turn, the preservice teachers collaborate with their host teacher in making decisions about how they will plan and deliver instruction in the assigned classroom. Linda, in conclusion, remarks that "No longer can we close our doors and 'do our own thing'! With 'push in' as a model, there are many people in any classroom at any given time. We truly need to think and work collaboratively so the work we do with students is the best we can provide."

Critical Thinking is Critical!

On the Cassidy's "What's Hot" list, Critical Thinking was subsumed under comprehension, which received one check for what is occurring now, but the respondents advocated two checks for the emphasis that it needs to be given. A number of our members agree. Rita Bean, University of Pittsburgh, feels that the current focus on accountability using "simple" measures reduces the focus on higher-level thinking and helping students learn to learn. She advocates that we professionals need to pursue other types of measures to assess effectiveness and that address the critical thinking skills we want students to possess. Linda Gambrell, Clemson University, feels that not only do students in our schools need to be critical thinkers but that the "current political climate suggests that it is more important than ever that we prepare literacy teachers who are critical thinkers."

Ray Reutzel, Utah State University, goes a step further by posing critical questions that we should ask ourselves. His initial comment is that he is "not so concerned about stepping outside the box . . . but stepping on the box! There are some among us who seem to want to step on, burn, or otherwise toss this box right out the door . . . why (has there been) such a virulent reaction from some of us in reading education against the biggest box of federal funding for reading we have ever seen?" He continues with questions for us each to consider:

> What are we "for" instead of what are we "against" in the field of reading? Will our continued "reading wars" within our scholarly community disarm us and discredit us without? Why is there a cry for scientific evidence in practice education? Why isn't there a cry for more interpretive and artistic practice in education? What is at work here? We need to have more honest conversations and fewer dogmatic pronouncements coming from the profession. We are at a crossroads in literacy and reading education. How much longer will Washington DC or state legislators have patience with a profession that can't seem to agree on whether the sun is shining today? Will we join hands at this point in time, or will we once again "circle the wagons and start shooting inward?" How can we come together, or will we as in the past, just start another organization where we can be with our own kind?

In other words, going back to our mouse parable, will the blind mouse that only "sees 'the something'" as a spear form his own spear group and the mouse that saw something as breezy as a fan form his own fan group? If so, mouse discourse and the hope of the mice listening again to each other and checking out the whole thing will no longer be one of the possibilities. It seems important that we reflect on Ray's questions and begin to discuss possibilities and inevitabilities with each other. What better forum is there than here at this CRA conference to do just that!

Technology and Media

As noted when I presented the Adolescent Literacy category, technology and media may be an important literacy vehicle for that group. Seventy two percent of the CRA members who answered my e-mail request noted technology as a category to consider in terms of its relationship to literacy instruction. Pat Koskinen, University of Maryland, feels that it is imperative that we need to help every family in the country become aware of the text in the form of captions on the highly motivating medium of television. She claims that the captions are free and plentiful as more than 1500 hours of TV programming per week are captioned. Research indicates that by just watching captioned TV at home, students' vocabulary and comprehension are enhanced. This incidental learning, however, can only occur if the captions are turned on by parents or other caregivers. She firmly believes that word needs to get out so that the potential of using captions as one way to support literacy learning can be realized.

Barbara Walker, Oklahoma State University, suggests we include multimedia and technology as tools to help us step outside the box. Creating multimedia responses to text can enhance critical thinking. Don Leu, University of Connecticut, goes a step further as he encourages one to consider the new literacies of the Internet and other Information and Communication Technologies (ICT) that are "rapidly redefining literacy in an information age and rapidly defining what students must know if we want them to succeed on life's journey." He continues to warn that "these new literacies include the new critical literacies required for evaluating and using information appropriately on the Internet. Ironically, the literacy community is the last to recognize the importance of the changes taking place around us." He also notes that it is difficult to build a consistent body of published research within traditional forums before the technology being studied develops into or is replaced by a newer technology.

Just before I left for this conference, I received a book about technology that I found impressive. It was *Technology for Literacy Teaching and Learning* (Valmont, 2003). William Valmont, University of Arizona, claims:

Constructing meaning as you read printed words alone is quite different from constructing meaning as you interact with multimedia, from which you construct meaning not only from words but also from graphics, photographs, animations, audio, and video almost simultaneously. (p. 1).

He further suggests that new skills are needed as we expect literacy to include multi-tasking, media literacy, visual literacy, global context, and being able to be telecollaborative. As just one example of the urgency of this need is that approximately 800+ billion E-mails are now sent each day throughout the world! In the past, we have considered survivor words such as poison, exit, H for hospital, and RR for railroad crossing. Valmont states that technology words are the survivor words of tomorrow. This new vocabulary includes such terms as cybersquatters, URLs, cobweb sites, netiquette, recursive, E-materials, metasearch engines, polysymbolic, and portrait mode. On-line glossaries are a resource that must become more familiar and more frequently used by literacy learners. It is also important that professors and teachers learn to use and apply technology and media. We must consider the possibilities of the best ways to model, teach, and use technology ourselves. We must resolve to find ways to eliminate gaps between the technological haves and have nots so we don't create struggling E-literates in the same vein that struggling readers exist today.

In the Reference section, I have included a short Webliography, another new survivor term, to offer you some additional sites that may be helpful. I highly encourage you to sign up for the CRA Listserv and to visit our newest CRA journal, *Literacy Cases Online*, and the CRA Website.

Today I have urged you to consider possibilities beyond what we are now doing in the areas of thinking and literacy. I have shared the ideas of some of our CRA members in the expressed categories of (a) definitions of literacy and instruction, (b) adolescent literacy, (c) collaboration instead of "discollaboration," (d) critical thinking is critical, and (e) technology and media. In essence, we cannot let our personal biases about what literacy is obscure or overlook where the world is going and, in many cases, has already arrived. We must encourage critical thinking so that we can evaluate and re-evaluate these changes. In looking at these five areas, we have concentrated on parts. We must be like that seventh mouse and put these parts into an integrated and balanced whole. If we do not, that SOMETHING which I will name literacy will not result in a cohesive, capable, functioning, and recognizable literacy elephant . . . or eventually in a literate society. Think possibilities . . . and be aggressive in making those possibilities you envision a reality that will benefit us all.

References

Hull, G. & Schultz, K. (2001). Literacy and learning out of school: A review of theory and research. *Review of Educational Research, 71,* 575-611.

McKissack, P., & McKissack, F. (1992). *Mary McLeod Bethune.* Chicago: Children's Press.

Valmont, W. J. (2003). *Technology for literacy teaching and learning.* Boston: Houghton Mifflin Company

Young, E. (1992). *Seven blind mice.* NY: Puffin Books.

Webliography

College Reading Association Sites

CRA Listserv majordomo@archon.educ.kent.edu Contact: Nancy Padak

CRA Website http://explorers.tsuniv.edu/cra/Contact: Marino Alvarez

Literacy Cases on Line www.literacycasesonline.org Editors: Sandee Goetze and Barbara Walker, Oklahoma State University

Other Literacy Related Sites

Beaucoup! http://www.beaucoup.com/1metaeng.html Conducts 11 metasearches at once; links to 20 more search engines

Langenberg.com http://www.langenberg.com/ Conducts metasearches and translates web pages in English, French, German, Dutch, Danish, Spanish, Finnish, Czech, Italian, or Portuguese. Engage in projects around the world.

ProFusion http://www.profusion.com/ Tips for conducting searches with links to nine search engines

The Global Schoolhouse http://www.gsn.org/ Free worldwide collaborative projects.

J. Estill Alexander Forum: Reflections, Remembrances, and Resonances Resulting from Mentorship

Dr J. Estill Alexander:
Lessons Learned

Cathleen Doheny

State University of West Georgia

I remember the first time I met Dr. J. Estill Alexander. He was the professor who taught one of the first doctoral courses I took at the University of Tennessee, Knoxville, during Fall semester, 1994. The course was, *The Psychology of Reading*. He sat at the front of the class; a sweet-faced, white-haired, professor-looking man with a mischievous smile and spark in his eyes that some would say was his love of teaching. He introduced himself, distributed the syllabus, and explained the requirements of the course. As he progressed through the assignments and readings, my anxiety rose. The requirements were rigorous. He expected students to read more than I thought was reasonable. And he looked cheerful about it.

Some students dropped the course during the semester. I chose to dig in and commit to long hours of preparation for group discussions based on required readings. I discovered during that first course that some faculty and graduate students referred to J. Estill Alexander as "Dr. Alex." I don't know why; I never learned why. I speculate that it was a term of endearment from those who knew him well and appreciated the man and his work. As I progressed through the doctoral program and took additional courses with Dr. Alexander, I adopted the shortened version of his name, Dr. Alex. I still think of J. Estill Alexander as Dr. Alex and that is how I write about his influence in my professional life.

This commentary is a tribute to Dr. J. Estill Alexander. It is a chronicle of personal reflections and interpretations about the influence that one professor had on shaping the professional persona of one graduate student. This paper is not a list of Dr. Alexander's lifetime achievements in the field of reading, his research agenda, or his monetary awards. Those who are active in the field are well aware of J. Estill Alexander's contributions to reading education. The intent of this paper is to express the gratitude I have for the commitment and care I received from Dr. Alex as he guided my learning.

During my first course with Dr. Alex, *Psychology of Reading*, I learned a lot about the role of affect in learning to read. I brought 13 years of public school teaching experience to Dr. Alex's class. As a public school teacher I often said, "I want my students to love reading." I never understood the complexity of that statement until Dr. Alex explained the importance of affect in learning. He led me to understand that when children are faced with reading tasks they cannot do, they have physiological responses that impede their ability to learn. He helped me to see that when children are expected to read books that are beyond their instructional levels, they are set up to fail. The effects of that failure are long lasting and severe. Failure defeats desire to read, creates animosity toward print, and reinforces negative feelings about one's self and one's ability. Dr. Alex taught me that a child's sense of his/her ability to learn is not a behavior modification task. It is a teaching task. Good reading teachers evaluate what students can do and then provide them with reading experiences that are successful and enjoyable.

Dr. Alex taught doctoral students important lessons that went beyond content. He taught us about the importance of developing professionally. I spent a lot of time at the University library that first semester. Invariably as I was reading yet another "seminal" or "current" or "state of the art" article on reading education, I ran into Dr. Alex. Sometimes he stopped and told me how wonderful it was to see me in the library. Other times he acknowledged me with his sparkling smiles as he headed toward the newspaper. One day I asked Dr. Alex if he went to the library every day. His face lit up. He said, "Oh yes! I come every day!" I discovered then that Dr. Alex loved to read. He loved to learn.

The second course that I took with Dr. Alex was *Theoretical Processes and Models of Reading.* There were only 4 or 5 students in the course and all but one were doctoral students. Though I learned a lot about different reading theories at the time, what I remember most are the conversations about professionalism. Since the group was small I felt more comfortable asking questions that went beyond content. I wanted to know what it was like to be a professor. I wanted to know what kinds of roles and responsibilities professors had. I asked Dr. Alex why his syllabi were so imposing, his expectations demanding. Dr. Alex, in his kind and humble way, talked about his excitement in teaching students who were committed to working hard, who would contribute positively to the profession.

Upon reflection about what I learned as a doctoral student under the guidance of Dr. Alex I arrived at five basic lessons. I refer to those lessons as "The Five L's." What follows is a description of "The Five L's." Dr. Alex never said these words. They are my interpretation of Dr. Alex's approach to teaching graduate courses. The Five L's are as follows:

L1. Load the syllabus—Lose the loafers

This technique I learned through observation. After Dr. Alex introduced his quite rigorous syllabus, I noticed that the second class was smaller. Those students who were not committed, who lacked a work ethic dropped his courses. The courses were better for it. The students who remained were well-read and interested in learning.

L2. Love the Library

To be successful in Dr. Alex's courses, I learned that much time would be spent in the library. "Love it like your second home," I joked with others. "See you in the library," I said after classes were over for the day. In 1994, there weren't lots of articles on the internet. We spent hours reading micro-fiche and microfilm, journal articles, and book chapters.

L3. Learn the Leaders—Learn to Lead

During the reading theories course, I also learned about the importance of learning the names of historical and current leaders in the field of reading. Graduate students were expected to be able to connect leaders in the field with their work. Dr. Alex encouraged doctoral students to join professional organizations to get to know reading leaders and other professionals in the field. He provided calls for proposals from state, national, and international organizations. He believed that students had something important to con-tribute and equally important, more to learn. He encouraged us to contrib-ute to the profession by submitting proposals for conferences and manu-scripts for publication. Learning the leaders, past and present, he believed would enrich our education. Learning to lead would enrich the profession.

L4. Link Theory to Practice

The third course I took from Dr. Alex was called, *Administration and Supervision of Reading*. Content learned in this course required me to link theory to practice in a comprehensive way. I learned to look at programs and identify strengths and weaknesses. I struggled with how to develop a coherent program that was based on sound theory and research and included assessment, resources, personnel, instructional methods, scheduling, as well as staff development for effective implementation.

During the *Supervision of Reading* course Dr. Alex described a "catch-ing butterflies" approach to creating comprehensive reading programs. He defined that approach as going out with a net to gather whatever butterflies are captured. When you see what you have you decide what to do with them. He was critical of that kind of approach. Dr. Alex supported more purposeful and thoughtful ways to develop reading programs. Dr. Alex advised that I start with my own views about how reading and writing are best learned. When I was clear about my underlying beliefs it was easier to develop an instructional program to guide teaching practices. I still believe strongly in the importance of connecting teaching practices to sound theories of learning.

L5. Let them Learn

Professionally, again I learned more from observing Dr. Alex teach rather than talking with him about teaching. Dr. Alex was notorious among doctoral students for leaving assignments open-ended. He wanted us to choose our own directions, our own topics, and learn all that we could about them. He promoted depth of knowledge as opposed to breadth of knowledge. He taught us the essence of scholarship.

I was expected to develop a project that would be meaningful to me and respect the goals of the course. Dr. Alex read my ideas, asked questions, offered suggestions, referred authors and titles, and provided feedback along the way. But in the end, I made the final decisions about the finished product. He assured me that whatever I chose would be of high quality. And so it was. With Dr. Alex's expert guidance, I learned about supporting students to identify and pursue their own interests. In addition, I learned the importance of sharing what I had learned with others. I learned that collegiality, was the professional responsibility of scholars.

My last experience with Dr. Alex, at the University of Tennessee was my work in the reading clinic. It consisted of content focused on assessment and diagnosis of reading strengths and weaknesses and remediation of reading difficulties. There is where I also learned the most about Dr. Alex, the man. Throughout my studies with Dr. Alex, he rarely spoke about himself and his accomplishments. It wasn't until I began working in the reading clinic that I began to learn about Dr. Alex from people who had known him for decades. I found out how dedicated Dr. Alex was to the establishment of a reading clinic. I saw plaques of appreciation from community and professional organizations for his contributions to their goals. I heard about how caring and kind he had always been to the secretaries and staff who worked in the clinic. I met people who had been students of Dr. Alex years ago. I found out that those who knew Dr. Alex the longest, loved and respected him the most.

I found similar sentiments from professionals at College Reading Association meetings. It seemed so many people had such high regard for this humble and quiet man with the sparkling eyes and mischievous smile. He was truly respected by esteemed colleagues in the reading profession. His commitment to the psychology and history of reading is well known in the field. His dedication to sharing his time and energy to improve reading education has been established.

The greatest lesson I learned from Dr. Alex is not included in the "Five L's Approach." What I learned from Dr. Alex about being a professor and a person was simple and profound. He never said these words to me. I gleaned them from my interpretation of my experiences with Dr. Alex and those who were touched by the way he lived his life, lived his profession. His legacy to my professional growth is this: It's not what you say you do that will earn honor and respect from your students and colleagues. Ultimately it's what you do and how you treat people that will be spoken about and remembered. I have a long way to go to realize this goal as I continue to learn and grow as a literacy teacher educator, with respect and gratitude to Dr. J. Estill Alexander.

J. ESTILL ALEXANDER:
MENTOR, COLLEAGUE, FRIEND

Sabiha T. Aydelott

Academic Bridge Program
The Qatar Foundation

Like any other year, I was attending the annual conference of the College Reading Association (CRA), and like any other year I ran into Betty Heathington. She had been a professor at The University of Tennessee, Knoxville (UTK), when I was a doctoral student, advised and mentored by J. Estill Alexander. We exchanged the normal pleasantries and promised to catch up with each other's news later. The later came the next day, when Betty sought me out to ask me to step into the void left by Bob Cooter who was unable to attend the conference. Betty, Bob, and Cathleen Doheny were scheduled to pay tribute to Alexander (Alex) at "The J. Estill Alexander Forum for CRA Leaders in Literacy: Reflections, Remembrances, and Resonances Resulting from Mentorship." The request was most unexpected and somewhat daunting as I would be speaking about my mentor to an audience consisting of the gurus of the reading world!

I welcomed the request to speak about Alex (he had finally asked me to call him that when he came to visit me in Egypt, during the time I taught at the American University in Cairo). It gave me the opportunity to reflect on and ponder over the years I had known him and the influence he had had on my work.

The first time I met Alex was in the Fall of 1985. I was "shopping" at UTK, in order to decide the major for my doctoral studies, and Alex was one of the professors I met with in order to decide my future. He spent considerable time with me, providing me with important information about the reading program at UTK. The information he shared convinced me that Reading was a field I wanted to pursue, and that it was in keeping with my interests, experience, and qualifications. Another factor that played an important role in convincing me to enter this field was his love and passion for it—he was totally absorbed by it. January of 1986 saw me as a student of the reading program and an advisee of J. Estill Alexander (his agreeing to mentor and advise me had been the deciding factor in my selecting Reading as my major). As a result of my work in the first term, he offered me an assistantship to work in the Reading Clinic. I was delighted; this assistantship proved to be invaluable for me as it provided me with the knowledge and experience that I could utilize in my teaching.

During the two years I spent at UTK (Jan. 1986–Dec. 1988), Alex was there to guide me through my studies and counsel me about professional matters. His attitude and conduct were exemplary, as a mentor, teacher, colleague, and as a friend. He was responsible for encouraging me to publish, by offering me the opportunity to develop an appendix for his (and Heathington's) book *Assessing and Correcting Reading Problems* (Alexander & Heathington, 1988), and by co-authoring an article with me for *Tennessee Reading Teacher*. He also encouraged me to present at conferences and to offer in-service workshops for several public schools in and around Knoxville. In addition to encouraging me to publish and make conference presentations as well as lead in-service workshops, he asked me to team-teach courses with him. I was, of course, flattered and thrilled to do so. Today, I have several publications, workshops and conference presentations to my name. For these achievements, I owe a debt to Alex. I have much to thank him for, as none of this would have been possible if he had not provided me with the encouragement and opportunity.

As a teacher and mentor, Alex was always calm, positive and encouraging. His interaction with his students and advisees was congenial and, at the same time, individualistic. He made each of his students feel special. He always had his office door open, which made us feel that we could approach him at any time, and he always had a smile to receive us. I think that one of the things that I will always appreciate about him, and which I have tried to emulate since, is his approachable nature. We never found his door closed . . . he was always there to guide us and help us. Often he would set aside what he was doing in order to attend to our questions, concerns, and problems.

We often discussed issues related to reading and the teaching of reading in and out of class. It was through his own work and interest in the affective domain that he inspired several of his students to explore this area. He felt that this aspect of reading was not given as much importance as were some of the other areas; therefore, he advocated that we, as teachers, should try to foster a love for reading in our students. He thought that there were several things that reading teachers should consider actively as these would make an impact on their students and encourage learning. In *Ten Best Ideas for Reading Teachers* (Alexander, 1991), he highlighted ideas to be practiced by reading teachers. These ideas, enumerated below, have proved to be of a universal and timeless nature, as they are just as important today as they were over a decade ago.

1. Consider affective responses to learning as basic as cognitive responses;
2. Use "short term" skills groups when working on cognitive skills;
3. Foster lifelong reading;
4. Utilize diagnostic teaching procedures;
5. Build background (schemata) for new learning experiences;
6. Consider the impact of your (teacher's) attitudes, nonverbal behavior, and modeling behaviors on student learning;
7. Utilize ecologically valid assessment tools;
8. Teach students to use a variety of decoding strategies;
9. Develop and reinforce reading skills in content areas; and
10. Utilize whole class, small group, and individualized instruction appropriate to student and class needs (Alexander, 1991, p. 30).

Alex was active in the public schools, in and around Knoxville, his adopted city (Lexington, KY, was his home and he never missed an opportunity to let us know that). He encouraged these schools to send students who were struggling with reading skills to the Reading Center at UTK. His purpose was two-fold: to provide a much needed service to the community and to provide his students with the laboratory they needed in order to conduct diagnosis and remediation of reading problems. Apart from the services provided by the Reading Center, he offered workshops on a fairly regular basis. Often, we, his graduate students, would come across teachers who had either studied with him or had been participants at his workshops and talks. Consequently, he had a major impact on the field of teaching reading.

As a colleague, he was a wonderful person to work with. Team-teaching courses with him (as a graduate student) was an exciting and invigorating experience. I learned much from him during that time. Years later, I returned to UTK (from Cairo) to teach courses on reading and language arts for a summer term. He was the Department Chair then. Once again, he was an encouraging and supportive colleague. His guidance, during my student days and later, was always extremely helpful and much appreciated. I could always count on him when I needed counseling and guidance on any issue related to reading and research. Alex and I kept in touch with each other even after I left UTK and even after I left the US. Though we were miles apart, he still played a major role in my professional life. He knew what I was doing professionally and was always pleased to hear about my work. I regret that I did not let him know that the book that I had co-edited had been published—I had thought that I would present him with a copy when I saw him in the summer of 2001. Before that summer, and every summer when I returned to the States, I would make it a point to look him up and he would find the time to be with my family and me for at least an evening.

Today, when my students show evidence that they enjoy reading and that it has become a part of their lives, it is a tribute to J. Estill Alexander's advocacy of the affective domain. He is sorely missed by the reading world, especially by his many students and colleagues, around the world.

References

Alexander, J. E., & Heathington, B. S. (1988). *Assessing and correcting classroom reading problems.* New York: Scott Foresman.

Alexander, J. E. (1991). Ten best ideas for reading teachers. In E. Fry (Ed.) *Ten best ideas for reading teachers* (p. 30). Menlo Park, CA: Addison-Wesley.

RESEARCH
AWARDS

Constructive Comprehension and Metacognitive Strategy Reading Instruction in a Field-Based Teacher Education Program: Effecting Change in Preservice and Inservice Teachers—Participant One

Michelle M. Fazio

Northwestern State University of Louisiana

Abstract

The purpose of this study was to examine the impact of constructive comprehension and metacognitive strategy reading instruction on preservice/ inservice teachers' beliefs and behaviors before and during their field experience and in their first year of teaching. The participants were two teachers viewed over a period of 2.5 years; however, this article focuses on only one of the participants. The teacher participant's theoretical beliefs were summarized in three overarching themes and were compared to her personal artifacts and instructional practices to search for areas of congruence and dissonance. In Phase I, the participant's beliefs and practices were congruent in terms of (a) balancing objectivist and constructivist instruction, (b) implementing constructive comprehension and metacognitive strategy instruction, and (c) modeling best practice by providing effective instruction for her students. In Phases II, III, and IV, the researcher found complete congruence in the participant's beliefs and behaviors.

It has been well-documented that children who are read to at home, who engage in multisensory experiences, and who are immersed in print-rich environments early in life have clear advantages when learning how to read. Still, every year teachers are faced with the difficulty of teaching *all* children to read, including those that have not been privileged with rich literacy experiences before coming to school. One intervention that can be implemented to support such readers is the use of constructive metacognitive strategy instruction (Brooks & Brooks, 1993; Smith, 1997; Vygotsky, 1978). As a result, students learn to interact/transact with text, self-monitor comprehension, and take ownership of their learning (Rosenblatt, 1994).

Few would argue that children thrive in classrooms where best practices are modeled, though definitions of best practices differ significantly (Cunningham & Allington, 1999). Even if definitions are cloudy, it is clear that beliefs about best practices impact instructional behaviors (Azjen, 1988; Lortie, 1975). Believing that how they were taught as children was appropriate, many teachers model the same teacher-centered practices—lecture, independent work, and isolated activities—regardless of what research has to say about how children learn. However, if teachers experience some type of dissonance with their beliefs and current educational research, it is possible for them to adopt student-centered practices such as inquiry-based learning, cooperative learning, and student-driven instruction.

The purpose of this study was to examine the impact of constructive comprehension and metacognitive strategy reading instruction on preservice/inservice teachers' beliefs and behaviors before and during their field experience and in their first year of teaching. Conducted over a period of 2.5 years, the study was divided into four phases and included two preservice/inservice teachers. This article focuses on only one of the participants. Questions the researcher sought to answer included: (a) How does participating in a constructive comprehension and metacognitive strategy instruction course impact preservice/inservice teachers' beliefs and behaviors?; (b) Specifically, how does participating in reflective activities impact preservice teachers' beliefs about teaching and learning?; (c) How does participating in a course modeling best practice of constructive comprehension strategy instruction impact preservice teachers' instructional behavior in their field experience?; (d) How does participating in a course modeling best practice of constructive comprehension strategy instruction impact inservice teachers' behavior in their first year of teaching?; and (e) Which factors appear to be most influential in impacting preservice/inservice teachers' beliefs and instructional behaviors?

Impact of Teacher Beliefs on Classroom Instructional Behaviors

When preservice teachers enter college, they already have strong beliefs about teaching and learning (Doyle, 1997; Maxson & Sindelar, 1998) which stem from (a) personal experience (Clandinin, 1986), (b) experience with schooling and instruction (Anning, 1988; Lortie, 1975), and (c) experience with formal knowledge (Crow, 1987). These beliefs influence content preservice teachers learn in their pre-professional education because steadfast beliefs determine what the preservice teachers will be willing to embrace and how they will teach in the future (Maxson & Sindelar, 1998; Richardson, 1996). Thus, it is critical that teacher educators explore preservice teachers' perceptions about effective teaching in order to reinforce beliefs that are grounded in current educational research and challenge beliefs that are inappropriate (Green, 1971; Richardson, 1996).

Though appropriate practices can hardly be summed in a single paragraph, instruction is considered to be effective when it appropriately and effectively utilizes a variety of strategies, among them: (a) active learning, (b) whole-to-part-to-whole instruction and authentic learning, (c) social learning, (d) teacher as facilitator, (e) content integration, and (f) high level thinking (Castor, 2000; Cornett, 1999; Heuwinkel, 1996). Teachers who model best practices tend to provide experiences for students to negotiate learning through hands-on, relevant experiences and teach in holistic, relevant contexts. Such teachers are also likely to use cooperative learning and let children take initiative in their own learning (Bredekamp & Copple, 1997; National Association for the Education of Young Children, 1998). Finally, they integrate curricula, ask high level/open-ended questions, and encourage children to solve real-life problems.

If beliefs about good teaching drive instructional behaviors, it seems natural that teachers implement reading instructional practices they deem effective. Many teachers who implement constructive comprehension and metacognitive strategy reading instruction find that their students experience growth in reading comprehension. As students are exposed to strategies that help them make sense of the world, they become proficient readers. They tend to:

- engage in actively constructing their own personal meanings by relating new information to preexisting knowledge structures (Anderson & Pearson, 1984);

- know that meaning lies neither within the text nor within the reader. Rather, it is constructed as the result of an interaction/transaction with text (Rosenblatt, 1994);

- self-monitor/use metacognitive processes as they read by questioning, reviewing, and rereading to increase comprehension (Baker & Brown, 1984; Flavell, 1981); and

- negotiate plans for comprehension. In other words, they thoughtfully select from a collection of strategies that they deem will best facilitate understanding under the given circumstances (Flood & Lapp, 1991).

Using these strategies, skilled readers are aware of what they do not understand and know what to do when they have trouble comprehending. Finally, they understand that reading is an active process that depends on their personal experiences and purposes for reading.

Methodology

This descriptive case employed qualitative methodology within a case study design, followed by a cross-case analysis. Interviews with Holly were the primary data source for gleaning information concerning beliefs, while observation was used to examine instructional practices as they related to beliefs and intentions. Finally, artifact collection and surveys were examined for congruency with beliefs and with other data collected.

The participants were selected through purposeful sampling (Patton, 1990). The researcher sought to ensure that the participants' unique characteristics and circumstances would provide the most inclusive picture the researcher sought to investigate. Criteria for selecting participants were based on age and experience because beliefs are thought to become more steadfast over time without intervention. It was assumed that the older a preservice teacher was, the more exposure she would have had to traditional instructional practices, and the greater reluctance she would experience with the use of constructivist comprehension and metacognitive strategy instruction (Cochran-Smith, 1991; Pajares, 1992). Thus, participants were initially selected so that a wide age range would exist.

The participant pool began with all of the students enrolled in the researcher's undergraduate level Comprehension and Literacy II course (RDG 370) during the Spring and Summer 1999 semesters; the pool was reduced to five Caucasian females who ranged in age from early twenties to mid thirties. Two of the preservice teachers held degrees external to the field of education; none of them had teaching experience. In Phase II the pool was reduced to Jennifer and Holly, both in their thirties, who continued to participate during their residency in Spring 2000 and first year of teaching in academic year 2000-2001. This article describes Holly's teaching experience.

In Phase I, Holly enrolled in the researcher's undergraduate Comprehension and Literacy course. In an introductory essay, she revealed that she had obtained a degree in Business approximately 20 years before. She worked part-time until finding out that she was pregnant and then decided to stay at home for the next 15 years. Following her child's entrance into high school, she decided to go back to college to get a degree in teaching. Because she was both a non-traditional student and a mother, she felt she had much to offer the teaching profession; she had certainly waited a long time to become one. Holly was an eager student; she never missed class. She seemed hungry to fill her files with student-centered strategies, and she was especially drawn to hands-on and cooperative activities. Connecting the class with the real world, she was the first student to realize that she could use the strategies the researcher was modeling in class with her own future students.

Over the course of the semester, Holly engaged in:

- analyzing and evaluating a state-adopted reading basal and making instructional recommendations;
- teaching five small- or whole-group reading comprehension lessons to public school children;
- reflecting on the lessons by sharing what went well, what her challenges were, and what she would do differently next time she taught the lesson;
- compiling a comprehension strategy notebook which consisted of explanation handouts and self-constructed artifacts;
- designing an integrated lesson plan that included all of the multiple intelligences; learning styles; quality children' literature; a basal story; visual or performing arts; and authentic listening, speaking, reading, and writing experiences;
- constructing a portfolio to demonstrate knowledge and skills as they related to the state teacher competencies;
- completing dialogue journals; and
- taking exams.

In Phases II and III, Holly enrolled in two semesters of field-based student teaching. Located in a rural area, the middle school she taught in served a predominantly low socioeconomic population; it was also a professional development school for the College of Education. Excited to have earned her degree and obtained teaching certification, Holly was hired in a rural elementary school that serves predominantly a middle class population in Phase IV.

Experiencing luck few new teachers know, Holly's first classroom was double the size of a typical classroom. She organized the room predominantly by centers, and she brought furniture from home. A queen-sized mattress with jersey sheets and oversized pillows served as one reading center, while a more formal desk and chairs comprised another. A variety of charts hung on the wall, along with Word Walls, pictures, and posters. Desks were arranged in pods so children could work on projects together, and a comfortable rug area filled the front of the room for morning group time. Clearly, it was an inviting classroom for children and adults alike.

Interviews

Interviews with Holly provided the primary source of data for the study. Ethnographic notes were taken during the interviews, and the conversations were tape-recorded and later transcribed. Before each conversation, the re-searcher shared data collected and analyzed from previous interviews and observations along with tentative emergent themes. Holly offered construc-tive feedback on analysis that had occurred, and the researcher refined the themes accordingly. The researcher also utilized the inter-rater reliability process (Merriam, 1998) and engaged in discussion with an external researcher until at least 90% agreement occurred on data analysis.

Conversations with Holly were semi-structured in nature. The interview guide (see Appendix A) included specific, open-ended questions to begin the process, but probes were used additionally to elicit more specific infor-mation when needed. Holly was free to add any information she deemed appropriate to the conversation. Finally, interviews were conducted until data saturation was reached.

Classroom Observations

Classroom observations were conducted in the natural setting to exam-ine for congruency among Holly's beliefs, intentions, and instructional be-haviors. Observations were scheduled until saturation of data was reached, and the researcher took the role of participant observer. Facets examined in each observation included: (a) the lesson topic and content, (b) the teacher's role, (c) the students' roles, (d) the instructional practices, and (e) compre-hension/metacognition focus. Appendix B provides a description of the observation guide.

Artifact Collections

Interested in Holly's instructional implementation, the researcher collected and analyzed artifacts such as dialogue journal entries, lesson plans, and her public school students' work. Following each observation, Holly's lesson plans and some of her public school students' work were collected and discussed during the interviews. During this time Holly had the opportunity to make connections among her teaching beliefs, instructional behaviors, and the artifacts collected. This provided another perspective for triangulating the data for validity and reliability purposes.

Survey

The researcher created an open-ended survey (see Appendix C) to glean information from preservice teachers regarding their beliefs and intentions concerning comprehension strategy instruction and constructivism. The sur-vey was used to collect written responses from the participants in the semes-ter they took the researcher's Comprehension and Literacy II course, and it contained four prompts. Content validity was established by giving copies of the instrument to a professor and to ten doctoral students, all who were certified teachers. They responded to the survey by indicating areas that were strong and areas that needed clarification and made suggestions for improvement. Appropriate changes were made to the draft survey before its first implementation. Reliability of the results was obtained through the inter-rater process.

Analysis for Each Data Source

Data from the interviews, observations, artifacts, and surveys were first individually analyzed using the constant comparative method of qualitative analysis (Glaser & Strauss, 1994). In this process, the researcher was involved in simultaneous collecting, coding, and analyzing of data. In the first stage, the researcher coded the data according to categories as they emerged. The researcher then shared the categories with Holly and the external researcher for inter-rater reliability purposes. In the second stage, the researcher compared incidents with incidents to determine how they related to one another. In the third stage, the researcher compared incidents and categories to integrate related information and deleted irrelevant information. This was done until the categories were saturated. Finally, the researcher capitalized on her field notes, coding schemes, and categories to formulate overarching themes.

Analysis across Data Sources

Data were also analyzed across sources. Categories constructed for each data source were compared to categories generated for the other sources; this enabled the researcher to examine for congruency of the phenomena across data sources. Ultimately, the researcher wanted to know how information obtained from observations, artifacts, and surveys compared to information gleaned from interviews with Holly. Further, the researcher employed constant comparative analysis to compare and contrast findings for each of the participants and organize the findings as congruent or dissonant (Glaser & Strauss, 1994).

Results

Phase I (Preservice University Course)

Space limits discussion of Phase I Data Analysis to broad overarching themes and subcategories. The students completed dialogue journal entries on the first day of the semester and at the conclusion of the course. The prompts included: (a) Discuss your attitudes and beliefs about teaching reading, (b) how can we use trade books to teach?, and (c) tell me what you feel are the most important things you learned in this course. They also completed an open-ended survey on the last day of the course. The four prompts were: (a) With which constructive metacognition and comprehension strategies are you familiar?; (b) which constructive metacognition and comprehension strategies do you plan to use during your internship and residency?;

(c) in your own words, tell me what you think a constructivist teacher is; and (d) how will you be a constructivist teacher during your internship, residency, and in your first year of teaching? (See Appendix D for a description of the strategies taught during the semester.)

Data gleaned from Holly suggested that she planned to implement research-based reading practices. Using her knowledge of comprehension strategies she gained that semester, Holly revealed, "I will use comprehension strategies so my students can regulate their own learning without my having to tell them everything. They'll have a lot of strategies to choose from so they can work according to their learning styles." She also intended to implement effective instructional practices. Demonstrating her knowledge of content integration, Holly wrote, "I plan to integrate literature with every lesson." Additionally, she considered student-centered instruction. Noting the importance of active learning, Holly shared, "This is a teacher who lets her/his students construct their own knowledge." Further data analysis indicated that she intended to teach to her students' affective domain, individualize instruction, and maximize her students' learning potential.

Phase II Internship
(First Semester of Field-Based Student Teaching)

Data collected in Phase II were limited to interviews, observations, and artifact collections. During interviews, Holly revealed that effective teachers balance objectivist and constructivist instruction. She explained, "I think it's important for the kids to construct their own knowledge. I can't just stand up there in front of the class and lecture the whole time because they won't listen to me or even behave if they get bored . . . I think they need to be actively involved in whatever we're doing." Observations and artifact collection also supported this notion. Holly effectively balanced teacher talk and student talk, and her students engaged with meaning-making strategies such as semantic webs, possible sentences (Stahl & Kapinus, 1991), and Venn diagrams.

Holly also indicated in interviews that children's comprehension can be maximized with constructive comprehension and metacognitive strategy instruction. She indicated that when her students experienced difficulty with comprehension, she often had them revisit the text to find answers; she added that participating in constructive comprehension and metacognitive strategy instruction in RDG 370 had encouraged her to use the comprehension strategies she had learned.

Observations and artifact collection provided further evidence of strategies. In her first lesson, she asked the students to construct possible sentences with vocabulary words rather than copy definitions from textbooks. After writing their sentences, the students shared them with partners, discussed whether the sentences were appropriate, and then re-wrote them if necessary. In the same lesson, students skimmed the chapter in their texts and worked in small groups to construct semantic webs to demonstrate knowledge of vocabulary and content. In her second lesson, the students compared and contrasted Revolutionary British and American armies using Venn diagrams before answering questions on a worksheet.

Holly also pointed out that teachers who model best practice use a variety of strategies to implement effective instruction. She noted, "Children should be actively involved in learning." Observations and artifacts supported her students' active learning. She included movement activities, designed cooking experiences, and varied instructional approaches according to students' needs.

Phase III Residency
(Second Semester of Field-Based Student Teaching)

During Holly's second semester of field-based student, she again affirmed her beliefs that objectivist and constructivist instruction should be balanced. She considered herself to be primarily constructivist and commented, "I try real hard to be student-centered. My students do a lot of talking in class." Observations and artifacts reinforced this notion. Though she did lecture for a few minutes at the beginning of her fourth lesson, Holly also had the class complete word sorts in small groups. As the students discussed their word sorts, Holly circulated around the room checking for understanding and doing informal assessments. The students' next opportunity to talk came as they created and shared sketch to stretch pictures (Short, Harste, & Burke, 1996).

Holly also reaffirmed that using constructive comprehension and metacognitive strategy instruction could maximize students' reading comprehension. When asked how she thought comprehension was best facilitated and/or taught, Holly mentioned the strategies she learned in RDG 370. She indicated that she used ". . . [The] Dots [Have it], lots of different graphic organizers, Venn diagrams, K-W-L charts, concept squares, and semantic webs . . . flip charts, brainstorming, and sketch to stretch" to help build her students' comprehension. Observations, lesson plans, and the children's work documented that she used these strategies with her children.

Finally, Holly again addressed the importance of using a variety of strategies to provide effective instruction. In interviews, she specifically addressed integrating the arts across the curriculum and encouraging cooperative learning: ". . . I also like to use paired learning and cooperative groups as much as possible. I like to pair stronger learners with weaker learners. They help each other, and they help me, too." Observations and lesson plans made visible Holly's repertoire of instructional strategies. She used classroom discussion, cooperative learning, and hands-on activities to stimulate her children. Believing high order thinking skills were important, she was careful to construct questions at each level of Bloom's Taxonomy to ensure her students were challenged.

Phase IV (First Year of Certified Teaching)

During her first year of certified teaching, Holly again referred to herself as a constructivist. She revealed, "It takes a lot more time to plan a constructivist lesson plan than it does to write an objectivist plan, but I know it's worth it." She went on to say that her current students spent about 20% more of their overall time on constructivist activities than did her students the previous semester. Observations and artifacts revealed that her students spent significant amounts of time talking and learning. For example, Holly constructed a K-W-L chart and Venn diagram on the board and asked the students to supply pertinent information. The students also had an opportunity to talk while sharing leaf rubbings and creative writing pieces. In her sixth lesson, the students read and summarized a story. Actively engaged, the students participated in buddy reading and constructing their own questions. They stood in front of the class and shared their questions, giving their peers opportunities to answer. Finally, they orally completed a beginning, middle, end summarization of the story.

When asked how she thought comprehension was best taught, Holly responded, "Comprehension with first graders must be creative. Summarizing verbally or in pictures seems to work best for my students." She noted that she also used a variety of graphic organizers to facilitate text comprehension. Observations and artifacts revealed that Holly's students used strategies quite often. Not only did her students complete K-W-L charts, cloze charts, and Venn diagrams, they also created story maps and eight page books. They participated in buddy reading, writing their own questions, and looping, and they engaged in brainstorming; creative writing; and beginning, middle, end activities. Examining the state-adopted textbook, teacher's manual, and student workbook, the researcher found that the students also practiced the following strategies: sequencing, What happened next?, Who said what?, character description, fantasy and reality, drawing conclusions, making inferences, and determining cause and effect.

In an early spring interview Holly confessed, "I understand now more than ever that each child learns differently." Sharing some of her favorite lesson plans with the researcher, Holly described strategies she had experienced the most success with; she specifically addressed the multiple intelligences and integrating the arts across the curriculum. As Holly shared her experiences, the researcher examined some of the children's artifacts. Holly was particularly fond of a lesson focusing on trees, leaves, fall, and spring, in which the children went outside to collect leaves and make rubbings. Holly commented, "I wish I had had a bigger variety of leaves for them to do rubbings with. It would have been better if we had had time today to look in the books to see what kinds of trees the leaves came from. We'll get to that though." She believed that the leaf rubbings were an effective hands-on way for her students to internalize curricular content.

Summary of Data Analysis for the Study

The researcher found that Holly's beliefs and practices for all three overarching statements throughout the study appeared to be congruent. Holly seemingly experienced no conflict between the way she believed she should teach and how she actually taught. As the study progressed, Holly shared her thoughts about how she was growing as a teacher. She was fully aware that she had room for growth, though she seemed so proud that her understanding of how children learn was continuously being enhanced. She established goals each semester to plan student-centered lessons, and she often forced herself to "sit on her hands" while her students took risks and made mistakes. At the end of the study, Holly was thrilled to have finished her first year of certified teaching, and she anticipated refining her teaching skills in the next academic year.

Impact of Reflective Activities on Preservice Teachers' Beliefs and Instructional Behaviors. In class conversations at the beginning of the semester, the RDG 370 students took primarily an objectivist stance toward teaching. Thus, the researcher carefully selected dialogue journal entry prompts for the students to reflect on, which enabled the researcher to be privy to the future teachers' thoughts. The researcher also hoped that the preservice teachers would feel cognitive dissonance about the way they were taught as children and how that type of instruction relates to current research on reading comprehension instruction. The researcher concluded that through the reflective activities, the preservice teachers were forced to consider the "why behind the what" as they contemplated why they would implement certain types of instruction in their future classrooms. The reflective activities further served to strengthen their intentions of using constructive comprehension and metacognitive strategy instruction in their future classrooms.

Impact of Constructive Comprehension Course on Holly's Preservice Instructional Behaviors. Holly utilized comprehension strategies in every lesson she taught, and in many lessons she used more than one strategy. She modeled some strategies for the students while the children orally participated, while other times the students engaged in hands-on comprehension instruction as they created their own artifacts. Thus, the researcher concluded that participating in a course modeling best practice of constructive comprehension strategy instruction impacted Holly's instructional practices in her field experience by encouraging her to use such instruction in each lesson she taught.

Impact of Constructive Comprehension Course on Holly's Inservice Instructional Behaviors. Holly made specific connections between the way she taught and some of the reading strategies the researcher modeled in the comprehension and literacy course. For example, during an interview, Holly thanked the researcher for sharing the strategies with her in class. She commented that she would not have known how to begin to teach comprehension without the strategies. Thus, the researcher concluded that participating in a course modeling best practice of constructive comprehension strategy instruction encouraged Holly to use such instruction in her first year of teaching.

Influential Factors in Impacting Holly's Preservice/Inservice Beliefs and Instructional Behaviors. Holly's preservice/inservice beliefs and behaviors were influenced by a number of environmental factors. Figure 1 depicts the relationships between Holly's beliefs and practices during Phase I. While enrolled in university coursework, Holly was exposed to constructive comprehension and metacognitive strategy instruction. Further, she engaged in reflective activities that encouraged her to align beliefs with future practices. Figure 2 describes the relationships between Holly's beliefs and practices during Phases II and III. While student teaching, Holly was exposed to her mentor teachers' theoretical beliefs and instructional practices. Her beliefs and practices may also have been impacted by the presence of her university liaisons and the researcher. Figure 3 demonstrates the relationship between Holly's beliefs and practices during Phase IV. During her first year of teaching, Holly was influenced by content contained in the state adopted reading basals with which she was required to teach, though she did not always take the basal teacher recommendations to heart. All factors considered, the researcher concluded that the most influential factors on Holly's teacher beliefs and practices were (a) her university coursework, including the reflective activities; (b) her student teaching experience; and (c) the presence of the researcher in the classroom.

Figure 1. Teacher Development Model for Holly Phase I

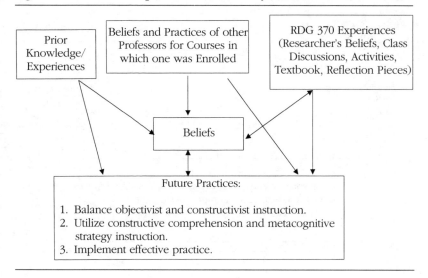

Figure 2. Teacher Development Model for Holly Phases II and III

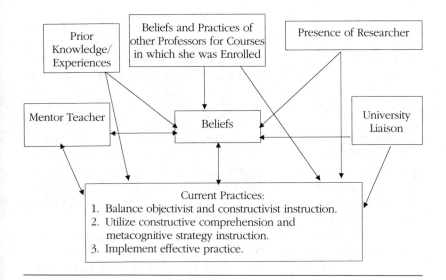

Figure 3. Teacher Development Model for Holly Phase IV

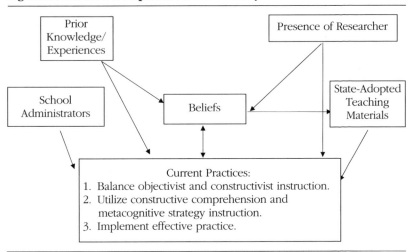

Discussion

Data collected suggested that Holly's beliefs and practices for all three overarching statements throughout the study were congruent. During observations, it was clear that she implemented instructional practices that reflected what current research has to say about best practices, and she engaged her students in purposeful, authentic activities, a notion expounded upon in Heuwinkel's (1996) research. She also allowed her children to work in groups, which facilitated social construction (Johnson & Johnson, 1994; Slavin, 1999). Finally, she believed in sensory based learning (Cornett, 1999).

While some of the findings of this study were congruent with other research studies, findings also emerged that differed from other research examinations. For example, observations of Holly in the final three phases were inconsistent with Durkin's (1978) findings that teachers spend little time on reading comprehension instruction. Durkin found in her study that teachers spend a great deal of time asking their students low level questions and assessing their students. In the current study, Holly consistently asked her students high level questions and engaged them in constructive comprehension and metacognitive strategy instruction.

The current study also differed from Durkin's (1984) findings that teachers tend not to teach vocabulary words in context or in meaningful situations that lead to in-depth understanding (Lloyd, 1996). In Holly's first lesson, rather than having her students copy definitions from social studies textbooks, a decontextualized activity, she first instructed them to write possible sentences for the words (Stahl & Kapinus, 1991); the students then created semantic webs to demonstrate their knowledge of how the words were related. In Holly's third lesson, she had her students examine vocabulary words in the context of their textbook. They then engaged in discussion, making hypotheses about what they thought the words meant. Finally, they created flip charts and recorded personal definitions for the words. In Holly's eighth lesson, she tied the new content to her children's prior knowledge by playing a looping game with them.

Finally, findings of this study were incongruent with Durkin's (1984) findings that few teachers capitalize on their students' prior knowledge and congruent with Lloyd's (1996) findings that most teachers make connections between old and new knowledge in their lessons. It appeared that Holly consistently began her lessons by providing her students with opportunities to connect new information with old information, a practice condoned by Anderson and Pearson (1984). She achieved this in a variety of ways, among them: (a) asking questions, (b) reading stories, (c) explicitly relating new knowledge to prior knowledge, and (d) having students share their own experiences with the class. The roots of this practice may be rooted in the way the researcher modeled capitalizing on prior knowledge in the comprehension and literacy course or in the dialogue journal entries Holly used to reflect on her beliefs and future practices. Or, perhaps Holly taught this way because her mentors modeled this behavior or because the researcher's presence encouraged her to do so.

Findings that emerged in the current study were congruent with other research studies on teacher beliefs about effective instruction. First, research supports the notion that a preservice teacher's field experience impacts preservice teachers' beliefs and practices (Linek, Nelson, Sampson, Mohr, & Zeek, 1999). Further, preservice teachers' field experiences can play a primary role impacting preservice teacher achievement and teacher performance in the first year of teaching (Richardson, 1996). Holly stated that many of the strategies she used were ones she had learned in preservice teacher seminars on campus.

Second, research suggests that the educational beliefs teachers hold impact what type of instruction they implement (Reutzel & Sabey, 1996). Holly's beliefs and practices were congruent throughout the study. She consistently balanced objectivist and constructivist instruction, utilized constructive comprehension and metacognitive strategy institution, and modeled best practice by implementing a variety of instructional strategies.

Limitations

This investigation was implemented with several limitations. First, Holly was involved in experiences external to the study that may have impacted her beliefs and instruction. Second, Holly was under the direction of a university liaison, mentor teachers, and others who could have affected her beliefs and instructional behaviors during her field experience. Third, self-reported data may be inaccurate because Holly may have elected to report data she deemed more appropriate than her true beliefs and behaviors, or she may provided answers she felt met the researcher's expectations. Fifth, the researcher's presence may have caused Holly to model instructional behaviors and create artifacts that were incongruent with her true beliefs in order to meet the researcher's expectations. Finally, because Holly was a volunteer, her theoretical beliefs and instructional behaviors may be atypical of all classroom teachers.

Case study design was selected because it was deemed most appropriate to answer the research questions (Merriam, 1998; Stake, 1995). Case studies are prevalent in the education field because they allow for in-depth understanding of a variety of phenomena; they provide a thick, rich description of the environment, the participants, and their behavior. Such qualitative research paints a more holistic picture than the use of quantifiable variables alone. Further, case studies accommodate the opportunity for an in-depth study of a person's knowledge, attitudes, beliefs, and behavior. Finally, case studies have significant potential for influencing future practice and research. It was the hope of this researcher to impact not only the lives of the preservice and inservice teachers in the area but also the students in their classrooms now and in the years to come. The intent of this study was not to generalize findings; rather, it was to describe in detail Holly's experience of transitioning from a university student, to a preservice teacher, and finally to a certified teacher.

Suggestions for Further Research

Results of this study uncovered several areas worthy of teacher, researcher, and political examination. First, research concerning how to increase the efficacy of mentoring programs for new teachers is needed. Perhaps if more teachers who model developmentally appropriate practice are paired with new teachers in order to scaffold their learning, support their instruction, and offer constructive feedback, the chances of new teachers implementing authentic literacy practices would be increased.

Second, more research is needed concerning self-efficacy. Results of this study showed that teachers who have high levels of self-efficacy are more willing to take risks in implementing effective instruction. More research is needed to examine the relationship between these two variables so that professors in preservice teacher education programs can make necessary interventions to boost their students' perceived levels of self-efficacy.

References

Anderson, R. C., & Pearson, P. D. (1984). A schema-theoretic view of basic processes in reading comprehension. In P. D. Pearson (Ed.), *Handbook of reading research* (pp. 255-291). New York: Longman.

Anning, A. (1988). Teachers' theories about children's learning. In J. Calderhead (Ed.), *Teachers' professional learning* (pp. 128-145). London: Falmer.

Azjen, I. (1988). *Attitudes, personality, and behavior.* Chicago: Dorsey.

Baker, L., & Brown, A. L. (1984). Metacognition skills and reading. In P. D. Pearson (Ed.), *Handbook of reading research* (pp. 353-394). New York: Longman.

Bredekamp, S., & Copple, C. (Eds.). (1997). *Developmentally appropriate practice in early childhood programs* (Rev. ed). Washington, DC: National Association for the Education of Young Children.

Brooks, J. G., & Brooks, M. G. (1993). *The case for constructivist classrooms.* Alexandria, VA: Association for Supervision and Curriculum Development.

Castor, B. (2000). Quality teaching key to education reform. *Educational Horizons, 78*(3), 135-136.

Clandinin, D. J. (1986). *Classroom practice: Teacher images in action.* London: Falmer.

Cochran-Smith, M. (1991). Reinventing student teaching. *Journal of Teacher Education, 42*(2), 104-118.

Crow, N. A. (1987, April). *Preservice teachers' biography: A case study.* Paper presented at the annual meeting of the American Educational Research Association, Washington, DC.

Cornett, C. E. (1999). *The arts as meaning makers: Integrating literature and the arts throughout the curriculum.* Upper Saddle River, NJ: Merrill.

Cunningham, P. M., & Allington, R. L. (1999). *Classrooms that work: They can all read and write* (2nd ed.). New York: Longman.

Doyle, M. (1997). Beyond life history as a student: Preservice teachers' beliefs about teaching and learning. *College Student Journal, 31,* 519-531.

Durkin, D. (1978). What classroom observations reveal about comprehension instruction. *Reading Research Quarterly, 14,* 481-533.

Durkin, D. (1984). Is there a match between what elementary teachers do and what basal reader manuals recommend? *The Reading Teacher, 37,* 734-744.

Flavell, J. H. (1981). Cognitive monitoring. In W. P. Dickson (Ed.), *Children's oral communication skills.* New York: Academic Press.

Flood, J., & Lapp, D. (1991). Reading comprehension instruction. In J. Flood, M. Jensen, D. Lapp, & J. R. Squire (Eds.), *Handbook of research on teaching the English language arts* (pp. 732-742). New York: Macmillan.

Glaser, B. G., & Strauss, A. L. (1994). Case histories and case studies. In B. G. Glaser (Ed.), *More grounded theory methodology: A reader* (pp. 233-245). Mill Valley, CA: Sociology Press.

Green, T. (1971). *The activities of teaching.* New York: McGraw-Hill.

Heuwinkel, M. K. (1996). New ways of learning = New ways of teaching. *Childhood Education, 73,* 27-31.

Johnson, D. W., & Johnson, R. T. (1994). *Learning together and alone: Cooperative, competitive, and individualistic learning* (4th ed.). Boston: Allyn and Bacon.

Linek, W. M., Nelson, O., Sampson, M. B., Mohr, K., & Zeek, C. (1999). Developing beliefs about literacy instruction: A cross-case analysis of preservice teachers in traditional and field-based settings. *Reading Research and Instruction, 38*(4), 371-386.

Lloyd, C. V. (1996). How teachers teach reading comprehension: An examination of four categories of reading comprehension instruction. *Reading Research and Instruction, 35,* 170-184.

Lortie, D. (1975). *Schoolteacher: A sociological study.* Chicago: The University of Chicago Press.

Maxson, M. M., & Sindelar, R. (1998). Images revisited: Examining preservice teachers' ideas about teaching. *Teacher Education Quarterly, 25*(2), 5-26.

Merriam, S. B. (1998). *Qualitative research and case study applications in education.* San Francisco: Jossey-Bass.

National Association for the Education of Young Children. (1998). Learning to read and write: Developing appropriate practices for young children-A joint position statement of the International Reading Association (IRA) and the National Association for the Education of Young Children. *Young Children, 53*(4), 30-46.

Ogle, D. (1986). K-W-L: A teaching model that develops active reading of expository text. *The Reading Teacher, 39,* 564-570.

Pajares, M. F. (1992). Teachers' beliefs and educational research: Cleaning up a messy construct. *Review of Educational Research, 62*(3), 307-332.

Patton, M. Q. (1990). Qualitative evaluation methods. (2nd ed.). Thousand Oaks, CA: Sage.

Reutzel, D. R., & Sabey, B. L. (1996). Teacher beliefs and children's concepts about reading: Are they related? *Reading Research and Instruction, 35,* 323-342.

Richardson, V. (1996). The role of attitudes and beliefs in learning to teach. In J. Sikula, T. Buttery, & E. Guyton (Eds.), *The handbook of research on teacher education* (pp. 102-119). New York: Simon & Schuster.

Rosenblatt, L. M. (1994). The transactional theory of reading and writing. In R. B. Ruddell, M. R. Ruddell, & H. Singer (Eds.), *Theoretical models and processes of reading* (4th ed., pp. 1057-1092). Newark, DE: International Reading Association.

Short, K. G., Harste, J. C., & Burke, C. L. (1996). *Creating classrooms for authors and inquirers* (2nd ed.). Portsmouth, NH: Heinemann.

Slavin, R. F. (1999). Comprehensive approaches to cooperative learning. *Theory into Practice, 38*(2), 74-79.

Smith, F. (1997). *Reading without nonsense* (3rd ed.). New York: Teachers College Press.

Smith, K. (1999). *Phonics friendly families.* Spring, TX: Absey & Company.

Stahl, S. A., & Kapinus, B. A. (1991). Possible sentences: Predicting word meanings to teach content area vocabulary. *Reading Teacher, 45*(1), 36-43.

Stake, R. E. (1995). *The art of case study research.* Thousand Oaks, CA: Sage.

Stauffer, R. (1976). *Teaching reading as a thinking process.* New York: Harper & Row.

Vaughan, J. L., & Estes, T. H. (1986). *Reading and reasoning beyond the primary grades.* Boston: Allyn and Bacon, Inc.

Vygotsky, L. S. (1978). *Mind in society: The development of higher psychological processes* (M. Cole, V. Jon-Steiner, S. Scribner, & E. Souberman, Eds., and Trans.). Cambridge, MA: Harvard University Press.

Appendix A. Interview Questions with Preservice/Inservice Teachers

1. Tell me how your internship/residency/first semester of teaching is coming along.
2. How do you think comprehension is best facilitated in the classroom?
3. How do you teach comprehension in your classroom?
4. What percentage of time would you say your students are engaged in constructivist activities?
5. How do you think students can be best taught to refine their metacognitive skills?
6. How do you encourage students to use metacognitive strategies in your class?
7. Some teachers say that using constructive comprehension and metacognitive strategy instruction takes too much time and effort. How do you feel about this statement?
8. How supportive are your mentor teachers/peer teachers about constructive comprehension and metacognitive strategy instruction?
9. In an ideal situation, how would you teach comprehension?
10. If one of your peer teachers were to ask you why you use constructive comprehension and metacognitive strategy instruction, how would you react to this question?
11. How has participating in constructive comprehension and metacognitive strategy activities in RDG 370 impacted the way you teach now?

Appendix B. Sample Observation Guide Used to Collect Data in Phase II

DATE	PURPOSE	QUESTIONS	OBSERVATION FOCUS
9/14/99	Introduce researcher to setting. Reintroduce preservice teacher to study. Describe preservice teacher's classroom practices as they relate to constructive comprehension and metacognitive strategy instruction.	Beliefs about constructive comprehension and metacognitive strategy instruction. Plans for using constructive comprehension and metacognitive strategy instruction.	Organization of room; design and content of lesson; role of teacher; role of student; instructional practices; comprehension and/or metacognition focus
12/3/99	Describe preservice teacher's classroom practices as they relate to constructive comprehension and metacognitive strategy instruction. Check researcher's perceptions about instructional beliefs and classroom practices as they relate to constructive comprehension and metacognitive strategy instruction.	Beliefs about constructive comprehension and metacognitive strategy instruction. Plans for using constructive comprehension and metacognitive strategy instruction.	Organization of room; design and content of lesson; role of teacher; role of student; instructional practices; comprehension and/or metacognition focus

Appendix C. Reading 370 Survey

The following questions relate to your Reading 370 experience. Please answer each item thoughtfully. While there are no right or wrong answers, clever responses are encouraged. Your feedback will be used to determine the effectiveness of the course. You do not have to participate, and confidentiality will be maintained.

1. With which comprehension strategies are you familiar?

2. Which comprehension strategies do you plan to use during your internship and residency?

3. In your own words, tell me what you think a constructivist teacher is.

4. How will you be a constructivist teacher during your internship and residency?

Appendix D. Comprehension Strategies Taught in RDG 370 Comprehension and Literacy I

1. **KWL (Ogle, 1986):** The students create a chart that shows what they *know* about a subject, what they *want* to know about a subject, and what they *learned* about the subject.

2. **Directed Reading-Thinking Activity (DR-TA) (Stauffer, 1976):** The students *predict* what they think will happen in the story, *verify* or *change* their predictions as they read, *make judgments* about the story, and then engage in *extension activities* with the story.

3. **Story Map (Smith, 1999):** During or after reading a selection, the students participate in an activity in which they discuss the story grammar (characters, plot, setting, conflict, theme, etc.)

4. **Venn Diagram (Smith, 1999):** The students create a chart with two or more overlapping circles in which they compare and contrast ideas pertaining the selection read.

5. **Semantic Mapping:** The students create a graphic organizer, usually with circles or rectangles, to indicate important ideas of what they have read and to show how the ideas are related.

6. **Interactive Notations System for Effective Reading and Thinking [Insert Strategy] (Vaughan & Estes, 1986):** The students use symbols such as question marks, exclamation points, stars, etc. to indicate their thoughts about the text (e.g., what they do not understand, what they deem important in the selection, what they disagree with, etc.)

7. **Concept Squares (Vaughan & Estes, 1986):** The students explore four aspects of a text. The questions or concepts they work with may be chosen by the students or by the teacher.

8. **Directed Listening-Thinking Activity (DL-TA) (Stauffer, 1976):** In this activity, the students listen as the teacher reads aloud. The students *predict* what they think will happen in the story, *verify* or *change* their predictions as they listen to the story, make *judgments*, and participate in *extension activities.*

9. **Brainstorming:** The teacher asks, "What do you think of when I say _____?" and the students respond on paper or aloud to the teacher as she records the responses.

10. **LINK (List-Inquire-Note-Know) (Vaughan & Estes, 1986):** The teacher presents the students with a concept. The students then *list* everything they know about it and share aloud with the teacher, who records the responses. Other students then *inquire* about any concepts they need clarification on, while the students who originally offered the responses *note* what they know about the topic. Following the lesson, the students are then given one minute to list everything they now know as a result of the lesson and discussion.

11. **Sketch to Stretch (Short, Harste, & Burke, 1996):** The students read or listen to a story and then draw a picture that "appeared" in their minds as the story was read. They then share their pictures with the class.

12. **Cubing (Vaughan & Estes, 1986):** The students describe an object or story using six different categories, one for each level of Bloom's Taxonomy.

13. **Trifold (Smith, 1999):** The students fold a piece of paper into thirds to explore three concepts of a narrative or expository text (e.g., beginning, middle, end).

14. **Eight Page Book (Smith, 1999):** The students fold a piece of paper and make strategic cuts with scissors to create small books that have 8 pages. They then record information from a text or write their own stories based on a text.

15. **The Dots Have It (Smith, 1999):** The students used colored sticker dots to mark words in texts of which they do not know the meaning. They then write what they think the words mean using context clues before verifying their hypotheses with dictionary definitions.

16. **Flip Charts (Smith, 1999):** Students use two staples and three pieces of folded paper to create flip charts. They then explore 6 facets of a topic or record important information about a book they're read or the current topic of study.

17. **Heart Strategy (Smith, 1999):** Students use scissors and paper to create hearts with flaps. They then analyze and synthesize by creating analogies and comparing and contrasting themselves with characters they read about in narrative texts.

18. **Setting Bookmarks (Smith, 1999):** On strips of paper, students illustrate the setting from a text, then use descriptive words from the selection to support their illustrations.

A Description of Vocabulary Learning in At-Risk College Freshmen Cooperatively Involved in Generative Study of Self-Selected Words

Janet L. Pariza

Northeastern Illinois University

Abstract

Vocabulary development at the post-secondary levels is a fundamental key to success. Many students find the demands of college-level vocabulary difficult, putting them at-risk for course failure. This study examines college freshman enrolled in a developmental reading course and their methods for developing vocabulary skills. Perceptions and opinions about vocabulary learning were examined during the course of the research, and the participants engaged in activities that revealed which strategies were utilized most effectively in word learning.

Introduction

One consistent goal of education, from the earliest beginnings of formal education to the present time, has been vocabulary development (Aristotle, 1991; Kennedy, 1983; Marrou, 1956; Quintilian, 95/1899). During the last century, researchers in education established a clear relationship between word knowledge and reading comprehension (Davis, 1944, 1968; Thorndike, 1917). Contemporary theorists and researchers have both acknowledged and built upon that relationship (Anderson & Freebody, 1981; Graves, 2000; Johnson & Pearson, 1978; Kameenui, Carnine, & Freschi, 1982; McKeown, Beck, Omanson, & Perfetti, 1983; Pearson & Johnson, 1978), allowing one group of contemporary researchers to conclude, "Vocabulary development is at the heart of all learning" (Wheatley, Muller, & Miller, 1993, p. 93).

Word knowledge is fundamental for successful reading comprehension, and successful reading comprehension is fundamental for academic success, particularly at the postsecondary level where textbooks are integral to independent knowledge acquisition (Burrell, Tao, Simpson, & Mendez-Berrueta, 1997; Voss & Silfries, 1996). Yet many postsecondary students find the vocabulary demands of college-level study challenging enough to jeopardize successful course completion (Nist, Holschuh, & Sharman, 1995; Sartain et al., 1982). College reading programs attempt to address the vocabulary needs of students both by increasing the overall size of the students' vocabularies and by developing independent word-learning strategies.

Although vocabulary has been called "one of the four instructional cornerstones of the college developmental reading program" (Stahl, Brozo, Smith, Henk, & Commander, 1991, p. 24), there is no strong research foundation upon which to build curriculum and instruction in such programs. Little vocabulary research has focused on college-level learners, and virtually no research has attempted to explore college students' perceptions of word learning or their development of independent word-learning strategies. Writing for the most recent edition of the *Handbook of College Reading and Study Strategies* (Flippo & Caverly, 2000), Simpson and Randall (2000) acknowledged the lack of a research into these areas and specifically called for "more research on student-centered vocabulary approaches...like Haggard's (1982) self-collection strategy" (p. 61). They further asked for descriptive studies that would go beyond standardized testing to interview students "to discover their opinions" about vocabulary instruction, to "share their perceptions of how they learn new words," and to describe "their strategies for learning unknown words" (p. 61). The research reported here was conducted in response to the directives of Simpson and Randall (2000) as well as in response to a recognized need in the researcher to better understand vocabulary learning in at-risk college freshmen as a prerequisite for the design of effective vocabulary instruction for this population.

Methodology
Research Design and Questions
The research reported in this study was conducted from the theoretical perspective of constructivism, using qualitative methods of data collection and a constant comparative method of data analysis. In the research, the researcher served three distinct roles: course designer, teacher, and researcher. The researcher had developed the curriculum for the semester-long developmental reading course that was the context of the study. Questions about the most efficacious plan for vocabulary instruction initially prompted the study. The researcher taught the two sections of the college reading course in which data were collected. The researcher designed the research to be minimally intrusive in classroom procedures.

This research was conducted in the context of a developmental reading course mandatory for some freshmen alternatively admitted to a large, state-supported, doctoral extensive research university in the Midwest. The reading course ascribes to a philosophy well stated by Bartholomae and Petrosky (1986) who recognized that some students experience "basic problems with advanced literacy (the problems of students who, while they can read and write, fail to read and write in ways that serve the ends or meet the expectations of university education)" (p. iv).

The reading course that served as the context for this research focused on the development of effective reading and study strategies through explicit instruction, teacher modeling, and the independent application of those strategies to college-level material. The reading course employed an intertextual approach to the semester-long exploration of a theme. The vocabulary component of the reading course was a modification of Haggard's (1982) Vocabulary Self-Collection Strategy (VSS) in which the students were required to select words from the assigned readings and to engage cooperatively in the determination of word meanings and the generation of mnemonic associations. Word knowledge was assessed informally through student self-reports of word learning.

This descriptive study that was designed to examine perceptions about vocabulary learning and independent word-learning strategies of at-risk college freshmen was initially guided by two overarching questions:

1. How do at-risk college freshmen perceive vocabulary learning?
2. What vocabulary learning strategies are independently selected and applied by at-risk college freshmen?

In addition, two subordinate questions guided the research:

3. How does working cooperatively to generate associations for targeted words impact student learning?
4. How was students' metacognitive awareness of word learning affected by the generative study of self-selected words?

Once data collection began, the research was also guided by the participants' on-going revelations of their perceptions about word learning.

Data Collection and Analysis

Data were collected consistently over one 16-week semester from 36 college freshmen enrolled in two sections of a college reading course taught by the researcher. Five of those students, Aracelli, Jay, LeRoy, Michael, and Tomika, (all pseudonyms) formed one working classroom group and served as key participants in the research. Data included three interviews with each of the five key participants; classroom observations, including audiotapes of the key group's weekly vocabulary sessions; document review, including journal entries and informal vocabulary assessments with responses to reflective vocabulary questions from all 36 participants and examination of vocabulary journals, reader response journals, formal essays, and essay exams from the five key participants; and both descriptive and reflective field notes written almost daily during the data collection process (see Appendix for data collection prompts).

Data analysis began simultaneously with data collection and continued after the collection period. Data analysis most closely resembled the constant comparative method, beginning with open coding and ending with the development of grounded theoretical propositions (Glaser & Strauss, 1967; Strauss & Corbin, 1990). As categories emerged from the data, they were examined analytically using questioning strategies to determine the characteristics of each category and the relationships among the categories, with the researcher employing alternative proposing and checking, using both inductive and deductive reasoning in the development of theoretical propositions (Cresswell, 1998). This study adhered to dictates for rigor and trustworthiness established in research literature (Bassey, 1999; Bogdan & Biklen, 1998; Lincoln & Guba, 1985; Merriam, 1998).

Descriptions
The Alternative Admittance Program

The reading course that was the context for the research reported here was mandatory for some students admitted through an alternative admittance program to a large state-supported doctoral extensive research university in the Midwest. In the Fall of 2000 when this research was conducted, 530 students were admitted to the university through the alternative admittance program. Of that number, 66% were African American, 12% were Hispanic/Latino, another 12% were Asian, 8% were Caucasian, and 3% were of an unspecified or non-reported ethnicity. Fifty-four percent of the entering freshman were female, and 29% of the total represented the first members in their respective families to ever attend college.

The program, which has been in existence since 1969, has a six-year graduation rate of 28%. This compares to a six-year graduation rate of 50% for the general university population. The alternative admittance program has a 76% first-year retention, a 50% second-year retention, and a 40% third-year retention. About 35% of the students in the program leave the university in good academic standing. In an effort to support these at-risk students, the alternative admittance program provides them with academic counseling, tutorial assistance, a freshman experience course taught by program counselors, financial aid advice, academic monitoring through the undergraduate years, and exit counseling for students withdrawing or transferring.

In addition, freshmen are placed into developmental courses in reading, writing, and mathematics when their test scores indicate a need for developmental work in these areas. Although the counselors and instructors who work with these students try hard to keep them in school, moving toward graduation, the majority of the students admitted through this program do not graduate from the university.

The Reading Course

The reading course in which this research was conducted was redesigned by the researcher in 1999 and was loosely patterned on a combined reading and writing course developed at the University of Pittsburgh, first taught in the Fall of 1978, and thoroughly described in *Facts, Artifacts, and Counterfacts: Theory and Method for a Reading and Writing Course* by Bartholomae and Petrosky (1986). The original course at the University of Pittsburgh served students who experienced "basic problems with advanced literacy (the problems of students who, while they can read and write, fail to read and write in ways that serve the ends or meet the expectations of university education)" (Bartholomae & Petrosky, 1986, p. iv). While several generations removed from the original model developed at Pittsburgh, the course attempted to adhere to the underlying philosophy of the original design by presenting students with extensive reading and writing on a central theme, by avoiding the kinds of "trivial or mechanical work" (Bartholomae & Petrosky, 1986, p. iii) that are still to be found in many developmental reading courses, and by presenting students with "the kinds of reading and writing that characterize college study" (Bartholomae & Petrosky, 1986, p. iii). It deviated from the original design by focusing more on reading than on writing, by more explicitly teaching active reading strategies, and by specifically focusing on connections between and among texts and between texts and personal experience.

The reading course used an intertextual approach to the exploration of the theme of personal identity development with course requirements addressing all forms of communication through three interrelated components: reading, writing, and vocabulary study.

The reading component required students to read four main texts and six satellite texts in addition to the course text. The main texts were all book-length memoirs that related aspects of the identity development of the subject of the memoir and, in some texts, that of the author as well. These four texts presented a diverse look at people from widely varying backgrounds and from overlapping time periods, spanning the whole twentieth century. Three of the memoirs were read and discussed by the whole class. A fourth memoir, chosen by each student from a short list, was read independently during the first half of the semester.

The book-length memoirs read by the full class, presented in the order in which they were read, were: *The Color of Water: A Black Man's Tribute to His White Mother* by James McBride (1996), *Bound Feet and Western Dress: A Memoir* by Pang-Mei Natasha Chang (1996), and *Duty: A Father, His Son, and the Man Who Won the War* by Bob Greene (2000). The list of books from which the students each selected an additional memoir included: *Always Running La Vida Loca: Gang Days in L. A.* by Luis Rodriguez (1993), *The Autobiography of Malcolm X as Told to Alex Haley* by Malcolm X (1964), *I Know Why the Caged Bird Sings* by Maya Angelou (1969), *Lakota Woman* by Mary Crow Dog (1990), and *Living Up the Street* by Gary Soto (1985).

The six satellite texts were four whole chapters from college-level textbooks, an excerpt of a few pages from an additional college-level textbook, and a five-page article from a college-level subject encyclopedia. The textbook selections presented theories that could be used to interpret the identity development of the people whose lives were revealed through the memoirs. Each text was selected because it offered a different perspective on the theme of personal identity development. For example, one text presented a theory of racial identity development while another presented several theories on gender identity development. The encyclopedia article offered historical background to enrich the comprehension of one of the memoirs.

The satellite texts, again presented in the order in which they were read, included "Identity Formation: Erikson's Theory of Psychosocial Development" from *Discovering Psychology* by Hockenbury and Hockenbury (1998); "Identity Development in Adolescence" and "Racial Identity in Adulthood," two chapters from *"Why Are All the Black Kids Sitting Together in the Cafeteria?" and Other Conversations about Race* by Tatum (1997); "Early Childhood Gender Socialization" from *Women, Men, and Society* by Renzetti and Curan (1999); "Women in China" by Kay Ann Johnson (1998), published in *Encyclopedia of Asian History;* and "Socialization" from *Sociology: Micro, Macro, and Mega Structures* by Jones, Gallagher, and McFalls (1999).

The course design necessitated class time devoted to group activities that engaged students in elaboration of concepts and ideas presented in the texts. Students engaged in focused small group collaboration on tasks such as group construction of graphic organizers or group brainstorming sessions to discover and support connections between and among the many texts as well as between the texts and personal life experiences. In this way, students first worked through small sections of text (daily readings) in dyads or triads to ensure and enhance text comprehension. Following the completion of a whole text, student groups engaged in broader scale interpretation, analysis, application, synthesis, and evaluation as they interpreted the lives presented in the memoirs using the theories from the textbook excerpts. Students were also asked to make connections between their own experiences and the texts as well as between and among the three texts already read. Perceived connections were further explored in journal entries.

The pattern of independent reading followed by classroom activities and journal writing to extend comprehension was maintained throughout the semester, as each new text and successive readings of textbook chapters added increasing depth to the students' understanding of the theme, personal identity development. Successful completion of the course required students to read over 1,000 pages.

The writing component of the course had a number of requirements. Students maintained a reading response/reflection journal throughout the semester. Students wrote a minimum of three entries each week in a reading response/reflection journal. Two entries were in response to journaling assignments provided by the course text; students wrote a third entry on a topic of their own choosing that related in some way to the course reading. As part of the semester journal requirement, students participating in this study also wrote three entries specifically addressing vocabulary issues (see Appendix for data collection prompts).

In addition to reflective journal writing, students composed two formal essays that required analysis, application, and synthesis of course concepts. To complete the writing component of the course, all three exams given in the course were essay exams, again requiring students to engage in analysis, application, and synthesis of course concepts as well as to write in the language that had been used in course texts and discussions.

For the vocabulary component of the reading course, students were required to construct a vocabulary notebook of self-selected words. Students were required to record a semester total of 120 words taken from the assigned readings. Each word record included the word, a text page reference, the context from which the word was taken, a definition of the word, and a mnemonic association. Each week, students were given some time in class to work with a group of peers on sharing words, negotiating definitions, and generating associations.

Each week, students were informally assessed on vocabulary knowledge. This assessment most often took the form of students' self-reporting word learning. Students were asked to cover everything in their notebooks except the listing of words. From the list of words, they were asked to choose three or four remembered words from the most recently recorded words and another two to three remembered words from words recorded earlier in the semester. For each remembered word, they wrote the meaning of the word and how or why they remembered it. Additionally, during the weekly informal assessments, students were frequently asked to respond in writing to specific questions about some aspect of vocabulary learning.

The vocabulary requirement of this course was an adaptation of Haggard's

(1982) VSS. Her strategy required students to contribute two words each to a weekly class list. The words could be from any source; the only requirement was that the student contributing the word needed to believe that it was a valuable word that all students in the class should know. These words, once compiled, became the basis for further vocabulary study, employing practice exercises and testing designed by the instructor. In the adaptation of VSS reported in this study, students contributed individually self-selected words taken from the course readings to the group. They engaged in group discussion and negotiation of meanings, additional generative work with the selected words, and informal assessments.

In addition to the regular course vocabulary requirement, the participants in this study regularly engaged in brief word activities that served as mental warm-up exercises at the beginning of class sessions. These activities provided a means to direct and keep student focus on words and to encourage flexibility and facility with word usage as well as to stimulate increased interest in words. Both Britton (1970) and Haggard (1980, 1986) described the seemingly natural propensity of children, adolescents, and adults to play with words. Stahl (1999) encouraged word play as "a way to create interest in words" (p. 23), and Haggard (1986) further suggested that stimulating interest in words could foster "interest in word learning" (p. 64).

Findings and Discussion

Throughout the semester, through interviews, journal entries, group and course work, the five key participants permitted a better understanding of how encounters with new words can lead to vocabulary growth. In sharing their individual ideas about word learning, they revealed their perceptions about language and vocabulary development. By describing the specifics of what they do when they encounter unfamiliar words, the participants revealed independent word-learning strategies. Through increased attention to vocabulary development, they revealed their metacognitive awareness of such development. By reflecting on their own reasons for new word learning, they revealed student motivation for attending to and learning unfamiliar words as well as multiple sources for new word learning. The ideas expressed by the key participants were significantly reinforced by the Total Student Population (TSP) of the two sections of college reading taught by the researcher.

General Perceptions about Language

The 36 participants in this study revealed two universally held general perceptions about language. They revealed seemingly intuitive understandings that words reveal the person and that language should be context appropriate. Michael knew that he needed to learn more words so that he would be able "to sound more mature . . . more professional" (Interview 3, 12/4/00). Jay said specifically that the level of vocabulary used can "make a person. You know . . . the words you use sell yourself, make an image of yourself" (Interview 3, 11/29/00).

The participants in this study understood that such characteristics as social class, levels of education, intelligence, and sophistication can all be revealed through language. Language, as the "the core of socialization" (Jones et al., 1999, p. 254), plays a major role in a person's acquisition of basic life skills necessary to function in any segment of society. Such awareness can be a motivating factor for continued vocabulary growth since, as students aspiring to professional careers, the participants knew that they must become fluent in the language of mature, adult professionals.

The second universally held language perception is somewhat related to the idea that words reveal the person. Students seemed almost instinctively to understand that different situations call for different levels of language and, conversely, that certain language is inappropriate in certain situations. Michael demonstrated his understanding of this perception during his first interview. He observed that he learned slang words very quickly, but he would not give any examples even though some came readily to mind. He said he would feel "too uncomfortable" saying those words to a teacher (Interview 1, 10/11/00). This same event of refusal to use certain terms in an academic setting occurred occasionally in the classroom when the students were engaged in word warm-up activities; the students would think of inappropriate words or phrases that met the needed criteria for the activity but would not break the rules of language appropriateness by sharing context inappropriate language.

It is not surprising that the participants of this study universally understood the rules of context appropriate language. In one study involving preschool children, Cox and Dixey (1994) concluded that "[t]hrough social and linguistic experiences, humans intuitively develop pragmatic knowledge about how language changes to meet the expectations of different contexts" (p. 162).

Perceptions about Vocabulary Instruction

Other perceptions about vocabulary, particularly those about vocabulary instruction, were not so universally held. Students' perceptions of traditional vocabulary study were split dichotomously. Some students believed traditional approaches to vocabulary study were beneficial while many others were in total agreement with Scott and Nagy (1997), who described as "pedagogically useless" (p. 187) the time-honored practice of presenting students with a list of words on Monday, requiring them to look up words in the dictionary, to record definitions and write original sentences using the words, all in preparation for a vocabulary quiz on Friday.

Of the key participants, Aracelli was most in harmony with the views of Scott and Nagy (1997). About the traditional approach to vocabulary study, she wrote, "I felt it was busy work. Most of the time it was pointless because everyone would study them [the words] the moment before the test and forget them by the time class was over" (Vocabulary Journal 2). Other students from the TSP agreed with her perception. One student wrote, "I think it was good for us to learn them [the words] at the time, but if you don't use them you forget them, so most of the words I don't remember" (TSP, Vocabulary Journal 2). This student, like some of the other participants, seemed to understand Nagy's (1988) second and third properties of effective vocabulary instruction: repetition and meaningful use. Since the instruction required only superficial levels of processing, no permanent learning was occurring.

In contrast, other students from both the key participant group and the TSP reported that they liked the traditional approach to vocabulary study. Many students liked the routine of the work, the regular exposure to new words, and the feeling of competence they garnered from successful performance. Confusing memorizing with permanent learning, some students who supported traditional methods seemed to believe that what they were doing was steadily improving their overall vocabulary knowledge. This misunderstanding about the nature of learning is not uncommon among at-risk college students who rely on memory for academic tasks even when those tasks require deeper levels of processing (Simpson, Olejnik, Tam, & Supattathum, 1994).

Other students from both the key participant group and the TSP seemed unwilling or unable to admit that what they had been asked to do was a waste of their time from which they had learned little or nothing. One student followed his account of a very traditional approach with this commentary: "I'm sure it was very helpful, but out of those hundreds of words, I hardly remember any" (TSP, Vocabulary Journal 2). And yet he was so convinced of the value of this work that he kept those vocabulary lists and had even brought them with him to the university.

In contrast to the dichotomy expressed about traditional methods, students' perceptions about the adaptation of Haggard's (1982) VSS approach used in this research were predominantly positive for various reasons. All of the members of the key participant group expressed their approval for the approach to vocabulary instruction used in this research. LeRoy thought it was definitely better for the students to choose their own words: "I think it's a better system cause it's words that I really want to know, not just words that so and so said I have to look up. It's words that I think I should know" (Interview 1, 10/16/00). In her development and subsequent study of VSS, Haggard (1982) concluded that personal selection of words allowed for increased interest in word study. In addition, personal interest is one of the characteristics of effective vocabulary instruction for college-age students (Ruddell & Shearer, 2002; Simpson, Nist, & Kirby, 1987; Simpson & Randall, 2000). Research has shown that when students are permitted to select their own words, they not only choose words previously unknown (Fisher, Blachowicz, & Smith, 1991; White, Slater, & Graves, 1989) but also make selections of words that are "important, challenging, [and] interesting" (Shearer, Ruddell, & Vogt, 2001, p. 569).

Focusing upon another aspect of the instructional approach, Tomika liked working with a group for vocabulary. She wrote, "I like the fact that if I didn't understand what the word meant, someone paraphrased the definition to make me understand" (Vocabulary Journal 3). Other students from both the key participant group and the TSP agreed that working with a small group was beneficial. The comments of some of the students on aspects of group instruction are suggestive of two of Stahl's (1999) principles for effective vocabulary instruction: involve the learner in actively processing new words and use discussion to actively teach new words. These students were also responding to the positive effects of dialogue found beneficial by Palinscar and Brown (1984).

The participants of this study found the generation of an association for each word was the most difficult and time-consuming part of the vocabulary requirement. But they later reported that the associations helped them learn and remember the targeted words. In his work on generative processes of reading comprehension, Wittrock (1990) emphasized the importance not only of generating a connection between the text and "one's memories, knowledge, and experience" but also the importance "for the learners to learn to control their own generative processes" (p. 353). Although the students complained about the difficulty of generating an association for each word, they discovered the power of well-chosen associations to anchor the meanings of new words.

Although there was not total agreement about any one aspect of the approach to vocabulary instruction used in this study, the majority of the students who responded to the final vocabulary journal preferred the approach used here to any they had previously experienced in high school (86% of 30 total responses). In an unsolicited comment about the approach, one student wrote, "I'm really glad I have this assignment because now I can't just skip over the word I don't know. I'm challenged by the words now" (TSP, Journal 9.3). And finally, one student from the TSP expressed his sentiments by writing, "I thought it was helpful because I learned how to learn vocabulary easier" (TSP, Vocabulary Journal 3).

Word-Learning Perceptions

Throughout the data collection period, multiple reflective questions were asked in an attempt to uncover students' perceptions about word learning. In the following paragraphs three key aspects of the students' perceptions about word learning will be addressed individually although it is understood that the various aspects of word learning do not function independently.

Several of the students from both the key participant group and the TSP seemed to perceive the socially mediated nature of word learning (Britton, 1970; Vygotsky, 1962). Perhaps Aracelli's discussion of word learning best exemplifies this perception. During our second interview she revealed that she was learning words from her teachers, "who use big words and . . . repeat themselves a lot" (Interview 2, 10/30/00). During a later interview, she provided specific examples of words she had learned with great ease in social contexts (Interview 3, 11/29/00). Like Aracelli, the other participants in this study seemed to have an understanding that one kind of word learning occurs without conscious effort on the part of the learner, but rather as a natural outcome of being in a social context where unfamiliar words are regularly encountered. Aracelli used an appropriate metaphor for this perception when she declared, "I've noticed that the rubbing off of huge words is coming on me" (Interview 3, 11/29/00).

The participants of this study acknowledged an aspect of language learning that is noticeably missing from the literature on vocabulary acquisition. The literature predominantly addresses vocabulary acquisition through reading or through explicit instruction while ignoring the incidental word learning that results from aural encounters with words in daily life experiences. Yet reading professionals' acknowledgement of this kind of learning is evident in the continuously repeated recommendation to teachers to create language-rich environments (Blachowicz & Fisher, 2000; Stahl, 1999).

A second area of inquiry into word learning explored the perceptions students have about what causes an encounter with one word to result in permanent word learning while single or even multiple encounters with another word apparently have no lasting effect upon vocabulary growth. A student from the TSP provided the language for this question in a reader response entry in his journal when he reported that "the word . . . has stuck in my head like gum on a desk" (TSP, Journal 3.1). The student's vivid analogy of word learning prompted a follow-up question for all participants. Although many students were able to recall specific words that had stuck to them, they were not always able to explain why one word sticks while another doesn't.

Explanations given by the participants for specific word learning fell into categories that are very well aligned with the recommendations for effective instruction offered by prominent scholars in the field (Beck, Perfetti, &

McKeown, 1982; Blachowicz & Fisher, 2000; Haggard, 1980, 1982; Nagy, 1988; Stahl, 1999). The students perceived the socially mediated nature of word learning and the effects of personal interest in word learning. The students understood that multiple encounters with a word can be beneficial but may not be sufficient for permanent word learning. The participants understood that word learning is facilitated by personal, meaningful connections to words and their meanings. And finally the participants reported the value of explanations that include both definitional and contextual information.

The third and final area of perceptions about word learning involved the question of whether word learning occurs more easily from listening or from reading. Many students reported that they learn words more readily from listening, relying upon the aural/oral component of language. Some students, including all five of the key participants, indicated that knowing how the word is pronounced is necessary for vocabulary acquisition but perhaps not sufficient when it is the only information available. Both Aracelli (Vocabulary Journal 1) and Tomika (Vocabulary Journal 3) exhibited behaviors demonstrating their need for an aural/oral stimulus to support vocabulary learning. Both girls worked through the dictionary pronunciations during group vocabulary sessions, trying to say the words smoothly and frequently asking for confirmation of their pronunciations. And both girls often enunciated with exaggerated precision words under consideration, repeating the target word as many as seven times.

Other students from both the key participant group and the TSP also revealed the perception that hearing the word or being able to pronounce the word was vital for word learning. The opportunity to hear a word pronounced appeared to be absolutely essential to word learning for some of the participants of this study. Other researchers have reached a similar conclusion. Miller and Gildea (1987) declared, "[I]n order to learn a word a child must be able to associate its sound with its meaning" (p. 94). Additionally, Shefelbine (1990), Lewkowicz (1985), and Ruddell and Shearer (2002) all found that increasing older students' abilities to decode polysyllabic words, thereby providing the aural connection, aided in both reading comprehension and vocabulary acquisition.

In addition to an exploration of the perceptions about word learning held by the participants, this study examined the metacognitive awareness of word learning in the participants. The participants' responses to questions about actual word learning indicated limited yet varying degrees of metacognitive awareness. The participants seemed to be largely unaware of word learning until they actually used a new word. Similarly, students' written comments about the nature and amount of overall word learning that had occurred during the semester further revealed a lack of conscious awareness of word learning. Representative of the responses of many, one student from the TSP wrote, "I think the growth just happened" (TSP, Journal 15.3). These students seemed unaware of any role they may have played in their own vocabulary growth. They didn't give credit either to the vocabulary component of the course or to the large amounts of reading, writing, and talking about text in which they had engaged for course requirements. That they can only explain vocabulary growth by saying it just happened is indicative of their low levels of metacognitive awareness. Metacognitive awareness is not strongly developed in students of this age and ability (Nist & Simpson, 1997; Pintrich, 1989) and attribution of learning to strategy use or other student-regulated behaviors is an indication of higher levels of awareness (Winne, 1995; Zimmerman, 1998).

And yet the semester-long focus on vocabulary did foster an increase in metacognitive awareness. The participants consistently reported that the vocabulary requirement of the college reading course had forced them to pay more attention to unknown words in print. Increased awareness to unfamiliar words has been documented in other studies where students spent time discussing word meanings either as a class or in small, collaborative groups (Haggard, 1982, 1986; Ruddell & Shearer, 2002; Zientarski & Pottorff, 1994). Whether such increased awareness leads to greater gains in overall vocabulary learning has not been documented.

Independent Word-Learning Strategies

In addition to general language perceptions and perceptions about word learning, the participants in this study revealed the independently selected strategies they use in encounters with unfamiliar words. These students reported using a full range of strategies, including those that parallel vocabulary instructional practices and those that are not aligned with instructional practices. The participants reported using context clues, morphemic analysis, dictionary reference, and various combinations of these instructionally prescribed strategies to understand unfamiliar words. The participants of this study also reported two strategies that are not generally instructionally prescribed: skipping unfamiliar words and asking someone to explain unfamiliar words.

One of the most interesting findings of this study and one that has serious implications for educators involves the relationship between one instructionally prescribed strategy and one not generally prescribed by instruction. The majority of the participants in this study reported dictionary use as the primary strategy applied when encountering unfamiliar words in print. Yet when asked to describe their most recent reading sessions and the number of times they had, in fact, referred to a dictionary, students frequently admitted very limited or no dictionary usage. This discrepancy puzzled the researcher and caused much subsequent questioning. Resulting data and analysis lead the researcher to conclude that the students were providing what they believed to be the expected response and what the researcher subsequently termed the conditioned response.

Further investigation into participants' use of the dictionary revealed that many of them, like students of all ages, experienced difficulty gaining usable information from the dictionary (McKeown, 1993; Miller & Gildea, 1987; Scott & Nagy, 1997; Shore & Durso, 1990). They reported frustration and confusion with dictionary definitions. Frequently during class vocabulary sessions, a working group would call the researcher to clarify what they had just read in the dictionary, clearly demonstrating the participants' inability to gain the kinds of definitional and contextual information needed for word learning from the dictionary (Blachowicz & Fisher, 2000; Nagy, 1988; Stahl, 1999).

What was revealed as a more successful strategy for the participants was asking someone to explain the unfamiliar word. Asking someone, the second most commonly reported independent strategy, is closely aligned with the Vygotskyian view of socially mediated learning and is also aligned with current recommendations for effective vocabulary instruction (Blachowicz & Fisher, 2000; Nagy, 1988; Stahl, 1999). However, asking someone to explain a word is not aligned with common vocabulary instructional practices, and students may, in fact, be discouraged from asking a knowledgeable educator about unfamiliar words by having that educator tell them to use the dictionary, thereby providing students with the conditioning for their responses, and thereby denying students one of the most helpful independent word-learning strategies while encouraging/requiring one of the least helpful.

Other strategies reported by the participants include the use of context clues and morphemic analysis. Use of context clues, while not always successful, is a most common occurrence in reading, and a great deal of research supports readers' spontaneous use of context in the construction of meaning from texts that contain unfamiliar words (Herman, Anderson, Pearson, & Nagy, 1987; Nagy, Anderson, & Herman, 1987; Nagy & Herman, 1987; Nagy, Herman & Anderson, 1985). Only a very few of the participants in this study reported that they attempted to analyze a word's parts in trying to ascertain its meaning. Few of these at-risk college freshmen seemed to have sufficient knowledge of word parts to successfully use morphemic analysis as a primary or solitary strategy. This finding concurs with the findings of Nagy, Diakidoy, and Anderson (1993), who concluded that high school students did not have enough knowledge of the most common suffixes to be able to use them to gain meaning from unknown words in contexts.

The participants of this study initially reported a full range of independent strategies, and later, in journal entries and other reflective writings, they acknowledged small changes in strategy selection with the overall trend reflecting a more active role for the learner. When asked at the end of the 16-week semester how their approach to unfamiliar words had changed, several participants responded with comments like the following, "I actually approach the words instead of just leaving them alone" (TSP, Vocabulary Journal 3) and "Now I don't just read past the unfamiliar words, but stop and try to understand it" (TSP, Journal 15.3). These students may be developing into self-regulated learners able to adopt new strategies and/or adapt previously used strategies for more successful learning (Winne, 1995).

Implications for Educators

Several implications for educators can be distilled from the findings of this study:

1. Allow at-risk college freshmen to self-select words for vocabulary study.
2. Present words orally and give students the opportunity to verbally repeat the words.
3. Avoid telling students to use the dictionary. Instead, provide students with explanations of words that include both definitional and contextual information.
4. Find opportunities to repeat words under study during classroom talk.
5. Provide multiple opportunities for students to talk and write about course topics.
6. Encourage/require student-generated associations for targeted words.
7. Promote metacognitive awareness through reflective writing that focuses students' attention on their own learning as well as on the strategies they are using.
8. Promote interest in words through teacher behaviors that include being enthusiastic about word learning, engaging in puns and word play, and encouraging discussion about words.

Conclusions and Suggestions for Future Research

This study distinguishes itself by a thorough examination of postsecondary students' perceptions of word learning and further validates Haggard's (1982) VSS method of vocabulary instruction. The thorough investigation into student perceptions reported here distinguishes this study from other research in the field of vocabulary that has focused primarily on the processes of vocabulary acquisition, such as incremental learning, and the practices of vocabulary instruction.

This study further validates Haggard's (1982) VSS and extends her findings. Although the vocabulary instructional approach used in the course that provided the context for this study was a modification of Haggard's VSS, it was a student-centered approach in which the students selected vocabulary words for study and engaged in classroom discourse to negotiate meanings and generate associations for those words. It differed from Haggard's approach in that it required words to be selected from course reading materials, that the discussions of word meanings were conducted in small groups rather than in a whole class format, and that students were required to generate a mnemonic association for each word. However, inasmuch as the two instructional approaches were the same, the findings are in agreement with Haggard's primary conclusions that VSS fosters a greater attention to unfamiliar words, stimulates independent vocabulary growth, and promotes word-learning strategies. This study went beyond the scope of Haggard's (1986) study to document changes in self-selected independent word-learning strategies.

All research is subject to limitations. In the study reported here, three limiting factors were identified and addressed. One limiting factor of this study is the necessity to use language to speak about language learning. A certain level of metacognitive sophistication is necessary to be able to examine the processes that occur during word learning. Also a certain level of verbal articulation is necessary in order to be able to coherently express thoughts, ideas, and feelings about the processes that occur during word learning. Because the participants in this study were students enrolled in a developmental reading course, they may have been limited in the ways they were able to think and talk about their own language functioning.

The nature of the relationship between the researcher and the participants inherently produces a second limiting factor. Because the researcher was the classroom instructor who was responsible for the participants' course grades, responses may have been influenced by the students' perceptions of what they thought the teacher wanted to hear. Although the students were told repeatedly that their responses would in no way influence their course grades and that the researcher was seeking truthful responses to questions, the desire to please is a strong one. A third limiting factor of this study is researcher bias. As in any research the assumptions and preconceptions of the researcher, both those acknowledged as well as those undiscovered, can color the analysis. These limitations were addressed through a strict adherence to the dictates for rigor and trustworthiness first described by Lincoln and Guba (1985) and later enumerated by Bassey (1999).

Future research should build on the findings of this study by going beyond mere descriptive reporting to seeking to understand what kinds of vocabulary/reading instruction could lessen older students dependence upon aural/oral stimuli, to understand the relationship between students' perceptions of the efficacy of instruction and the resultant student learning and to understand what kinds of vocabulary instruction and student reflection could promote the development of more successful independent word-learning strategies and greater metacognitive awareness. Given the importance of continued vocabulary development to successful completion of postsecondary education and given the underlying goal of college reading programs to promote the development of self-regulated learning behaviors, it is most important that college reading professionals understand which independent word learning strategies allow for student success and what kinds of instruction could best foster the development of those strategies.

References

Anderson, R. C., & Freebody, P. (1981). Vocabulary knowledge. In J. Guthrie (Ed.), *Comprehension and teaching: Research reviews* (pp. 77-117). Newark, DE: International Reading Association.

Angelou, M. (1969). *I know why the caged bird sings.* New York: Bantam Books.

Aristotle (1991). *On rhetoric: A theory of civic discourse* (G. A. Kennedy, Trans.). New York: Oxford University Press.

Bartholomae, D., & Petrosky, A. (1986). *Facts, artifacts, and counterfacts: Theory and method for a reading and writing course.* Portsmouth, NH: Boynton/Cook.

Bassey, M. (1999). *Case study research in educational settings.* Buckingham, England: Open University Press.

Beck, I. L., Perfetti, C. A., & McKeown, M. G. (1982). The effects of long-term vocabulary instruction on lexical access and reading comprehension. *Journal of Educational Psychology, 74,* 506-521.

Blachowicz, C. L., & Fisher, P. (2000). Vocabulary instruction. In M. L. Kamil, P. B. Mosenthal, P. D. Pearson, & R. Barr (Eds.), *Handbook of reading research* (Vol. 3, pp. 503-523). Mahwah, NJ: Erlbaum.

Bogdan, R. C., & Biklen, S. K. (1998). *Qualitative research for education: An introduction to theory and methods* (3rd ed.). Boston: Allyn & Bacon.

Britton, J. (1970). *Language and learning.* London: Penguin Press.

Burrell, K. I., Tao, L., Simpson, M. L., & Mendez-Burrueta, H. (1997). How do we know what we are preparing our students for?: A reality check of one university's academic literacy demands. *Research and Teaching in Developmental Education, 13,* 55-70.

Chang, P. N. (1996). *Bound feet and western dress: A memoir.* New York: Anchor Books.

Cox, B. E. G., & Dixey, B. P. (1994). Preschoolers doing "code-switching." In C. K. Kinzer & D. J. Leu (Eds.), *Multidimensional aspects of literacy research, theory, and practice* (pp. 162-171). Chicago: National Reading Conference.

Creswell, J. W. (1998). *Qualitative inquiry and research design: Choosing among five traditions.* Thousand Oaks, CA: Sage.

Crow Dog, M. (1990). *Lakota woman.* New York: Harper Perennial.

Davis, F. B. (1944). Fundamental factors of comprehension in reading. *Psychometrika, 9,* 185-197.

Davis, F. B. (1968). Research in comprehension in reading. *Reading Research Quarterly, 3,* 499-545.

Fisher, P. J. L., Blachowicz, C. L. Z., & Smith, J. C. (1991). Vocabulary learning in literature discussion groups. In J. Zutell & S. McCormick (Eds.), *Learner factors/teacher factors: Issues in literacy research and instruction* (pp. 201-209). Chicago: National Reading Conference.

Flippo, R. C., & Caverly, D. C. (Eds). (2000). *Handbook of college reading and study strategy research.* Mahwah, NJ: Erlbaum.

Glaser, B. G., & Strauss, A. L. (1967). *The discovery of grounded theory.* Chicago: Aldine.

Graves, M. (2000). A vocabulary program to complement and bolster a middle-grade comprehension program. In B. M. Taylor, M. F. Graves, & R. Van Den Broek (Eds.), *Reading for meaning: Fostering comprehension in the middle grades* (pp. 116-135). New York: Teachers College Press.

Greene, B. (2000). *Duty: A father, his son, and the man who won the war.* New York: Morrow.

Haggard, M. R. (1980). Vocabulary acquisition during elementary and post-elementary years: A preliminary report. *Reading Horizons, 21,* 61-69.

Haggard, M. R. (1982). The vocabulary self-collection strategy: An active approach to word learning. *Journal of Reading, 27,* 203-207.

Haggard, M. R. (1986). The vocabulary self-collection strategy: Using student interest and world knowledge to enhance vocabulary growth. *Journal of Reading, 29,* 634-642.

Herman, P. A., Anderson, R. C., Pearson, P. D., & Nagy, W. E. (1987). Incidental acquisition of word meaning from expositions with varied text features. *Reading Research Quarterly, 22,* 263-284.

Hockenbury, D. H., & Hockenbury, S. E. (1998). *Discovering psychology.* New York: Worth.

Johnson, D. D., & Pearson, P. D. (1978). *Teaching reading vocabulary.* New York: Holt, Rinehart, & Winston.

Johnson, K. A. (1998). Women in China. In A. T. Ainslie (Ed.), *Encyclopedia of Asian history* (pp. 219-224). New York: Scribner.

Jones, B., Gallagher, B. J., & McFalls, J. A., Jr. (1999). *Sociology: Micro, macro, and mega structures.* Ft. Worth, TX: Harcourt Brace.

Kameenui, E. J., Carnine, D. W., & Freschi, R. (1982). Effects of text construction and instructional procedures for teaching word meanings on comprehension and recall. *Reading Research Quarterly, 17,* 367-388.

Kennedy, G. A. (1983). *Greek rhetoric under Christian emperors.* Princeton, NJ: Princeton University Press.

Lewkowicz, N. K. (1985). Attacking longer words: Don't begin at the beginning. *Journal of Reading, 29,* 226-237.

Lincoln, Y. S., & Guba, E. G. (1985). *Naturalistic inquiry.* Beverly Hills, CA: Sage.

Marrou, H. I. (1956). *A history of education in antiquity* (G. Lamb, Trans.). New York: The New American Library.

McBride, J. (1996). *The color of water: A black man's tribute to his white mother.* New York: Riverhead Books.

McKeown, M. G. (1993). Creating effective definitions for young word learners. *Reading Research Quarterly, 28,* 16-33.

McKeown, M. G., Beck, I. L., Omanson, R. C., & Perfetti, C. A. (1983). The effects of long-term vocabulary instruction on reading comprehension: A replication. *Journal of Reading Behavior, 15,* 3-18.

Merriam, S. B. (1998). *Qualitative research and case study applications in education*. San Francisco: Jossey-Bass.

Miller, G. A., & Gildea, P. M. (1987). How children learn words. *American Scientific, 257(3)*, 94-99.

Nagy, W. E. (1988). *Teaching vocabulary to improve reading comprehension*. Urbana, IL: National Council of Teachers of English, and Newark, DE: International Reading Association.

Nagy, W. E., Anderson, R. C., & Herman, P. A. (1987). Learning word meanings from context during normal reading. *American Educational Research Journal, 24*, 237-270.

Nagy, W. E., Diakidoy, I. N., & Anderson, R. C. (1993). The acquisition of morphology: Learning the contribution of suffixes to the meanings of derivatives. *Journal of Reading Behavior, 25*, 155-170.

Nagy, W. E., & Herman, P. A. (1987). Breadth and depth of vocabulary knowledge: Implications for acquisition and instruction. In M. G. McKeown & M. E. Curtis (Eds.), *The nature of vocabulary acquisition* (pp. 19-35). Hillsdale, NJ: Erlbaum.

Nagy, W. E., Herman, P. A., & Anderson, R. C. (1985). Learning words from context. *Reading Research Quarterly, 20*, 233-253.

Nist, S. L., Holschuh, J. L., & Sharman, S. J. (1995, April). Making the grade in undergraduate biology courses: Factors that distinguish high and low achievers. Paper presented at the annual meeting of the American Educational Research Association, San Francisco, CA.

Nist, S. L., & Simpson, M. L. (1997). *Developing vocabulary concepts for college thinking* (2nd ed.). Boston: Houghton Mifflin.

Palinscar, A. S., & Brown, A. L. (1984). Reciprocal teaching of comprehension-fostering and comprehension-monitoring activities. *Cognition and Instruction, 1*, 117-175.

Pearson, P. D., & Johnson, D. D. (1978). *Teaching reading comprehension*. New York: Holt, Rinehart and Winston.

Pintrich, P. R. (1989). The dynamic interplay of student motivation and cognition in the college classroom. In C. Ames & M. L. Maehr (Eds.), *Advances in motivation and achievement: Motivation enhancing environments* (Vol. 6, pp. 117-160). Greenwich, CT: JAI Press.

Quintilian. (1899). *Institutes of oratory; or, Education of an orator* (J. S. Watson, Trans.). London: George Bell and Sons. (Original work published 95)

Renzetti, C. M., & Curan, D. J. (1999). *Women, men, and society*. Boston: Allyn & Bacon.

Rodriguez, L. (1993). *Always running la vida loca: Gang days in L. A.* New York: Simon & Schuster.

Ruddell, M. R., & Shearer, B. A. (2002). "Extraordinary," "tremendous," "exhilarating," "magnificent": Middle school at-risk students become avid word learners with the Vocabulary Self-Collections Strategy (VSS). *Journal of Adolescent & Adult Literacy, 45*, 352-363.

Sartain, H. W., Stahl, N., Ani, U. N., Bohn, S., Holly, B., Smolenski, C. S., et al. (1982). *Teaching techniques for the language of the disciplines*. Pittsburg, PA: University of Pittsburg.

Scott, J. A., & Nagy, W. E. (1997). Understanding the definitions of unfamiliar verbs. *Reading Research Quarterly, 32*, 184-200.

Shearer, B. A., Ruddell, M. R., & Vogt, M. E. (2001). Successful middle school intervention: Negotiated strategies and individual choice. In J. V. Hoffman, D. L. Schallert, C. M. Fairbanks, J. Worthy, & B. Maloch (Eds.), *National reading conference yearbook, 50* (pp. 558-571). Chicago: National Reading Conference.

Shefelbine, J. L. (1990). A syllabic-unit approach to teaching decoding of polysyllabic words to fourth- and sixth-grade disabled readers. In J. Zutell & S. McCormick (Eds.), *Literacy theory and research: Analysis from multiple paradigms* (pp. 223-229). Chicago: National Reading Conference.

Shore, W. J., & Durso, F. T. (1990). Partial knowledge in vocabulary acquisition: General constraints and specific detail. *Journal of Educational Psychology, 82,* 315-318.

Simpson, M. L., Nist, S. L., & Kirby, K. (1987). Ideas in practice: Vocabulary strategies designed for college students. *Journal of Developmental Education, 11(2),* 20-24.

Simpson, M. L., Olejnik, S., Tam, A. Y., & Supattathum, S. (1994). Elaborative verbal rehearsals and college students' cognitive performance. *Journal of Educational Psychology, 86,* 267-278.

Simpson, M. L., & Randall, S. N. (2000). Vocabulary acquisition and the college student. In R. F. Flippo & D. C. Caverly (Eds.), *Handbook of college reading and study strategy research* (pp. 43-73). Mahwah, NJ: Erlbaum.

Soto, G. (1985). *Living up the street.* New York: Bantam Doubleday Dell Books.

Stahl, N. A., Brozo, W. G., Smith, B. D., Henk, W. A., & Commander, N. (1991). Effects of teaching generative vocabulary strategies in the college developmental reading program. *Journal of Research and Developmental Education, 24,* 24-32.

Stahl, S. A. (1999). *Vocabulary development.* Cambridge, MA: Brookline Books.

Strauss, A., & Corbin, J. (1990). *Basics of qualitative research: Grounded theory procedures and techniques.* Newbury Park, CA: Sage.

Tatum, B. D. (1997). *Why are all the black kids sitting together in the cafeteria? and other conversations about race.* New York: Basic Books.

Thorndike, E. L. (1917). Reading as reasoning: A study of mistakes in paragraph reading. *The Journal of Educational Psychology, 8,* 323-332.

Voss, J. F., & Silfreis, L. N. (1996). Learning from history text: The interaction of knowledge and comprehension skill with text structure. *Cognition and Instruction, 14,* 45-68.

Vygotsky, L. S. (1962). *Thought and language* (E. Hanfmann & G. Vakar, Trans.). Cambridge, MA: MIT Press. (Original work published 1934)

X, M. (1964). *The autobiography of Malcolm X, as told to Alex Haley.* New York: Ballantine Books.

Wheatley, E. A., Muller, D. H., & Miller, R. B. (1993). Computer-assisted vocabulary instruction. *Journal of Reading, 37,* 92-102.

White, T. G., Slater, W. H., & Graves, M. F. (1989). Yes/no method of vocabulary assessment: Valid for whom and useful for what? In S. McCormick & J. Zutell (Eds.), *Cognitive and social perspectives for literacy research and instruction* (pp. 391-397). Chicago: National Reading Conference.

Winne, P. H. (1995). Inherent details in self-regulated learning. *Educational Psychologist, 30,* 173-187.

Wittrock, M. C. (1990). Generative processes of comprehension. *Educational Psychologist, 24,* 345-376.

Zientarski, D. P., & Pottorff, D. D. (1994). Reading aloud to low achieving secondary students. *Reading Horizons, 35,* 44-51.

Zimmerman, B. J. (1998). Academic studying and the development of personal skill: A self-regulatory perspective. *Educational Psychologist, 33,* 73-86.

Appendix. Vocabulary Prompts for Data Collection

Initial and follow-up vocabulary journals completed during class time

Vocabulary Journal 1 **(09/01/00)**

1. How do you learn new words?
2. Do you know when you learn a word?
3. Can you give an example of a time when you learned a new word?
4. Do you learn words better from listening or from reading?
5. What do you do when you encounter a word you don't know while reading?
6. What do you do when you encounter a word you don't know while listening, like in a lecture?
7. Is there a particular process that you use to learn the meaning of unknown words? If so, describe it.

Vocabulary Journal 2 **(09/09/00)**

Please write about the specific vocabulary work you did in high school and how you felt about doing it.

Vocabulary Journal 3 **(12/08/00)**

1. What do you think about the approach to vocabulary used this semester?
2. Do you think it would have been better if we had done vocabulary work as a whole class? Why or why not?
3. What did you like about working on vocabulary with a group?
4. What didn't you like about working on vocabulary with a group?
5. Do you think you would have learned more words if we'd had traditional vocabulary quizzes?
6. Do you think this work has improved your overall vocabulary?
7. Honestly describe for me what you do when you're reading and you encounter an unknown word?
   a. If you said you use the dictionary—think back to your last reading session and tell me how many times you referred to the dictionary while you were reading.
8. Is there any change in your approach to unfamiliar words from the beginning of the semester?
9. Has the work in vocabulary this semester made your more aware of unfamiliar words you encounter in your reading?
10. Describe anything interesting that happened with vocabulary during the past week or so.

Sample Interview Protocol

Protocol for Second Interview with Tomika on 10/30/00

1. During our last interview you told me that you enjoyed knowing a word that others didn't know? Do you know why such situations please you? Have you found yourself in such a situation lately? Tell me about it.

2. Also during our last interview, you explained how your roommate watches TV with the captions on. Have you experienced any word learning from that?

3. Michael told me that he learns slang words more readily than school words. Do you find that to be true with you also? Can you remember any specific slang words you learned quickly?

4. Aracelli told me that she and her roommate have a word-a-day calendar that they use to try to improve vocabulary. Have you ever heard of such a thing? Do you think such a technique could be worthwhile?

5. Can you explain to me what you do when you encounter unfamiliar words in print?

6. Do you ever remember being taught phonics? Decoding skills?

7. The last time we talked, I asked you to put out your antenna, to try to be more aware of what happens when you encounter unfamiliar words. Did you do that? Do you have anything to report?

Journal Assignments From Course Text That Focused on Vocabulary

Journal Week 3 *(Metacognitive)*

First think about your vocabulary. Let your mind explore possible answers to the following questions before you begin to write: Are you finding yourself surrounded by unknown words as you move through the school day? Are you able to understand the textbooks you are being asked to read? Do you understand the words your instructors use in lecture? How strong is your vocabulary? How do you learn new words? What are your strengths and weaknesses in learning new words? What strategies have you developed to deal with unknown words in your reading? In lectures? In class discussion? What ideas do you have about how you can develop a stronger vocabulary? Or about how you can develop effective strategies for dealing with unknown words in reading and in listening.

Next write about your vocabulary. Step back and analyze your vocabulary and your abilities to learn new words.

Journal Week 7 *(After first reading of Johnson's "Women in China")*

First think about reading difficult texts. Let your mind explore possible answers to the following questions before you begin to write: Did "Women in China" present you with a reading challenge? How did you feel when you were faced with this challenge? What did you do to with those feelings? Did you allow them to control your behavior or did you take control of your feelings? What specifically about the reading challenged you? How did you overcome these difficulties? What were you able to take away from your first reading of this text? Was it enough? What was your purpose in reading this text? Do you think a second reading would benefit you or is there something else you should do to access the information in this text?

Next write about reading and you. Without specifically answering the reflective questions, analyze your approach to difficult texts. Tell WHAT you do as well as WHY and HOW.

Journal Week 9

First think about encounters with new words. Let your mind explore possible answers to the following questions before you begin to write: Has your awareness of words changed since the beginning of the semester? How? Why? What do you do when you encounter a word you don't know? Is your response different when you are reading from when you are listening? What strategies are you using to deal with unknown words? Are you successfully learning some of the new words you encounter? Can you describe how you learn new words?

Next write about your encounters with new words. Remember analysis requires an examination of the **how** and the **why** as well as the **what**.

Journal Week 15

First think about encounters with new words. Let your mind explore possible answers to the following questions before you begin to write: Has your awareness of words changed since the beginning of the semester? How? Why? What do you do when you encounter a word you don't know? Is your response to unfamiliar words in print different from your response to unfamiliar words in conversation? What strategies are you using to deal with unknown words? Are you successfully learning some of the new words you encounter? Can you describe how you learn new words?

Next write about your encounters with new words. Remember analysis requires an examination of the **how** and the **why** as well as the **what**.

CELEBRATING ELEMENTARY
AND SECONDARY CLASSROOMS

"I want that book!": First-Graders' Preferences for Expository Text

Kathleen A. J. Mohr

The University of North Texas

Abstract

This report describes a study of book preferences among 190 first-graders. Students were exposed to nine different, high-quality, picture books of various genres (including multicultural texts) and then asked to select one to own. A mixed subgroup of students had the texts read to them during read-aloud sessions, but the majority simply perused the books. Of the total, 122 students were also interviewed about their selection processes. An overwhelming majority selected informational, rather than narrative books. The students evidenced a strong preference for books on animals and learning about the world around them, making the book's content or topic the primary selection rationale. This finding adds to the growing research that informational texts have a strong role to play in the literacy development of even the youngest readers and counters the common notions that primary students favor multicultural and narrative texts.

Students' self-selection of books and preferences for independent reading materials has been a recurring research interest among literacy professionals (Burgess, 1985; Campbell, 1990; Laumbach, 1995; Reutzel & Gali, 1998; Simpson, 1996). Attending to what students prefer to read is justified because the opportunity and ability to self-select books supports the motivation to read. It is commonly acknowledged that if teachers expose students to a variety of books and can direct students to books that interest them, students will spend more time reading independently.

A related concern in this area is whether students have sufficient exposure to a variety of texts and the opportunity to apply appropriate literacy skills and strategies necessary for reading (Caswell & Duke, 1998; Duke & Kays, 1998; Pappas, 1993; Yopp & Yopp, 2000). Duke's (2000) investigation of first-grade classrooms evidenced a paucity of expository text in those environments, which she hypothesized may contribute to a lack of experience with informational texts. Students who are not comfortable with or well equipped to comprehend informational text may be at a distinct disadvantage when faced with the varied text structures and concept load in reading materials expected of students in and beyond the intermediate grades.

One reason for the scarcity of expository text in early grades may be that teachers carry a bias for storybooks and that they make the assumption that young children prefer hearing or reading stories rather than informational passages. Another possible explanation for the dominance of narrative text in early grades is that basal readers and classroom anthologies have long included a majority of narratives (Hoffman et al., 1994; Moss & Newton, 1998), serving as the basis to teach reading. There may also be a developmental factor. Many assume that young children are more likely to understand and appreciate stories (Egan, 1993; Moffett, 1968) and that a strong diet of narrative texts may be the best way to initiate young students to reading. However, it is important that educators reconsider traditional practices, question common assumptions, and investigate ways to ensure a "healthy literacy diet" for even the youngest of readers (Duke, 2000). The high literacy expectation that our society places on learners necessitates continued efforts in understanding what is involved in making youngsters life-long readers who are able to read competently and choose to do so.

Early research in this area identified students' book preferences to be based on the physical text features (e. g., title, cover page, illustrations, etc.) and various story elements (e.g., genre, plot, theme) (Greenlaw & Wielan, 1979; Lawson, 1972; Peterson, 1971; Stewig, 1972). Later studies investigated how students' selected their recreational reading materials (Hiebert, Mervar, & Person, 1990; Lysaker, 1997; Timion, 1992; Wendelin & Zinck, 1988). The results of this research indicated that friends and family were consistent sources for book recommendations and that students relied on familiar authors and books as they made their reading choices (Isaacs, 1992). Teachers were identified as only moderately successful in determining students' interests and consequently a focus was placed on guiding students to be successful selectors of their own reading materials (Ohlhausen & Jepsen, 1992).

Along with basic text features, research has considered related factors, including students' age, gender, and reading ability with regard to book preferences. One summary of such research is that as children mature their range of reading interests broadens. Thus, while emergent readers are reported to prefer fairy tales and fantasy, the preferences of older readers include more realistic literature (Purves & Beach, 1972). In general, research has demonstrated that as age increases, genre preferences expand.

Research from various nations has identified gender differences in students' book preferences that emerge around age nine (Haynes, 1988). Such studies indicate that children hold gender stereotypes and that boys prefer to read about male characters and girls prefer female protagonists. With regard to genre preferences, boys have shown a preference for nonfiction books, particularly books about science, animals, and history. Girls have typically shown stronger interest in fiction, especially books dealing with families, home-life, and animals.

More recent studies have investigated how various types of readers select their independent reading materials and whether the selected texts match the individual reader's reading level (Fresch, 1995; Kragler, 2000; Lehmann, 1991; Lysaker, 1997; Swanton, 1984). While there are differences in the books preferred by proficient versus struggling readers, the research in this area recommends that teachers guide students in becoming strategic book selectors by modeling their own decision-making and highlighting literary elements. In most of these studies, determining differences among ethnically diverse students was not considered.

There is sparse research about whether students' prefer books that match their race or ethnic origins. In their children's literature textbook, Stoodt-Hill and Amspaugh-Corson (2001) cite no research on this aspect of book preferences. However, they posit a well-accepted hypothesis:

> The research results regarding the racial and ethnic differences in children's reading interests are dated and inconclusive. The availability of literature with minority characters as protagonists was so limited in the past that children had little opportunity to exhibit differences in reading interests. We do know, however, that children enjoy reading about people who are like themselves, so with exposure to multicultural literature, researchers find a good chance that minority children will prefer it. (p. 62)

Many advocates of children's literature recommend the use of multicultural books that afford readers both "windows and mirrors" (Bishop, 1990) through which to view the world and themselves (Hopson & Hopson, 1993; Katz, 1983; Radencich, 1985; Ramsey, 1987; Rudman, 1984). It is largely assumed, however, that students want to see themselves in books or that they prefer books that allow them to vicariously experience the social milieu around them. Actual research supporting this intuition is quite limited. The larger project, of which this report is a part, sought to investigate the position that children prefer books that mirror them in important ways. In addition, the project investigated whether even young students can explain how and why they select a book. Another aspect addressed if such students can classify picture books by genre. The basic research questions guiding this portion of the study were:

1. Given a wide variety of high-quality picture books, which book (type) would first-graders select to keep as their own?

2. Given a wide variety of books from which to choose one, would first graders evidence a preference for particular genres?

3. What are students' rationales for selecting a book to own?

Methodology

Texts

The initial task of this project was to review and select appropriate picture books to use for the selection process. The researcher consulted with a regional Teachers' Choice coordinator and an experienced children's librarian and bookstore owner before reviewing dozens of recently published picture books. The criteria governing the selection of books included: published within the last year; high-quality illustrations; content appropriate for first-graders; similar in quality and price; and representative of different genres, genders, ethnicities, and languages (Spanish and English).

The final text selections were made with the approval of the other professionals mentioned. Nine recently published picture books were selected for their high-quality illustrations, text content, and appeal to first-graders to serve as representatives of a variety of genres and multicultural children's literature. Four of the texts were classified as nonfiction: an A-B-C collection of poems about classroom pets, an informational text featuring photographs and short descriptions of dangerous animals, a partial biography of Abraham Lincoln's early life, and a comical description of mothers illustrated with dinosaur characters. The other five selections were classified as fiction, but of these, there were both fanciful and realistic narratives with male and female characters that were Asian, Hispanic, Black, or Caucasian. The selected books evidence themes popular with young children: family relationships, school activities, magic, and animals. Two hard-back copies of each book were purchased for demonstration purposes. The books selected for use in the study are listed in Appendix A.

These texts were representative of the following attributes:

- Gender (male and female characters)
- Genre (fanciful and realistic fiction, informational and biographical nonfiction, and poetry)
- Ethnicity (Anglo, Asian, Black, and Hispanic)
- Language (English and Spanish)
- Theme (family, school, nature, history, magic)

Subjects

For this project, the researcher made arrangements for the first-grade classes in a semi-rural, economically diverse school district in the southeast portion of the United States to participate in the study close to the end of the school year. This afforded most of the students the benefits of nearly two full years of regular classroom instruction and the commensurate exposure to a variety of books prior to participating in the study. Many of these first graders also participated in the district's preschool program, which afforded yet another year of exposure to teacher-selected children's literature.

In the ten first-grade classrooms of this school, there were 190 students with a mean age of 7.7 years at the time of the study. Of this total, 56 students (30%) were Hispanic, predominantly Mexican by descent. Twenty-eight (50%) of the Hispanic students were classified as Limited-English-Proficient (15% of the total first-grade population). For these students, the instructions and interview protocol items were presented in English or Spanish, as appropriate.

Within these first grades there were 104 (55%) males and 86 (45%) females. The same percentages applied to the numbers of males (31=55%) and females (25=45%) in the Hispanic subgroup.

Procedures

The researcher requested that the school principal schedule the first-grade classes for the book selection process in one-hour time slots during one week toward the end of the school year. The researcher set up a table outside the respective classrooms so that individual students could come out into the hallway to look at the books and then make their selections. The students were given as much time as needed to select their favorite book and the hallway traffic was minimal.

In addition to the text selection process, a majority of the students (n=122, 64%) agreed to answer questions about their choices. These brief interviews took place between the researcher and the student on chairs near the books situated in the hallway. Students consenting to the interview were asked several questions. The questions related to the student's selection relative to choice and rationale. The list of interview questions is included in Appendix B.

The first graders participating in the study were asked to look at all the books available and to decide which one they would like to have as their own. When the students made their individual selections, the researcher made note of the choices and continued with the brief interview of those students who had parental permission and gave personal consent to answer the questions. The interviews were conducted while another student was looking at the books. The researcher asked the questions seeking the students' reasons for their respective book selections and wrote the students' responses verbatim on the students' data sheets. Students without parental participation consent were able to choose a book, but were not interviewed. Again, all the first-grade students on this school campus were asked to select a free, hard-back, picture book to keep as their own. After selections were made from among the presented texts, orders were placed and the books were delivered to the students at the school about a week later.

As a subset of the larger study, two of the ten first-grade classrooms, with a total of 41 students (22% of the first-grade population) were selected by the school principal to hear the books read aloud in class as a part of the regular read-aloud time. The researcher read three books aloud at a time for three mornings in these classes. The book review and selection procedures were then conducted as with the other eight classes.

The results of the students' preferences and the comparison of selections between Hispanic and non-Hispanic students are reported elsewhere (Mohr, 2003). This report addresses the students' responses to the interview questions, specifically their rationales for their book preferences. The researcher/interviewer read the interviewed students' comments several times, developing codes for categories for their rationales and compiling them on a data sheet. Some of the codes were then reduced into generalized categories. Simple descriptive statistics were generated and representative comments were noted.

Results

An overwhelming number of these first-grade students selected nonfiction, expository texts, rather than fictional narratives. Of the 190 students, 159 (84%) selected from among the nonfiction titles. One title, *Animals Nobody Loves* (Simon, 2001), accounted for nearly half (46%) of the children's choices. Another 34% of the students preferred the poetry book or the fanciful description of what mothers can't do. The remaining choices, (including the five multicultural narratives and the biography) were preferred by fewer than 10 students each.

Even among the students who had the texts read to them and then perused the texts to select one for keeping, the overwhelming preference (90%) was for nonfiction. In fact, even more of these students who had had the books read to them in class, preferred the nonfiction books, particularly *Animals Nobody Loves* (Simon, 2001).

The preferences of both girls and boys were for nonfiction books, but the percentages do indicate a gender difference. Of the boys, 100 of the 104 (96%) selected nonfiction, while 59 of the 86 girls (69%) selected a nonfiction title. The percentage of Hispanic students (88%) selecting the expository texts exceeded that of the non-Hispanic students, (84%). The Hispanic girls were more dispersed in their selections than Hispanic boys. Of the nine books presented, the Hispanic girls' selections included seven different titles, although some of these books were picked by just a few students. The Hispanic boys chose only four different titles and most were interested in the nonfiction animal book.

Interview Results

Of the 190 participants in the study, 122 (64%) consented to being interviewed following their selection of a book. After noting a student's selection, the researcher/interviewer first asked the question, "What kind of book is it?" Most of the students had difficulty with this question. Perhaps they were not accustomed to classifying books with genre terms, such as fiction, nonfiction, narrative, story, information, or expository. Most were not able to give a response until prompted with, "Is this book a story book or an information book?" When a student responded to this prompt, the interviewer would ask the student, "How do you know?" to elicit a justification for the student's classification.

Once given the either/or classification prompt, 85% (n=54) of the students who selected *Animals Nobody Loves* (Simon, 2001) classified it as an informational text. Thus, these first graders seemed fairly sure that they had selected an informational book and were correct in assuming so. Additionally, 82% of the students (n=17) selecting the fictional narratives classified them as fiction. Thus, the majority (58%) of students appeared to understand the genre of the books they had selected, even if they did not (on their own) have the terminology to describe it.

Students' classification of some of the other titles, however, was much less clear. In fact, all four of the girls selecting the biography classified it as a story. This is a reasonable designation since the book is a partial biography and is presented as a story about young Abraham Lincoln. Still, none of the students used the term "biography" even when they mentioned Abraham Lincoln as the subject. A majority of students (82%) selecting the other nonfiction books, *There's a Zoo in Room 22* (Sierra, 2000) and *What Moms Can't Do* (Wood, 2000) also classified these books as story books. It was with these two texts that the first graders were most confused about the genre of their selections. It appears that young students may be easily confused by such hybrid texts—books of mixed genre— especially fantasy/poetry books.

Boys in this study tended to be more accurate than girls in classifying their selected texts, 70% versus 32% correct. However, this discrepancy could be due to the fact that more girls selected the two mixed-genre texts (*There's a Zoo in Room 22* and *What Moms Can't Do*). In other words, accuracy of genre identification was dependent on text selection.

When asked, "What do you think this book is about?," a minority of students (n=20 or 16%) replied, "I don't know." This group included an equal proportion of boys and girls. Many of the students who had a response made limited guesses about their books' content and seemed to rely on the front cover, the title, or some of the illustrations. The content guesses from some students were very general topics, while other students posited a very narrow topic relying on a specific page reference. See Appendix C for examples of students' responses.

Question #4 of the interview included a two-part prompt for their selection rationales, "Why did you pick this book to keep?" and "Why is this book your favorite one in this group? " Students' rationales fell into five broad categories: content, text features, genre, family connections, and undefined. In other words, these first graders gave reasons for selecting their respective books based on the kind of book it seemed to be, on visible features of the book (e.g., illustrations), the content of the book, whether it would appeal to someone in their families, or the students were not able to give any particular selection rationale. Only six (<5%) students could not give a clear reason for their book choices. Sixteen students (13%) gave more than one reason for their respective selections. These students' comments were categorized by their first or primary rationale (see Table 1).

Table 1. Categories of Book Rationales Among First-Graders Interviewed

1ST-GRADER INTERVIEWS	CONTENT/ TOPIC	TEXT FEATURES	GENRE/ BOOK	SOCIAL CONNECTIONS	UNSURE/ "I DON'T KNOW."	TOTALS/ NUMBER OF STUDENTS
Males	47	20	1	3	0	71
Females	23	16	4	2	6	51
Total	70	36	5	5	6	122

None of the students indicated that he or she selected a book because it mirrored him or her in any way. Many students, however, indicated that they had selected a book because they wanted a window to the world, especially the animal kingdom. Of the 140 student rationales provided, 106 (76%) related to the book's content, generally the topics of animals, humor, and family. Most of the students' rationales were direct statements about wanting a book about animals (see Appendix C).

Only 12% of the students (n=15) mentioned the illustrations, even though all the books were high-quality, well-illustrated picture books. Only 6% of the students (n=7) made mention of specific genre (i.e., wanting a storybook or a book that was real) as the reason for the respective decisions. A few students (n=6) said they wanted a particular book because they wanted to share it with someone in their families.

Interestingly, readability of the texts did not seem to be an issue with these first graders, despite the fact that they were all young readers. These students, for the most part, wanted informational books about animals and were not intimidated by the structure or vocabulary and did not seem to think that their ability to read the text was a reason not to own a book.

This study's results might have been limited by the collection of books that was offered to the students. Given only nine from which to choose, the students were forced to select from a minimal number of picture books. To mitigate against these possible limitations, the researcher sought professional recommendations and selected excellent examples of various genres from among recently published picture books. Another limitation may be that the students were relatively young and, therefore, perhaps less able to articulate their selection rationales. To facilitate the students' ability to respond to the interview questions, the researcher posed questions in both English and Spanish, when necessary, and employed several different questions to elicit students' thinking.

Discussion

The results of this study indicate a strong preference for nonfiction, particularly informational, texts among first graders. This finding counters previous research that concluded that younger children prefer fairy tales and other narrative works. These students, with a mean age of 7.7 years were very interested in animals, not just animal characters, but real and potentially dangerous creatures in the world around them. Thus, the majority selected a book that provided a window to the animal kingdom.

In contrast to conjectures that students would prefer books that mirror them in important ways, these students made practically no mention of text features or content that related to their ethnic or language backgrounds. Perhaps, other age groups would evidence more of a preference for seeing themselves in books, but such was not present here.

Another interesting and perhaps surprising finding is that these students made their selections based more on content than on illustrations. It was the book's topic that attracted the majority of students. The overarching preference was for animal books, not for type of illustration, fanciful story, readability of text, or superficial text features.

These findings add to the research on young students' reading preferences. It challenges the intuitive notion that students want to see themselves in books and substantiates more recent research that there is reason to share more expository text with young learners. This study evidences first graders' preference for informational books, especially those that feature animals or present animals in humorous or interesting perspectives. One extension to this study would be to offer young students another set of books that does not include animals to determine whether the preference for informational texts would be duplicated. Further research could help determine whether a preference for books that mirror personal attributes is a developmental need or an assumption made by concerned adults.

Another project could be to challenge children to sort a set of books into fiction and nonfiction categories or more explicit genres. A salient issue of this study is the confusion some students evidenced when talking about their selected book. It was apparent that these older first graders were not particularly familiar with common book terminology and had some difficulty classifying books. Perhaps teachers of primary students could model book sorting and classification for youngsters and encourage them to use appropriate terminology. Such instructional activities might help early readers to better understand their reading preferences and better appreciate the variety of books that are available. Knowing more about books and genre could certainly support productive reading habits in students, even those at the earliest stages.

References

Bishop, R. S. (1990). Mirrors, windows, and sliding glass doors. *Perspectives, 6,* ix-xi.

Burgess, S. A. (1985). Reading but not literature: The Child Read survey. *School Library Journal, 31,* 27-30.

Campbell, R. (1990). *Reading together.* London: Open University.

Caswell L. J., & Duke, N. K. (1998). Non-narrative as a catalyst for literacy development. *Language Arts, 75,* 108-117.

Chavarria-Chairez, B. (2000). *Magda's tortillas.* Houston, TX: Pinata Books.

Chen, K. (2000). *Lord of the cranes.* New York: North-South Books.

Duke, N. K. (2000). 3.6 minutes per day: The scarcity of informational texts in first grade. *Reading Research Quarterly, 35,* 202-224.

Duke, N. K., & Kays, J. (1998). "Can I say 'Once upon a time'?": Kindergarten children developing knowledge of information book language. *Early Childhood Research Quarterly, 13,* 295-318.

Egan, K. (1993). Narrative and learning: A voyage of implications. *Linguistics and Education, 5,* 119-126.

Fresch, M. J. (1995). Self-selection of early literacy learners. *The Reading Teacher, 49,* 220-227.

Greenlaw, M. J., & Wielan, O. P. (1979). Reading interests revisited. *Language Arts, 56,* 432-434.

Haynes, C. (1988). Explanatory power of content for identifying children's literature preferences. *Dissertation Abstracts International, 49-12A,* 3617. University Microfilms, No. DEW8900468.

Herrera, J. F. (2000). *The upside down boy: El nino de cabeza.* San Francisco: Children's Book Press.

Hiebert, E. H., Mervar, K. B., & Person, J. (1990). Research directions: Children's selections of trade books in libraries and classrooms. *Language Arts, 67,* 758-763.

Hoffman, J. V., McCarthey, S. J., Abbott, J., Christian, C., Corman, L., Curry, C., et al.

(1994). So what's new in the new basals? A focus on first grade. *Journal of Reading Behavior, 26,* 47-73.

Hopson, D. P., & Hopson, D. S. (1993). *Raising the rainbow generation: Teaching your children to be successful in a multicultural society.* New York: Simon & Schuster.

Isaacs, K. T. (1992). Go ask Alice: What middle schoolers choose to read. *The New Advocate, 5,* 129-143.

Katz, P. A. (1983). Developmental foundations of gender and racial attitudes. In R. L. Leahy (Ed.), *The child's construction of social inequality.* New York: Academic Press.

Kragler, S. (2000). Choosing books for reading: An analysis of three types of readers. *Journal of Research in Childhood Education, 14,* 133-141.

Laumbach, B. (1995). Reading interests of rural bilingual children. *Rural Educator, 16,* 12-14.

Lawson, D. V. (1972). *Children's reasons and motivation for the selection of favorite books.* Doctoral dissertation, University of Arkansas. *Dissertation Abstracts International, 32-09, 4840.* University Microfilms, No. AAT8900468.

Lehman, B. A. (1991). Children's choice and critical acclaim: A united perspective for children's literature. *Reading Research and Instruction, 30,* 1-20.

Lysaker, J. T. (1997). Learning to read from self-selected texts: The book choices of six first graders. In C. K. Kinzer, K. A. Hinchman, & D. J. Leu (Eds.), *Inquiries in literacy theory and practice: The forty-sixth yearbook of the National Reading Conference.* (pp. 273-282). Chicago: National Reading Conference.

Moffett, J. (1968). *Teaching the universe of discourse.* Boston, MA: Houghton Mifflin.

Mohr, K. A. J. (2003). Children's choices: A comparison of book preferences between Hispanic and non-Hispanic first graders. *Journal of Reading Psychology 24*(2), 163-176.

Mollel, T. (2000). *Subira, subira.* New York: Clarion Books.

Moss, B., & Newton, E. (1998, December). *An examination of the informational text genre in recent basal readers.* Paper presented at the National Reading Conference, Austin, TX.

Ohlhausen, M. M., & Jepsen, M. (1992). Lessons from Goldilocks: "Somebody's been choosing my books but I can make my own choices now." *The New Advocate, 5,* 31-46.

Pappas, C. C. (1993). Is narrative "primary"?: Some insights from kindergartners pretend readings of stories and information books. *Journal of Reading Behavior, 25,* 97-129.

Peterson, G. C. (1971). *A study of library books selected by second grade boys and girls in the Iowa City, Iowa Schools,* Doctoral dissertation, University of Iowa. *Dissertation Abstracts International, 32-09 4847.* University Microfilms, No. AAT7208307.

Purves, A., & Beach, R. (1972). *Literature and the reader: Research in response to literature, reading interests, and the teaching of literature.* Urbana, IL: National Council of Teachers of English.

Radencich, M. C. (1985). Books that promote positive attitudes toward second language learning. *The Reading Teacher, 38,* 528-530.

Ramsey, P. (1987). *Teaching and learning in a diverse world: Multicultural education for young children.* New York: Teachers College Press.

Reutzel, D. R., & Gali, K. (1998). The art of children's book selection: A labyrinth unexplored. *Reading Psychology, 19,* 3-50.

Rudman, M. K. (1984). *Children's literature: An issues approach.* New York: Longman.

Sierra, J. (2000). *There's a zoo in room 22.* San Diego, CA: Harcourt.

Simon, S. (2001). *Animals nobody loves.* New York: Seastar Books.

Simpson, A. (1996). Facts and fictions: An investigation of the reading practices of girls and boys. *English Education, 28,* 268-279.

Stewig, J. (1972). Children's preferences in picture book illustration. *Educational Leadership, 30,* 276-277.

Stoodt-Hill, B. D., & Amspaugh-Corson, L. B. (2001). *Children's literature: Discovery for a lifetime* (2nd ed.). Upper Saddle River, NJ: Merrill Prentice Hall.

Swanton, S. (1984). Minds alive! What and why gifted students read for pleasure. *School Library Journal, 30,* 99-102.

Timion, C. S. (1992). Children's book selection strategies. In J. W. Irwin & M. A. Doyle (Eds.), *Reading and writing connections: Learning from research* (pp. 204-222). Newark, DE: International Reading Association.

Van Steenwyk, E. (2000). *When Abraham talked to the trees.* Grand Rapids, MI: Eerdmans Books.

Wendelin, K. H., & Zinck, R. A. (1988). How do students make book choices? *Reading Horizons, 23,* 84-88.

Wong, J. (2000). *The trip back home.* San Diego, CA: Harcourt.

Wood, D. (2000). *What moms can't do.* New York: Simon & Schuster Books for Young Readers.

Yopp, H. M., & Yopp, H. K. (2000). Sharing informational text with young children. *The Reading Teacher, 53,* 410-423.

*This investigation was supported by a Research Initiation Grant
sponsored by the University of North Texas*

Appendix A. Selected Picture Books Offered to First Graders in Study

TITLE/ATTRIBUTES	AUTHOR
1. *Magda's Tortillas* (realistic Hispanic family fiction; female protagonist, in English and Spanish)	Becky Chavarria-Chairez
2. *Lord of the Cranes* (Asian fantasy fiction; male protagonist)	Kerstin Chen
3. *The Upside-Down Boy* (realistic, Hispanic family/school fiction; male protagonist in English and Spanish)	Juan Felipe Herrera
4. *Subira Subira* (fanciful Black family fiction; female protagonist)	Tololwa Mollel
5. *There's a Zoo in Room 22* (school/animal poetry)	Judy Sierra
6. *Animals Nobody Loves* (information nonfiction)	Seymour Simon
7. *When Abraham Talked to the Trees* (biography; male protagonist)	Elizabeth Van Steenwyk
8. *The Trip Back Home* (realistic Asian family fiction; female protagonist)	Janet Wong
9. *What Moms Can't Do* (humorous family nonfiction)	Douglas Wood

Appendix B. Children's Book Preferences: Text Attributes That Matter to Students

Interview Protocol

Initial instructions: *I have many books here for you to look at. Look carefully at all these books and then decide which one book you would like to have as your own. You can only pick one of these books to keep, so take your time to choose your favorite one.*

(Each student is given time to look at the selected picture books. The researcher will wait until the student has picked a favorite. When the student is ready, the researcher will continue with the following interview protocol.)

1. *Did you pick one book that you would like to keep? Show me which one is your favorite.* (Record book selection.) *I would like to ask you a few questions about this book and I want to write down some of what you say. Is that okay?* (Unless the student objects, the interview will continue.)

2. *What kind of book is it?* (Record student comments, especially related to genre or type.)

3. *What do you think the book is about?* (Record student comments about book's focus or plot.)

4. *Tell me, why did you pick this book to keep? Why is this one (book) your favorite one in this group (of books)?* (Record details of selection rationale.)

5. *What makes this book so special? What do you like about this book?* (Record noted text attributes.)

Appendix C. Selected Quotes from Student Interviews

Question #2—What kind of book is it?

It's a Seymour Simon book.

It's a critter book.

It's a snake book.

It's a book that I should need for GT (Gifted and Talented Program) because it has all the animals I need to know about.

It's a Mother's Day book.

It's a reading book; it tells you how to make cookies.

It's kinda [sic] a Chinese book.

It's a hardback book.

It's a country book.

Is it a Spanish book?

Is it a story book or an information book? How do you know?

It's an information book because I am a good reader.

It's an information book because it has real pictures.

It's an information book because it's something people don't know and whoever wrote it is telling them.

I just think in my brain it's information. It kinda [sic] asks you questions.

It's information because on the side are some pictures that are real and then on the word side is some information.

I'm not sure. It's probably just a story because it gots [sic] lots of animals in it.

It's information because it only tells about one animal on each page.

I think it's a story book because it tells you lots of things. No, it's an information book because it tells you lots of things; that's what information means.

It's a story because it has pictures.

I think it's an information book because the title says, *What Moms Can't Do.*

It's not no [sic] information book; it's too much like a kid's book.

It's just a plain story book.

It's a story. It gots [sic] a picture of a dinosaur and dinosaurs aren't real.

It's a story because that couldn't be real. They wouldn't get so many pets in a class.

It's not real; it's fantasy. It's information and that means it's not real.

It's a story because it has colored, make-believe pictures. And, it doesn't have chapters.

It's a story book and an information book together because it tells you what Magda did with her tortillas and how to make tortillas—you roll them up.

It's a story book because usually it's a story in books.

It's a story because trees cannot talk. You can imagine that they do, but they don't.

Mi mam< me dijo que todos los libros que tenemos son cuentos. (My mom told me that all the books we have are stories.)

Question #3—What do you think this book is about?

It's about all sorts of animals; some eat meat and some don't.

It's about animals boys like.

Question #4—Why did you pick this book to keep? Why is this book your favorite?

It is information and my mom is a science teacher and I want to be a science teacher.

I want this one because you get to see the information. If you go to a place and there's [sic] these animals, you need this information.

It's my favorite because it's not real. I like things that are fake—that wouldn't happen for real.

It looks like it's a true story and I like true stories.

Question #5—What makes this book so special? What do you like about this book?

I kinda [sic] like dangerous things.

If I see something and I don't know what it is, I can look in it (the book) and know what it is.

I think my brothers will like it.

I have two other books that have moms and things people can do.

I wanted to learn what moms can't do.

It's Mother's Day in one more day and I thought I could get a Mother's Day book.

We're going to the zoo and I like animals.

It looked cool and it looked inspiring.

TEACHING FLUENCY FIRST: READER'S THEATER, PARTNER READING, AND TIMED "WRITERS' CRAFT" PASSAGES— HOW ONE TEACHER INCORPORATED FLUENCY INTO HER READING CURRICULUM

Lorraine Griffith

West Buncombe Elementary School
University of North Carolina, Asheville

Timothy Rasinski

Kent State University

Abstract

One fourth grade teacher found that her struggling readers were not performing well on reading achievement tests, even when following curricular guidelines for improving both word attack and critical thinking skills. The results of this intense work with at-risk readers seemed to yield "critically thinking non-readers." After attending a workshop with Dr. Timothy Rasinski, she began a ten-week teacher-action research study centered on the teaching of fluency through reader's theater. Because of the success of that ten-week trial, she continued reader's theater throughout that school year eventually seeing a program design evolve. For three years, new features were added to the program. The second year she added practice timed reads and some partner reading, with even more success. This article was completed during the third year of program. Throughout the entire implementation of the evolving program, data were collected by a third party assessing "silent reading comprehension" using the Qualitative Reading Inventory II (Leslie & Caldwell, 1995). Based on the current results of the program, the authors feel that placing fluency in the forefront of reading instruction yields fluent readers who have the ability to think critically and comprehend well.

Reading fluency is the ability to read accurately, quickly, effortlessly, with appropriate expression and meaning (Rasinski, 2003). It has been identified by the National Reading Panel (2000) as a key ingredient in successful learning instruction. Reading fluency is important because it impacts students' reading efficiency (Rasinski, 2000) and comprehension (Rasinski, 2003).

The theory of automaticity in reading (LaBerge & Samuels, 1974) provides a theoretical rationale for the importance of reading fluency. According to this theory, readers have a limited amount of attention they can devote to cognitive tasks such as reading. Reading itself requires at least two critical tasks to be accomplished by the reader—decode the words and comprehend the text. Given the limited amount of attentional resources available to any reader, attention that is given to the decoding requirement cannot be used for comprehension. Thus, readers who must spend considerable cognitive effort to decode words, even if they are successful at that task, may compromise their comprehension because they are not able to devote a sufficient amount of their attention to making sense of the text.

One goal of reading instruction then (i.e., the fluency goal) is to develop decoding to the point where it is an automatic process—requiring minimal attentional resources. When decoding is automatized, readers can maximize their attentional resources devoted to comprehension. A recent review of the research related to reading fluency confirms that fluency is indeed a significant factor in reading related to comprehension and achievement (Kuhn & Stahl, 2000).

Although fluency has been identified as a key element in successful reading programs, it is often the case that it is not a part of the reading program (Allington, 1983; Rasinski & Zutell, 1996). When I (Timothy) speak about reading fluency to groups of teachers, I usually receive comments from participants that fluency is not something that was taught in their teacher training program and is not part of their implemented reading curriculum—in short they indicate a lack of familiarity with the notion of fluency.

When I talk with teachers about reading fluency, I often hear later from many of them about what they are trying in the way of fluency instruction. Lorraine Griffith is one of those teachers. After her initial contact with me over three years ago, we have kept up an ongoing correspondence about reading instruction in general and reading fluency in particular. What she has done to make reading fluency an integral part of her curriculum has been, in my opinion, exceptional and a great example of classroom scholarship. In this article we hope to share how she has transformed her curriculum for the betterment of her students' reading development.

Critically Thinking Non-Readers

Year after year, children streamed into my (Lorraine's) rural 4th grade classroom reading below grade level. Teaching in North Carolina, a high stakes assessment state, I felt the increasing pressure to pull them up efficiently and effectively. But I was failing to meet their needs in bridging the gap between where they were and where they needed to be. I used a combination of silent reading, sporadic partner reading, and teacher read alouds in my instruction. Students discussed their stories with me and with their classmates. I implemented classroom instruction to be sure my kids were test-prepped by the best "comprehension" tools: multiple choice questions at multiple levels of depth and "question stems" from the North Carolina State Department of Education's sample lists. I worked hard on having the students think about their thinking, seeing them truly learn about inferences and make judgments on a text.

But the tears would flow during the tests, as frustrated, struggling children realized they could never read the three-page grade level articles to get to the questions. They experienced two and a half hours of hopeless misery. I had taught my at-risk children to think critically. But they just couldn't read fluently! They were unable to get to the point where they could put their thinking skills to good use.

As I reflected on my practice, I realized the "at-risk" readers, children whose silent reading comprehension levels were below fourth grade, were probably more dependent on the teacher read-alouds during guided reading or picture-enhanced text, than the independent, grade level chapter book texts themselves. If I didn't read the text aloud, they would depend on the class discussion and summary of the text before answering the multiple-choice questions.

During the three years before shifting to an emphasis on reading fluency (Fall 1997 through Spring 2000), my Title One at risk readers averaged a gain of 0.83 years on the word recognition (word list subtest) and 1.17 years in silent reading comprehension (see Table 1) according to an Informal Reading Inventory (Scott & McLeary, 1993) used by our district at the time and administered by a third party, a trained Title One teacher. But I knew I needed a better strategy for closing the reading gap. In order for children up to three years below grade level to catch up by middle school, the gain in silent reading comprehension needed to increase by more than just one year. And the catch-up plan needed to be more than just effective, it needed to be efficient. As a result of using a balanced literacy model, the instructional day was already full, so I could only consider substituting changes in practice during the existing blocks of time.

**Table 1. Average Annual Gains in
Reading Achievement for At-Risk Students**

	FLUENCY-ENHANCED READING PROGRAM (2000-2003)	TRADITIONAL READING PROGRAM (1997-2000)
Improvement in Silent Reading Comprehension (Qualitative Reading Inventory)	2.87	1.17
Improvement in Word Recognition (Qualitative Reading Inventory)	1.67	0.83

Note. Gains are reported in grade level units

A Strategy Shift to Fluency with Reader's Theater: Year One

In July of 2000, I heard Tim Rasinski (Rasinski, 2000) speak on "Strategies for Struggling Readers" at a local district supported workshop. During Dr. Rasinski's presentation, I was struck by the data he reported on fluency, and especially by one of the studies discussed from *The Reading Teacher* article, "I Never Thought I Could Be a Star: A Reader's Theater Ticket to Reading Fluency" (Martinez, Roser, & Strecker, 1999). I was amazed to see the study's second graders made remarkable progress in their reading comprehension after only a ten-week implementation of an oral reading fluency strategy, reader's theater.

I knew that the eventual goal of reading instruction was for children to be able to critically think about a text. But there was a step missing in my reading instruction between simply decoding text and being able to think critically about that text. The at-risk readers were not reading well enough nor fluently enough to have the luxury of thinking deeply about text while reading independently. Re-telling was about all they could handle. Out of sheer frustration with such an emphasis by our district to skip directly from reading the text silently to critically thinking about the text, I was ready to try a shift in my reading instruction techniques—from a focus on continual instruction in phonics for the lowest students, continuous attempts to engage them in silent reading, and training them to answer difficult multiple-choice questions to an emphasis on fluency instruction. I decided to emulate the Martinez et al. (1999) study I had heard about and then try reader's theater for the first ten weeks of the 2000-2001 school year.

I did not alter my guided reading block. I continued to use a varied combination of novels, short stories, non-fiction, and the basal reader as texts. I continued to teach those same critical thinking techniques in discussion of real text. But I added an emphasis on reading fluency through reader's theater.

At first I wondered how I would find enough reader's theater scripts to keep my children reading for ten weeks. I was amazed to find free reader's theater scripts on an Internet site such as Aaron Shepard's (1996). I found a number of age-appropriate script collections for purchase, especially enjoying the scripts by Braun and Braun (2000a, 2000b) and Dixon, Davies, & Politano (1996). But I soon discovered that scripts were quite easy to arrange on my own, especially when using poetry such as Maya Angelou's (1990) poem, "Life Doesn't Frighten Me at All." Moving beyond poetry into content-related topics, I found that scripts I arranged could be integrated quite effectively between the language arts block and science or social studies.

I followed a simple weekly procedure. At the beginning, every child had the same script. I wanted the more accomplished readers to model fluent reading for the others. After copying enough scripts, one for each child, I highlighted the assigned parts using a variety of highlighters. I quickly and randomly handed out reader's theater scripts on Monday mornings, with the child's part highlighted. I assigned a nightly 10-minute practice read. The children logged their practice times in reading logs, usually rehearsing with a parent or sibling. On Fridays, just before lunchtime, the kids rehearsed in groups for about 15 minutes. Because each child received a script randomly with only his/her part actually marked, and then practiced independently during the week, they actually "met" their fellow performers just before lunch on Fridays during rehearsal and performance. While they practiced, I coached individuals and small groups of students.

Initially, it was effective to have all of the children in the same script. One child would see her part interpreted a number of different ways. She would see the potential drama in the written word. As the weeks went on I developed a wider variety of script resources. Eventually I divided the children into different performance troupes each week. Each group of readers had a different script to perform allowing for a much more interesting Friday production. But I still paid no attention to the child's reading level as I assigned parts. It was truly not an "ability grouped" activity. Because the text was practiced so often throughout the week and the lines were limited in number, even a low reader could perform well on Friday. I wanted all of the children to consider themselves as equals during the performances, differing only on the level of dramatic interpretation of the texts. I found that some of my lower readers were the most dramatic, finding the first opportunity ever to shine as a star performer in reading.

Traditionally, our grade level had enjoyed a "Fun Friday" reward time on Friday afternoons. The students would engage in a fun activity such as cooking or watching a movie correlated with the unit of study. With a new group of students at the beginning of a school year, I announced that we would have a special celebration of reading every Friday afternoon. To make the performance an "occasion," the children took turns bringing in refreshments. They were thrilled with Fridays, loved to perform in a "dinner theater" atmosphere, and I had managed to substitute a meaningful reading intervention for an otherwise mish-mash of activities.

In only ten weeks, I saw positive results similar to the second grade study I had attempted to emulate. But I also saw a deepened interest in reading. I began to see the expressiveness seep into the children's oral reading during the guided reading block. At one point while partner reading Ashley Bryan's (1989) *Pourquoi Tales* during guided reading, one of my English as a Second Language (ESL) students whispered to another struggling reader, "Let's read that part again, only this time like 'reader's theater.'" In all of my years in fourth grade, I had never heard a child come up with the idea to re-read a passage simply for the pleasure of reading it.

Thrilled with the initial 10-week progress, I decided to keep data for the rest of the school year. Because we were a Title One school and my greatest concern was with the at-risk kids (children who were not learning disabled but were reading below grade level), I was able to take advantage of their testing program for the targeted students (those reading significantly below grade level). I had not seen a yearlong study of the effect of reader's theater on at-risk students in the intermediate grades and wondered if the reading enthusiasm and emphasis on expressive flow would last. I also wondered what kind of impact it would make on testing with the targeted Title One kids for one full school year.

After the first year of implementation, my four targeted Title One students experienced a 2.5 year increase in their silent reading comprehension as measured by an informal reading inventory (Scott & McLeary, 1993). I was thrilled to find that this relatively small intervention had more than doubled the gain I might normally have expected students to make in one year of instruction. Ironically, with a lessened stress on phonics instruction during the 30 minute Title One block and a greater stress on reading with meaning and expression, the children's average gain in word list recognition was 1.25 years, substantively more than in previous years.

A Continued Shift To Fluency Development: Year Two

Feeling wildly enthusiastic about the improvement of more than a year simply using one new strategy, reader's theater, I continued my quest for a deepened understanding of fluency development. I had read Dr. Rasinski's October, 2000 article in *Reading Teacher*, "Speed Does Matter in Reading." During the 2001-02 year, I decided to investigate the role of speed in a child's reading comprehension. I tested my children's reading speed by doing a one-minute reading probe. The process was simple: I simply had the children read a grade level passage and recorded notes on words omitted or pronounced incorrectly. I counted the words read correctly. I was surprised to find out that 44% of my children read below the average reading speed of 99 words correct per minute for the beginning of 4th grade on 4th grade level material (Rasinski, 2003). Fifteen percent of my children were at risk, reading below 74 words correct per minute.

I decided to keep track of the reading rate of all of my children and the silent reading comprehension of my five Title One students (see Table 2). I also began to use two other interventions to increase reading fluency: short term use of timed reads and partner reading.

Table 2. Gains in Fluency and Comprehension for At Risk Students

2001-2002 School Year At-Risk Readers	Rate	Silent Reading Comprehension (QRI-II)
Beginning of Fourth Grade (August)	62.4 words per minute	2.2 grade level
Middle of Fourth Grade (January)	103.8 words per minute (+ 41.4 words)	4.8 grade level (+2.6 years)
End of Fourth Grade (April)	109.8 words per minute (+ 6.8 words)	5.4 grade level (+0.6 years)

Having read a book on using "writer's craft passages" as an integral part of the writing block (Fletcher & Portalupi, 1998), I selected exemplary passages from books to be used for writing each week. I also used the same passages for the timed reads each day. In this way I was hitting the proverbial second bird with the same stone.

For the first week of using the timed reads, I ran copies from the opening scene of *Roll of Thunder, Hear My Cry* (Taylor, 1976). I read the passage aloud to the children with attention to the syntax and expressive nature. After doing a mini-lesson on the characterization of Little Man, we discussed the author's style of writing and the way the author opened with such a telling statement about Little Man. We talked about how we could use that technique to open a story we wrote.

The following day, the children each read the passage to a partner for one minute and made a mark in the passage where they ended reading. After each child had read, we discussed the way different children read the passage. Sometimes they would model read for the class to show how expressive and interpretive they could be. We then moved on to the writing at hand, because we were still in the writing block, using the passage as a model for writing narrative. We read the same passage daily through Friday. The children noted their increasing reading rate each day and we talked about how important reading with energy is to understanding what we read.

The children loved competing against themselves each day and recording the number of words they could read expressively in one minute of reading time. The children were cautioned not to read as fast as they could for the sake of reading fast, but to read expressively and with meaning. Students began to internalize the characteristics of the writer's techniques and vocabulary as the children practiced reading again and again. There were times when the oral interpretation was so moving, I would have to blink back tears. I was seeing the benefits of theatrical performance interwoven with this emphasis on reading rate and writer's craft.

Children read orally with partners daily during the time I had the 30 minute Title One block. The Title One teacher would sometimes read with a small group doing novels and encouraged children to read aloud as they desired. But she also covered skills necessary for the understanding of text through programs used in our district. The rest of the children read in pairs or small groups of similar reading levels. The chosen book would be read together orally at school and then read silently at home. A few of the children in Title One requested to move into partner reading with their friends, simply reading the whole thirty minutes instead of having the small group time. This request was granted because for the first time these at-risk children desired to participate in a reading culture. They were beginning to realize a social aspect to reading. During this particular block, I conferenced with the reading pairs who were not in the Title One group.

In the year 2001-02, the additional short-term interventions of timed readings and encouraging reading at a higher rate and with expression seemed to have a direct impact on the word recognition and the silent reading comprehension. Title One students experienced substantial gains in reading rate and oral interpretation of connected text on the Qualitative Reading Inventory II (Leslie & Caldwell, 1995). The average gain in word recognition (word list) reading was 2.4 years. An even higher gain was found in silent reading comprehension, now up to 3.20 years gain. It was interesting to me that the two Title One students who requested to move out into the partner reading, made the greatest gains of the five Title One students. (This observation led to an overall implementation of partner reading among all Title One students the following year.) I also observed a strong correlation between the at-risk students' word count per minute data and their silent reading comprehension as measured by the Qualitative Reading Inventory II (Leslie & Caldwell, 1995) (see Table 2).

My room was becoming a reading-centered culture. And the parents were also realizing the impact of this heightened emphasis, telling me touching stories from home. One January afternoon, a parent of a reluctant reader had been working on a work-related project at the computer all day. She had been amazed to see her daughter Sally curled in a chair reading a book for most of the day. Late in the afternoon, Sally piped up, "Mom! We have to get out of here and do something!" Her mom fully expected a suggestion like going shopping or roller-skating! But instead Sally suggested, "How about if we go to Barnes and Noble to have hot chocolate while I read and you work?" Sally had learned there was joy in sustained and extended periods of silent reading!

Fluency First: A Three-Pronged Effort in Year Three

After the positive results of the past two years of the program, I have concluded that the three-pronged fluency effort (reader's theater, partner reading, and one minute practice readings) is a worthwhile set of strategies for preparing fourth graders to be life-long, critically thinking readers. This year, 2002-03, I am simply continuing the efforts made in the past few years but with some additional modifications.

Reader's Theater

I have continued handing out reader's theater scripts every Monday morning and having a performance on Friday afternoons. The children continue to love the performances, although they have begun doing reader's theater in several of the classrooms below fourth grade. The medium does not seem to lose its fascination and challenge. This time block simply continues to replace a reward time used traditionally in my grade level.

This year the children are writing and arranging their own scripts more often than before. One of the more intense writing projects, was an assignment I gave to create a reader's theater concerning what "really" happened to the Lost Colony. The children were assigned to heterogeneous groups and required to write from an assigned point of view: John White's, the colonists', the Native Americans', or the bears watching behind the trees. Ironically this activity probably did more to teach "point of view" than all of the testing strategies I formerly depended upon. In addition, the activity truly integrated teaching of communication skills and social studies.

Partner Reading

I have developed a more organized plan to partner read with the children. Instead of having the partner reading going on during the 30 minute Title One block, I now have it scheduled during the "sustained silent reading" block. My Sustained Silent Reading (SSR) block in the past had been plagued with "fake readers," students who pretend to read but do not. These "fake readers" are the very students who need the daily practice of reading the most. It seemed to me that partner reading provided a means to require all students to read and the opportunity for me to observe their reading. And so, I began the year by pairing up my children so that they could cooperatively learn to read and understand text.

Partners are paired according to interests, reading ability, reading rate, and social compatibility. Although the assignment of reader's theater parts is not connected to a student's reading ability, partner reading is homogeneous. Because partner reading was substituting for the SSR time, I wanted the children to be reading on their own with material that challenged them somewhat and required them to collaborate with a partner to negotiate the text and construct meaning (Vygotsky, 1978). Because I closely supervise the reading time and discussion, I also act as a "problem-solver," but with a twist— the children first strive to solve problems with text collaboratively and then call me over if they need more aid.

During partner reading, the pairs of children choose reading materials they are interested in reading together. They read aloud together for thirty minutes, usually taking turns as one is reading and the other follows along tracking the words. They have the choice of how they want to read, whether chorally, taking turns, or reading dialog in parts. Because I have spent time modeling how to discuss books, the children have learned to monitor their own reading comprehension. When they do not understand a passage, they stop and ask a partner what it means. Or they might choose to simply go back to re-read. Sometimes if they are really stumped, they look around and call me over.

In the meantime, I rotate throughout the classroom and conference with various partners. This is a wonderful opportunity to eavesdrop on oral reading and ask truly meaningful questions based on the text they are reading that day. Here I have a chance to interject those critical thinking questions, necessary for test preparation but within the context of their own choice of text. I take notes on children's reading progress and comprehension, noting mini-lessons that may be needed for a small group or noting strategies that may need to be re-taught.

At the close of the partner reading time, the children make commitments to each other about how many pages they are going to read in the evening. All of my children are required to read 20 minutes at night. Because the children have similar reading rates, they can come up with an appropriate number of pages to read. Parents have affirmed this accountability system. Children tend to be more serious about reading commitments to a friend than they are to the teacher or a parent.

Because partner reading is simply a bridge between guided reading and independent silent reading, I encourage kids who are reading on grade level to begin silent reading during the partner reading/SSR block in January. All of the children participate in a "silent reading marathon" once a week to develop their ability to silent read for a sustained hour of uninterrupted reading time.

"Writer's Craft"/Timed Reads

Despite the results from last year's exercise in using timed reads to improve reading rate, I consciously decided to downplay reading rate this year, hoping to see the same results using other methods. I was uncomfortable with some of the techniques I was hearing about from other schools with children beginning to feel that reading was a race or a hurtful time of comparison to others. Although I had not seen adverse affects in my own classroom, I shied away from the timed reads this year. I did continue to do one-minute probes each month. I have been very surprised this year to see that the progress in reading rate is not happening as steadily as it did last year. I have concluded that the ones who are really struggling simply need the "kick in the pants" provided by timed reads.

Student achievement in this third year has continued the trend that began when I introduced fluency into my reading curriculum. The student achievement results in Tables 1 through 3 include data from the third year.

Table 3. Progress in Instructional Reading Level for At-Risk Students

	Fluency-Enhanced Reading Program (2000-2003)	Traditional Reading Program (1997-2000)
Average Instructional Reading Level at Beginning of the Year	2.93	3.00
Average Instructional Reading Level at End of Fourth Grade	5.80	4.17
% of At-Risk Students Exiting 4th Grade On or Above Grade Level	93%	22%

Note. Gains are reported in grade level units.

Third Year Conclusions

Based upon three years of implementing a reading curriculum that includes reading fluency as an integral element, I have come to the following conclusions:

- Reader's theater provides a highly motivational opportunity for repeated reading, with an emphasis on the dramatic interpretation of text.
- Reader's theater offers an arena for children to develop public speaking skills in a safe community of learners.
- Reader's theater scripts and poetry seem to help children to develop a greater understanding of mood and author's purpose when orally interpreting text.

- Reader's theater scripts can be interwoven into the content areas, providing more background knowledge for reading than can be covered during class time.
- Writing reader's theater scripts is a natural way to scaffold students' writing by allowing them the support of a well-written text from which their script is drawn.
- Partner reading brings in the social aspects of a book culture to children, encouraging mutual enjoyment of a text with multiple perspectives on a passage and monitoring of comprehension by consistent book discussions.
- Partner reading helps children to stay motivated to read novels by sharing the responsibility of reading text.
- Partner reading offers valuable time on task practice for phonetic development, especially for the reader's who have gaps in their word attack skills.
- Partner reading reinforces the importance of syntax as connected text is interpreted orally.
- Writer's craft/timed reading reinforces the beauty of the well-crafted word in connected text, offering a model for writing story leads, exploding moments within a text, and powerful endings.
- Writer's craft/timed reading assures the student's understanding of the reflexive nature of reading and writing.
- Writer's craft passages, when timed, seem to help the children develop a pace more consistent with skilled, on grade-leveled reading.
- The combination of any or all of these techniques have significantly enhanced the at-risk students' performance to the point where most are now reading on grade level. (see Table 3).

Although the primary focus of my three-year program has been on students who qualify for the Title One reading program, I have seen encouraging changes in all of my readers' comprehension as I have focused on fluency. What began as an intervention for at-risk readers, has enhanced the performance of all of my children. Each year children of all levels have become more involved with community theater and church plays. With the shift of the focus from an intervention technique to a mediating strategy, children seem to be climbing the independent reading levels at break-neck speed. One child at the high end of my 2002-2003 class began the school year at an 8th grade reading level and finished at a 12th grade reading level. Most importantly, our class is passionate about reading and because of that, we have come full circle. As children of all reading levels have increased in fluency, their attention to the structure of the text, the development of story, and the deeper meaning of text is made possible. All my fourth graders are reading fluently, and consequently thinking meaningfully and critically about text.

Over the course of the past three years I have come to see that reading fluency is indeed an important part of the reading curriculum for all students, and especially for those who experience difficulty in reading. I have also learned that reading fluency can be taught in a variety of ways. Teachers interested in making fluency an integral part of their instructional curriculum for reading should rely on certain key principles in designing such instruction: fluency requires opportunities for students to hear fluent, expressive, and meaningful reading from their teacher, their parents, and their classmates; fluency requires opportunities for students to practice reading texts multiple times; fluency requires opportunities for students to be coached in fluent, expressive, and meaningful reading by their teacher and their classmates; and fluency requires opportunities for students to engage in meaningful and critical discussions of the texts they read and meaningful performances of the texts they practice. How these principles are turned into actual practice depends on the individual teacher. In my own classroom, I found that that these principles came to life in reader's theater, timed reading, and partner reading and that they had a positive impact on my students' reading development.

References

Allington, R. L. (1983). Fluency: The neglected goal of the reading program. *The Reading Teacher, 36,* 556-561.

Angelou, M. (1990). Life doesn't frighten me at all. In J. Agard (Ed.), *Life doesn't frighten me at all* (pp. 2-3). New York: Henry Holt.

Braun, W., & Braun, C. (2000a). *Readers theatre: Scripted rhymes and rhythms.* Winnipeg: Portage & Main Press.

Braun, W., & Braun, C. (2000b). *Readers theatre: Treasury of stories.* Winnipeg: Portage & Main Press.

Bryan, A. (1989). *Pourquoi tales: The cat's purr, why frog and snake never play together, the fire bringer.* Boston: Houghton Mifflin.

Dixon, N., Davies, A., & Politano, C. (1996). *Learning with readers theatre.* Winnipeg: Portage & Main Press.

Fletcher, R., & Portalupi, J. (1998). *Craft lessons: Teaching writing K-8.* Portland: Stenhouse.

Kuhn, M. R., & Stahl, S. A. (2000). *Fluency: A review of developmental and remedial practices.* Ann Arbor, MI: Center for the Improvement of Early Reading Achievement.

LaBerge, D., & Samuels, S. A. (1974). Toward a theory of automatic information processing in reading. *Cognitive Psychology, 6,* 293-323.

Leslie, L., & Caldwell, J. (1995). *Qualitative reading inventory-II.* New York: Allyn and Bacon.

Martinez, M., Roser, N., & Strecker, S. (1999). "I never thought I could be a star": A readers theater ticket to reading fluency. *The Reading Teacher, 52,* 326-334.

National Reading Panel (2000). *Report of the national reading panel: Teaching children to read. Report of the subgroups.* Washington, DC: Department of Health and Human Services, National Institutes of Health.

Rasinski, T. V. (2000). Speed does matter in reading. *The Reading Teacher, 54,* 146 - 151.

Rasinski, T. V. (2000, July). *Strategies for struggling readers.* Workshop session presented at the staff development session of Buncombe County Public School District, Asheville, North Carolina.

Rasinski, T. V. (2003). *The fluent reader.* New York: Scholastic.

Rasinski, T. V., & Zutell, J. B. (1996). Is fluency yet a goal of the reading curriculum? In E. Sturtevant & W. Linek (Eds.), *Growing literacy: Yearbook of the college reading Association* (pp. 237-246). Harrisonburg, VA: College Reading Association.

Scott, J., & McCleary, S. (1993). *Diagnostic reading inventory for primary and intermediate grades.* Akron, OH: Scott & McCleary Publishing Company.

Shepard, A. (1996). *Aaron Shepard's world of story.* Retrieved August 2000, from http://www.aaronshep.com/rt/index.html

Taylor, M. (1976). *Roll of thunder, hear my cry.* New York: Penguin Books.

Vygotsky, L. S. (1978). *Mind in society: The development of higher psychological processes.* Cambridge: Harvard University Press.

Urban Filmmakers: The Mutigenre Process in a New Setting

Joanne Kilgour Dowdy
Sunny-Marie Birney

Kent State University

Abstract

This urban filmmaking class represents the multigenre writing process in a new setting. Students were introduced to the skills of an independent film-making industry and encouraged to write, script, design, edit, and cast their productions for a final screening six months after they began their journey in the classroom. Evidence of their growth as writers and producers is given in their testimony to the new levels of awareness of the way in which they have improved as writers and young people who are capable of achieving high ideals in and out of the classroom. This project is a reminder that the writing process can be revamped to meet the standards of media literate adolescents in the urban setting, given time, expertise, and the support of the successful adults in the independent filmmaking industry.

Teachers of urban youth have long extolled the virtues of using culturally relevant content to ensure that students stay motivated and committed to learning the craft of writing (Bean, Valerio, Senior & White, 1997; Mahiri & Sablo, 1996; Nurss, Abbott-Shim, McCarty, & Hicks, 1999; Szustak, 1993; Taggart, 1994). By ensuring that students see their lives valued in the class-room, and that their voices are given adequate scope for development in the many writing genres that youth are inclined to experiment with, teachers build a community of writers. Given this mandate for developing student writing in the urban school districts that we serve, it is important to note the quality programs that enhance learning among youth wherever they exist.

One way to catch the attention of young writers is to call on their extensive expertise in television and film literacy. Because of the long hours that our young people have spent watching stories created for the movies (i.e., Walt Disney animated films and action movies) that highlight superheroes like Superman, they bring a "natural" sensitivity and critical awareness of what works in television. Lund (1998) is especially enthusiastic about the efficacy of video production in the service of increasing writing skills in the urban high school because it puts the students in the seat of the knowledge-able expert. The production process of filmmaking is also documented as a means to promoting the composing process (Cox, 1985), assessing content knowledge, writing skills, and research skills (Doig & Sargent, 1996), and can therefore be seen as a way to enhance the language arts.

Given the flexibility of the production process that leads to the screen-ing of films, teachers of language arts and proponents of collaborative learn-ing skills for urban youth would do well to think of filmmaking as a multigenre journey. Not only do students have to do research for their story, write a screenplay, develop storyboards, design costumes, choose music, and cast actors in their final productions, but they must also be savvy at directing their talent in acting scenes and using editing equipment so that they can realize their stories. As Cox (1985) reminds us, film composition is one way a child learns the importance of giving ideas a form and shaping their thoughts.

The Multigenre Research Paper

In Romano's (1995) *Writing With Passion: Life Stories, Multiple Genres*, we are introduced to the concept of research as a "many splendored" en-deavor. The production of "crots" or self-contained pieces lined up in a se-ries (i.e., like a filmstrip), is the product of a process that allows students to "meld fact, interpretation, and imagination" into a meaningful whole (p. 109). Each of the crots is an individual composition of varying length and genre, each "making a point of its own, separated from the text by white space, unconnected . . . by transition devices" (cited in Grierson, 1999, p. 51). The student, much like the film and video director, is led by his/her own vision in the organization and presentation of the research.

Multigenre projects are the result of extensive reading and research. As students begin to imagine the lives beyond the facts that they gather, they start the hard work of good writing. Their final presentations of visual com-positions are the result of intensive reflection and personal investment in thinking like a character. Further, students are encouraged to bring their voices to the final work, in written form, and to reflect the nature of their "innova-tive, risk-taking behavior" (Grierson, 1999). The student is encouraged to create a fictive world out of the materials that are documented in books and other records. Visioning the life that inspired these documents becomes a personal journey that unearths the student's personal life-view. No two students, there-fore, are expected to write the same way about the experiences of public personalities like Tupac Shakur or Queen Latifah.

The Media Project

The Media Project gave students from the inner city a chance to be exposed to the techniques of film production and an opportunity to learn the industry from the experience of insiders. The students were offered classes in film theory, managing equipment used in film studios, writing film scripts, casting actors in the roles for their short films, and editing their own short films. Also, a final screening day was organized for the finalists in the six-month journey. The young filmmakers presented their short films at a community hall where family, friends, local film production veterans, and supporters of the local independent film industry turned out to celebrate their success.

Setting and Participants

This study was conducted over eight months from 2001-2002, in a major city of the Southern United States. The sponsor, IMPRINT film and video company, worked out an agreement with Grant State university to hold the classes in a classroom at their main campus. Students were also allowed to use the premises for classes, filming scenes, and rehearsing their actors.

The Instructor

The instructor for the program, Nick, was selected because of his national reputation as an independent filmmaker. Among his credentials is a film trilogy which looks at Black men and violence in the United States. He also had experience teaching film courses at a local university and had developed educational video programs for a federal agency on people with disabilities.

The Students

The six students who were able to complete the six-month journey came from diverse neighborhoods in the city. The youngest, Nia, was fourteen years old at the time that she began the program. The oldest, Jai, was in his first year at Grant State College and had already declared his interest in film studies. Another female student, Yani, was also in her first year as a Grant college student and was an acting major. Mandy, the third girl, was just finishing high school and was certain that she would be pursuing communication studies in college. The other two students, Fiona and Robert, were juniors in high school and were also members of a dance company that frequently performed and traveled to other states during the film project.

IMPRINT Film and Video Company

This privately run film and video company provides classes and salons on video, and screens films in the community. It sponsors an annual film festival, a major event in the Southeastern United States, and acts as an organizing arm for independent filmmakers in the community. IMPRINT employs local film professionals to teach classes on film production and video workshops at its headquarters in the heart of the city where it is located.

The Professionals

Several professionals were enlisted by the instructor, Nick, to facilitate the coaching, filming and editing of the student productions. Lorna, a professional producer, volunteered on production for two of the short films. John, a director and producer, did a lecture on the role of the production manager and later acted in one of the teen films as a doctor. Sylvia, a cinematographer, began as a volunteer on camera but later was hired as an assistant producer to facilitate the successful completion of the six student films. Althea, an independent video director and editor, assisted one of the students on his editing journey during a crucial part of the final stages of the project. Finally, Dr. Fola did a class on media literacy for the students from her perspective as a representative of youth media at a national broadcasting company.

The Principal Investigator

As a Black, female associate professor of literacy studies, an actress, a graduate of the Juilliard School, and a researcher with an interest in media literacy, I was interested in documenting the progress of the film students over the six months. By June, three months in to the journey, I was enlisted as an actor in one of the short films produced by Mandy. The opportunity to observe this young woman direct scenes from her film and manage the difficulties that came with volunteer actors and crew, gave me a better appreciation of the process that the students were being exposed to as filmmakers.

The Film Class

Students began their filmmaking journey by watching films from different genres and discussing the film styles that each represented. They also analyzed the effects that different styles had on them and the way in which these styles were represented in modern films. Next, they were introduced to the stereotypes of Black people in contemporary television and feature films. Such characters as the Buffoon, Mammy, Saffire, and Buck were presented through familiar television shows like *Fresh Prince of Bel Air* and *Boston High*. They were then asked to write the dialogue in a scene from a popular movie. This exercise allowed them to hone their skills in listening and observing the details of the shots that they were representing in their text (i.e., they would note if the scene was interior or exterior, day or night, and any details of the camera angle).

Study Method

I interviewed Nick three times, for approximately one hour each time, to get information on his plans for the instruction of the students and an orientation to the project from his perspective. His interviews were conducted over a year. Following a review of his first two transcripts my assistant and I created questions that we would ask the six students, and the adults who worked with them during the project in the seventh month of the project. We also interviewed two mothers, eight months into the project, who were willing to share their experience of the journey as they watched their daughters become more involved in the filmmaking class. The six students were interviewed one more time, five months after their initial interview. Each interview lasted for about forty-five minutes.

The sampling strategy of Goetz and LeCompte (1984) led us to follow the film project over the course of eight months by talking to the principal participant, Nick, at the beginning, middle and end of the project. We spoke with the other groups at the end of the project. The choice to reference IMPRINT instructors as the experts who would name the case study participants was taken from the protocol suggested by Merriam (1984).

Lincoln and Guba (1985) provided several recommendations for data analysis, i.e., triangulation, prolonged engagement, peer debriefing, member checks, and thick description. The study developed inductively with categories and questions emerging from the data provided by Nick, and then being refined into focused questions that were addressed to the students, professionals, mothers, and IMPRINT personnel, who constituted the network of the Media Project (MP).

The Interview Protocol

Two members of the team used three broad questions with the students to cover the beginning, middle, and end of the journey in the film class. We wanted to understand the filmmakers' journey through their own stories. The three questions were based on the protocol described by Seidman (1991), i.e., "How did you come to be in this project?"; "What is it like now that you have done at least half of the project"; and "Now that you have reached the end of the journey, what has it been like?"

One interviewer asked students follow-up questions about their writing process eight months after the screening of their films. The writing process questions got the students to think about the steps that they took to develop their scripts, the way in which they depended on class discussions to do their revisions, the kinds of exercises that were done in the class to help them improve their stories, and the way in which they proceeded to direct their films once they were done writing.

The interviews were audio and video taped and the sessions lasted from forty to sixty minutes each and were later transcribed for analysis. Each transcript was delivered to the person who was interviewed and changes were made if there was wrong information that needed to be corrected. The participants also had the option to remove any answers that they felt would reflect on them in a negative way or cause harm to others in the program.

After reading the transcripts of the audio-taped interviews, each member of the research team did preliminary coding based on emerging themes. Using constant comparison (Strauss & Corbin, 1990), each member of the team compared and discussed their findings with the lead investigator and coordinated initial codes. The entire team then re-analyzed data to confirm categories, make final changes, and reach consensus on the descriptions that would be used to represent the data's themes. During the second review of the transcripts close attention was paid to the descriptions of the life changes that the students talked about as a result of completing their short films and sharing them with a wider community. The following report focuses on the responses of the students who reflected on the journey as writers in a filmmaking class.

Data Analysis

Several themes related to the writing process that led to the final film scripts are presented here. These themes include: (a) the class exercises that prepared the students to begin their script writing, (b) class critiques of the drafts, (c) the process of peer critiquing that helped the writers polish their scripts, (d) the result of the writing process, and (e) changes in the students at the end of the class.

The Writing Class

On the subject of the writing exercises that Nick, the instructor, presented to the students, Jai shared some personal insights on his journey:

> I think that I had trouble trying to create different characters that were all well rounded in themselves because my tendency was just to have a character that said this, and another character that said this, and almost had the same type of personality, they did not have any individuality in that. And so trying to create a full rounded character outside of yourself is very hard. (March, 2002).

Nia had another way of analyzing her process:

> Well, I developed my skill through like bits and pieces of things that I saw on television and like how I wanted to make that story better. And I went to class one day and the director of the class, he helped me out. We brainstormed a little bit and then from there I just wrote my own script (May, 2002).

Yani remembered the surprise of free writing in class:

> One of the main things that [Nick] did was he helped us write. [He said] don't think about your writing, don't have a focus when you start to write, but to just write. You know how you're taught in school to come up with a thesis and then write based on that. He took it from. . . . you know, it was a different type of brain storming, to just write (Oct, 2001).

Themes in the Student Writing

Once the scripts began to come into focus for the students, they found that they brought in more of their own history to make the ideas ring true. Nick remembered that:

> Jai had a girlfriend kind of relationship that didn't go well, but I don't think it was anywhere near the complexity of what he wrote about in *Joy Kill*. I want to say probably Rob did something that was pretty similar to real life, in that all of his characters were named after [people he knew] and the main character was named after himself, and [the character's] friends were [given names of] people that were in the class [with Rob], . . . and he gave people personalities based on people that he knew (March, 2002).

Robert also commented on how his writing looked to his own life for inspiration:

> I wanted to have myself in there so bad but Nick said that directors can't be the main characters. Of course, you saw [my personality] in there a few times. . . . So I had [the character] dress kind of like me, I had him talking like I would talk (March, 2002).

Class Critiques

When it came to critiquing each other's scripts and polishing the writing, Nick recalled how the process required the students to sit and listen to their dialogue being read by their peers. He told them that they couldn't "explain anything, everything has to come through the script and the dialogue." (March,2002). The job of the writers during these sessions was to take notes about the dialogue and its effect on the class, and to make changes to their scripts after the readings.

Yani had deep respect for the peer editing process:

> You know when you're only judging yourself you tend to be either less or more critical. You know it just depends on you and a lot of times you might not see . . . you know, how much you may need to cut or how average or mediocre your film or writing is. And so we had each other to just help to make it less mainstream as I keep pointing out. (March, 2003).

Nia had to admit that she was challenged by the critiquing, too:

> The script writing was also kind of hard for me because, its like you had to write from other people's point of view and not just your own. You couldn't just put your opinion. You had to put like how someone else would think about that one thing. And trying to make it fit one person's personality and keep in that one character [was really difficult]. (May, 2002).

The class critique of each other's editing during the production process also led to some revisions by the young filmmakers. Yani's reaction to the grueling process of video editing was summed up like this:

> Editing was also kind of difficult cause after seeing all that I had on tape, you know, it was a lot of stuff that I wanted to put on the [final] tape but it wasn't needed. And, I don't know, you have so much material but its like a lot of it is garbage, bottom line. (March, 2002).

The Final Products

The actual products of this long process of revision and readings led to some interesting scripts and difficult production issues. Nick thought highly of Jai's script because of the originality of the language. As he explained:

> Jai's film had this language that I was particularly intrigued by, because they spoke in a kind of I guess, for lack of a better word, a Shakespearean kind of dialect. They used a lot of words to express something simple. And everyone in the film spoke that way to each other and these were young adults, teenagers, you know, having a conversation and there was this kind of Shakespearean tragedy in it. (August, 2001).

Robert however had serious issues with the practical details of getting his scenes to look real. He complained that:

> I wanted like a real party scene, to go to a party and just shoot or whatever. But there was no time to find a party and go to one. So we just had to work with our people we already had, which was like seven people. And Nick was doing the camera that day so he made it look like it was a real party. (April, 2002).

Changes in the Students

One of the main results of the filmmaking course can be seen in a change in student attitudes toward themselves, their life perspectives, and their abilities. Yani and Nia were very sure about their personal growth and the lessons learned in the filmmaking field. Nia talked about herself from the vantage point of a maturing director:

> I think I've become more mature because I had to deal with stuff [on] the spot like, when a lot of my actors quit on me I had to think fast and

get more people. And most fourteen year olds didn't know how to deal with that, and I think I dealt with it great and having to work with . . . everyone in the class was older than me. And I think I did a good job of coping with that. (April, 2002).

Jai thought about his philosophical shift since studying Black stereotypes in film:

What I've learned from the class that really helped me not only in being a filmmaker, but also in being a media person . . . and that's just learning about stereotypes about Black people [in film] and that was very, very helpful to learn...we learned about that the first few weeks of class. And simply learning about how Blacks have been thought about and how they have been stereotyped helps in [my creative process]. (March, 2002).

Yani reflected on the growth in her confidence level in this way:

The main thing that has changed in my life is, I think, I'm at a higher level of confidence in my approach to doing new things. Like a lot of work goes into making a film and . . . when you see your finished product and you realize and go back and . . . , you reflect on all that you've done. It's like dang oh, wow! I did all that? I can do anything you know. (March, 2002).

Finally, Nia brings all the wisdom of her fifteen years to bear on the experience of being a first-time filmmaker by saying that: " I really didn't consider film[making] as one of my options, but now that I see and I kind of like it, I mean I'm not really sure what I want to do when I grow up but this is definitely one of my options." (May, 2002).

The Plans for Future Films

Further discussion of the role of this film class and the experiences that it provided for the students led them to talk about the way in which their careers would incorporate the life lessons learned. Robert shared these ambitions for his school career: "When I go to college, if I go to Grant State, I know I want to minor, I would probably take a film class or something, because I know that would be easy, not easy, but because I know a little literacy, kind of, it wouldn't be nothing new." (May, 2002).

Yani already had ideas for a new film that she would do in her community and school:

I want to do a script about a girl . . . [and] I think I want it to be silent. Like the film will focus on this woman she is in her early twenties, and we just see her like go through a regular day from the moment she wakes up to the moment she goes to sleep and the thing is . . . we will hear like random voices of people hating on her. And she'll . . . like she wouldn't hear it. (March, 2002).

Discussion

The multigenre project that these students embarked on during the film-making class allowed them to bring their personal interests and passions to the challenge. Unlike the students in the urban classrooms cited by Fine (1992), Camitta (1993), and Mahiri and Sablo (1996), who found the subject matter of their writing assignments unworthy of their attention or serious interest, the young filmmakers wrote stories that told about their success in the face of difficult situations. Yani wrote about a married couple having a child after several failed attempts to add to their family, Jai wrote about a young couple overcoming a misunderstanding and coming together in spite of a friend's attempt to destroy their relationship, Mandy wrote about a young woman who used the frustrations of her everyday life in a single-parent family by writing and performing poetry about the people and experiences that she valued most in her life. Each student took the opportunity to bring their experience of life into their work.

Further, the fact that the filmmaking process is a multigenre enterprise (i.e., students have to design crots that represent scripts, costumes, music, set design, camera shots, story boards, and publicity flyers), ensured an engagement with their craft which touched them in intimate places. Like the work that calls on the holistic considerations of meanings in texts (Applebee, 1984; Calkins, 1986; Poplin, 1988) the craft of filmmaking and production led the students to make connections on deep levels with themselves and their communities. If they were to lay down each frame of their films on a piece of paper they would, in effect, demonstrate in crots the results of their research into the lives of the characters that they created. They let their personal lives inform their choice of characterization, music scores, costume design, graphics, and choice of actors.

By showing the students how to use technology (i.e., the video camera and the editing program), the instructor gave them a form that they could adapt to their individual artistic visions. The filmmakers were exposed to camera techniques and point-of-view shots that helped to tell their stories from the most powerful angles. These techniques became the composing skills of the young directors and helped to expand their tools for sharing their stories with audiences who were media literate like themselves.

The evidence of the success of this method of teaching composing techniques can be found in the way that the students talk about their appraisal of their work at the end of the film course. Yani says: "We weren't afraid to explore, experience every little thing there was to experience about making your first film with each other." (March, 2002). And in this statement she uncovers the exhilaration of discovering a new means of communicating successfully with the world. She also lays bare the vulnerability of surrendering to a new form of expressing her ideas.

When Jai talks about his discovery of the need to go outside of himself in order to create a believable character, he is making a journey that his English teacher may have longed to see him begin since he entered the Language Arts classroom. As Jai reflects on his composing process, "My tendency was just to have a character that said this, and another character that said this, and almost had the same type of personality." (March, 2002). We see him begin to grapple with the reality of using his intellectual knowledge of the character and learning to transpose that information into realistic dialogue based on the way that real people interact with each other. It is a writing task that takes on new meaning to him as he struggles with the challenge of being an artist.

The students also made a commitment to the projects that brought them to a new sense of themselves as active participants in their lives. As Yani intimates in this statement, "It's like dang oh, wow! I did all that? I can do anything you know." (March, 2002). These students came to see their abilities as successful writers and producers. They came to value their intrinsic potential and knew that it would take them on to other victories. This point is best expressed by Nia when she says, "I mean I'm not really sure what I want to do when I grow up but [filmmaking] is definitely one of my options." (May, 2002). Jai best describes the heightened appreciation for the filmmakers when he talks about the fact that "the best thing was watching like, the family just smile at [the film], you know, really be proud of me." (October, 2001).

Rather than ignore the pressing concerns of the students in the film class, as it happens in many urban school settings (Sola & Bennett, 1994), the instructor created a workshop environment that encouraged students to "act like" professional independent filmmakers. Nick, the instructor, reminded the students that they needed to go beyond the mainstream images of Black people that they had grown accustomed to seeing. They were given free reign to bring their imaginations to the task of representing their communities in a positive light. In response to the concerns of Gordon (1993) and Bartolome (1994) that schools might misinterpret the need for culturally relevant materials in urban settings and implement pre-packaged curricula and strategies, this filmmaking workshop offered a formula for teaching writing and composing skills in many areas of design and craftsmanship that silenced those fears.

In fact, this group of filmmakers showed in their work that issues of the family and personal relationships are far up on the list of hot topics that Black students find important to their lives. By sidestepping the traps of showing gun fights, baby mama dramas, drug addiction, and stories of over-consumption of material goods by black teens, these students put the lie to the tale about "the raw and sometimes cruel reality" that black students have at their fingertips (Macedo, 1994, p. 120). By going to the intimate experience of their personal stories they revealed a side of the Black community that very few independent or mainstream film producers are yet to take a risk on showing to the nation.

Toward The New Urban Storyteller

In a country where people of color are hard pressed to find positive images of themselves in films and video presentations, it is refreshing to find one group of urban filmmakers who are committed to changing the stereotype that they are identified with in the media. Whether these young people make it to the Hollywood production houses that have shaped their ideas about success, or they remain in their neighborhoods as lights of inspiration, they will make a difference where they are.

For the teachers who are concerned about the implications of this filmmaking journey and its importance to the literacy levels of the students, it is important to note that three of the six students are now involved in college classes that focus on communication studies, film, and theater. Clearly, the filmmakers have achieved a level of literacy that is higher than the high school achievement that they were enjoying when the film course began. The youngest of the students has continued to do independent projects at her high school that allow her to express her artistic and production talents. We are looking forward to her graduation from high school and successful college career.

Now that these six students know how to create their multigenre stories and produce them with video equipment and editing software that is available in most high schools and colleges, they will always be able to impact the environments where they work as artists. Their very presence as graduates of a filmmaking class that allowed them to bring themselves, intimate and complex, to the task of speaking to their community will enhance the work that they do in college and beyond. Their success, small in numbers but large in implications for further investment in the youth video field that is exploding across the country, can force us to look to young people to tell stories of the spirit of the urban child in the poem by Angelou and Basquiat (1993) "Life doesn't Frighten Me." These young people know that:

> If I am afraid at all
> It's only in my dreams. . . .
> Life doesn't frighten me at all
> Not at all
> Not at all
> Life doesn't frighten me at all. (p. 2)

References

Angelou, M., & Basquiat, J. M. (1993). *Life doesn't frighten me*. New York: Stewart, Tabori & Chang.

Applebee, A. (1984). *Contexts for learning to write: Studies of secondary school instruction*. Norwood, NJ: Ablex.

Bartolome, L. (1994). Beyond the methods fetish: Toward a humanizing pedagogy. *Harvard Educational Review, 64*(3), 173-194.

Bean, T. W., Valerio, P. C., Senior, H. M., & White, F. (1997). *Secondary English students' engagement in reading and writing about a multicultural young adult novel.* Paper presented at the meeting of the National Reading Conference, Scottsdale, AZ.

Calkins, L. (1986). *The art of teaching writing.* Portsmoth, NH: Heinemann-Boynton/Cook.

Camitta, M. (1993). Vernacular writing: Varieties of literacy among Philadelphia high school students. In B. Street (Ed.), *Cross-cultural approaches to literacy* (pp. 228-246). Cambridge: Cambridge University Press.

Cox, C. (1985). Filmmaking as a composing process. *Language Arts, 62*(1), 60-69.

Doig, L., & Sargent, J. (1996). Lights, camera, action. *Social Studies Review, 34*(3), 6-11.

Fine, M. (1992). *Disruptive voices: Transgressive possibilities of research.* Ann Arbor, MI: University of Michigan Press.

Goetz, J. P., & LeCompte, M. D. (1984). *Ethnography and qualitative design in educational research.* Orlando, FL: Academic Press.

Gordon, B. (1993). African American cultural knowledge and liberatory education: Dilemmas, problems, and potentials in postmodern American society. *Urban Education, 27*(4), 448-470.

Grierson, S. T. (1999). Circling through text: Teaching research through multigenre writing. *English Journal, 89*(1), 51-55.

Lincoln, Y. S., & Guba, E. G. (1985). *Naturalistic inquiry.* Beverly Hills, CA: Sage.

Lund, D. J. (1998). Video production in the English language arts classroom. *English Journal, 87*(1), 78-82.

Macedo, D. (1994). *Literacies of power: What Americans are not allowed to know.* Boulder, CO: Westview Press.

Mahiri, J., & Sablo, S. (1996). Writing for their lives: The non-school literacy of California's urban African American youth. *Journal of Negro Education, 65*(2), 164-180.

Merriam, S. B. (1984). *Case study research in education: A qualitative approach.* San Francisco, CA: Jossey-Bass.

Nurss, J. R., Abbott-Shim, M., McCarty, F., & Hicks, D. (1999). *An effective staff development plan to encourage writing in the transition classroom.* Atlanata, Georgia: Georgia State University, Center for the Study of Adult Literacy.

Poplin, M. S. (1988). Holistic constructivist principles of the teaching/learning process: Implications for the field of learning disabilities. *Journal of Learning Disabilities, 21*(7), 401-416.

Romano, T. (1995). *Writing with passion: Life stories, multiple genres.* Portsmouth, NH: Boynton/Cook.

Seidman, I. E. (1991). *Interviewing as qualitative research.* New York: Teachers College Press.

Sola, L., & Bennett, M. (1994). The struggle for voice: Narrative, literacy and consciousness in an East Harlem school. In J. Maybin (Ed.), *Language and literacy in social practice* (pp. 117-138). Clevedon Avon, England: Multicultural Matters.

Strauss, A., & Corbin, J. (1990). *Basics of qualitative research: Grounded theory procedures and techniques.* Newbury Park, CA: Sage.

Szustak, S. (1993). *Using blues in the classroom: Giving form to feeling.* Paper presented at the meeting of the National Council of Teachers of English, Pittsburgh, PA.

Taggart, L. (1994). Student autobiographies with a twist of technology. *Educational Leadership, 51*(7), 34-35.

The Effects of Engaged Reading on Secondary Students' Standardized Test Scores

Lisbeth A. Dixon-Krauss

Florida International University

Linda McClanahan

University of Central Florida-Daytona Beach

Abstract

This paper presents a study initiated in a suburban high school to survey students' reading habits and improve reading scores on the Florida Comprehensive Achievement Test (FCAT). A survey was conducted to determine the amount of time tenth grade students spent daily doing classroom reading, homework reading and leisure reading. Student and teacher interviews were used to clarify the types and amount of content reading assignments in and outside of class. The relationship between students' daily reading habits and their reading achievement showed a positive relationship between classroom reading and FCAT reading achievement. Interview data showed teachers relied on methods of content presentation that did not require extensive textbook reading. An intervention activity of fifteen minutes text reading per class was then implemented school-wide for one year to increase students' classroom reading time. An increase in FCAT reading scores was reported following the classroom reading intervention.

Regardless of the designated time slots allotted for reading during the school day, the reported amount of time students actually spend reading in the classroom is minimal. Guthrie and Greaney (1996) reported seven to eight minutes of reading per day in the elementary grades and only fifteen minutes in the middle grades. At the secondary school level, the National Assessment of Educational Progress (NAEP) 1998 *Reading Report Card* data showed 43% of twelfth graders reported reading eleven or more pages per day while 33% read five or fewer pages (Donahue, Voelki, Campbell, & Mazzeo, 1999). The idea that increasing the amount of reading would produce better readers seems to be a rather simple, yet rational approach to improving reading performance. This study addressed the question of how much time secondary students spend reading, both in and out of the classroom, and how that time spent reading relates to their achievement.

Literature Review

McCormick (1995) recommended students should be engaged in reading connected, authentic texts at least one-third of every class period, particularly struggling readers enrolled in special programs. But, several factors related to the curriculum and classroom practice have contributed to the diminishing amount of time designated for text reading. In primary grades, students spent more time in activities assumed to be related to reading, (e.g., copying, circling, phonics drill, etc.), than they did in actual text reading (Allington, 2001). Expanding information in today's society has resulted in more content to teach in the higher grades, with lengthier subject area textbooks that require an even greater amount of time needed for reading them (Ryder & Graves, 1998). Across all grades, time-consuming classroom interruptions, in the form of discipline problems, announcements, etc., steal approximately thirty minutes of engaged instructional time each day, resulting in a loss of two whole school days every month (Allington, 2001). Teachers surveyed in Texas reported that the huge amount of time schools spend in test preparation, in response to their state mandated high-stakes test, minimized the time for teaching and learning and was especially harmful for at-risk students (Hoffman, Assaf, & Paris, 2001).

The term, *engaged reading,* refers to students' motivation to read for a variety of purposes, along with their strategic use of various approaches to comprehension. Guthrie and Wigfield (2000) described engaged reading as the students' coordination of their strategies and knowledge (cognition) within a community of literacy (socialization) in order to fulfill their personal goals (motivation). Inherent in this definition of engaged reading is the individual student's motivation to read and exert control over his or her own reading situation.

The role of motivation in increasing children's literacy development has been documented (Gambrell, 1996; Guthrie & Anderson, 1999). Guthrie and Wigfield (2000) pointed out that motivation is the link between reading and achievement; noting that motivation leads to frequent reading, frequent reading leads to competence, and competence increases motivation. In a study of over 1,700 sixth graders, Ivey and Broddus (2001) found middle school readers valued time for personal reading. They preferred silent reading because it increased their understanding, but were frustrated because they were provided limited opportunities to select their own reading material and read at their own pace in school.

The strong relationship between reading engagement and reading achievement has been documented by the 1998 NAEP data for 9, 13, and 17 year olds (Donahue, Voelki, Campbell, & Mazzeo, 1999). The more highly engaged readers in all three age groups showed higher achievement than less engaged readers, while high reading engaged middle school students even had higher achievement than lower reading engaged high school students. Also, highly engaged readers from low income families had higher achievement than low engaged readers from high income families. This finding suggests that reading engagement may even compensate for low family income and educational background (Guthrie & Wigfield, 2000).

The National Reading Panel (NRP) findings regarding voluntary reading were less conclusive than those reported by the NAEP. The NRP Report of the Subgroup on fluency verified the importance of repeated and guided oral reading to increase fluency and reiterated the importance of increasing students' reading fluency as an aid to comprehension (National Reading Panel, 2000). However, the NRP report concluded from their data analysis that there is no evidence to support the claim that encouraging students to do more voluntary silent reading actually improves reading achievement (National Reading Panel, 2000). In response, Krashen (2001) pointed out the panel's analysis used only 10 studies comparing only 14 groups of students and lasting for less than one year. Krashen reported that when studies lasting at least one year or longer were examined, thirty-five out of thirty-six comparisons showed improvements, and voluntary reading was most effective with younger, less mature readers.

Extensive reviews of research also supported both oral and silent repeated reading of texts of moderate to easy levels. For both beginning readers and students with reading difficulties, reading rate, accuracy, and comprehension improved significantly with repeated text reading (Allington, 2001; Klenk & Kibby, 2000). In a study examining the reading achievement of students aged 9 to 14 and the quality of their schools in thirty-two nations, Elley (1992) found the greater the amount of time allocated for reading and writing during the school day, the higher the achievement. Also, the amount of free voluntary reading that students engaged in was the second most powerful predictor of school achievement, following parental cooperation.

Regardless of how the data is interpreted, the need for more research on the relationship between students' reading of connected text and achievement is evident. The report of the NRP subgroup on fluency called for more research to evaluate the effectiveness of students' engagement of wide reading on reading achievement (National Reading Panel, 2000). More specifically, Guthrie and Wigfield (2000) pointed out the need for more investigations using contextualized observations or measures that would be more responsive to classroom and environmental events, as well as school-wide inquiry into reading engagement. The study reported here was a school-wide inquiry initiated in one suburban high school to improve reading scores on the Florida Comprehensive Achievement Test (FCAT), the primary criteria used to calculate school performance grades in Florida (Bureau of Education Information and Accountability Services, 2000-2001). The purpose of the study was to examine the relationship between students' daily reading habits and their FCAT reading achievement scores.

Method

This school-wide inquiry study was conducted in two phases that lasted for one complete year. In the first phase, a reading habits survey was conducted to determine the amount of time tenth grade students actually spent daily engaged in reading connected text both in and outside of their classes. In the second phase, intervention activities were implemented school-wide for one year to increase students' engaged reading time in school. Following the year of reading time intervention, the school FCAT reading scores were examined.

Reading Habits Survey

Subjects. Participants in the reading habits survey phase of the study included 76 tenth grade students from English II College Prep and English II Honors classes. This sample included all students of average reading ability, ranging from the 4th to 8th stanines on the Stanford Achievement Test. The teachers participating included three English teachers, four teachers from the academic classes (two biology, two world history), and two from performance classes (drivers education, ROTC).

Instruments. The following three instruments were used in the study:
1. Student Record of Reading Time was a daily self-report checklist of the time the students spent reading recorded in 15-minute increments (see Appendix A). The checklist included recorded minutes for: (a) classroom reading time (CRT), the number of minutes spent reading during each class period; (b) homework reading time (HRT), the number of minutes spent reading during an after-school homework assignment; and (c) leisure reading time (LRT), the number of minutes spent reading text of personal choice and interest.

2. Student Survey of Reading Habits was a survey containing 15 items on students' reading habits outside of classes, perceptions of their own reading abilities, and reading preferences (see Appendix B).

3. Teacher Survey of Reading Assignments was a survey containing 10 items on the amount and type of homework and classroom reading assignments the teachers used in their respective classes (see Appendix C).

Data collection procedures. The Student Survey of Reading Habits, Record of Reading Time, and Teacher Survey of Reading Assignments were administered by the school reading specialist during a two-week period in the spring after students took the FCAT. Initially, the students completed the Survey of Reading Habits questionnaire administered in their English classes. The Record of Reading Time checklist was completed by each student every day for two weeks in English II class during *bellwork*, the first five minutes of classes when the teachers were preparing the class period attendance reports. The fifteen minute time increments were used for the checklists to help ensure efficiency and accuracy in students' daily recordings of their reading times. Individual Interviews were conducted by the reading specialist with a random sample of 20% of the student participants two weeks after the Student Record of Reading Times was completed. The interviews were conducted to verify and clarify results of the Student Survey of Reading Habits and to help clarify and interpret possible bias in the self-report data from Student Record of Reading Time and Teacher Survey of Reading Assignments.

Results

A multiple regression analysis was used with the Student Record of Reading Time data to evaluate how well classroom reading time (CRT), homework reading time (HRT), and leisure reading time (LRT) predicted the FCAT Reading Scores. The linear combination of classroom reading, homework reading, and leisure reading times was not significant, $F(3,72) = 2.577$, $p = .06$. These results indicated there was no relationship between students' FCAT reading scores and their actual text reading for their schoolwork in the classroom, for their homework, and for their own purposes outside of school. As shown in Table 1, only the partial correlation coefficient between classroom reading time CRT and FCAT Reading was significant ($p < .05$), and this partial coefficient of .23 for classroom reading time CRT/FCAT reading was low. The minimal relationship found between reading times and FCAT could indicate the test does not reflect actual text reading ability of students, or it could be due to students' inaccurate reporting of their own reading times.

Table 1. Summary of Coefficients of Each Predictor with FCAT Reading Scores

Reading Time	Beta Coefficient	*t*	*p.*	Partial Coefficient
Classroom Reading Time	.246	2.024	.047	.232*
Homework Reading Time	.096	.769	.445	.090
Leisure Reading Time	.055	.473	.638	.056

Note: $*p < .05$

Means were reported in Table 2 to further clarify daily patterns of average reading times. Students' total daily classroom reading time for all four classes they attended ($M = 90$ min.) did not meet the one-third of each class period goal (120 min.) suggested by McCormick (1995). Students averaged 35% of their total class reading time in their English classes. This group of tenth graders spent an average of only fifteen minutes daily in leisure reading time and thirty-seven minutes in homework reading time (approximately 9 minutes per class). The total amount of daily reading time reported by students was low, less than one hour outside of school and only one and one-half hours in school.

Table 2. Reading Time Means

	MEAN	STANDARD DEVIATION	N
FCAT Reading	309.62	32.53	76
Classroom Reading Time	90.42	43.50	76
Homework Reading Time	37.91	32.38	76
Leisure Reading Time	14.99	15.46	76

Note: Classroom Reading Time Mean was less than goal (1/3 of class time = 120 minutes)

Reading time means, reported by SAT stanines in Table 3, indicated that students with higher reading ability tended to read more both in and out of school. Only those students with SAT reading scores at the 8th stanine met the recommended 120 minutes daily of classroom reading time. Leisure reading time was minimal, with a range from nine to eighteen minutes daily across students in all stanines.

Table 3. Mean Minutes Read Per Day

	READING TIME			
STANINE	CLASSROOM	HOMEWORK	LEISURE	TOTAL
4	70	27	13	110
5	88	37	15	140
6	88	33	13	134
7	98	41	21	160
8	157	87	18	262

Note: Stanine 8 Classroom Mean was greater than goal (1/3 of class time = 120 minutes)

Responses to the Student Survey of Reading Habits were tallied, reported in percentages, and analyzed to clarify the self-reported data on reading time. Students reported that when homework was assigned it was twice weekly per class, with 13% having homework in only one of their classes, 38% in two classes, 31% in three classes and 13% in four classes. Less than half of the students, 47%, reported that they enjoyed reading. Of those who read books for leisure, 28% reported reading one or more books per month while 44.7% read six or fewer books per year. Most students reported reading popular teenage magazines for leisure, and only 20% were reading a book. These responses support the low means obtained for homework and leisure reading time reported on the student record of reading time checklist. Almost all students interviewed, 92%, reported they read well enough to function adequately, but 57% indicated that they would like to read better.

In the follow-up interviews, twenty-one students clarified and verified their answers on the reading habits survey. Students reported a range of zero to forty-five minutes of time assigned daily for classroom reading (total for all four classes), with thirteen students reporting thirty to fourty-five minutes. This finding is less than the classroom mean minutes read per day reported in Table 3. Fourteen of the students ranked English as their most difficult class, and all students reported the most reading was required in the class they ranked most difficult. All twenty-one students reported they had homework at least twice a week in one or two classes. When asked about the type of homework assigned, fifteen students reported they had reading plus worksheets, three reported problems to solve (math or chemistry) and only one reported having writing for homework. This is also consistent with the report of low homework reading time means found on the Student Record of Reading time checklist. In the area of leisure reading, nine students reported they liked to read for escape or imagination, four reported they sometimes liked to read depending on the book and not for school, and seven did not like to read because they thought reading was boring or they preferred more physical activity in their leisure time.

Analysis of the Teacher Survey of Reading Assignments supported the student reports of reading times. The English teachers reported requiring daily classroom individual reading, while the other teachers listed two to three times weekly of teacher reading followed by individual student oral reading. One science teacher reported daily individual student reading during bellwork, which consisted of approximately five minutes per day. Eight of the ten teachers reported that they assigned homework two times per week, while the Honors classes received homework more than three times weekly.

Three important findings related to the teachers' homework and classroom reading assignments were evident: (a) the teachers indicated that 90% of honor students completed their homework while only 30% to 40% of the other students completed their homework, (b) most students read well enough to do what they needed in class, and (c) 80% of the teachers summarized class texts and gave students notes over the material or put students in groups so the more proficient readers could read and summarize the material for others rather than requiring text reading. The teachers placed importance on students' acquiring subject information and learning the objectives tested on their subject area exams required to pass their courses rather than on students reading their textbooks.

School Reading Time Intervention Activities

Results of the Reading Habits Survey led to the conclusion that students in this high school needed to spend more class time reading challenging texts and responding to this reading. In response, the following four-step school-wide reading improvement program was implemented in the fall of the following year with the new class of tenth graders:

Specify a plan. Students were required to read grade level materials for at least fifteen minutes daily per class for four days per week and respond to this reading in class discussion, written assignment, a test, an essay, etc. Within the school district, county mandated FCAT preparation curriculum initiatives and prepackaged FCAT materials were being implemented in other schools. In this school's specified plan, no mandated or prepackaged FCAT materials were used in order to control for other curricular changes that might affect the school FCAT reading scores that were collected following intervention. The plan was approved by the principal of the school.

Recruit departmental support. The plan was explained to the subject area department heads and suggestions were encouraged to ensure success of the intervention activities. Teachers were reluctant to devote class time to reading; normally reading was assigned as homework, and class time was used to prepare students for county subject area curriculum exams and FCAT exams. Department heads agreed to the plan because reading in class would involve materials tested on the county exam rather than FCAT-prep materials.

Train teachers. The teachers were informed that their students needed to read material appropriate for their grade level under the supervision of a teacher in order to improve their reading comprehension. Examples of reading response strategies were distributed during subject area department meetings. The response strategies included discussion questions, graphic organizers, essay and note taking. A checklist was used weekly for teachers to record text pages read and how students responded to the reading.

On-going support. The reading specialist provided support by helping teachers write graphic organizers or compose questions. She ordered books and magazines for science, history, and elective classes. She visited all areas of the school and talked daily with the teachers about their reading and responding activities. The school television station was also used to promote reading. The reading specialist prompted teachers bi-weekly to complete their checklists of text pages read and collected the checklists at the end of each week.

Reading achievement results. Reading achievement was examined after the school-wide reading time intervention activities were implemented for one year. The post intervention achievement data analyzed were school FCAT reading scores reported as the number of students who took the FCAT within each achievement level category ranging from Level 1 through Level 5. The school FCAT reading scores for year 1, before intervention, and for year 2, after intervention, are reported in Table 4. Level 1 and Level 2 performance categories represent failure, and the number of student FCAT scores in Levels 1 and 2 are used to determine the school's accountability rankings of A through F in Florida (Bureau of Education Information and Accountability Services, 2000-2001). In the first year, 77% of the scores were in the Level 1 and Level 2 failure categories. In year 2, following intervention, 66% of the scores fell in Level 1 and Level 2 for an 11% improvement after the first year of increased classroom reading time.

Table 4. School FCAT Reading Scores

	Scale Score	Score Levels				
		Level 1	Level 2	Level 3	Level 4	Level 5
Before Intervention (Year 1)	295	40%	37%	15%	5%	2%
After Intervention (Year 2)	308	30%	36%	20%	6%	8%
Difference	13	-10%	-1%	+5%	+1%	+6%

Discussion and Implications

Findings from this study support the claims that students who read more have higher reading achievement (Donahue, Voelki, Campbell, & Mazzeo, 1999; Elley, 1992; Guthrie & Wigfield, 2000). The students with higher achievement read more both in class and for homework, but only the above average achievers in the 8th stanine exceeded 120 minutes which would equal the one-third of class time of reading per day recommended (McCormick, 1995).

Reading Time and Reading Achievement

Findings on the relationship between reading time and FCAT scores were inconclusive. The significant relationship between classroom reading time and FCAT reading scores suggested that classroom reading time does predict FCAT reading. However, the relationship between FCAT reading scores and the combination of all three reading time variables, both in and outside of the classroom, was not significant. Also, the strength of the relationship between the one significant predictor, classroom reading and the FCAT reading test, was low. Although this finding could be due to students' inaccurate daily reporting of their reading times, the initial student surveys, follow-up interviews, and teacher surveys all showed reports of similar reading times. This finding leads to questions about whether the FCAT reading test actually does assess students' ability to read connected text.

The increase in the school's overall FCAT reading scores following the intervention of only fifteen minutes per class of daily classroom reading and response further suggests a relationship between classroom reading time and reading achievement, but this finding needs more research and extensive clarification. The lack of relationship found between the FCAT scores and reading outside of class or homework reading further complicates the issue. In the interviews, students reported fifteen or more minutes of homework twice weekly per class, but that homework included completing worksheets and math problems as well as reading. These findings lead back to questions previously raised by other researchers about the relationship between authentic text reading, classroom reading instruction, and high-stakes testing (Allington, 2002; Hoffman, Assaf, & Paris, 2001).

For students in this study, leisure reading time was minimal. Less than half of the students interviewed reported that they enjoyed reading. Those who did read for leisure selected popular adolescent magazines, *Seventeen, Teen,* or *People,* that contain several pages of advertisements and very little challenging text. This is consistent with the 1998 NAEP report that the amount of leisure reading decreases substantially and the relationship between reading self-selected materials and achievement test scores decreases by high school age (Donahue et al., 1999).

Teachers' Classroom Reading Practices

The Teacher Survey data revealed some interesting findings about the teachers' beliefs regarding classroom reading time, their curriculum, and their classroom practices. Most of these teachers (80%) emphasized the need for students to acquire information in the subject areas and learn the objectives tested on the final exams rather than read their content textbooks. Although the teachers recognized that many of their students needed to read better in order to actually read their textbooks and complete their homework, they had devised a system of notes and summaries to sidestep textbook reading entirely. The constraints imposed on the teachers' classroom practices by the mandated standard county curriculum and exams for core subject area courses were also evident in the implementation of the school-wide intervention plan. In order to get teachers to participate in the fifteen minutes of reading time per class, the text materials used for the reading and response had to be related to the county curriculum. These findings on the beliefs and practices of the teachers in this school reflected the pervasive applications of the traditional teacher-centered, transmission of information style approach in content area classrooms documented by other researchers (Bean, 2000).

In summary, the most conclusive finding in this study was the minimal amount of time these average achieving tenth grade students spent engaged in classroom, homework, and leisure reading. A more obscure finding in the interview data that also merits further investigation was all students ranked the course requiring the most text reading as their most difficult course. This is particularly puzzling when we consider that 92%, almost all students, reported they read well enough to function adequately. Findings from this study raise important questions regarding the relationship between classroom reading time and achievement, as well as questions about whether the FCAT reading test does actually reflect students' ability to read connected text.

References

Allington, R. L. (2001). *What really matters to struggling readers: Designing research-based programs*. Boston, MA: Allyn and Bacon.

Allington, R. (2002). Accelerating in the wrong direction: Why thirty years of federal testing and accountability hasn't worked yet and what we might do instead. In R. Allington (Ed.), *Big brother and the national reading curriculum: How ideology trumped evidence* (pp. 235-263). Portsmouth, NH: Heinemann.

Bean, T. W. (2000). Reading in the content areas: Social constructivist dimensions. In M. L. Kamil, P. B. Mosenthal, P. D. Pearson, & R. Barr (Eds.), *Handbook of reading research III* (pp. 629-666). Mahwah, NJ: Lawrence Erlbaum.

Bureau of Education Information and Accountability Services. (2000-2001). *Florida School Indicators Report*. Retrieved August 15, 2003, from http://info.doe.state. fl.us/fsir2002/school_report.cfm

Donahue, P., Voelki, K., Campbell, J. R., & Mazzeo, J. (1999). The NAEP 1998 reading report card for the nation and the states. *Education Statistics Quarterly, 1,* 21-27.

Elley, W. B. (1992). *How in the world do students read? IEA study of reading literacy*. The Hague, Netherlands: International Association for the Evaluation of Educational Achievement.

Gambrell, L. (1996). Creating classroom structures that foster reading motivation. *Reading Teacher, 50,* 14-25.

Guthrie, J. T., & Anderson, E. (1999). Engagement in reading: Processes of motivated, strategic, knowledgeable, social readers. In J. T. Guthrie & D. Alvermann (Eds.), *Engaged reading: Processes, practices, and policy implications* (pp. 17-45). New York: Teachers College.

Guthrie, J. T., & Greaney, V. (1996). Literacy act. In R. Barr, M. L. Kamil, P. B. Mosenthal, & P. D. Pearson (Eds.), *Handbook of reading research II* (pp. 68-96). Mahwah, NJ: Lawrence Erlbaum.

Guthrie, J., & Wigfield, A. (2000). Engagement and motivation in reading. In M. L. Kamil, P. B. Mosenthal, P. D. Pearson, & R. Barr (Eds.), *Handbook of reading research* III (pp. 403-422). Mahwah, NJ: Lawrence Erlbaum.

Hoffman, J. V., Assaf, L. C., & Paris, S. G. (2001). High-stakes testing in reading: Today in Texas, tomorrow? *The Reading Teacher, 43,* 482-492.

Ivey, G., & Broddus, K. (2001). "Just plain reading:" A survey of what makes students want to read in middle school classrooms. *Reading Research Quarterly, 36,* 350-377.

Klenk, L., & Kibby, M. W. (2000). Re-mediating reading difficulties: Appraising the past, reconciling the present, constructing the future. In M. L. Kamil, P. B. Mosenthal, P. D. Pearson, & R. Barr (Eds.), *Handbook of reading research III* (pp. 667-690). Mahwah, NJ: Lawrence Erlbaum.

Krashen, S. (2001). More smoke and mirrors: A critique of the National Reading Panel Report on fluency. *Phi Delta Kappan 83(2),* 119-122.

McCormick, S. (1995). *Instructing students who have literacy problems.* Englewood Cliffs, NJ: Prentice Hall.

National Reading Panel. (2000). Teaching children to read: Report of subgroups. Washington, DC : National Institute of Child Health and Human Development.

Ryder, R., & Graves, M. (1998). *Reading and learning in the content areas.* Upper Saddle River, NJ: Prentice Hall.

Appendix A. Student Record of Reading Time

Complete this survey by checking the number of minutes you read for classwork, homework assignments, and leisure.

DAY/ PERIOD	CLASSWORK (CHECK NUMBER OF MINUTES)	HOMEWORK (CHECK NUMBER OF MINUTES)	LEISURE (CHECK NUMBER OF MINUTES)	TYPE OF LEISURE READING
M – 1	1-15___ 16-30___ 31-60___ 60+___	1-15___ 16-30___ 31-60___ 60+___	1-15___ 16-30___ 31-60___ 60+___	
M –2	1-15___ 16-30___ 31-60___ 60+___	1-15___ 16-30___ 31-60___ 60+___	1-15___ 16-30___ 31-60___ 60+___	
M – 3	1-15___ 16-30___ 31-60___ 60+___	1-15___ 16-30___ 31-60___ 60+___	1-15___ 16-30___ 31-60___ 60+___	
M – 4	1-15___ 16-30___ 31-60___ 60+___	1-15___ 16-30___ 31-60___ 60+___	1-15___ 16-30___ 31-60___ 60+___	
Total				

DAY/ PERIOD	CLASSWORK (CHECK NUMBER OF MINUTES)	HOMEWORK (CHECK NUMBER OF MINUTES)	LEISURE (CHECK NUMBER OF MINUTES)	TYPE OF LEISURE READING
T – 1	1-15___ 16-30___ 31-60___ 60+___	1-15___ 16-30___ 31-60___ 60+___	1-15___ 16-30___ 31-60___ 60+___	
T – 2	1-15___ 16-30___ 31-60___ 60+___	1-15___ 16-30___ 31-60___ 60+___	1-15___ 16-30___ 31-60___ 60+___	
T – 3	1-15___ 16-30___ 31-60___ 60+___	1-15___ 16-30___ 31-60___ 60+___	1-15___ 16-30___ 31-60___ 60+___	
T – 4	1-15___ 16-30___ 31-60___ 60+___	1-15___ 16-30___ 31-60___ 60+___	1-15___ 16-30___ 31-60___ 60+___	
Total				

DAY/ PERIOD	CLASSWORK (CHECK NUMBER OF MINUTES)	HOMEWORK (CHECK NUMBER OF MINUTES)	LEISURE (CHECK NUMBER OF MINUTES)	TYPE OF LEISURE READING
W – 1	1-15___ 16-30___ 31-60___ 60+___	1-15___ 16-30___ 31-60___ 60+___	1-15___ 16-30___ 31-60___ 60+___	
W – 2	1-15___ 16-30___ 31-60___ 60+___	1-15___ 16-30___ 31-60___ 60+___	1-15___ 16-30___ 31-60___ 60+___	
W – 3	1-15___ 16-30___ 31-60___ 60+___	1-15___ 16-30___ 31-60___ 60+___	1-15___ 16-30___ 31-60___ 60+___	
W – 4	1-15___ 16-30___ 31-60___ 60+___	1-15___ 16-30___ 31-60___ 60+___	1-15___ 16-30___ 31-60___ 60+___	
Total				

Appendix B. Student Survey of Reading Habits

DIRECTIONS: Please answer the following questions by writing on this survey.

1. The four classes I am taking this term are _____, _____, _____, and _____.

2. List the classes you have homework in at least twice a week.

3. Does your homework usually require you to read from a textbook or an article that has been Xeroxed?

4. When do you do your homework?

5. Where do you do your homework?

6. While I do my homework, I usually listen to the radio or stereo. ___yes ___no

7. While I do my homework, I usually watch television. ___yes ___no

8. Do you have a job?
   If so, where do you work?   How many hours a week do you work?

9. Do you read any magazines regularly?
   If so, which ones?

10. Do you read the newspaper regularly?

11. Do you read books for your own enjoyment or information?
    If so, how often do you read or how much time do you spend reading? (Check one)
    ___one book a week to two weeks
    ___one book a month
    ___one book every two or three months
    ___two or three books a year

12. Most of my reading is for school (homework or classwork) or for pleasure. (Circle one)

13. I enjoy reading.   ___yes ___no

14. I read well enough to do what I need to do.   ___yes ___no

15. I wish I could read better.   ___yes ___no

Appendix C. Teacher Survey of Reading Assignments

1. List the classes you teach and the approximate number of students in each class.

2. List the classes for which you assign homework and tell how often you assign homework that involves students reading a passage, article, chapter, or story.

3. Approximately what percentage of students complete most or all of the homework assigned?

4. How do you count homework?

5. How do you verify that students do the reading assigned?

6. If you do not assign homework regularly, what are some of the reasons why you do not require homework?

7. How often do students read passages, articles, chapters in textbooks, stories, etc., during the class period?

8. Do students do most of their reading independently or do you read to them as they follow along in the textbook?

9. Do you summarize passages or chapters and require students to take notes or study notes rather than reading the entire passage? If so, how often?

10. According to your expertise as a classroom teacher, how would you rate the reading level of the students you teach? (Circle one)
    A) My students read well enough independently to complete their homework successfully.
    Or
    B) My students have difficulty reading independently; therefore, I must make allowances for their limitations in reading.

LITERACY LEARNING AND THE METAPHOR OF APPRENTICESHIP

Edward H. Behrman

National University

Abstract

This paper explores the usefulness and limitations of extending the apprenticeship metaphor to classroom-based literacy instruction. First, it discusses traditional apprenticeship from the perspective of Lave and Wenger's (1991) concept of legitimate peripheral participation and Wenger's (1998) social theory of learning. Then it presents and analyzes an exemplar of a reading apprenticeship recently published in Harvard Educational Review *(Greenleaf, Schoenbach, Cziko, & Mueller, 2001). In contrast to traditional apprenticeships, the reading apprenticeship appears to emphasize identity more than practice, and community more than meaning. The reading apprenticeship is characterized by social formation, rites of passage, and cultural systems. Less evident is concern for everyday activity in real-life settings, coordination of activity with community purpose, and the interaction of learners with environmental resources. It is proposed that other educational programs such as community-based project learning are more aligned with the principles of legitimate peripheral participation.*

What's in a name? Although the Bard may be correct that changing the name of something does not alter its salient characteristics, using a metaphor to describe an object or event does have a profound impact upon our conceptualization of the object or event. Metaphors are more than just literary devices, they influence how we think and how we act (Lakoff & Johnson, 1980, 1999; Tripp, 1990). So when educational researchers describe an instructional practice metaphorically, such as speaking of *scaffolding* instruction or *coaching* students, they are intentionally or unintentionally altering the perceptions of teachers, administrators, school board members, and policy makers at the state and national levels.

Several recent efforts to improve the reading and writing abilities of both elementary students (Dorn, French, & Jones, 1998; Knapp & Windsor, 1998) and secondary students (Greenleaf, Schoenbach, Cziko, and Mueller, 2001; Jordan, Jensen, & Greenleaf, 2001; Lee, 1995; Schoenbach, Greenleaf, Cziko, & Hurwitz, 1999) have drawn upon the metaphor of *apprenticeship* to describe classroom-based instructional practices. A common feature of these literacy apprenticeships is the designation of the classroom teacher or adult volunteer as a mentor who demonstrates the desired behavior and then monitors the students' attempts to replicate the behavior. Literacy apprenticeship is founded upon Vygotskian learning theory, which asserts that higher psychological processes, such as reading and writing, begin in a social context of interaction between the learner and a more advanced other (Dorn et al., 1998; Jordan et al., 2001; Knapp & Windsor, 1998). Literacy apprenticeship also follows directly from the cognitive apprenticeship method proposed by Allan Collins and colleagues in which the teacher first "models" the skill or activity, "coaches" the novice during initial practice, and then "fades" as the student becomes more independent (Brown, Collins, & Duguid, 1989; Collins, 1988, 1991; Collins, Brown, & Holum, 1991; Collins, Brown, & Newman, 1989).

Because apprenticeship carries with it a number of positive cultural values—for example, learning that is practical, well rehearsed, and progressing toward an acknowledged standard—the metaphoric designation of apprenticeship to any instructional program may assign to the program these positive values, whether or not they are reproduced. This paper will explore the usefulness and limitations of extending the apprenticeship metaphor to classroom-based literacy instruction by contrasting traditional apprenticeships in non-school settings as described by Lave and Wenger (1991) with an exemplar of reading apprenticeship recently published in *Harvard Educational Review* (Greenleaf et al., 2001). Specifically, this analysis will consider how well instructional programs that promote literacy development in school settings are aligned with principles of legitimate peripheral participation and a social theory of learning that undergird apprenticeship learning in non-school settings.

Theoretical Perspective

Current interest in apprenticeship as a form of learning has been stimulated by the emergence of situated cognition as an important perspective within educational psychology. In contrast to a purely cognitive position that identifies the locus of learning within individuals (Reynolds, Sinatra, & Jetton, 1996), situated cognition places learning not only within individuals but also within the social context of the learning situation (Kirshner & Whitson, 1998). Although situated cognition does not offer a unified theory of learning, two assumptions ground most work in situated cognition: (a) learning cannot be separated from the activity in which the learning takes place, and (b) learning occurs on both the social and individual planes (Greeno, 1991, 1997; Kirshner & Whitson, 1998; Putnam & Borko, 2000). Amount and quality of learning depend upon physical setting, available tools or resources, and interpersonal transactions engaged between learner and community members (Brown et al., 1989; Cobb & Bowers, 1999; Greeno, 1997; Greeno, Collins, & Resnick, 1996; Putnam & Borko, 2000). From a situated perspective, transfer of learning occurs not because of structures that are represented in the mind but because structures of activity from the target situation are repeated in the transfer situation (Greeno, Moore, & Smith, 1993).

Within this tradition of situated cognition, Jean Lave and Etienne Wenger have analyzed traditional apprenticeship to better understand learning as activity-in-practice (Lave & Wenger, 1991). They were concerned that in its increasing use among educational researchers as a synonym for situated learning, apprenticeship had become too ill-defined to meaningfully contribute to learning-research problems. For that reason, they felt it was necessary to distinguish between the metaphorical use of apprenticeship in educational research and specific historical forms of apprenticeship. In their analyses of five apprenticeships (i.e., midwives, tailors, quartermasters, butchers, and recovering alcoholics), Lave and Wenger developed the concept of learning as legitimate peripheral participation in communities of practice. In their view, legitimate peripheral participation contributes to situated learning theory by proposing that practice should not be conceived within processes of learning, but that learning be considered an integral aspect of practice. Newcomers are initially placed at the periphery of the practice, eventually moving from less-engaged to more-engaged involvement. Peripherality implies relevant participation in the community practice that has not yet developed into full participation. Learning is both an evolving form of membership in the community and a vehicle for becoming a different person in terms of relations with the social world. Therefore, mastery of new tasks or new understandings is only part of learning, since "identity, knowing, and social membership entail one another" (Lave & Wenger, 1991, p. 53). Legitimate peripheral participation also implies learning be viewed as a process of community reproduction and change, as newcomers move to old-timer status.

Wenger (1998) has offered a social theory of learning which expands upon the concept of legitimate peripheral participation by categorizing learning in communities of practice along four dimensions: community (learning as belonging), meaning (learning as experience), identity (learning as becoming), and practice (learning as doing) (see Figure 1). Each of the four dimensions is mutually dependent upon and overlapping with the other dimensions. According to Wenger, learning occurs at the intersection of these four dimen-

Figure 1. A Social Theory of Learning (adapted from Wenger, 1998)

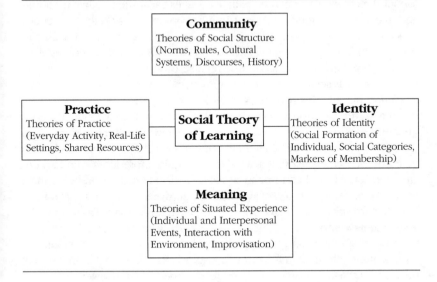

sions. Learning as participation is "caught in the middle" (Wenger, 1998, p. 13) between theories of social structure (rules, norms, cultural systems, discourses, and history) and theories of situated experience (individual or interpersonal events, interaction with environment, and improvisation). Learning as participation is also caught between theories of identity (social formation of individual, social categories, and markers of membership) and theories of practice (everyday activity in real-life settings, and shared resources).

Traditional Apprenticeships

Each of the five contemporary apprenticeships analyzed by Lave and Wenger (1991) illustrates how learning, or failing to learn, may be understood through the lens of legitimate peripheral participation. In the case of Yucatec Mayan midwives, the apprentices are daughters or granddaughters of midwives. The apprentice is integrated into daily life so seamlessly that there is no recognizable teaching involved, nor is the youngster formally recognized as an apprentice. Young girls grow up observing the practices of midwifery, such as giving prenatal massages or administering herbal remedies. The girls may be asked to run errands or procure supplies. As she grows older, usually after the birth of her own child, the apprentice may be allowed to assist in delivery or give a prenatal massage. The decision to become a midwife herself does not occur until after the apprentice is more fully involved in the practice.

In contrast, the parents of apprentice tailors in West Africa enter into a formal agreement with a master tailor, who takes the apprentice into his house and allows the apprentice to work in his shop. In the shop the apprentice observes the process of making garments. At first, the apprentice learns to sew by hand, sew by machine, and press clothes. A typical pattern involves learning the steps of production in reverse order, moving from finishing activities such as sewing buttons or hemming cuffs, to sewing pieces together, to cutting pieces. This reverse process is intended to show the apprentice how each step contributes to the overall product. In the case of apprentice quartermasters in the US Navy, some apprentices first attend a specialized school, while others receive all their training aboard ship. Interestingly, two quartermaster chiefs felt that it was better to train apprentices who had not attended school but had prior experience as deckhands. Apprentices must learn to work cooperatively with other quartermasters to plot a ship's position. Aboard ship they receive both on-the-job training as well as school-like assignments with workbooks and exercises. Novices first learn to work as fathometer operators and bearing takers, through each of six positions that represent the information flow from sensor to chart. In time the novice may be allowed to stand watch with a more seasoned quartermaster.

The case of apprentice meat cutters in a US trade union was the one apprenticeship in which Lave and Wenger (1991) found unsuccessful learning. The apprentice butcher begins in a trade school that combines classroom-based instruction with practice in a shop. However, much of the classroom instruction and shop practice is outmoded, such as learning to make wholesale cuts that are not used in retail stores or learning to sharpen knives when knife-sharpening is now provided by an outside contractor. After receiving a certificate from the trade school, the apprentice continues with on-the-job training in a retail store. In the store, the apprentice's responsibilities tend to be low-level and repetitive, such as working at an automatic wrapping machine for years until a new apprentice comes along to replace him. Journeymen butchers are usually not granted time to train the apprentices. Furthermore, the physical layout of most butcher departments prevents the apprentice from observing the entire work process.

The last case of apprenticeship is unusual in that recovering alcoholics are not learning a trade but the "skill" of not drinking. More so than in the other apprenticeships, a transformation of identity is more overtly a feature of the recovering alcoholic apprenticeship. Several times a week the apprentice joins other apprentices and old-timers at a meeting of Alcoholics Anonymous (AA). At the meeting the apprentice hears old-timers give testimony, telling stories of their lives as alcoholics. The personal story is seen as a critical part of the reconstruction of identity from drinking non-alcoholics to non-drinking alcoholics. The apprentice listens to these personal stories and must confront whether he or she is also an alcoholic. In due course the apprentice will be expected to tell a personal story. Telling stories is learned through imitation rather than explicit teaching. The apprentice is encouraged to follow the Twelve Steps to sobriety, beginning with a pledge not to drink alcohol for the next 24 hours and ending with a recruiting visit to a current alcoholic to encourage him or her to join AA.

For Lave and Wenger (1991), legitimate peripheral participation provides access to community learning resources and a wide range of activities in the course of practice. From their peripheral perspective, apprentices are able to progressively structure an overview of the enterprise. Lave and Wenger point out that neither an explicit master-apprentice relationship nor routinized reproduction of simple tasks are inherent attributes of apprenticeship. Learning in apprenticeship occurs through social participation, but only in the case of tailors are there clearly defined master-apprentice roles. Yet even with tailors, it is often the relationship with other apprentices or experienced tailors that contributes most directly to learning. Evident in legitimate peripheral participation is acquisition of particularized knowledge or skills to be used for an immediate purpose that contributes to overall production, but rarely is there direct teaching. Learning is largely improvised, so "a learning curriculum unfolds in opportunities for engagement in practice. It is not specified as a set of dictates for proper practice" (Lave & Wenger, 1991, p. 93). From the learners' standpoint, legitimacy is established by interaction with adept practitioners and realization that there is a field of mature practice for what they are learning. The newcomer learns initially from participation in activities that are useful to the community but pose little risk. Over time the newcomer takes on more difficult tasks, moving from peripheral to full participation. The role of "instruction" is to provide learners opportunities to participate in legitimate events as members of communities of practice.

Legitimate peripheral participation therefore identifies two critical aspects of apprenticeship learning: (a) participation in meaningful, actual practice within a social community; and (b) identity formation/transformation of both the apprentice and the community (Wenger, 1998). An implication for education is that learning may be viewed as an aspect of practice, not only in identifiable apprenticeships but also in other learning situations. Practice in this sense may be defined as limited co-production in authentic activity that has meaning to the learner and the community of practice.

Exemplar: A Content-Area Reading Apprenticeship for Ninth Graders

Greenleaf et al. (2001) have reported on an academic reading curriculum for underachieving secondary students. The program they describe is called alternately Academic Literacy or Reading Apprenticeship. Its goal is to improve content-area reading abilities of all ninth graders at a college preparatory urban high school. In contrast to a remedial reading program featuring isolated skill-based instruction, the Academic Literacy course requires students to read narratives, commercials, and historical texts. The class meets for one 50-minute and two 90-minute periods per week. Throughout the course students are challenged to consider two guiding questions: What is reading? and What do successful readers do when they read?

The curriculum is divided into three units: Reading Self and Society, Reading Media, and Reading History. In the first unit, students read narratives by famous Americans, interview family and community members about the role of reading in their lives, and read self-selected books during sustained silent reading. In the second unit, students analyze commercials to discover how this form of visual text addresses audience and purpose. Students then create their own commercials to target specific audiences. In the third unit, students read textbooks and primary source documents to interpret events related to totalitarianism, genocide, and hate crimes.

Four different teachers instruct twelve sections of Academic Literacy. Two are English teachers, one is a history teacher, and one's discipline is not identified. One instructional strategy used throughout the course is Reciprocal Teaching or RT (Brown, Palinscar, & Armbruster, 1994), whereby the teacher and students take turns questioning, summarizing, clarifying, and predicting. A second instructional strategy is described as "explicit, integrated instruction in self-monitoring, cognitive strategies, and text analysis" (Greenleaf et al., 2001, p. 95). Teachers use "think-alouds" (Baumann, Jones, & Siefort-Kessell, 1993; Davey, 1983; Silven & Vaurus, 1992) to model how they read and analyze texts. Students are encouraged to discuss their own reading processes. Teachers give instruction in and demonstrate a number of generic reading skills that are presumed to have application across academic reading situations, such as mapping the rhetorical pattern of organization or identifying morphemic structure of unfamiliar vocabulary. A strong emphasis on self-monitoring is apparent throughout the course. For example, during sustained silent reading students maintain a "metacognitive log" detailing what confuses them during the reading. Students are asked to share the metacognitive logs with other students. Also, each month students write a letter to the teacher explaining what they are finding out about themselves as readers.

Interviews with eight students are used to gain insight into how the course affects their reading processes. A specific intent of the interviews is to evaluate "the degree to which students are appropriating the reading practices available to them in the instructional setting" (Greenleaf et al., 2001, p. 98). Greenleaf et al. present extensive data from an interview with one student named Rosa. In describing Rosa, her teacher explains:

> She didn't bring the strategic thinking and competence and engagement that I knew she had in other aspects of her life. . . . You see this with so many kids. In the hall, in the cafeteria, in their communities, in all these places these are active, engaged, bright, funny kids. They come into the classroom and they turn into a ghost of themselves. . . . Then there are the kids who don't become ghosts—they're demons. They're acting out, they're bringing their most angry selves into the classroom. (p. 99)

During each interview, students are assigned four tasks: reading aloud, reading silently, being read to, and thinking aloud while reading. During Rosa's interview she is asked to read a passage on totalitarianism. The interviewer tries to assess the extent to which Rosa uses the predicting, summarizing, questioning and clarifying strategies of Reciprocal Teaching. In describing how her reading habits have changed, Rosa contrasts Academic Literacy with a history class:

> Um, usually in like a regular history class. . . . Okay, read from page so-n-so to so-n-so, answer the red square questions and the unit questions and turn them in. . . . Now it's like, you have to talk about it. You have to explain what you read. You have to make a tree about it, okay? . . . You have to get more into the book than you realize. (p. 101)

The interviewer next asks Rosa to explain how she would read the text as a class assignment. Rosa responds:

> I guess I'd have to start by the title. And then, um, just try to relate the first paragraph, second paragraph. . . . So if I understand like the first paragraph, then I would see what like the subheadings are about. . . . Then I would start reading. . . . Just keep reading and if I have any questions just try to answer them within the reading. Pretty much do what we do with RT. (p. 102)

The interviewer then asks Rosa to demonstrate how she would use specific RT strategies such as predicting and summarizing. Rosa also shows how she uses context cues to help her with unfamiliar vocabulary but requires assistance from the interviewer. Later in the interview, when Rosa encounters a passage she finds confusing, the interviewer asks her to explain what was going thorough her mind:

I was trying to like stay focused. . . . Because I knew that, 'cause when I got half way through that excerpt from the book, I started losing the beginning and I started turning fuzzy. And I knew that I was going to lose it by the end of the reading. So I was like, "Okay, I have to go back." So I went sort of back, skimmed through it, got the main idea, went, kept on reading . . . and just kept skimming back. (p. 108)

The researchers conclude that in this interview with Rosa, "we are able to see clear reflection of the instructional practices that the Academic Literacy course constructed to support her reading development" (p. 109). They praise her use of both the cognitive and metacognitive strategies she was taught.

Discussion

The Academic Literacy course identifies itself as an apprenticeship primarily on the basis of the explicit support provided by the teacher, who demonstrates and then supervises the use of cognitive and metacognitive strategies during reading. It is therefore closely aligned both in philosophy and approach with the cognitive apprenticeship method, which asserts that whereas in a traditional apprenticeship the tasks to be learned are readily observable, in a cognitive apprenticeship the mental activities of the expert are not overt and must be made "visible" to the novice (Collins et al., 1991). On the other hand, Lave and Wenger (1991) note, "In apprenticeship opportunities for learning are, more often than not, given structure by work practices instead of strongly asymmetrical master-apprentice relations. Under these circumstances learners may have a space of 'benign community neglect' in which to configure their own learning relations with other apprentices" (p. 93). Lave and Wenger's observation suggests important differences between literacy apprenticeship and traditional apprenticeship in terms of both practice and identity.

Practice

In the reading apprenticeship, learning is structured more by the hierarchical interpersonal relationship between learner and master than by learners' and master's co-participation in meaningful community activity. The master knows how to do something (read an academic text) and expects the student to learn this technique. Yet the master is not actually participating in a work practice, as there is no ultimate work product for which the teacher is responsible, such as an academic essay to be published or presented. The teacher cannot demonstrate an authentic reason for reading the text other than as instructor. Thus, the field of mature practice is not clear. At one level, the field of mature practice may be the future classroom in which students will face academic reading tasks. At another level, the field of mature practice may be the out-of-school arena in which academics practice their disciplines, the historian practicing historical analysis or the literature scholar practicing literary criticism. But the literacy apprentice does not learn in either of these settings. Learning to read academic text occurs in a reading improvement class, as preparation for upcoming activity. In this sense the reading apprenticeship operates much as the trade school for butchers. The teacher must make assumptions about the future work practices that apprentices will face, but as in the trade school, there is no assurance that the practices of the preparatory situation will parallel those of the transfer situation. For example, in her content-area class, Rosa may not be expected to "make a tree" of the rhetorical structure; she may very well be asked to read and answer the chapter questions.

The removal of apprentice from the arena of mature practice is founded upon two ubiquitous assumptions that underlie the pedagogy of explicit teaching of reading strategies. First is the sense that since the strategies are deemed effective by the mentor, both mentor and apprentice should focus on strategic use more than the product of strategic use. Students can implement these strategies with any text selected by the teacher or by themselves. Students seem to be considered successful to the extent that they employ the favored strategies. In contrast, in traditional apprenticeship strategy emanates from practice, but it does not constitute practice. A second assumption is the notion that strategies can be universally applied across a range of disciplines, text types, reading situations, and reading purposes. The reader may select from a menu of pre-taught strategies and if one does not work, try another, but responsive adaptation in the performance of practice, such as the creation of a new situation-specific strategy, does not seem to be encouraged. Related to this assumption of strategy generality is the belief that a mentor can therefore be a generalist; an English teacher can be considered the expert in reading history and the history teacher can be the expert in reading literary narrative. Only in the restricted sense that an English teacher has successfully completed college, and perhaps has taken one or two history courses, could an English teacher be considered a expert-in-practice of history. Thus, in the reading apprenticeship the activity of academic reading, rather than being viewed as context-dependent, takes on an almost context-independent nature.

Perhaps because of this removal from mature practice and concurrent emphasis on strategy implementation, students seem to have a diminished opportunity to interact with a full range of environmental resources. For instance, when asked by the interviewer how she would use RT if she were stuck on the meaning of a word, Rosa explains, ". . . since I didn't understand it someone would have to like describe it and if we didn't know we would ask

Ms. Cziko and Ms. Cziko would tell us the definition" (Greenleaf et al., 2001, p. 104). In her response Rosa acknowledges that RT as the favored strategy encourages her to first attempt to use context cues, then depend on social resources. In fact, during the interview Rosa asks the interviewer to tell her the meaning of *regime.* Interestingly, though, Rosa admits that "if it was home, I would pretty much use the dictionary" (p. 104), recognizing that the community of the classroom encourages a different set of environmental resources than those available to her in her out-of-school practice.

Another significant departure from traditional apprenticeship is that reading apprenticeship, in its strong adherence to the principles of adult as mentor or coach, does not appear to foster the "benign neglect" that would stimulate broader social interaction. While the reading apprenticeship does provide for some limited forms of apprentice interaction, such as class discussion, sharing of metacognitive logs, and peer consultation, these activities are teacher-structured and teacher-controlled. For example, an explicit part of the RT approach reported by Rosa is, when you get stuck, get help from another student, but if you're still stuck, ask the teacher. What appears absent from the reading apprenticeship is the looser and more organic social interaction of a traditional apprenticeship in which novices are often left to figure things out on their own, asking other apprentices or observing more experienced practitioners. In traditional apprenticeship "there is little observable teaching; the more basic phenomenon is learning" (Lave & Wenger, 1991, p. 92). Put another way, "Mastery resides not in the master but in the organization of the community of practice of which the master is part" (Lave & Wenger, 1991, p. 94).

Identity

Although the reading apprenticeship features a hierarchical master-apprentice relationship, it nonetheless does appear to place strong emphasis on identity development. Students move from a position of unfamiliarity to one of familiarity in relation to a way of reading. Their sense of being "good readers" is reinforced continually by the teacher and by the learning activities. Students are guided by the question, "What do successful readers do when they read?" and are encouraged to themselves become successful readers. They are asked to keep reading logs and assess their reading success. Although there are no tangible markers of membership such as certificates or titles, there is still a pervading sense that one is either a good academic reader, a developing academic reader, a struggling academic reader, or an uncommitted academic reader. When Rosa explains to the interviewer, "You have to get more into the book than you realize" (Greenleaf et al., 2001, p. 101), she is admitting to an implicit rite of passage in both the social and individual formation of her identity as a reader. Identity appears bound to competence in performing the academic tasks prescribed by the mentor.

By tying identity formation to competence as defined by the mentor, rather than by successful completion of a task that is important for a community need, the reading apprenticeship fosters reproduction of a culture of schooling, not a culture of practice. A clear social structure of adult not only as expert but also as authority figure is maintained. Students are encouraged to question, seek advice, and receive validation from the adult. Students are inculcated into the cultural mores of being a learner in an academic community: you read for a purpose established by the community and you accomplish your task a certain way. You not only try to understand what you are reading, but you should question why the author wrote the text. You should be prepared to discuss how you connect the text to other texts and your prior knowledge. You must share your response to the text with adult and, upon the adult's instructions, with other students as well. When you have learned to do these things, you become accepted into the community as an improving academic reader. Through this process of enculturation into being an academic reader, the traditions of the school community are maintained and renewed.

Identity formed through mentor expectations and cultural reproduction of a community of schooling tend to diminish the agency of individual learners. Thus, in reading apprenticeship, there seems to be little evidence of meaning as a dimension of learning. Meaning here must not be confused with understanding or comprehension of text, which may require connecting the text to outside knowledge. Meaning involves the way the individual interacts with the environment to make sense of it and orchestrates personal activity during participation in community practice to better understand the world (Wenger, 1998). Students offer little resistance to the imposed cultural norm. They do not question the validity of the strategies they are taught. Their interpretation of activity is fully dependent upon the teacher's acceptance of their performance and their own self-monitoring using the culturally determined criteria. Even when students take limited opportunities to connect the immediate learning to other aspects of their lives, as with the community interviews or the writing of commercials, these activities are nonetheless class "assignments" rather than learner-initiated attempts to create meaning. Thus, along a scale of culture at one end and agency at the other, literacy apprenticeship appears weighted more toward culture.

From the perspective of Wenger's (1998) social theory of learning, the reading apprenticeship, in contrast to traditional apprenticeship, appears to emphasize identity more than practice, and community more than meaning. The reading apprenticeship is characterized by social formation, rites of passage, and cultural systems. Less evident is concern for everyday activity in real-life settings, coordination of activity with community purpose, and the interaction of learners with a full set of environmental resources.

Conclusion

A pedagogical issue challenging the application of situative theory to school-based instruction is whether "real problems" and "authentic contexts" can be imported into the classroom without fundamentally changing the nature of the activity. As Greeno et al. (1996) have noted, "A crucial issue in the nature of learning is whether, and in what ways, the peripheral participation of beginners is legitimate" (p. 23). Gee (2000) has suggested that a measure of the authenticity of school-based literacy practices is the extent to which they relate to literacy practices outside school.

Yet Lave and Wenger (1991) are careful to distinguish that legitimate peripheral participation is a theory of learning as social practice, not an instructional approach to be "implemented" or "operationalized" by schools. Legitimate peripheral participation raises questions about the contexts of schooling and the contexts of communities of practice. For example:

There are vast differences between the ways high school physics students participate in and give meaning to their activity and the way professional physicists do. The actual reproducing community of practice, within which school children learn about physics, is not the community of physicists but the community of schooled adults (Lave & Wenger, 1991, p. 100).

In schools, teachers are removed both physically and socially from the mature practice they are demonstrating. For Lave and Wenger (1991), limited participation that disconnects the learner from the culture of practice results in knowledge being viewed as abstract. The presumption that cognitive and metacognitive strategies can be appropriated from one situation and then readily transferred across a range of new literacy situations may be more consonant with empiricist and rationalist views of transfer than the sociohistorical and ecological views of transfer underlying situated cognition theory (Greeno et al. 1993). Therefore, applying the learning-as-apprenticeship metaphor to school-based literacy programs appears inconsistent with perspectives of knowledge and transfer upon which school curricula are usually based. Literacy apprenticeship, while acknowledging the importance of social interaction in learning, nonetheless assumes the primacy of cognitive structure as an element of transfer. Literary apprenticeship in school settings and traditional apprenticeship in non-school settings therefore represent fundamentally different conceptions of knowing and learning: for one, theories, models, or other abstractions may be taught, learned, and rehearsed prior to application in the transfer situation; for the other, theory-practice and knowing-doing being embedded in each other are indivisible.

Legitimate peripheral participation may nonetheless suggest that literacy development of school-age learners can be fostered in communities of authentic practice, in which learners are exposed to a wide variety of social and physical resources in non-school settings. The practices being observed and eventually performed by the novice would be meaningful to both the learner and the broader community. The learner would interact with mentors, other experienced adults, and peers in a less-formal structures that would place focus upon the activity. Learning would thus become a by-product of participation. Such literacy learning opportunities already exist in any number of out-of-school contexts, such as the home, religious organizations, museums or other cultural institutions, youth groups, and common-interest affiliations such as chess clubs, 4-H clubs and the like. Other literacy learning opportunities aligned with principles of legitimate peripheral participation could be school-based but would require students to participate in non-school contexts as well. Importantly, the rationale for participation in the non-school context must be not to fulfill a school assignment, but to contribute to the community practice. A community-based learning project could require students to participate in the planning of a museum exhibit, the relocation of a homeless shelter, or the preservation of a wildlife habitat. For example, Pedraza and Ayala (1996) have described the Young Scientists Club, in which youngsters are co-planning the development of a vacant lot into a neighborhood park. Hogan (2001) has described a service learning project in which students work with a local environmental council to develop a watershed management plan. Both the Young Scientists Club and the watershed service project offer rich opportunities for situated literacy development through participation in meaningful community practices. Only when the focus of involvement shifts from explicit teaching to learning through meaningful participation can the metaphor of apprenticeship be more fully applied.

References

Baumann, J. F., Jones, L. A., & Siefort-Kessell, N. (1993). Using think alouds to enhance children's comprehension monitoring abilities. *The Reading Teacher, 47,* 184-193.

Brown, A. L., Palinscar, A. S., & Armbruster, B. B. (1994). Instructing comprehension-fostering activities in interactive learning situations. In R. B. Ruddell, M. R. Ruddell, & H. Singer (Eds.), *Theoretical models and processes of reading* (4th ed., pp. 757-787). Newark, DE: International Reading Association.

Brown, J. S., Collins, A., & Duguid, P. (1989). Situated cognition and the culture of learning. *Educational Researcher, 18*(1), 32-42.

Cobb, P., & Bowers, J. (1999). Cognitive and situated learning perspectives in theory and practice. *Educational Researcher, 28*(2), 4-15.

Collins, A. (1988). *Cognitive apprenticeship and instructional technology* (Report No. BBN-R-6899). Cambridge, MA: BBN Labs, Inc. (ERIC Document Reproduction Service No. 331465)

Collins, A. (1991). *A cognitive apprenticeship for disadvantaged students* (Tech. Report No. 10). New York: Center for Technology in Education. (ERIC Document Reproduction Service No. 338729)

Collins, A., Brown, J. S., & Holum, A. (1991). Cognitive apprenticeship: Making thinking visible. *American Educator, 15*(3), 6-11, 38-46.

Collins, A., Brown, J. S., & Newman, S. E. (1989). Cognitive apprenticeship: Teaching the craft of reading, writing, and mathematics. In L. B. Resnick (Ed.), *Knowing, learning, and instruction: Essays in honor of Robert Glaser* (pp. 453-492). Hillsdale, NJ: Erlbaum.

Davey, B. (1983). Think aloud: Modeling the cognitive processes of reading comprehension. *Journal of Reading, 27,* 44-47.

Dorn, L. J., French, C., & Jones, T. (1998). *Apprenticeship in literacy: Transitions across reading and writing.* Portland, ME: Stenhouse.

Gee, J. P. (2000). Discourse and sociocultural studies in reading. In M. L. Kamil, P. B. Mosenthal, P. D. Pearson, & R. Barr (Eds.), *Handbook of reading research, vol. 3* (pp. 195-207). Mahwah, NJ: Erlbaum.

Greenleaf, C. L., Schoenbach, R., Cziko, C., & Mueller, F. L. (2001). Apprenticing adolescent readers to academic literacy. *Harvard Educational Review, 71*(1), 79-129.

Greeno, J. G. (1991). Number sense as situated knowing in a conceptual domain. *Journal for Research in Mathematics Education, 22,* 170-218.

Greeno, J. G. (1997). On claims that answer the wrong questions. *Educational Researcher, 26*(1), 5-17.

Greeno, J. G., Collins, A. M., & Resnick, L. B. (1996). Cognition and learning. In D. C. Berliner & R. C. Calfee (Eds.), *Handbook of educational psychology* (pp. 15-46). New York: Macmillan.

Greeno, J. G., Moore, J. L., & Smith, D. R. (1993). Transfer of situated learning. In D. K. Detterman & R. J. Sternberg (Eds.), *Transfer on trial: Intelligence, cognition, and instruction* (pp. 99-167). Norwood, NJ: Ablex.

Hogan, K. (2001, April). Contrasting cultures of school and community-based environmental science learning. Presented at the annual meeting of the American Educational Research Association, Seattle, WA.

Jordan, M., Jensen, R., & Greenleaf, C. (2001). "Amidst familial gatherings": Reading apprenticeship in a middle school classroom. *Voices from the Middle, 8*(4), 15-24.

Kirshner, D., & Whitson, J. A. (1998). Obstacles to understanding cognition as situated. *Educational Researcher, 27*(8), 22-28.

Knapp, N. F., & Winsor, A. P. (1998). Reading apprenticeship for delayed primary readers. *Reading Research and Instruction, 38*(1), 13-29.

Lakoff, G., & Johnson, M. (1980). *Metaphors we live by.* Chicago: University of Chicago.

Lakoff, G., & Johnson, M. (1999). *Philosophy in the flesh.* New York: Basic.

Lave, J., & Wenger, E. (1991). *Situated learning: Legitimate peripheral participation.* Cambridge, MA: Cambridge University Press.

Lee, C. D. (1995). A culturally based cognitive apprenticeship: Teaching African American high school students skills in literary interpretation. *Reading Research Quarterly, 30,* 608-630.

Pedraza, P., & Ayala, J. (1996). Motivation as an emergent issue in an after-school program in El Barrio. In L. Schauble & R. Glaser (Eds.), *Innovations in learning: New environments for education* (pp. 75-91). Mahwah, NJ: Erlbaum.

Putnam, R. T., & Borko, H. (2000). What do new views of knowledge have to say about research on teacher learning? *Educational Researcher, 29*(1), 4-15.

Reynolds, R. E., Sinatra, G. M., & Jetton, T. L. (1996). Views of knowledge acquisition and representation: A continuum from experience centered to mind centered. *Educational Psychologist, 31,* 93-104.

Schoenbach, R., Greenleaf, C., Cziko, C., & Hurwitz, L. (1999). *Reading for understanding: A guide to improving reading in middle and high school classrooms.* San Francisco: Jossey-Bass.

Silven, M., & Vaurus, M. (1992). Improving reading through thinking aloud. *Learning and Instruction, 2,* 69-88.

Tripp, S. D. (1990). *Metaphor and instruction.* Ames, IA: Iowa State University of Science and Technology, Ames. Coll. of Education. (ERIC Document Reproduction Service No. ED 323953)

Wenger, E. (1998). *Communities of practice: Learning, meaning, and identity.* Cambridge, England: Cambridge University.

CELEBRATING
DIVERSITY

GENDER ISSUES IN CHILDREN'S NARRATIVE WRITING

Barbara A. Illig-Aviles
Indiana University of Pennsylvania

Kay A. Chick
Penn State Altoona

Michael Arnall
Beth Hutson
Indiana University of Pennsylvania

Abstract

Research has shown that students' gender schema can change as a result of literacy experiences. In this study, the researchers examine the influence of plot and character development mini-lessons using quality children's literature on the narrative writing of fifth graders. Picture books with strong female or sensitive male characters were shared during each mini-lesson. Three narrative writing samples were gathered. The first writing sample was collected prior to the mini-lessons, another during the mini-lessons and the third sample after the mini-lessons. An analysis of students' narrative writing samples is presented with an emphasis on gender themes and stereotypes. Recommendations for teachers and researchers are discussed.

One purpose of schooling is to provide children with opportunities to experience new identities, especially as they engage in textual worlds in multiple ways (Hicks, 2001). Reading, writing, and discussion practices that encourage children to transact with text may indeed be able to extend students' concept of self and nurture new possibilities for living and knowing (Bender-Peterson & Lach, 1990). These new possibilities may be especially important with regard to gender roles. As children are learning gender identity, they are also learning to read (Pidgeon, 1994). Books have the potential to shape children's views on gender, and early studies suggest that when non-sexist stories are shared with children, they display less stereotyped attitudes and behaviors (Barclay, 1974; Campbell & Wirtenberg, 1980).

Research indicates that boys and girls prefer different kinds of books (Chick & Heilman-Houser, 2000; Guthrie & Greaney, 1991; Lynch-Brown, 1977; Zimet, 1966). Boys tend to like adventure, science fiction, and sports stories, whereas girls prefer realistic fiction with themes about family and school life, as well as romance and career stories. Boys generally choose books with male protagonists, while girls will cross gender lines and choose books with either male or female protagonists, especially as they mature as readers.

A significant number of research studies also suggest a "pattern of gender conformity in children's narrative writing" (Peterson, 2001, p. 452). Girls have been shown to enjoy writing more than boys, are more often involved in writing activities before they start school, and are more willing to write as a leisure activity. Both males and females prefer to write about same gender characters (Millard, 1997). Girls' narrative writing evidences characters that share, help, or empathize with others while characters in boys' narrative writing are adventurous and often engage in aggressive or dangerous actions (Fleming, 1995; Gray-Schlegel & Gray-Schlegel, 1995-96; McAuliffe, 1994; Trepanier-Street, Romatowski, & McNair, 1990). Girls' narrative writing focused on topics, like relationships, that were within their lived experiences while boys' narrative writing usually involved topics and/or character actions that were not part of their lived experiences. Peterson's (2001) interviews with fourth grade writers may partly explain this phenomenon. She reports that while the fourth graders in her study were willing to consider alternative gender roles, their discussions were based on the assumption that gender roles were natural and they seemed to recognize the possibility of negative social consequences if gender lines were crossed even within their narrative stories.

On the other hand, Young (2000) contends that critical literacy activities can provide spaces for children to think about and critique gendered roles. If teachers engage students in multiple dialogues around appropriate texts that highlight how gender is represented, they might begin to question what defines male versus female and perhaps even begin to debunk gender stereotypes.

This current study examines children's narrative writing samples for gender differences. The researchers chose to initiate writing experiences with a series of mini-lessons on plot and character development so that the students could use what they had learned to create more well-developed stories. To determine the influence of the stories themselves on students' gendered beliefs, the researchers purposely did not initiate discussion regarding gender roles. However, in each mini-lesson, students reacted to gender issues and discussed gender stereotypes that were evident within the stories.

Specifically, this study seeks to answer the following questions. Does the narrative writing of boys and girls differ with respect to gender-fair and gender-stereotyped character development? What affect do plot and character development mini-lessons using quality children's literature have on gender development in fifth graders' narrative writing?

The picture books selected for the study were identified by the researchers as having strong female or sensitive male characters who demonstrated non-stereotypical traits or behaviors. Picture books were selected for two reasons. First, the stories could be shared in less time than longer texts and would be more easily analyzed by all students during the mini-lessons that followed the read-aloud. Second, we were working closely with the classroom teacher whose focus at the time of the research was the development of her students' narrative writing. These picture books then had the potential to become models for their narrative writing experiences. Fifth grade students in this study wrote three different stories that the researchers then analyzed for instances of gender stereotypes or the breaking of gender barriers.

First, descriptions of subjects, setting, and research methods are presented. Plot and character development mini-lessons are then provided along with details of the children's literature selections. Next, analysis and results of students' narrative writing samples are discussed, with particular attention to gender themes. Finally, discussion, conclusions, and recommendations for teachers and researchers are presented.

Subjects and Setting

The subjects in this study were a class of 13 multi-ethnic fifth-graders in a laboratory school in western Pennsylvania. Gender lines were split with seven females and six males. Two females were Chinese with limited English proficiency, and in fact, one wrote her first piece using Chinese characters. Two of the thirteen, one male and one female, were identified as students with special needs and their IEP's (Individual Education Program) indicated significant learning difficulties.

Methods

The research took place during the Fall semester, 2001, with the final student narrative writing completed in early 2002. Before this study began, the classroom teacher had discussed elements of story as part of her initial work with narrative text. As a prewriting activity, prior to the initiation of our study, she had students complete a graphic organizer that included setting, primary character, other characters, primary character's goal, moral dilemma (conflict), and resolution. Students were then instructed by their teacher to create a story with a clear conflict and resolution using information in their graphic organizer. This narrative became the researcher's baseline writing sample.

After the baseline writing Sample A was gathered, the researchers taught a series of four mini-lessons, one per week. One researcher taught the lessons, while the other acted as observer and recorder. The protocol for the mini-lessons included an introduction to the book that made connections to students' background knowledge, a read-aloud of the text with opportunities for student response throughout the reading, then a strategy lesson that either emphasized plot or character development via text analysis. For example, the primary objective of the first mini-lesson was to introduce students to how authors develop characters by analyzing the main character in Karen Winnick's (2000) *Sybil's Night Ride*. In this historical fiction story, based on a true incident, Sybil completes a "night ride" to help muster a New York militia in defense of a British invasion. The researcher began the lesson by reciting *The Midnight Ride of Paul Revere* (Longfellow, 1861/2001). Before completing the first stanza, students' hands shot up as they called out the name of the poem. Most students not only knew of Paul Revere's adventure, but also shared additional historically accurate information concerning the incident. The researcher then asked if anyone had heard of Sybil Ludington. No one had. After the read-aloud the researcher again asked the question, "Why do you suppose few people know about Sybil Ludington?" Students concluded that Sybil's lack of fame was due to her gender, but that girls today could do the same things as boys. The text was then used as a model to discuss how authors develop characters. Students identified examples of appearance, settings, actions/behaviors, and dialogue that Winnick used to develop Sybil's character. Two other texts were provided by the researchers for independent classroom reading that also portrayed examples of strong female characters. These two picture books, *Brave Margaret: An Irish Adventure* (San Souci, 1999) and *Kate and the Beanstalk* (Osborne, 2000) were available to students throughout the research project.

The second mini-lesson again focused on character analysis using Allen Say's (2000), *The Sign Painter*. After the fifth graders compared and contrasted the characters of the sign painter and his apprentice, who was a sensitive young man and an artist at heart, we supported the students in the development of a character map as a prewriting activity for their next narrative. The character map encouraged students to think of three traits that would describe the main character in their story, with evidence (i.e., appearance, actions, dialogue, and setting) that they could include within their text that would help to develop the character. For example, in Figure 1, Emily developed her character, Kayley, to be affectionate using actions/behaviors and dialogue. Her evidence indicated that (a) Kayley gave cards to people in the hospital, (b) that she will never stop caring for others, and (c) that everyone says she is an affectionate person.

After a read-aloud of Hazen's (1989) book, *The Knight Who Was Afraid of the Dark*, discussion explored how authors develop plot. In this story, a young knight had difficulty courting his true love because he was afraid to

Figure 1. Prewriting Activity for Sample B

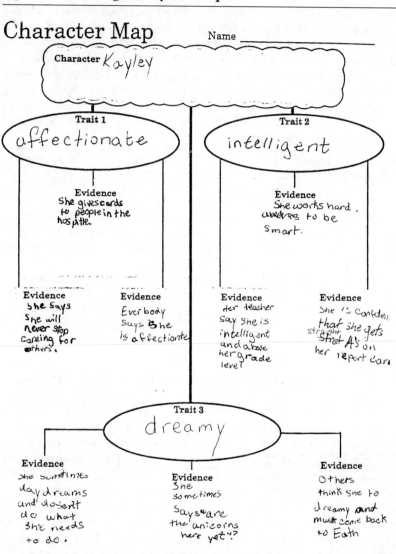

Character Map

Name _____

Character Kayley

Trait 1
affectionate

Evidence
She gives cards to people in the hospitle.

Evidence
She says She will never stop careing for others.

Evidence
Everybody says she is affectionte

Trait 2
intelligent

Evidence
She works hard and wes to be smart.

Evidence
Her teacher say she is intelligent and above her grade level

Evidence
She is confiden that she gets straight A's on her report card

Trait 3
dreamy

Evidence
She sometimes day dreams and dosen't do what she needs to do.

Evidence
She sometimes says "are the unicorns here yet"?

Evidence
Others think she to dreamy and must come back to Eath

go out after dark. To prove his love, however, he found the courage and faced his fear. In this third mini-lesson students quickly understood how important well-developed characters were to the design of plot as they engaged in creating a plot line for the text. During the third and fourth mini-lessons, students continued their writing and revision of narrative writing.

The fourth mini-lesson continued the instruction on plot development but now used the strong female character in Diane Stanley's (1997), *Rumpelstiltskin's Daughter*. Following the read aloud and large group discussion, students worked in small groups to analyze the plot of the text and design their own plot lines for the story. These were then shared with the large group. The instructor reminded the fifth graders to use their new knowledge of plot development as they revised their own narratives. The final writing Sample C, was completed after a three-week semester break (see Table 1).

Table 1. Mini-lesson sequence

MINILESSON	LESSON FOCUS	CHILDREN'S LIT. SELECTION	WRITING SAMPLE
			Baseline (Sample A)
1	character analysis	Sybil's Night Ride	
2	character analysis and development	The Sign Painter	character map (prewriting for Sample B)
3	plot analysis	The Knight Who Was Afraid of the Dark	Draft of Sample B
4	plot analysis and development	Rumpelstiltskin's Daughter	Completion of Sample B Sample C (at conclusion of semester break)

Analysis

Data were first analyzed using qualitative methods suggested by Bogdan and Biklen (1992). First the authors independently read all three writing samples and coded each for story theme, gender of student author, gender of story characters, and the specific instances in the narratives that represented reinforcing or breaking male and female stereotypes. The authors then met to discuss and reconcile differences in coding. If after discussion of each instance of writing that a researcher considered reinforcing or breaking a stereotype, the researchers could not agree, the instance was coded as neutral (neither reinforcing nor breaking a male or female stereotype). These instances were not included in the analysis due to their inconclusive nature. Data were entered using Microsoft Access 2000 for the descriptive analysis. A relational database with two tables was developed – one with student data and one with writing sample data. Fields were identified based on the coding discussed above. The program permitted the researchers to sort and retrieve the data in a variety of ways, i.e., individual student writers, all male or all female writers, instances of male or female stereotypes, or instances of breaking gender role barriers. Finally, a descriptive analysis was developed from the raw data and our field notes to answer our research questions.

Results

In this study the research questions sought to determine whether there were differences in the narrative writing of boys and girls and what influence plot and character development mini-lessons using quality children literature had on gender development in the students' narrative writing. Analysis of data indicated that there were definite differences in how boys and girls developed their story themes and characters. In addition, gender-fair children's literature appeared to affect gender development in the girls' narrative writing.

Female Writing Samples

As depicted in Table 2 (Reinforcing and Breaking Female Stereotypes) the seven female students developed both male and female characters in each of their writing samples. The girls' stories portrayed stereotyped female characters with decreasing frequency throughout the series of samples. Concurrently, the instances of portrayal of female characters that break female stereotypes increased. For example, in Emily's baseline story, the main character is Angela, a lawyer, and her friend Wendy, who were victimized by a male bank robber. Emily wrote:

> Suddenly a loud voice said, "Freeze everyone! This is a holdup! Hands over your head". "Oh, don't hurt us" said Wendy, but the robber pushed her down to the ground. As he stashed the money from the teller into his bag, everyone heard the police sirens. John had secretly called the police on his cell phone. The robber was arrested and taken away.

Table 2. Reinforcing and breaking female stereotypes (Girls n = 7 Boys n = 6)

Narrative Writing Sample	Same/Mixed Gender Characters in Girls Writing Samples	Same/Mixed Gender Characters in Boys Writing Samples	Girls Who Reinforced Female Stereotypes	Boys Who Reinforced Female Stereotypes	Girls Who Broke Female Stereotypes	Boys Who Broke Female Stereotypes
A	2 same 5 same	5 mixed 1 mixed	5	1	5	1
B	3 same 1[a]	4 same	4	3	4	0
C	3 same 4 mixed	6 same 0 mixed	3	0	7	0

Note. Total instances > n
[a] *1 student absent*

Note that John, a male character, is the one who quickly calls the police on his cell phone and the robber is apprehended. In her final Sample C story, the main characters were Elaine and Kayla who are involved in another robbery. This time, however, Kayla, a Tae Kwon Do expert, kicks a knife out of the robber's hand and pins him to the floor while Elaine calls the police. Now Emily writes:

> When Elaine and Kayla walked into the apartment, Elaine went to the kitchen, and then she heard a noise. There stood a man dressed up as a beggar, carrying Elaine's jewelry cases and a purse, which contained some money. She screamed, and the man said, "If you shout again, I will hurt you." Suddenly, Elaine was struggling with the man to get her things. By then, Kayla who had heard the scream rushed into the kitchen and jumped on the robber. He pulled out a knife to cut Kayla, but she kicked it out of his hands, caught his arms, and pinned him to the floor. Elaine quickly called the police and they came shortly to take the screaming robber away.

The males in the girls' stories generally demonstrated stereotypical male behaviors (see Table 3). For example, in one of Jenny's stories she writes "My dad had already left for work; he is a veterinarian. My mom works around the house and sometimes baby-sits". In another example, Carole included Lloyd, "a very mean kid . . . who runs around everywhere and never pays attention. One time he cut a girl's braid off." Female writers consistently reinforced male stereotypes in their stories (see Table 3).

Table 3. Reinforcing and breaking male stereotypes (Girls n = 7 Boys n = 6)

Narrative Writing Sample	Same/Mixed Gender Characters in Girls Writing Samples	Same/Mixed Gender Characters in Boys Writing Samples	Girls Who Reinforced Female Stereotypes	Boys Who Reinforced Female Stereotypes	Girls Who Broke Female Stereotypes	Boys Who Broke Female Stereotypes
A	2 same 5 same	5 mixed 1 mixed	3	6	0	3
B	3 same 3 mixed 1[a]	4 same 2 mixed	2	6	1	5
C	3 same 4 mixed	6 same 0 mixed	4	6	1	1

Note. Total instances > n

[a] *1 student absent*

The analysis of themes for story Sample A supported the literature discussed in the introduction. Over 50% (4/7) of the girls wrote animal stories, two wrote adventure stories, and the final was a fantasy. By story Sample C, the end of the series, more girls (4/7) wrote adventure stories, two wrote about themselves as independent females, and one wrote a story with a relationship theme.

Male Writing Samples

An analysis of the writing samples of the six 5th grade boys revealed that they rarely used female characters in their stories. In the eighteen stories written by the males, only three contained female characters, therefore, there was little opportunity to reinforce or break female stereotypes (see Table 2). On the other hand, all the boys reinforced male stereotypes in each of the three writing samples (see Table 3). For example, Ian's second story in sample B was about Calicio, a young boy. In the story he and his father waited patiently at the table for their dinner to be served.

> Back at the hut, little Calicio sat exhausted at the dinner table waiting patiently, but hungrily for dinner to be served. Just then his father came in from working in the woods, sat down and started talking to his son. He said, "Chopping wood for the fire is awfully hard work Cal, if you would want to, you could come help too in the forest tomorrow? By the way, where is your mother?" "Oh, mother's in the kitchen cooking dinner, "answered Cal. . . . "Dinner's ready," Mother shouted from the kitchen.

Even in Ian's third story in sample C, he continued to reinforce male stereotypes. In this alien space adventure, Ian is "a scientist, and a general of a small force of naval, ground and air troops." When an "alien mass destroyer" attacked their ship, Ian wrote, "'Find them,' I said icily looking over the horizon with cold fury in my eyes, 'find them,' I repeated, 'find them and destroy the aliens'." Karl also consistently reinforced male stereotypes. Male stereotypes were reinforced in his Sample B writing with a character named Kevin, "who had a chainsaw in each hand" and "destroyed every single tree" in his path, and later in Sample C with Commander Keith who flies his space ship too fast and crashes it. "Whoa Ha! This is absolutely fun!" said Keith. "Well what are you waiting for? Let's go faster!"

An interesting phenomenon occurred with narrative Sample B, which was written during the teaching of the mini-lessons. In that writing sample, five of the six boys broke male stereotypes, yet in narrative Sample C, written after semester break, only 1 of the 6 boys broke a male stereotype. For example in Ian's story discussed above, his character, Calicio, helped his mother wash the dishes. Cal also "sat weeping next to the body of once an honorable and loyal friend" [a wolf]. Karl also broke male stereotypes when

his character Bill, through dialogue, encouraged "chainsaw Kevin" to reconsider his violent ways, and Kevin says, "Well thanks for giving me the
advice . . . I'll talk to my boss and show the disaster."

An analysis of themes for the male writing samples indicates a predilec-
tion for adventure stories and, more specifically, violent fantasy space stories. For example, in Matt's story the "Anquillians," a hostile alien race, plan
to blow up the solar system. As the story draws to a close, the male heroes
kill the alien cannibals and defuse the bomb.

Read Aloud Response

As discussed in the methods section, the researchers, in most cases, purposely did not raise the issue of gender directly with students. However, as
students analyzed story characters or plots, they spontaneously reacted to
gender issues. During the read aloud of *The Knight Who Was Afraid of the
Dark* (Hazen, 1989), all students discussed their fears. Several girls made note
of the fact that it took courage for the knight to admit his fear of the dark to
his sweetheart, while the boys commented on the creative ways the knight
created his own light via "a fistful of fireflies, a glowworm-studded shield,
and his faithful electric eel wound around his arm" (p. 19). As students analyzed the plot in *Rumpelstiltskin's Daughter* (Stanley, 1997) the girls were
intrigued by Hope's ability to thwart the king, and the boys were struck by
her "cool-headed determination" to improve the lives of the country folk in
the kingdom. Additionally, several boys were surprised that Hope didn't want
to be a queen, but "Wow, the prime minister instead!"

Discussion and Conclusions

This study, like those of other researchers (Gray-Schlegel & Gray-Schlegel,
1995-96; Yeoman, 1999; Young, 2000), suggests that students' gender schemas
can change over time when provided with experiences that help them to
reflect on and question gender roles. Boys often have a narrower range of
gender appropriate thoughts, feelings and behaviors than girls, who are more
willing to be gender "disruptive" (Yeoman, 1999). In this small sample there
were differences in the narrative writing of boys and girls. Children's literature with strong female and sensitive male characters and narrative writing
experiences appeared to have an influence on the girls' abilities to write about
characters who were strong and independent females. The treatment, however, had no observable impact on the boys' writing samples. The boys appeared to be swayed by popular culture (i.e., movies like Harry Potter, Lord
of the Rings, and Star Wars that were released during the time of the study)
and the peer influence in their classroom.

Newkirk (2002) suggests that the fantasy, adventure, and popular culture that boys often include in their narrative writing do not always repre-

sent the aesthetic qualities that many educators seek, and boys often balk at making their characters more realistic. However, he emphasizes that it does not mean that boys do not identify with their writing. They, in fact, often get so into their stories that they describe the writing experience as if it is almost happening. In the wake of school shootings, many schools are banning boys from creating themes of violence in their narrative writing. This type of writing, once viewed as typical of boys, now is suspect and many offending boy authors are finding themselves in the guidance counselor's office.

This study had several limitations which should be considered when analyzing these results. First, the sample size was small (n=13) and only fifth grade students were included. Second, the intervention period was short, approximately five weeks. A longer intervention period with more narrative writing experiences may have had a significant impact on the results. Third, this study used only select children's literature titles with strong female and sensitive male characters. Additional titles and different types of mini-lessons may have had an affect on gender characteristics in the character development of student's writing.

Recommendations

Since this study suggests that experiences with children's literature with strong female characters and sensitive male characters encourage females to write outside traditional gender boundaries, such literature should be an integral part of any literacy program. In addition, "gender disruptive" literature should be included in school and classroom libraries and integrated throughout the elementary curriculum. Students should routinely participate in analysis activities and class discussions that emphasize the positive attributes of characters that break gender barriers. In addition, girls and boys would benefit from the critical analysis of gender-typed characters and classroom discussions concerning the influence of peers and the media on individuals' gender role development.

Although the boys in this sample maintained gender conformity in their writing, a longer intervention period might result in broader standards of what males deem acceptable in both theme and character development. Boys must be ensured a safe classroom environment in which to explore various types of literature and stories with female protagonists. Providing boys with story starters that include female characters may help them to gain a comfort level and increase the number of female characters in their narrative writing.

Although the results of this research support previous studies, they suggest that further research is needed to more fully assess the impact of children's literature with strong female characters and sensitive male characters on the narrative writing of children. As more children's authors write fiction and non-fiction texts that are gender-fair, their stories may have a positive influence on the way children express gender beliefs in their own writing.

References

Barclay, L. (1974). The emergence of vocational expectation in preschool children. *Journal of Vocational Behavior, 4*, 1-14.

Bender-Peterson, S., & Lach, M. (1990). Gender stereotypes in childrens's books: Their prevalence and influence on cognitive and affective development. *Gender and Education, 2*(2), 185-197.

Bogdan, R., & Biklen, S. (1992). *Qualitative research for education: An introduction to theory and methods.* Boston: Allyn and Bacon.

Campbell, P., & Wirtenberg, J. (1980). How books influence children: What the research shows. *IRBC Bulletin, 11*, 3-6.

Chick, K., & Heilman-Houser, R. (2000). Children's literature choices: Gender stereotypes prevail. *Pennsylvania Reads: Journal of the Keystone State Reading Association, 1*(2), 3-13.

Fleming, S. (1995). Whose stories are validated? *Language Arts, 72*, 590-596.

Hazen, B. S. (1989). *The knight who was afraid of the dark.* New York: Dial Books for Young Readers.

Hicks, D. (2001). Literacies and masculinities in the life of a young working-class boy. *Language Arts, 78*(3), 217-226.

Gray-Schlegel, M. A., & Gray-Schlegel, T. (1995-96). An investigation of gender stereotypes as revealed through children's creative writing. *Reading Research and Instruction, 35*(2), 160-169.

Guthrie, J., & Greaney, V. (1991). Literacy acts. In R. Barr, M. Kamil, P. Mosenthal, & D. Pearson (Eds.), *Handbook of reading research* (vol. II, pp. 68-96). New York: Longman.

Longfellow, H. W. (1861/2001). *The Midnight Ride of Paul Revere.* Brooklyn, NY: Handprint Books.

Lynch-Brown, C. (1977). Procedures for determining children's book choices: Comparison and criticism. *Reading Horizons, 17*(3), 243-250.

McAuliffe, S. (1994). Toward understanding one another: Second graders' use of gendered language and story styles. *The Reading Teacher, 47*(4), 302-310.

Millard, E. (1997). *Differently literate: Boys, girls, and the schooling of literacy.* Washington, DC: The Falmer Press.

Newkirk, T. (2002). *Misreading masculinity: Boys, literacy, and popular culture.* Portsmouth, NH: Heinemann.

Peterson, S. (2001). Gender identities and self-expression in classroom narrative writing. *Language Arts, 78*(5), 451-466.

Pidgeon, S. (1994). Learning reading and learning gender. In M. Barrs & S. Pidgeon (Eds.), *Reading the difference: Gender and reading in elementary classrooms* (pp. 20-37). York, ME: Stenhouse Publishers.

Trepanier-Street, M., Romatowski, J., & McNair, S. (1990). Children's written responses to stereotypical and non-stereotypical story starters. *Journal of Research in Childhood Education, 5*(1), 60-72.

Yeoman, E. (1999). How does it get into my imagination? Elementary school children's intertextual knowledge and gendered story lines. *Gender and Education, 11*(4), 427-440.

Young, J. (2000). Boy talk: Critical literacy and masculinities. *Reading Research Quarterly, 35*(3), 312-337.

Zimet, S. (1966). Children's interest and story preference. *Elementary School Journal, 67,* 122-130.

Selected Children's Literature

Osborne, M. P. (2000). *Kate and the beanstalk.* New York: Atheneum.

San Souci, R. (1999). *Brave Margaret: An Irish adventure.* New York: Simon & Schuster.

Say, A. (2000). *The sign painter.* New York: Houghton Mifflin.

Stanley, D. (1997). *Rumpelstiltskin's daughter.* New York: Morrow Junior Books.

Winnick, K. (2000). *Sybil's night ride.* Honesdale, PA: Boyds Mills Press.

LANGUAGE OF SILENCE: EXPRESSIVE LANGUAGE SKILLS AND READING

Arlene Hett

University of Portland

Abstract

The purpose of this ethnographic case study was to describe the expressive language characteristics of the preschool Native American girl. Additionally, the study investigated whether (a) these characteristics are specific to this population as compared to the Anglo children in the Head Start program, (b) these characteristics are gender specific, and (c) these characteristics handicap the preschool Native American girl when she enters a formal education program.

In this study, an ethnographic case study method was combined with quantitative test scores. Data were gathered through observation and interview as well as through analysis of test scores. The findings revealed that there are distinct language patterns of female Native American speakers. The observations indicated that Native American girls speak less than other groups of children. The interviews revealed that the Native American mothers described their daughters as "shy." The test scores showed a significant difference between the scores of Native American students and Anglo students, between Native American girls and Anglo boys, and most significantly, between Native American girls and Anglo girls.

> "There are silences that speak louder than words"
> Anonymous

Need

Educators who work with diverse cultures need to be aware that children respond to schooling within their dominant form of communication. Even when students speak the same language as the teacher, they may communicate through a completely different delivery system. These differences may result in a "language of silence" for some minority students when a traditional approach to reading instruction is utilized. In the classroom, this "language of silence" may speak louder than words.

While current teacher preparation programs require at least one course in multicultural education, the majority of in-service teachers received their degrees years ago and may not be prepared for the pluralistic society reflected in today's classrooms (Gay, 2000; Hollins, King, & Hayman, 1994; Ladson-Billings, 1994; Villegas, 2002). This lack of training may lead to unrealistic teacher expectations for minority students who have distinct language patterns. Native American female students who speak the "language of silence" may have difficulty in a classroom where girls are expected to be highly verbal. A quiet Native American girl, who remains silent when asked a question, for example, may be considered at-risk by her teacher. This silence in the classroom may speak louder than any words when used as informal classroom assessment. Therefore this study may be educationally relevant for early childhood classroom teachers of language arts and reading, university professors of early childhood language arts and reading education, and university professors of educational foundations interested in culturally relevant pedagogy.

Although the body of Native American research is growing, there continues to be a dearth of research concerning the expressive language skills of preschool Native American girls. This study provides an important contribution to Native American research as well as to the body of research that focuses on expressive language. Most importantly, this study may have significance for Native American students. This study may also provide educators with strategies concerning how Native American children can succeed in schools.

Review of the Literature

A review of the literature in the areas of language, culture, and education provides insights into this learning situation. In *The Invisible Culture*, Philips (1983) notes that "the children of the Warm Springs Indian Reservation are acculturated in their preschool years into modes of organizing the transmission of verbal messages that are culturally different from the Anglo middle-class children." She goes on to explain that "this difference makes it more difficult for them to then comprehend verbal messages conveyed through the American schools' Anglo middle-class modes of organizing classroom interactions" (p. 4). Philips' (1983) findings provided a foundation for this study of expressive language skills of Native American girls.

Connelly (1985) studied expressive and receptive language skills of young Indian children in grades one through three from four schools in rural southeastern Alaska. Two schools were primarily white and two were primarily Native American, with 200 students in the total sample. His results showed that, "Indian children tend to attain relatively low scores on tests which assess verbal skills and attain at least average scores on tests which assess nonverbal skills" (p. 9). It is imperative that assessment in the classroom be multi-dimensional by including more than test scores, i.e., using observation forms or interview forms with parents or teachers may add richness to the assessment (see Appendix A and Appendix B).

Another study completed in Alaska was based on observations of conversations between Native American and Anglo speakers. Nelson-Barber and Meier (1990) found that an Anglo speaker often asks a question, then pauses and waits for a Native American speaker to reply. When the Native American listener pauses too long before giving a reply the Anglo speaker resumes speaking. The Native American, who wished to reply but was accustomed to longer pauses between speakers, was not given an adequate opportunity to respond. On the other hand, when Native American speakers did have the floor, they were interrupted frequently because they took what were perceived by Anglos to be overly lengthy pauses between thoughts. One of the Native American women said, "While you're thinking about what you're going to say, they're already talking" (p. 35). Native American speakers often said very little while Anglo speakers seemed to do all the talking. What implications does this hold for the Native American/Anglo classroom? If an Anglo teacher does not make a conscious shift in the language pattern being used, there will be little opportunity for the Native American child to speak. It is important that these students do not feel as outsiders in their own classrooms simply because they may be out of sync with the interactive style used by the teacher.

Children learn their language through imitation of others in their environment. (Luria & Yudrovich, 1971; Purves, 1991; Winterowd, 1989). Vygotsky (cited in Wertsch, 1985) describes in detail how language evolves through sociocultural interactions. As language is learned, certain discriminations and experiences which are important to that culture are also learned. It becomes apparent that the culture of a child is greatly reflected in the child's expressive language. Both the verbal and the nonverbal behavior in communication reflects the culture of the person. It appears that preschool aged children have become so enculturated into modes of transmitting verbal messages that their form of communication is culture specific (Philips, 1983).

Our educational system assumes that children enter school with a shared developmental sequence of expressive language skills; however, that developmental sequence may be very diverse (Indian Nations at Risk Task Force, 1991). Educators who are working with diverse cultures in their schools need to look at curriculum policies to insure that students are taught within their dominant form of communication. This is much more complex than simply dealing with children who speak a language which differs from the dominant language. It deals with the "hidden" handicap of speaking the same language but with a completely different delivery system (Indian Nations at Risk Task Force, 1991).

Language has been used by parents, grandparents, pediatricians, and educators to assess development in children. Child development charts reassure parents that if the child produces specific words within a certain age range the child's development is progressing normally. The child who responds with different patterns of communication is often labeled as language delayed.

Many of the forms of assessment using language in the schools have been based on informal teacher judgment. However, during the past several decades, researchers have begun to standardize more formal assessments of children's use of language. These tests have been categorized as expressive or receptive measurements. Expressive tests measure the child's ability to express thoughts and ideas and receptive tests assess the child's ability to understand what others are expressing (Cazden, 1972).

The Expressive One-Word Picture Vocabulary Test (EOWPVT) measures expressive vocabulary for children ages 2-12 and takes approximately 15 minutes to administer. The test consists of 110 line drawings. The examiner's task is to give a one-word description of the objects pictured in each test plate. A base is established by eight consecutive correct responses while a ceiling is obtained when the child fails six consecutive items (Gardner, 1979).

Testing is not the only label-producing barrier for these children. Speaking the "language of silence" may actually be a larger barrier to school success for Native American girls. Studies of culturally sensitive education support the validity of a cumulative body of research that identifies the crisis in teacher education in the area of culturally responsive educators (Grant, 1992; Ladson-Billings, 2001). Therefore, educators, including pre-service teachers, need information regarding the cultural aspects of language and how to adjust their classrooms to meet the needs of all students (Edwards & Pleasants, 1998).

Language of Silence Study
Research Questions

1. What are the expressive language characteristics of the preschool Native American girl?

2. Are these characteristics specific to this population as compared to the Anglo children in the Head Start program and the Native American boys?

3. Do these characteristics handicap the preschool Native American girl when she enters a formal education program?

In this study the author analyzed the expressive language characteristics of 179 pre-kindergarten students. The study involved 58 Anglo males, 70 Anglo females, 30 Native American males, and 21 Native American females. The ethnographic case study was conducted during two semesters at two sites in Montana. Quantitative test scores from the EOWPVT (Gardner, 1979) were combined with the ethnographic study to provide a better foundation of data for the case study. The EOWPVT was selected because it has been used in providing a consistent estimate of a child's expressive vocabulary. This test is discussed in the 9th edition of the *Mental Measurements Yearbook* (Buros, 1985). The reliability coefficients ranged from .876 to .96. The corresponding standard error of measurement ranged from 3.38 to 5.41.

The major portion of the data for this study was gathered through descriptive research methods (Goetz & LeCompte, 1984; Guba & Lincoln, 1981; Merriam, 1988). Additional data were gathered through the administration of the EOWPVT. These data were analyzed through a simple t-test to determine if there were differences in the test scores of Native American girls as compared to Native American boys, Anglo girls, and Anglo boys. The statistic to be tested was the difference between the two means (Mitchell & Jolley, 1988; Wiersma, 1986). The significance level was set at .05. A t-test was utilized to insure robustness when analyzing unequal N sizes (Al-Harbi, 2003; Gall, Gall, & Borg, 2003).

The triangulation process included observation, interviews of teachers and parents, and testing. The selected population for this study was Head Start children with a mean age of four years and nine months. The tribal affiliation of the Native American students included Chippewa-Cree, Little Shell, and Blackfeet.

Method of Collecting Data

An ethnographic case study method was selected for this study because it provided a means of gaining the necessary information (Dixon, Bouma, & Alkinson, 1987; Merriam, 1988). Ethnographic case studies concentrate attention on the way particular groups of people confront specific problems, taking a holistic view of the situation (Merriam, 1988). In fact, one should expect "reality" to be different at different times, recognizing that the difference will depend on the situation and not merely on a lack of reliability in methodology. The naturalistic inquirer seeks multiple realities (Guba & Lincoln, 1981)

As a participant observer (Spradley, 1980) the author observed and recorded descriptive data and direct quotes, utilized interviews, video recorded interaction data, and analyzed video recordings of classroom interactions. Observation forms were utilized to provide a method of collecting the data (see Appendix A).

The videotapes were analyzed for quality, frequency, and types of conversation. The author used the observation form for evaluating the tapes in the same style that the daily visitations were also noted and recorded on the observation forms.

The teachers in the classroom were interviewed to gather information about what was happening between the class and the teacher from the teacher's perspective. Mothers of the girls were interviewed to discover ways in which they interact with their daughters (Edwards, 1989; Edwards, Franklin, & Pleasants, 1999). This information provided additional information about the girls' language usage. The interview form was recommended by Leedy (1989) as a method for gathering and organizing the available information (see Appendix B). The method of organizing the data from the observations and the interviews was proposed by Monette (1990). The responses from the observation and interview forms were assembled and tallied. The tallied results were analyzed to find common categories. The triangulation of this information with the quantitative data collected from testing provided a greater data base.

Observation Data

The main technique used to gather data in the classroom was through participant observation. By devoting time daily to the classroom over a period of two semesters, the author was able to become familiar with the routine of each classroom, gain an understanding of the teacher's style, and become so familiar in the classroom that the children began to accept the author as another teacher in the classroom. The time this took varied from classroom to classroom. Classrooms where parents were frequent volunteers took the shortest amount of time for students to accept the author because they were accustomed to having new adults in the classroom.

The observation form (see Appendix A) was utilized to collect the data on interaction between the students and the teacher. The author watched to see which students answered or asked questions, made comments either negative or positive, were involved in listening, and actually initiated conversation. An observational log was also written and videotape was recorded as an extension to aid the author.

The data from the observation form indicated that as a total group, the Native American girls talked less than the Anglo girls, the Anglo boys, or the Native American boys. Native American girls talked when prompted and were observed having a longer wait time in responding to conversation. It appeared that they were just listening more thoughtfully. Native American girls had the lowest language count of all four groups as demonstrated in Table 1.

Table 1. Data from observation form

Group	Number in Group	Language Count	Language Count Per Child
Native American Girls	21	103	5
Native American Boys	30	241	8
Anglo Boys	58	409	7
Anglo Girls	70	620	9

Interview Data

To describe the language characteristics of the Native American girls, the mothers of these girls were interviewed by the author. The interviews were completed in the spring. The interview form (see Appendix B) was followed and the one-on-one interviews lasted from a half hour to an hour. The mothers exhibited some of the same language characteristics as their daughters. Some of the mothers talked freely and others simply answered the questions. The interview started with a brief explanation of the study and a look at the test being used to measure expressive language. Next the questions from the interview form were asked. The final step was to summarize their responses.

The mothers of the Native American girls were interviewed regarding the students birth weight, siblings, tribal group, language spoken in the home, literacy in the home, television watched per day, discipline, and strengths and weaknesses. Table 2 reflects the data from the interview form.

Table 2. Data from Interview Form

Siblings	f	Tribal Group	f	Discipline	f	Strength	f	Weakness	f
0	4	Little Shell	1	Talk	6	Smart	5		
1	3	Blackfeet	7	Separation	4	Athletic	3	Shyness	6
2	2	Chippewa-Cree	6	Spank	2	Artistic	3	Others	4
3 or more	6	Gros Ventre	1	Reward	3	Cute	2		
						No Strength	2	No Weakness	5

Literacy and Reading Material

During the interview process, mothers of the Native American girls were asked how often they read to their daughters. The mothers reported reading to their daughters frequently or seldom with no middle approach taken. The majority said that they have been reading to their daughters since their daughters were born. Following are some of the mothers' comments.

- "She gets read to about every other day. Usually my mother or grand-mother reads to her."
- "We read once in a while, about three times a month. Her older brother reads to her all the time."
- "We read together, about three books a week. I use it as a punishment. If she doesn't listen, then I don't read to her."
- "I don't like to read myself."

When asked, "What do you read?" the mothers reported a variety of materials for reading, but the most frequently read were a current popular movie theme book. None of the mothers reported reading magazines or newspapers.

All the mothers reported that their daughters watched TV every day. There were a variety of times reported with cartoons being the most popular show. Comments from the mothers include the following.

- "She watches a lot of TV. In the morning, she watches cartoons before school and then in the afternoon and evening that is about all she does. We have a VCR so she likes to watch movies."
- "She watches mysteries with me."
- "She doesn't watch much. Maybe two hours every day."
- "She's a real couch potato. She likes to cuddle up with her pillow. She never watches in the morning before school because we never have time."

An analysis of the interviews with the mothers showed that they displayed a variety of parenting skills, much as might be found in any culture. If the children were present during the interview, they were on their mother's lap or near her. The mothers reported two extremes in reading; either they read to their daughters frequently or seldom. Additionally other information was gained during the mother's interviews such as withholding reading as a punishment or the parents dislike for reading. Because of the variance in response, it is not possible to claim a connection to the test scores. One area of consistency that surfaced during the interviews was that all the mothers reported that their daughters watched TV every day. The average number of hours watched each day was five. However, the majority of the mothers stated that "the TV was always on." Although the information is limited, it appears that watching television everyday for five hours may have an impact on expressive language skills.

The teachers were also informally interviewed each week concerning the Native American girls in their classrooms. The teachers consistently stated that the girls should talk more, that they were too quiet and shy, and that they seemed younger then they actually were. It appeared that the teacher thought the Native American girls spoke the "language of silence."

Test Results

A third set of data was gathered through the administration of the EOWPVT. These data were analyzed through a simple t-test to determine if there were differences on the test scores of Native American girls as compared to Native American boys, Anglo boys, and Anglo girls. The Language Standard Score (LSS) which indicated the extent to which a child's EOWPVT performance deviated from the average performance of children at that designated age level. Tables for language standard scores corresponding to raw scores were provided for each age level.

The mean LSS for the Anglo population was 93.16 and the mean LSS for the Native American population was 83.94. There was a significant difference between the populations (t= 4.03, df=85, p=.000). The LSS for the Anglo population was significantly higher than the LSS for the Native American population as demonstrated in this data from EOWPVT comparing means (see Figure 1).

Figure 1. LSS for Anglo Population Compared to Native American Population

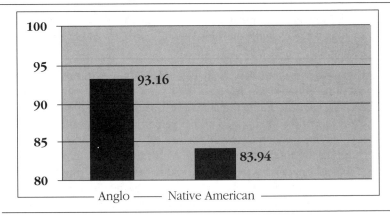

When the Native American girls were compared to the Native American boys, the females scored lower; however, there were no significant differences (t= 0.90, df= 49, p= 0.37). The mean LSS for the Native American girls was 81.86 and for the Native American boys it was 85.40 (see Figure 2).

**Figure 2. LSS for Native American Girls Compared
to Native American Boys**

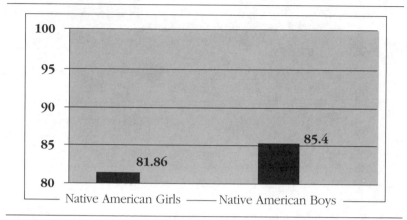

There was a significant difference when the Native American girls were
compared to the Anglo boys. The mean LSS for the Native American girls
was 81.86 and for the Anglo boys the mean LSS was 89.93 (t= 2.25, df= 77,
p= 0.027) (see Figure 3).

Figure 3. LSS for Native American Girls Compared to Anglo Boys

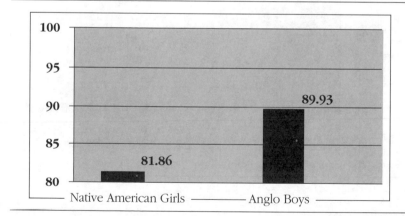

Anglo girls' LSS were then compared to Anglo boys' LSS. There was a
significant difference (t= 2.61, df= 177, p= 0.10). The mean LSS for the Anglo
girls was 95.84 and for the Anglo boys the mean LSS was 89.93 (see Figure
4).

The highest difference was between the Native American girls and the
Anglo girls. The mean LSS for the Native American girls was 81.86 and the

Figure 4. LSS for Anglo Girls compared to Anglo Boys

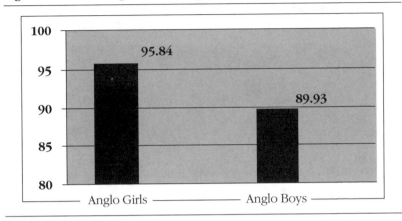

mean LSS for the Anglo girls was 95.84. This was a significant difference (t= 4.31, df= 89, p=0.001) (see Figure 5).

The findings of this testing describe the characteristics of the Native American girls as having the lowest Language Standard Score on the EOWPVT.

Figure 5. LSS for Native American Girls compared to Anglo Girls

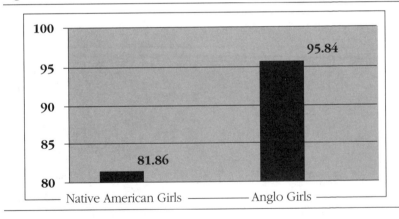

Limitations

The use of only two locations may limit the generalization of the study's quantitative findings. The interviewing of the Native American mothers by an Anglo investigator may be a limitation. The EOWPVT has certain limitations as disclosed in the *Mental Measurement Yearbook* (Buros, 1985).

Conclusion

The findings revealed that there are distinct language patterns of female Native American speakers. The findings from the observations, interviews, and testing described the expressive language characteristics of the 21 Native American girls at two sites. The categories explored with the observation form repeatedly led to the same conclusions: (a) Native American girls engage in conversation less than Native American boys, Anglo males and Anglo girls; (b) Native American girls use a longer "wait period" for conversations; and (c) Native American girls did not engage in self talk (talking to themselves as they performed activities).

A recurrent theme during the mothers' interviews was that they described their daughters as being shy. Several mothers said, "she is just shy around strangers," or "she wants to play with the children at school but she is too shy," or "she talks at home but she never talks to her teacher."

The third part of the data collection was the expressive language testing. In the testing there was a significant difference in Language Standard Scores between the Native American girls and the Anglo girls, between the Anglo students and the Native American students, and between the Native American girls and the Anglo boys.

Additionally, these language characteristics appear to be specific to Native American girls, as compared to the other Native American and Anglo students in the program. These characteristics appear to be gender specific to the Native American girls. Although the Language Standard Scores from the EOWPVT did not show a significant difference in scores between the Native American girls and Native American boys, the observations did lead to a different conclusion. The observation form tally revealed a language count of five per Native American girl and eight per Native American boy.

To find out if these language characteristics handicap the preschool Native American girl when she enters a formal education program, the teachers were informally interviewed each week concerning the Native American girls in their classrooms. The teachers consistently stated that the girls should talk more, that they were quiet and shy, with a few exceptions, and that they seemed younger than they actually were. These recurring statements led to the conclusion that the expressive language characteristics do handicap Native American girls in a formal education setting.

Recommendations

The Language of Silence study served to describe the expressive language characteristics of the preschool Native American girl. The recommendations are directed toward the teachers of Native American girls and the schools that serve those girls. With minorities expected to compose 40 % of the public school population, the failure of school districts to educate minority students is a major concern. With the number of potential dropouts growing in schools near Native American reservations, administrators and teachers are searching to discover culturally relevant techniques (Sparks, 2000). Assessment, curriculum policy, teaching methods, teacher education programs and in-service teacher development must all be addressed.

If Native American children tend to attain relatively low scores on tests that assess verbal skills and attain at least average scores on tests that assess nonverbal skills (Connelly, 1985), one major educational concern is to assess how we test Native American children. A method of assessment which would be beneficial to Native American children may also be better for other children. Assessment must be based on more than language scores. It must include a multitude of assessments for each child. These could include a portfolio, observation, and interview as well as testing. This could give us a more complete way to measure students' placement and success in school.

Although teachers seldom have the time to make observations other than informally in the classroom, observations should become a part of every assessment. By using an observation form such as the one used in the Language of Silence research, the teacher can gain important information by focusing on the language characteristics of one child at a time.

Likewise, parent-teacher conferences should be used as an interview rather than a reporting period. Parents know the child better than anyone else and can provide insights, which may be extremely important to the education of the student (Edwards et al., 1999).

While testing will still be a necessary part of education for statistical purposes, educators can minimize negative effects by making it only one part of the total assessment picture. Educators who value the importance of informal testing procedures in the classroom will ask questions concerning each child's expressive language skills. For example:

1. Is the child willing to participate in expressive language activities?
2. Can the child express ideas clearly?
3. Does the child use standard English?
4. Does the child have an adequate vocabulary to allow for the expression of ideas?
5. Does the child use the basic sentence patterns of English?
6. Does the child respect the rights of other participants in an oral language activity?

When teachers have Native American girls in their classrooms, they can provide appropriate teaching methods for those students and at the same time meet the needs of the other children in the class. Native American girls may not succeed in a highly verbal classroom. Other students in the classroom may also be more successful in a more visual classroom. The goal must be to increase participation by accepting short or non-verbal responses, present multiple choice tasks, give visual clues, and create a classroom atmosphere where all responses are considered with respect.

At the school level, an inventory of practices can be completed for major understandings of the current practice. The Northwest Regional Educational Laboratory (2002) has a comprehensive process, *Learn-ed Nation's Inventory: A tool for Improving Schools with American Indians and Alaska Native Students*. This instrument will be very helpful at the building or district level.

References

Al-Harbi, K. (2003, January). *Robustness*. Unpublished paper presented at the annual meeting of American Association of Colleges for Teacher Education, New Orleans, LA.

Buros, O. K. (1985). *The mental measurements yearbook*. Highland Park, NJ: Gryphon Press.

Cazden, B. (1972). *Child language and education*. New York: Holt.

Connelly, J. B. (1985). Receptive and expressive vocabularies of young Indian children. *Journal of American Indian Education, 24*(1), 33-37.

Dixon, B., Bouma, G., & Alkinson, G. (1987). *A Handbook of social science research*. New York: Oxford University Press.

Edwards, P. (1989). Supporting lower SES mothers' attempt to provide scaffolding for book reading. In J. B. Allen & J. Mason (Eds.), *Risk makers, risk takers, risk breakers* (pp. 222-250). Portsmouth, NH: Heinemann Educational Books.

Edwards, P., & Pleasants, H. (1998). How can we provide for culturally responsive instruction in literacy? In S. Neuman & K. Roskos (Eds.), *Children achieving: Best practices in early literacy* (pp. 98-120). Newark, DE: International Reading Association.

Edwards, P., Franklin, S., & Pleasants, H. (1999). *A path to follow: Learning to listen to parents*. Portsmouth, NH: Heinemann.

Gall, M., Gall, J., & Borg, W. (2003). *Educational research: An introduction*. Boston: Allyn and Bacon.

Gardner, F. (1979). *Expressive one-word picture vocabulary test manual*. Novato, CA: Academic Therapy Publications.

Gay, G. (2000). *Culturally responsive teaching: Theory, research & practice*. New York: Teachers College Press.

Goetz, J., & LeCompte, M. (1984). *Ethnography and qualitative design in educational research*. San Diego, CA: Academic Press, Inc.

Grant, C. (1992). *Research and multicultural education from the margin to the mainstream*. Bristol, PA: The Falmer Press, Taylor & Francis Inc.

Guba, E., & Lincoln, Y. (1981). *Effective evaluation: Improving the usefulness of evaluation through responsive and naturalistic approaches*. San Francisco: Jossey-Bass.

Hollins, E. R., King, J. E., & Hayman, W. C. (Eds.). (1994). *Teaching diverse populations: Formulating a knowledge base*. Albany, NY: State University of New York Press.

Indian Nations at Risk Task Force. (1991). *Indian nations at risk: An educational strategy for action. Final report.* Washington, DC: US Department of Education.

Ladson-Billings, G. (1994). *The dream keepers: Successful teachers of African American children.* San Francisco: Jossey-Bass.

Ladson-Billings, G. (2001). *Crossing over to Canaan: The journey of new teachers in diverse classrooms.* San Francisco: Jossey-Bass.

Leedy, P. (1989). *Practical research: Planning and design.* New York: Macmillan Publishing co.

Luria, A. R., & Yudrovich, F. L. (1971). *Speech and the development of mental processes in the child.* Harmandsworth: Penguin.

Merriam, S. (1988). *Case study research in education: A qualitative approach.* San Francisco: Jossey-Bass.

Mitchell, M., & Jolley, J. (1988). *Research design explained.* New York: Holt, Rinehart, and Winston, Inc.

Monette, D. (1990). *Applied social research: Tool for the human services.* Fort Worth, TX: Holt, Rinehart and Winston.

Nelson-Barber, S., & Meier, T. (1990). *Multicultural context: A key factor in teaching.* New York: Academic Connections.

Northwest Regional Educational Laboratory. (2002). *Learn-ed nations inventory: A tool* for improving schools with American Indian and Alaska native students. Washington, DC: US Department of Education.

Philips, S. (1983). *The invisible culture.* New York: Longman.

Purves, A. (1991). The textual contact: Literacy as common knowledge and conventional wisdom. In E. Jennings & A. Purves (Eds.), *Literate systems and individual lives.* Albany, NY: State University of New York.

Sparks, S. (2000). Classroom and curriculum accommodations for Native American students. *Intervention in School and Clinic, 35*(5), 259-263.

Spradley, J. (1980). *Participant observation.* New York: Holt, Rinehart, and Winston.

Villegas, A. (2002). *Educating culturally responsive teachers: A coherent approach.* Albany, NY: State University of New York Press.

Wertsch, J. V. (1985). *Vygotsky and the social foundation of mind.* Cambridge, MA: Harvard University Press.

Wiersma, W. (1986). *Research methods in education.* Newton, MA: Allyn & Bacon, Inc.

Winterowd, W. R. (1989). *The Culture and the politics of literacy.* Oxford: Oxford Press.

Appendix A. Observation Form

The observation form gathered information on location, number of children present, activity of teacher, activity of the group, comments and language observed. Tally marks were made in each of the following categories.

LANGAUGE OF SILENCE–OBSERVATION FORM

Date: _____

Time: _____

Location: _____

Children Present –

Activity of Teacher –

Activity of Group –

Comments –

Language Observed –

	1	2	3	4	5	6	7	8	9	10	11	12	13	14	15
Answers Question															
Asks Question															
Makes Statement															
Positive Comment															
Negative Comment															
Listening															
Initiates Conversation															

LANGUAGE OF SILENCE–OBSERVATION FORM
Definitions of Language Behaviors (Monette, 1990)

Questions –	Verbal behavior that demands or suggests a response from one or more group members
Statements –	Verbal behavior that gives information and does not call for a response from group members
Positive Comments –	Verbal behavior that followed the behavior of one or more group members and relates to this behavior to encourage similar responses. Suggests recognition, approval, or praise.
Negative Comments –	Verbal behavior that followed the behavior of one or more group members and relates to this behavior to discourage similar responses. Suggests disapproval or displeasure.
Listening –	Silence on the part of the group member either while another member verbalizes or while waiting for another member to verbalize.

Appendix B. Interview Form

LANGUAGE OF SILENCE – INTERVIEW FORM

Date: _____

Time: _____

Location: _____

Interview Concerning: _____

Person Being Interviewed: _____

Student's Age: _____

Date of Birth: _____

Birth Weight: _____

Mother's Name: _____

Father's Name: _____

Siblings: _____

_____

Address: _____

Tribal Group: _____

    Urban _____

    Reservation _____

Language Spoken in Home:

    English _____   Other _____

Literacy:

    How often do you read together? _____

    What do you read?

        Books _____   Magazines _____   Newspapers _____

    How much TV do you watch per day? _____

Is there any other information you can share regarding your daughter?

Relating African American Students' Scores on State-Mandated Reading and Writing Tests to Standardized Measures of Reading and Oral and Written Language

Monica Gordon Pershey

Cleveland State University

Abstract

Mandated testing is prominent among educational initiatives. Questions arise about testing students who face economic disadvantages, are of racial, ethnic, or language minority status, or are at risk for academic failure because their schools provide limited opportunities for academic advancement. This study used normed tests to measure oral and written language and reading abilities in 263 grade four and six African American students and compared results to performance on criterion-referenced mandated testing of reading and writing.

For normed and mandated tests, group mean scores were at times below expectations. Principal components analyses determined language capabilities underlying performance on testing. Factors that accounted for the variance in scores included vocabulary, knowledge of the conventions of written language, knowledge of sentence syntax, and reading comprehension.

Prominent among current educational initiatives is the importance of preparing students to meet curriculum standards and perform well on mandated testing (National Education Goals Panel [NEGP], 1994; United States Department of Education [USDOE], 2001; USDOE, 2002). The effort to establish summative tests of academic performance overlaps the current school accountability movement, which holds schools and educators responsible for students' progress (National Center on Educational Outcomes [NCEO], 2001; USDOE, 2002).

Testing figures prominently into the lives of pupils in Ohio. Districts have been required to administer the *Ohio Proficiency Test* (OPT) (Ohio Department of Education, 1995; *Ohio Student Testing Requirements,* 1991) to measure how students perform on learning outcomes identified by the state. The OPT is a criterion-referenced test of content areas and reading and writing given in grades four, six, nine, ten, and twelve. Testing is supposed to correspond with what is taught and measure cumulative learning and overall school achievement. However, preparing students to demonstrate the applied process skills tested by the OPT reading and writing subtests has been a challenge (e.g., summarization, finding paragraph details, writing a friendly letter) (Pottle, 2001).

The OPT has become the standard by which pupil competency and school accountability have been assessed. The state of Ohio ranks school districts according to twenty-seven performance standards, twenty-five of which apply to achieving a 75% pass rate on the subtests of the OPT in all grades. The other two standards are attendance and graduation rates. A district is then assigned to one of four performance categories (i.e, effective, continuous improvement, academic watch, academic emergency). At the time of this study 69 of the state's 607 districts met eight or fewer standards and were in academic emergency (Ohio Department of Education, 2000).

The author of this study provided professional development seminars to teachers from a district that was in academic emergency. Enrollment in this district was virtually 100% African American. The teachers emphasized their impressions that students' consistently poor OPT performance was likely due to an inadequate oral language basis that impacted negatively upon reading and writing performance. Language development, as a factor in test performance, has been suggested by Meisels (1989) and Popham (1999); however, this appears to be a new area of research. Little data exist on how language capabilities correlate with performance on criterion-referenced tests of curriculum mastery. To explore this hypothesized connection, the author collected data on the oral and written language and reading skills of the district's fourth and sixth graders.

This study (a) explored whether students' normed test scores met age and grade level expectations, (b) identified where performance on the normed tests and the OPT were related, and (c) determined language capabilities that predicted OPT reading and writing performance.

Debates Attendant to Testing

Underlying a belief in high-stakes testing is the assumption that students score as they do because of exposure to school curriculum (Glaser, 1994). However, it is problematic to assume that exposure is of uniform quality across schools or is equally meaningful to all students. Questions arise about the appropriateness of testing students who face economic disadvantages, are of racial, ethnic, or language minority status, or are at risk for academic failure because their schools lack resources and provide limited opportunities for academic advancement (Bobbett, 1993; Denoyer & White, 1992; Gallagher, 1993; International Reading Association [IRA], 1999; Kohn, 2000; Ladson-Billings, 1994; Manning, Lucking, & MacDonald, 1995; McGee, 1997; Meisels, 1989; Popham, 1999; Raivetz, 1992; Roderick, 1995; Westbury, 1994; Winfield, 1990). Studies have shown that minority and low income students are more likely to fail high-stakes tests and remediation for those who fail is less likely to be effective (Morris, 2000; National Assessment of Educational Progress [NAEP], 1998; NAEP, 1999; NAEP, 2000; Schellenberg, 1998; Winfield, 1990). Tests reveal a widening gap between high and low income schools, especially on questions that require an extended verbal response (National Educational Research Policy and Priorities Board, 1999). Summative tests do not identify the academic supports that students would need to receive in order to perform better on curriculum demands and on subsequent testing (Barkley, 2001).

Several studies have shown that minority and low income students are more likely to fail mandated achievement tests and that remediation for those who fail is less likely to be effective (Morris, 2000; NAEP, 1998; NAEP, 1999; NAEP, 2000; Schellenberg, 1998; Winfield, 1990). However, the cause of test failure is not entirely clear. Jackson (1999) offered that risk is less dependent upon income and more directly related to residential and school segregation. Popham (1994,1999) ventured that testing outcomes tend to be biased in favor of children from economically advantaged, stimulus-rich homes, who have acquired language-based information outside of school. A strong language basis, promoted early on in children's education, prepares learners to be developmentally ready to profit from instruction (Meisels, 1989). The language of the school curriculum, including the discourses of literacy instruction, may be beyond the comprehension of children who lack substantial language backgrounds (Butler, 1999; Falk-Ross, 2002; Snow, Burns, & Griffin, 1998).

Characteristics of the OPT

As a criterion-referenced measure, the OPT resembles the NAEP (2000) in some ways. Both reading measures address how well a learner comprehends what is read, extends comprehension, and manipulates information (e.g., follows directions). Both writing assessments require the student to write to accomplish a variety of purposes (Commission on Behavioral and Social Sciences and Education, 1998; NAEP, 2000; Ohio Department of Education, 2000; *Ohio Student Testing Requirements*, 1991).

Despite this resemblance, questions of reliability, validity, and appropriateness arise when education agencies prepare their own criterion-referenced competency tests (Lanese, 1992; Snodgrass & Salzman, 1998). Instruments that are not normed can produce unstable results, particularly when testing African American students (Urdan & Davis, 1998). The *Ohio Statehouse Newsletter* (2000) reported that the passing rate on the OPT grade four reading test was 65% for Anglo-European children and 33% for African American children. Earlier grading scales left 20% of African American children passing compared to 53% of Anglo-European students, so grading was adjusted. Testing outcomes were thus an artifact of a variable performance standard and were far from absolute measurements.

A few authors compared the OPT with norm-referenced measures of school achievement but for students older than grades four and six. Robinson and Moore (1992) and Stroud (1995) found weak but significant correlations between reading and writing performance on the *Metropolitan Achievement Test* (Balow, Farr, & Hogan, 1992) and the grade nine OPT. Noel (1994) established that the grade nine OPT reading and writing tests correlated highly with the *California Achievement Tests* (CTB/McGraw-Hill, 1992) language and reading tests. Hull and Tache (1993) determined that the *Iowa Tests of Basic Skills* (Hoover, Hieronymus, Frisbie, & Dunbar, 1996) correlated significantly with OPT scores for reading and writing for 700 high schoolers.

The Research Study
Purpose
As Meisels (1989) and Popham (1999) suggested, poor scores on high-stakes testing may be due to a lack of language-based information learned in and out of school. The present study determined whether performance on a non-standardized test of curriculum mastery correlated with performance on standardized tests of oral language, writing, and reading capabilities.

Research Questions
This study answered the following questions. First, to reveal an overall impression of participants' written language and reading capabilities, did OPT reading and writing scores correlate? Second, were participants' oral and written language and reading capabilities adequate, as ascertained by standardized measures? Third, which subtests of the norm-referenced tests of oral and written language and reading correlated significantly with scores on the OPT? Fourth, which subtests of the norm-referenced tests correlated to reveal consistencies in participants' performance? Fifth, which subtests of the norm-referenced tests might predict performance on the OPT? Sixth, what language capabilities were derived as principal components of performance on the norm-referenced tests?

Method

Participants

A sample of 263 students participated in this study: 140 fourth graders (64 males and 76 females) and 123 sixth graders (56 males and 67 females). For fourth graders, the mean age was 10.1 years (range 9.3 to11.5 years) and for sixth graders the mean age was 12.1 years (range 11.2 to 13.7 years). None of the participants received special education or regular education supplemental services and parent/guardian permission was obtained for each participant.

Setting

Participants lived in an urban suburb about ten miles from the center of a moderately large city. According to the U.S. Census Bureau (2000), 90.4% of the population of the community was African American. Between one-third and one-half of African American residents were part of families that own homes. Home values averaged about $70,000 and rental properties were about $500 per month. The percent of children in this community listed as economically disadvantaged was 25.1%, compared to a state average of 13.4% (Ohio Department of Education, 2000; U.S. Census Bureau, 1990). About one-third of the children might live in homes with no husband present (U.S. Census Bureau, 1990). District enrollment was 3,100 students. Transience was noted in the schools. In 1998-1999 nearly 13% of all students were not in the district for half of the year; another 13% switched buildings in the district during the year (the state averages are about 11%) (Ohio Department of Education, 2000). Twenty-seven percent of students were eligible for free or reduced fee lunches and 31% qualified for Title I services. Special education services were provided to 30% of the student population.

The racial composition of the district staff was 41.1% non-minority, .5% Asian, and 58.4% African American (Ohio Department of Education, 1998). Although class size averaged about 24 students and annual spending per pupil was about 12% greater than the state average, the district was ranked as the fifth lowest of the county's thirty-one districts in academic accomplishments. The district met only seven of twenty-seven state academic standards. Meeting so few standards placed the district in "academic emergency," the lowest of four performance categories. About 11% of the state's districts fared this poorly.

The district met the standard for student attendance but failed the standard for graduation rate (only 75%, which was down by 5% over the past three years). In the year prior to this study, of all academic subjects tested by the OPT, the district achieved a passing rate (at least 75% of pupils tested pass) only for writing in grades six, nine, ten and twelve and reading in grades nine and ten. For grade four, 9.5% of students passed all OPT subtests; the state average was 31.9%. For grade six, 16.1% passed all subtests; the state average was 32.5%. These were the best fourth and sixth grade scores that the district achieved over the three years prior to the study. For grade nine, 41% passed all areas (the state average was 61%), and for grade twelve 15.5% passed (state average was 39.8%). At this rate, if one were to look around an elementary classroom of twenty-four children, six will not graduate. Of the eighteen who remain, fifteen won't pass the grade twelve test. The student body can be said to have been at considerable risk for academic failure. Clearly, large numbers of students were struggling to meet state academic standards.

Instrumentation

A battery of test scores was obtained for all participants. Each test will be described.

State mandated testing. The grade four OPT reading test assessed the ability to silently read fiction and nonfiction text and (a) summarize text, (b) use graphic aids and illustrations to interpret information, (c) retell text, (d) interpret text vocabulary, (e) analyze text, (f) infer from text, (g) respond to text, (h) predict text outcomes, and (i) discern main and supporting ideas. The grade six OPT reading test included the ability to read nonfiction and fiction text and (a) analyze aspects of text, (b) summarize text, (c) infer from text, (d) respond to text, (e) critique text for its organization and logic, and (f) evaluate author's purpose.

The OPT grade four writing test required the child to prepare a letter to a friend and a personal narrative. Writers were assessed through holistic scoring for (a) clarity, (b) adherence to topic, (c) logic and organization, (d) use of a variety of words, (e) use of a variety of sentence structures, (f) awareness of word usage, and (g) correct mechanics and spelling. The grade six writing test assessed the ability to write a fictional narrative and a set of directions to complete a task. Writers were holistically scored for how well they (a) focus on a topic, (b) support ideas by giving details or examples, (c) write with logic and organization, (d) choose appropriate wording, (e) use complete and varied sentence structures, and (f) demonstrate correct mechanics and spelling. The holistic scoring rubrics yielded a score of zero to four points; only scores of three and four are passing.

Norm-referenced tests: Oral language. All oral language subtests yielded standard scores. Tests used for the grade four assessment included the *WORD-R* (Huisingh, Barrett, Zachman, Blagden, & Orman, 1990) (a test of vocabulary) and the *Test of Language Development-Intermediary* (TOLD-I:3) (Hammill & Newcomer, 1997) (verbal reasoning, grammar, listening, vocabulary). Subtests and results are found in Table 1.

Table 1. Fourth Grade Descriptive Data

Assessment	Mean Standard Score	Standard Deviation
WORD-R	100 (range 55-145)*	15*
WORD-R Synonyms	86.2	<1 SD below
WORD-R Semantic Absurdities	84.9	1 SD below
WORD-R Antonyms	88.9	<1 SD below
WORD-R Multiple Definitions	76.6	<1 SD below
TOLD-I:3	10 (range 1-20)*	3*
TOLD-I:3 Sentence Combining	10.1	Normative mean
TOLD-I:3 Picture Vocabulary	8.7	<1/2 SD below
TOLD-I:3 Generals	8.8	<1/2 SD below
TOLD-I:3 Grammatic Completion	8.8	<1/2 SD below
TOLD-I:3 Malaprops	8.4	<1 SD below
SCALE-L	50 (range 28-72)*	10*
SCALE-L All Items	44.4	1/2 SD below
TOWL-3	10 (range 1-20)*	3*
TOWL-3 Vocabulary	9.3	<1/2 SD below
TOWL-3 Sentence Combining	9.8	<1/2 SD below
TOWL-3 Story Construction	9.0	<1/2 SD below
TORC-3	10 (range 1-20)*	3*
TORC-3 General Vocabulary	8.7	<1/2 SD below
TORC-3 Syntactic Similarities	8.9	<1/2 SD below
TORC-3 Paragraph Reading	8.3	1/2 SD below

based on normative values

Both tests were developed using a normative sample whose demographics mirrored the United States. African Americans represent just over 12% of the population (U.S. Census Bureau, 2000). The *WORD-R* was normed using a sample that was 13% African American. For the TOLD-I:3 the normative sample was 15% African American.

Assessment of oral language in grade six included the *WORD-Adolescent Test* (WORD-A) (Zachman, Huisingh, Barrett, Orman, & Blagden, 1989) (vocabulary and semantics). The test was normed on a sample that was 14% African American. *The Test of Adolescent and Adult Language* (TOAL-3) (Hammill, Brown, Larsen, & Wiederholt, 1994) Listening Vocabulary subtest was also used. The TOAL-3 normative sample was 15% African American.

Written language. Written language measures yielded standard scores. The *Scaled Curriculum Achievement Levels Test* (SCALE) (Doherty & Roid, 1992) estimates an academic functional level for students in grades three to eight in language and reading. The test manual does not indicate the demographics for the normative sample.

The Language Usage subtest, known as the SCALE-L, assesses five curriculum strands, Composition Structure, Composition Process, Grammar/

Usage, Punctuation, and Capitalization. All items on the SCALE-L are multiple choice. Items require students to recognize written language conventions or interpret the meaning of a written message.

The second instrument used to evaluate written language was the *Test of Written Language* (TOWL-3) (Hammill & Larsen, 1996). The TOWL-3 was normed on a sample which was 13% African American.

Sixth graders' writing capabilities were further assessed via administration of two TOAL-3 subtests. Writing Vocabulary presents the same task as the TOWL-3 Vocabulary subtest (write a given word in a meaningful sentence). Writing Grammar is a test of sentence combining. The TOAL-3 was used instead of the TOWL-3 because its administration required less time—if students begin with items selected for children near their own age, not eight-year-olds, they are likely to reach the ceiling in less time.

Fourth graders were given the *Test of Reading Comprehension* (TORC-3) (Brown, Hammill, & Wiederholt, 1995). This instrument identifies the reader's ability to apply word-level vocabulary processing skills, sentence-level syntactic processing skills, and paragraph-level comprehension skills. The TORC-3 yields standard scores. The test was normed on a sample that was 12% African American.

Sixth graders' reading competencies were assessed using the SCALE Reading subtest (SCALE-R) and the reading portions of the TOAL-3. The SCALE-R assesses reading for Word Meaning, Literal Comprehension, Interpretive Comprehension, and Evaluative Comprehension. TOAL-3 Reading Vocabulary assesses single-word comprehension. Reading Grammar assesses sentence-level comprehension. The TOAL-3 was used instead of the TORC-3 because its administration required less time—if students begin reading items selected for age peers, not seven-year-old readers, they are likely to reach the ceiling in less time.

Procedures

Data collection. Standardized testing began in February and continued through early June. Each participant left class for a total of three to four hours to complete testing. Children attended two to four testing sessions in order to prevent fatigue. Testing was conducted in empty rooms in the schools. In March, students took the OPT with their classes, which was scored by the state's outsourcing arrangements and reported to the district in mid-June.

The researcher and thirty graduate students served as testers. All students had completed coursework on testing procedures, had experience administering standardized tests, and had taken a course on language development in African American children. Testers participated for fifteen to sixty-five hours. Testing teams (usually four students plus the researcher) visited the schools weekly for up to three days per week.

Groups of about ten children rotated among the testing stations. Some began with one-on-one oral language testing, while small groups of others were given the reading and written language instruments first. Tests across and within each language modality were administered in randomized order to prevent order effects. Short breaks were given as needed.

Each participant completed all measures. Tests were scored by six of the testers who served as student workers. Occasional errors made it necessary to discard some scores on some subtests. There was never more than one subtest discarded per student. All protocols were reviewed by the researcher then scores were entered into the SPSS Base 10.0 (1999) program by a graduate student trained in statistics. The researcher reviewed the SPSS files and corrected data discrepancies before final data analyses were run.

Results

Findings provided response to the research questions.

Question 1—To reveal an overall impression of the children's written language and reading capabilities, did OPT reading and writing scores correlate?

A score of 75% is required to pass any of the OPTs. In the fourth grade, 93 pupils (66.4%) achieved a score of 75% or more. Scores ranged from 31% to 98%, with a mean of 75% (standard deviation [SD] 14.6. Forty-four students (31.4%) passed the OPT writing test. Scores ranged from 37.5% to 87.5%, with a mean of 62% (SD .13). There were thirty-seven children (26.4%) who passed both subtests.

In the sixth grade, forty-three pupils (34.9%) achieved a score of 75% or more on the OPT reading test. Scores ranged from 16% to 92%, with a mean of 65.5% (SD 14.6). One hundred and one students (82%) passed the OPT writing test. Scores ranged from 12.5% to 87.5%, with a mean of 65% (SD .17). There were sixty-one children (49.5%) who passed both subtests.

Fourth grade OPT reading and OPT writing scores correlated ($r = .447$, $p \leq .0001$), as did sixth grade OPT reading and OPT writing scores ($r = .380$, $p \leq .0001$), to reveal a moderately stable and representative measure of reading and writing performance. The overall result was that students in this sample did not perform very successfully on state-mandated tests.

Question 2—Were participants' oral and written language and reading capabilities age appropriate as ascertained by standardized measures?

Scores for grade four are found in Table 1. Fourth grade mean oral language scores were consistently below normative means. Tasks that required more complex verbal reasoning and vocabulary usage posed difficulty for students. Better scores were obtained for simpler verbal tasks, such as sentence combining, picture identification, and recognizing grammatic constructions. Moderately difficult tasks, such as identifying misuse of words and supplying synonyms and antonyms, brought scores below normative means. Deciphering multiple word meanings and semantic absurdities proved the most taxing.

Fourth grade written language was commensurate with oral language capabilities. Written sentence combining was near the normative mean, as was oral sentence combining. Vocabulary, recognizing written language meanings and conventions, and story writing were below expectations. Fairly good syntactic skills were displayed in reading for sentence meaning. However, the more complex task of reading paragraphs was an area of difficulty.

Scores for grade six are reported in Table 2. Mean scores were below expectations by varying margins. WORD-A assessed concepts related to daily living. Mean scores were close to normative means. But mean performance on TOAL-3 Listening Vocabulary, a test of multiple meaning words related to more complex concepts, was two SDs below the normative mean. This finding may signal considerable insufficiencies in vocabulary.

Table 2. Sixth Grade Descriptive Data

Assessment	Mean Standard Score	Standard Deviation
WORD-A	100 (range 55-145)*	15*
WORD-A Brand Names	95.9	<1/2 SD below
WORD-A Synonyms	91.3	1/2 SD below
WORD-A Signs of the Times	99.0	near normative mean
WORD-A Definitions	92.3	1/2 SD below
TOAL-3	10 (range 1-20)*	3*
TOAL-3 Listening Vocabulary	5.1	>1-1/2 SD below
TOAL-3 Writing Vocabulary	4.9	>1-1/2 SD below
TOAL-3 Writing Grammar	5.2	>1-1/2 SD below
TOAL-3 Reading Vocabulary	5.9	<1-1/2 SD below
TOAL-3 Reading Grammar	5.2	>1-1/2 SD below
SCALE-L	50 (range 28-72)*	10*
SCALE-L All Items	45.6	1/2 SD below
TOWL-3	10 (range 1-20)*	3*
TOWL-3 Story Construction	8.1	>1/2 SD below
SCALE-R	50 (range 28-72)*	10*
SCALE-R Level 4 Items	43.5	>1/2 SD below

based on normative values

Sixth graders showed notable insufficiencies in written language. TOAL-3 scores indicated that vocabulary usage and sentence construction were considerably below norms. The SCALE-L showed that participants' knowledge of written language conventions was not strong. The SCALE-R showed difficulties in reading for word meaning and passage comprehension.

Question 3—Which subtests of the norm-referenced tests of oral and written language and reading correlated significantly with scores on the OPT?

Subtest means that correlated at $p \leq$ .0001, $r \geq$ .4 (Pearson Product Moment correlations) are found in Tables 3 and 4. For grade four, several oral language mean scores correlated with OPT reading scores. Oral language development appeared relevant to test performance. Written language means also correlated with OPT reading scores. Knowledge of written language conventions, vocabulary, and sentence manipulation skills appeared related to performance on the mandated reading test. Correlations between OPT reading and standardized reading test scores occurred. Notably, a reading score, TORC-3 General Vocabulary, was the only standardized measure that correlated with the OPT writing score.

For sixth grade, oral and written language scores correlated with OPT reading, again attesting to the interrelatedness of these various language skills. There were no grade six reading measures that correlated with OPT reading. None of the grade six measures correlated with OPT writing. This points to the possible spuriousness of the OPT writing scores in comparison to the other tests given. It appears that the OPT writing mean was anomalously high.

Analysis of these correlations suggested that, in both grades, (a) vocabulary-driven measures of oral and written language correlated frequently and strongly with the OPT tests, and (b) subtests that measured written language usage and conventions correlated with the state's measure of reading abilities.

Question 4—Which subtests of the norm-referenced tests correlated to reveal consistencies in participants' performance?

Subtest means that correlated at $p \leq$ .0001, $r \geq$ .4 are found in Tables 3 and 4. For fourth graders, numerous correlations within tests affirmed the strength of the instruments. Correspondences between vocabulary and verbal reasoning were seen within and across oral and written language modalities. Reading scores correlated within the reading instrument and with oral and written language testing.

Correlations between vocabulary-driven oral language measures were found. Several measures of oral vocabulary and linguistic reasoning correlated with written vocabulary and written language scores. Correlations were evidenced between two sorts of composition skills: conceptual (meaning-based) and mechanical. Reading vocabulary correlated with oral vocabulary, oral measures of linguistic reasoning, and with overall written language skills. Reading comprehension at the sentence level correlated with oral tasks involving linguistic reasoning and with written sentence combining. Sentence processing and sentence construction were related skills.

For grade six, numerous oral language subtests correlated with one another, as did written language scores. There were multiple correlations

Table 3. Fourth Grade Correlation Matrix

	OPT RD	OPT WR	WORD SYN	WORD SEM	WORD ANT	WORD MDEF	TOLD SENCO	TOLD PVOC	TOLD GEN	TOLD GRM	TOLD MALP	SCALE L	TOWL VOCAB	TOWL SENCO	TOWL STORY	TOR C VOC	TORC SYNTX	TORC PARA
OPTRD																		
OPT WRIT																		
WORD SYN	.594																	
WORD SEM	.537		.649															
WORD ANT	.438		.674	.677														
WORD MDEF	.550		.515	.509	.466													
TOLD SENCO			.400															
TOLD PVOC			.532	.500	.441	.429												
TOLD GEN	.530		.546	.605	.517			.477										
TOLD GRM						.409												
TOLD MALP	.434		.489	.441	.449	.467		.496	.443									
SCALE	.546		.545	.426		.624				.403								
TOWL VOCAB	.485		.526	.453	.453	.494			.437		.520	.501						
TOWL SENCO	.406																	
TOWL STORY																		
TORC VOC	.451	.444	.515	.431	.449	.459		.400	.496		.413	.454	.543	.414				
TORC SYNTX	.406		.401	.480										.457		.458		
TORC PARA	.422																.458	

Note. Pearson r, significant at $p \le .0001$

Table 4. Sixth Grade Correlation Matrix

	OPT RD	OPT WR	WORD BRND	WORD SYN	WORD SOT	WORD DEF	TOAL LISTN	SCALE L	TOWL STORY	TOAL WVOC	TOAL WGRM	TOAL RVOCB	TOAL RGRM	SCALER
OPT READ				.458		.500	.418	.590		.455				
OPT WRIT														
WORD BRND				.571	.575	.593	.413							.444
WORD SYN	.458		.571			.773	.485	.466		.601		.548		.464
WORD SOT			.575			.561	.453							
WORD DEF	.500		.593	.773	.561		.498	.474		.552		.535		.499
TOAL LISTN	.418		.413	.485	.453	.498		.492		.555		.498		
SCALE L	.590			.466		.474	.492			.599	.465	.569	.484	
TOWL STORY														
TOAL WVOC	.455			.601		.552	.555	.599			.447	.568		
TOAL WGRM								.465		.447				
TOAL RVOCB				.548		.535	.498	.569		.568			.414	.569
TOAL RGRM								.484				.414		.484
SCALE R			.444	.464		.499						.569	.484	

Note. Pearson *r*, significant at *p* ≤ .0001

between vocabulary-driven oral measures. Vocabulary correlated with measures of conceptual understanding. Correlations between conceptual and mechanical composition skills were evidenced. Sentence combining skill correlated with other measures of written language skill.

Multiple measures of reading comprehension correlated, demonstrating the relationship between comprehension at the word, sentence, and paragraph levels. Reading vocabulary was related to oral vocabulary and to oral linguistic reasoning. Recognition of written language conventions and usage correlated with reading comprehension at the sentence level.

Question 5—Which subtests of the norm-referenced tests might predict performance on the OPT?

For grade four, linear regressions were run for the measures that correlated significantly ($p \leq .0001$) with the OPT reading and OPT writing scores. Predictors of OPT reading performance were WORD-R Synonyms ($R^2 = .353$), WORD-R Multiple Definitions ($R^2 = .303$), WORD-R Semantic Absurdities ($R^2 = .288$), TOLD-I:3 Generals ($R^2 = .281$), TOWL-3 Vocabulary ($R^2 = .235$), TORC-3 General Vocabulary ($R^2 = .204$), WORD-R Antonyms ($R^2 = .191$), TOLD-I:3 Malaprops ($R^2 = .189$), TORC-3 Paragraph Reading ($R^2 = .178$), TOWL-3 Sentence Combining ($R^2 = .165$), and TORC-3 Syntactic Similarities ($R^2 = .164$). Only TORC-3 General Vocabulary ($R^2 = .197$) was predictive of the OPT writing outcome.

To determine whether several factors taken together accounted for a percent of the variance in OPT reading scores for fourth graders, multiple regressions were run. Combinations of the variables that yielded the most powerful linear regressions were applied. To account for the impact of oral vocabulary as a variable in OPT reading performance, a multiple regression was run using the following scores as independent variables: WORD-R Synonyms, WORD-R Semantic Absurdities, WORD-R Antonyms, WORD-R Multiple Definitions, TOLD-I:3 Generals, and TOLD-I:3 Malaprops. The R^2 value for these factors was .458, $p \leq .0001$. When taken together, these vocabulary capabilities accounted for roughly 46% of the variance in OPT reading scores. Another multiple regression was run using TORC-3 General Vocabulary and TOWL-3 Vocabulary as independent variables. The R^2 value for these factors was .285, $p \leq .0001$, suggesting that reading and writing vocabulary accounted for about 29% of the variance in OPT reading performance. An additional multiple regression used TORC-3 Syntactic Similarities and TORC-3 Paragraph Reading as independent variables. The R^2 value for measures that required complex reading was .268, $p \leq .0001$, accounting for about 27% of the variance in OPT reading scores. Finally, a multiple regression was run using TOWL-3 Vocabulary and TOWL-3 Sentence Construction as independent variables, to explore the impact of written response quality on OPT reading outcomes. The R^2 value was .301, $p \leq .0001$, which accounted for about 30%

of the variance in OPT reading performance. Reading ability itself was not more important than vocabulary and the ability to use words and sentences to construct written responses.

Regarding sixth grade data, linear regressions were run for the measures that correlated ($p \leq .0001$) with OPT reading at $r = .4$ or better. Predictors were SCALE-L ($R^2 = .348$), WORD-A Definitions ($R^2 = .250$), WORD-A Synonyms ($R^2 = .210$), TOAL-3 Writing Vocabulary ($R^2 = .207$), and TOAL-3 Listening Vocabulary($R^2 = .175$).

Multiple regressions determined whether several factors taken together accounted for a percent of the variance in OPT reading scores for sixth graders. One multiple regression was run using TOAL-3 Listening Vocabulary and TOAL-3 Writing Vocabulary as independent variables. The R^2 value for these factors was .244, $p \leq .0001$, denoting that complex oral and written vocabulary knowledge and usage accounted for 25% of the variance in OPT reading scores. Another multiple regression used only oral vocabulary measures, TOAL-3 Listening Vocabulary, WORD-A Synonyms, WORD-A Definitions. The R^2 value for these factors was .292, $p \leq .0001$, accounting for approximately 30% of the variance in OPT reading outcomes. An additional multiple regression used the SCALE-L and SCALE-R as independent variables, to explore the importance of knowledge of written language conventions and reading abilities. The R^2 value for these variables was .347, $p \leq .0001$, suggesting that 35% of the variance in performance could be attributed to reading and written language abilities. A final regression used the TOAL-3 Writing Vocabulary and the SCALE-L as independent variables. The R^2 value for these variables was .363, $p \leq .0001$, denoting that written language capabilites accounted for over 36% of the variance in OPT reading performance. For sixth graders, comprehension of the meaning of written words as well as knowledge of the mechanics and conventions of written language were important factors, slightly overshadowing oral vocabulary alone as predictive variables.

For both grades, OPT reading performance can be predicted by word knowledge and word usage skills. The ability to manipulate compositional elements (i.e., choosing and ordering words to form sentences, using sentences to express multi-sentence ideas, choosing how to best convey a purpose, writing mechanics) had some predictive power. Reading comprehension testing was also predictive.

Question 6—What language capabilities were derived as principal components of performance on the norm-referenced tests?

Principal Components Analysis (PCA) was performed to determine the number and composition of language capabilities that were operative as children took the norm-referenced tests. PCA reduces the number of variables analyzed and identifies basic components of performance. This statistic determines the fundamental dimensions tapped by larger sets of variables, in this case the multiple normed subtests. PCA was performed separately by grade.

The number of components was determined using the Eigenvalue greater than 1 criteria as well as the logical interpretability of the resulting components (Tabachnick & Fidell, 1996). In fourth grade three factors representing language abilities accounted for 53% of the variance in scores. The first factor was labeled Vocabulary and had high loadings from WORD-R Synonyms, WORD-R Semantic Absurdities, WORD-R Antonyms, WORD-R Multiple Definitions, TORC-3 General Vocabulary, TOWL-3 Vocabulary, TOWL-3 Story Construction, TOLD-I:3 Sentence Combining, TOLD-I:3 Picture Vocabulary, TOLD-I:3 Generals, TOLD-I:3 Grammatic Completion, and TOLD-I:3 Malaprops. The second factor was labeled Written Language and had high loadings from SCALE-L. The third factor was labeled Syntax and had high loadings from TORC-3 Syntactic Similarities and TOWL-3 Sentence Combining.

For sixth grade three factors accounted for 53% of the variance in scores. The first factor was labeled Written Language and consisted of high loadings from SCALE-L, TOAL-3 Reading Vocabulary, TOAL-3 Reading Grammar, TOAL-3 Writing Vocabulary, and TOAL-3 Writing Grammar. The second factor was labeled Vocabulary and consisted of high loadings from WORD-A Brand Names, WORD-A Synonyms, WORD-A Signs of the Times, WORD-A Definitions, and TOAL-3 Listening Vocabulary. This factor also had a high cross loading from TOAL-3 Writing Vocabulary. The third factor was labeled Reading Comprehension and consisted of high loadings from SCALE-R. This factor also had a substantial cross loading from SCALE-L.

Factor scores were computed for each component and these scores served as composite variables in subsequent analyses. Factor scores derived from the above PCAs were entered simultaneously as independent variables in regression analyses, for the purpose of predicting OPT reading and OPT writing scores. In fourth grade, all language ability factors were significant predictors of OPT reading scores (Vocabulary $\_$=.42, $t(125)$=5.42, $p \leq .001$; Written Language $\_$=.30, $t(125)$=3.88, $p \leq .001$; $\_$=.18, Syntax $t(125)$=2.61, p=.01). Together these variables accounted for 46% of the variance in OPT reading scores (total Regression $F(3,125)$=35.27, $p \leq .001$). Only Vocabulary and Written Language predicted unique variance in OPT writing scores (Vocabulary $\_$=.21, $t(125)$=2.21, p=.03; Written Language $\_$=.22, $t(125)$=2.29, p=.02; Syntax $\_$=.07, $t(125)$=0.82, p=.41). Together these variables accounted for 15% of the variance in OPT writing scores (total Regression $F(3,125)$=7.54, $p \leq .001$). Language abilities accounted for substantially more variance in OPT reading than in OPT writing scores ($t(126)$=4.05, $p \leq .001$).

In grade six, all language ability factors predicted significant unique variance in OPT reading scores (Vocabulary $\_$=.22, $t(110)$=2.69, p=.008; Written Language $\_$=.37, $t(110)$=4.47, $p \leq .001$; $\_$=.24, Reading Comprehension $t(110)$=2.82, p=.006). Together these variables accounted for 44% of the variance in OPT reading scores (total Regression $F(3,110)=28.30$, $p \leq .001$). Only Vocabulary abilities were a marginally significant predictor of unique variance in OPT writing scores (Vocabulary $\_=.19$, $t(110)=1.81$, $p=.07$; Written Language $\_=.12$, $t(110)=1.14$, $p=.26$; Reading Comprehension $\_=.10$, $t(110)=0.92$, $p=.36$). However, together these variables accounted for 11% of the variance in OPT writing scores (total Regression $F(3,110)=4.33$, $p=.006$). Again, language abilities accounted for substantially more variance in OPT reading scores than in OPT writing scores ($t(111)=4.12$, $p \leq .001$).

Discussion

Limitations of the Study

This study was limited to African American students in one community. This participant selection factor may limit generalizability of findings to other groups and other communities. Results are pertinent to the OPT and cannot be applied to other state, commercial, or NAEP assessments.

Implications

Findings yield several implications for preparing students for mandated testing and for identifying and serving students who may be at risk for less adequate performance. First, the importance of building students' vocabularies cannot be underestimated. Results demonstrated the importance of vocabulary knowledge to reading comprehension (Johnson & Pearson, 1978; Nagy, 1988). Second, reading scores coincided with the ability to manipulate compositional elements. Knowledge of written language mechanics and conventions consistently correlated with reading scores. Students must learn how the mechanical conventions of language are used to convey meaning.

Third, oral and written language and reading scores were low, placing students at considerable risk for poor performance on high-stakes testing. Other studies have shown concerns relative to test performance for minority and low income students, especially when tests scrutinized verbal abilities (Morris, 2000; NAEP, 1998; NAEP, 1999; NAEP, 2000; Schellenberg, 1998; Winfield, 1990). The present study is significant in its relationship to published documentation which proposed that risk of academic failure can be linked to residential and school segregation (Jackson, 1999). Students sampled may have had a somewhat more elevated risk for school achievement concerns.

Fourth, the interrelationship of language development and academic achievement is apparent. Speech-language pathologists, reading specialists, learning disabilities specialists, and special educators can be called upon to assist regular education teachers in earlier identification of academically-relevant language deficiencies several years before children undergo grade four achievement testing.

Conclusions

The interrelationship of measures of language development and academic achievement has been demonstrated. Consistencies in performance were related to the underlying element of vocabulary. Future research on the relationship between language development and academic achievement is needed.

The USDOE (2001) suggests that innovations in high-stakes testing should include developing assessments that can yield better information about areas of school achievement that students may be struggling with and that can diagnose learners' specific problems. Perhaps this will result in the creation of instruments that are sensitive to how language learning impacts academic achievement.

References

Balow, I. H., Farr, R. C., & Hogan, T. P. (1992). *Metropolitan Achievement Test.* San Antonio, TX: Harcourt Brace Educational Measurement.

Barkley, R. (2001). The OEA [Ohio Education Association] on testing. *Ohio Schools, 79,* 12.

Bobbett, G. C. (1993, April). *The impact of community/school characteristics on student outcomes: An analysis of report cards on schools.* Paper presented at the annual meeting of the American Educational Research Association, Atlanta, GA.

Brown, V. L., Hammill, D. D., & Wiederholt, J. L. (1995). *Test of Reading Comprehension (TORC-3).* Austin, TX: Pro-ed.

Butler, K. (1999). From oracy to literacy: Changing clinical perceptions. *Topics in Language Disorders, 20*(1), 14-32.

Commission on Behavioral and Social Sciences and Education. (1998). *Equivalency and Linkage of Educational Tests Interim Report.* Washington, DC: National Academy Press. Retrieved August 5, 2001, from http://books.nap.edu/books/N1000906html/32.html

CTB/McGraw-Hill. (1992). *California Achievement Test.* Monterey, CA: CTB/McGraw-Hill.

Denoyer, R., & White, M. (1992). *Proficiency testing and the income gap.* (ERIC Document Reproduction Service No. ED35064)

Doherty, V. W., & Roid, G. H. (1992). *Scaled Curriculum Achievement Levels Test (SCALE).* Los Angeles, CA: Western Psychological Services.

Falk-Ross, F. C. (2002). *Classroom-based language and literacy intervention: A program and case study approach.* Boston: Allyn & Bacon/Longman.

Gallagher, M. P. (1993, April). *Proficiency testing and poverty: Looking within a large urban district.* Paper presented at the Annual Meeting of the American Educational Research Association, Atlanta, GA.

Glaser, R. (1994). Criterion-referenced tests: Part II. Unfinished business. *Educational Measurement: Issues and Practice, 13*(4), 27-30.

Hammill, D. D., Brown, V. L., Larsen, S. C., & Wiederholt, J. L. (1994). *Test of Adolescent and Adult Language (TOAL-3).* Austin, TX: Pro-ed.

Hammill, D. D., & Larsen, S. C. (1996). *Test of Written Language (TOWL-3)*. Austin, TX: Pro-ed.

Hammill, D. D., & Newcomer, P. L. (1997). *Test of Language Development-Intermediate (TOLD-I:3)*. Austin, TX: Pro-ed.

Hoover, H. D., Hieronymus, A. N., Frisbie, D. A., & Dunbar, S. B. (1996). *Iowa Test of Basic Skills*. Itasca, IL: Riverside Publishing.

Huisingh, R., Barrett, M., Zachman, L., Blagden, C., & Orman, J. (1990). *The WORD-R: A test of expressive vocabulary and semantics*. East Moline, IL: Linguisystems, Inc.

Hull, M., & Tache, D. (1993). *Are Iowa Test of Basic Skills stanines predictors of success on Ohio's Ninth Grade Proficiency Test?* (ERIC Document Reproduction Service No. ED35064)

International Reading Association (IRA). (1999). High stakes assessments in reading. *The Reading Teacher, 53*(3), 257-263.

Jackson, J. F. (1999). What are the real risk factors for African American children? *Phi Delta Kappan, 81*(4), 308-312.

Johnson, D., & Pearson, P. D. (1978). *Teaching reading vocabulary*. New York: Holt, Rinehart & Winston.

Kohn, A. (2000). *The case against standardized testing*. Portsmouth, NH: Heinemann.

Ladson-Billings, G. (1994). *The dreamkeepers*. San Francisco: Jossey-Bass Publishers.

Lanese, J. F. (1992, April). *Statewide proficiency testing: Establishing standards or barriers?* Paper presented at the Annual Meeting of the American Educational Research Association, San Francisco, CA.

Manning, M. L., Lucking, R., & MacDonald, R. H. (1995). What works in urban middle schools. *Childhood Education, 71*(4), 221-224.

McGee, G. W. (1997, March). *What state tests test*. Paper presented at the Annual Meeting of the American Educational Research Association, Chicago, IL.

Meisels, S. (1989). *Testing, tracking, and retaining young children: An analysis of research and social policy*. Washington, DC: National Center for Education Statistics.

Morris, D. R. (2000). *Assessing the implementation of high stakes reform: Aggregate relationships between retention rates and test results*. Paper presented at the Annual Meeting of the American Educational Research Association, New Orleans, LA.

Nagy, W. E. (1988). *Vocabulary instruction and reading comprehension (Tech. Rep. No. 431)*. Champaign, IL: University of Illinois, Center for the Study of Reading.

National Assessment of Educational Progress (NAEP). (1998). *Long-term trends in student reading performance*. Retrieved August 5, 2001, from http://nces.ed.gov/pubsearch

National Assessment of Educational Progress (NAEP). (1999). *NAEP 1998 reading report card for the nation and the states*. Retrieved August 5, 2001, from http://nces.ed.gov/pubsearch

National Assessment of Educational Progress (NAEP). (2000). *The NAEP guide*. Retrieved August 5, 2001, from http://nces.ed.gov/pubsearch

National Center on Educational Outcomes (NCEO). (2001). *Special topic areas*. Retrieved August 5, 2001, from http://www.coled.umn.edu/nceo

National Education Goals Panel (NEGP). (1994). *Goals 2000 The National Education Goals Report: Building a nation of learners 1994*. Washington, DC: Author.

National Educational Research Policy and Priorities Board. (1999). *Investing in learn-*

ing: A policy statement on research in education. Washington, DC: US Department of Education.

Noel, A. W. (1994). *Predictors of success on Ohio's Ninth Grade Proficiency Test.* (ERIC Document Reproduction Service No. ED392803)

Ohio Department of Education. (1995). *Fourth grade proficiency tests: Information guide.* Columbus, OH: Author.

Ohio Department of Education. (1998). *Staff profile.* Retrieved August 12, 2003, from http://www.ode.state.oh.us/htbinstaff_Profile.com?SELECTION=IRN&irn =045005+Warrensville+Heights+City+SD+%28Cuyahoga%29&county=01+Adams &ctytot=01+Adams&vepd=001+Apollo+JVSD+VEPD&years=1998

Ohio Department of Education. (2000). *State of Ohio 2000 school district report card.* Retrieved August 6, 2001, from http://www.ode.state.oh.us

Ohio Statehouse Newsletter. (2000, May). Columbus, OH: Author.

Ohio Student Testing Requirements. (1991). Columbus, OH: Ohio State Legislative Office of Education Oversight.

Popham, W. (1994). The instructional consequences of criterion-referenced clarity. *Educational Measurement: Issues and Practice, 13,* 15-18, 30.

Popham, W. (1999). Why standardized tests don't measure educational quality. *Educational Leadership, 56*(6), 8-15.

Pottle, P. (2001). Coping with a process-oriented mandate. *Primary Voices K-6, 9*(3), 32-37.

Raivetz, M. J. (1992). Can school districts survive the politics of state testing initiatives. *NASSP Bulletin, 76*(545), 57-65.

Robinson, M. A., & Moore, M. H. (1992, April). *State proficiency tests and standardized tests.* Paper presented at the Annual Meeting of the American Educational Research Association, San Francisco.

Roderick, M. (1995). *Grade retention and school dropout: Policy debate and research questions.* Phi Delta Kappa Center for Evaluation, Development, and Research, Research Bulletin No. 15. Retrieved June 16, 2001, from http://www.pdkintl.org/ edres/resbul15.htm

Schellenberg, S. J. (1998, April). *Does it matter where poor kids live? A look at concentrated poverty and achievement.* Paper presented at the Annual Meeting of the American Educational Research Association, San Diego, CA.

Snodgrass, D. G., & Salzman, J. A. (1998). *Graphical representations of data: Iowa Tests of Basic Skills, Ohio Sixth Grade Proficiency Tests, and SB 55.* Paper presented at the Mid-Western Educational Research Association Annual Conference, Chicago.

Snow, C. E., Burns, S., & Griffin, P. (1998). *Preventing reading difficulties in young children.* Washington, DC: National Academy Press.

SPSS Base 10.0 Applications Guide. (1999). Chicago: SPSS, Inc.

Stroud, R. E. (1995). *Correlations between the Metropolitan Achievement Tests, Seventh Edition, and the Ohio Ninth-Grade Proficiency Tests.* (ERIC Document Reproduction Service No. ED394992)

Tabachnick, B. G., & Fidell, L. S. (1996). *Using multivariate statistics* (3rd ed.). New York: HarperCollins.

U.S. Census Bureau. (1990). *U.S. Census Data.* Database C90STF1A. Retrieved June 16, 2001, from www.venus.census.gov

U.S. Census Bureau. (2000). *American FactFinder.* Retrieved June 16, 2001, from http:/ /factfinder.census.gov

United States Department of Education (DOE). (2001). *Back to school, moving forward.*

Retrieved December 5, 2002, from http://www.ed.gov/inits/backtoschool/index.html

United States Department of Education (DOE). (2002). *No child left behind.* Retrieved December 5, 2002, from http://www.NoChildLeftBehind.gov/

Urdan, T., & Davis, H. (1998). *Differences by race and grade level in motivation for taking standardized achievement tests.* Paper presented at the Bi-annual Meeting of the Society for Research on Adolescence, San Diego, CA.

Westbury, M. (1994). The effect of elementary grade retention on subsequent school achievement and ability. *Canadian Journal of Education, 19*(3), 241-250.

Winfield, L. F. (1990). School competency testing reforms and student achievement: Exploring a national perspective. *Educational Evaluation and Policy Analysis, 12*(2), 157-173.

Zachman, L., Huisingh, R., Barrett, M., Orman, J., & Blagden, C. (1989). *The WORD-Adolescent Test (WORD-A): A test of expressive vocabulary and semantics.* East Moline, IL: Linguisystems, Inc.

Acknowledgments

This research was supported by a New Faculty Research Award, NF-001, Cleveland State University.

The author thanks Anna Lisa Lincoln, statistician.

CULTURAL MEMOIR AND MULTIPLE LITERACIES: YOU AND I "FRONT AND CENTER"

Denise H. Stuart

The University of Akron

Abstract

Preservice teachers taking a course, Integrated Language Arts and Media, *developed their own cultural memoirs using a multiple literacies approach with a variety of print and non-print media. Students integrated the language arts as they read and wrote about, discussed and viewed artifacts, photos, documents, and other self-selected media that related to their culture. Process and product of the project are described including students' reflective writing that revealed what they learned about themselves, their own culture, and that of their peers through participation in the cultural memoir project. They learned about culturally responsive teaching as they considered the influence of culture in teaching and learning in the reading and language arts classroom.*

Introduction

Both a challenge and an opportunity continue for preservice teachers and teacher educators today as they prepare for teaching in the 21st century. They may be working with diverse groups of students, often differing from their own culture. Moreover, they will be using a variety of media, print, and non-print to develop content. Teacher educators are called upon to prepare preservice teachers to develop what Ladson-Billings (1995) and Delpit (1995) describe as culturally responsive teaching that draws on students' cultural strengths for learning. As a teacher educator I wondered how culture could be addressed in my classes. How could I model approaches useful for teaching Reading and Language Arts? How could I use a variety of media to explore culture? What would be learned by exploring students' cultural stories through memoir work and through use of a multiple literacies approach? I wondered if my preservice teachers were aware of the influence of their own culture in teaching and learning. Could this be effective in more deeply understanding the culture of themselves and others and become an approach useful in learning about the culture of their own students? These are the issues that guided the development of the cultural memoir project reported here.

Culturally Responsive Teaching

Our schools are increasingly diverse in student population yet less so in teacher population. Teacher educators need to address related issues in teacher preparation programs. The National Center for Educational Statistics (2002) found that 38.8% of students in America's public school classrooms in 2000-2001 were culturally diverse children. In six states (California, Hawaii, Louisiana, Mississippi, New Mexico, and Texas) and the District of Columbia, 50% or more of students were non-white. Yet as Nieto (2000) notes the "nation's teachers have become more monolithic, monocultural and monolingual" (p. 181). This is characteristic of the preservice teachers with whom I work who are primarily Caucasian, middle-class females. This trend away from diversity of teachers continues. The National Education Association (as cited in Nieto, 2000) reports that in 1971, 88% of teachers were Caucasion, 8.7% African-American and 3.6% other; while in 1996, 96.7 % were Caucasion, 7.3% African-American and 2% other.

The Standards for Teacher Education as set forth by The National Council for the Accreditation of Teacher Education (2002) require that programs address diversity in their curriculum, instruction, and fieldwork. This suggests that all courses need to be infused with meaningful content that addresses diversity. We need to empower the seemingly monolithic population of preservice teachers to know approaches that engage in culturally responsive teaching so they can best draw on the cultural strengths of the diversity of their students. Nieto (2000) concludes that few substantive efforts have been made toward these goals and asserts that issues of diversity, particularly equity, be placed "front and center" (p. 180) in teacher education.

Multiple Literacies

I argue that a multiple literacies approach expands ways of learning and can facilitate developing what Delpit (1995) describes as "cultural lenses" necessary for understanding culture and experience. How students use literacy, that is, construct meaning, involves interpretive and communicative processes. Multiple literacies create an "intersection among school, community and personal literacy" (Gallego & Hollingsworth, 1992, p. 207). This results in an environment where students not only engage in ways of interpreting and communicating in traditional school literacy, but where community literacy includes traditions of culture and personal literacy involves ways of knowing about one's self. This approach taps into cultural "funds of knowledge" (Moll, Amanti, Neff, & Gonzalez, 1992) for use in the classroom. These "historically accumulated and culturally developed bodies of knowledge and skills" (Moll et al., 1992, p. 133) become cultural and cognitive resources for understanding students in a more holistic way.

The case for multiple literacies has been evolving. Sheridan (2000) declares that "human literacies are multiple and varied, interdependent and equivalent, related and necessary. No single system for representing thought is powerful enough to explain all of our thoughts. Why constrain the human brain to a limited range of literacies?" (¶. 5). Kellner (1998) emphasizes that "we need multiple literacies for a multicultural society. We need to develop new literacies to meet the challenge of the new technologies" (p. 103). Kellner points to media literacy as an important area to learn about including print media of books, newspapers, and magazines and non-print media of film, photography, music, and technology as it provides critical cultural information. I perceived artifacts and objects to be valuable resources for learning, as well as for telling cultural stories and constructing memoirs.

In my effort to develop strategies to raise issues of culture and engage students in using multiple literacies, I learned about several projects. Allen and Labbo (2001) described how "photographs along with written memoirs might make [their] students' cultures visible" (p .42) and concluded cultural memoir work to be strategic in culturally engaged teaching. Bussert-Webb's (2001) project developed visual story through artwork that represented the values and interests of urban middle school students and their families. In their work with middle school Latina students, Daisey and Jose-Kampfer (2002) developed biographical storytelling through art, poetry, and reflective writing. They found "the power of story to make a difference in Latinos' thinking" (p. 584), particularly evident in the drawings of Latinas at work where, for example, images produced after storytelling shifted from 72% to 13 % factory/domestic/migrant worker and from 8% to 70% of professional/technical worker. Short and Pierce (1995) remind us of the need to use multiple literacies such as oral tradition, music, and visual image to be inclusive of the many ways of knowing among families.

I decided to use multi-media, a variety of print and non-print material, for my students to explore their own "funds of knowledge" (Moll et al., 1992), learn about their own culture and that of their peers. They developed multiple literacies (Kellner, 1998) as they took a critical look at the cultural material they shared through personal memoir work while they engaged in the language arts: reading, writing, listening, discussing, viewing, and creating visuals. They drew on multiple sources to construct memoirs and make personal, cultural connections. This work is described below.

The Cultural Memoir Project
Overview of the Project

Preservice teachers in my middle years education course, *Integrated Language Arts and Media,* engaged in thoughtful development of their own cultural memoirs. These undergraduate students were primarily juniors and seniors; several were non-traditional, returning to the University after pursuing other careers or raising children. While the class was composed primarily of Caucasian females, there were three African-American women and five Caucasian men.

My goal for the cultural memoir project was to engage students in exploring their own culture and its influence in their lives. Working with a variety of print and non-print media that students brought to class weekly, we learned to unpack the stories behind the materials through discussion and questioning. We developed critical literacy learning. For example, we explored why a picture was taken or what the symbols on the object represented or what the significance of the book was in family and cultural history. Students constructed meaning of culture, their own and that of their peers, through small and whole group discussion, individual writing, and reflection. The project evolved over the semester and, like a journey, had a beginning where we explored "culture," a middle where we interpreted and produced materials, and an end where we synthesized the experience and celebrated our journey. Lastly, students considered how they might apply this approach to their own teaching and to understanding the culture of their future students. I reviewed my students' products and reflective writing in an effort to understand what they gained from the project.

Several elements were integral to developing this cultural memoir project as outlined in Table 1. Early in the semester we brainstormed "culture," activating prior knowledge and offering me a sense of students' perceptions. What emerged were broad interpretations of the concept relating to ethnicity, religion, family, work choices, lifestyles, and life situations. For example, we talked about the culture of being a twin or the culture of being adopted, as well as the culture of Irish heritage or of the African-American experience. Students then wrote their first reflective work describing themselves in relation to culture. This was collected, then returned and revisited toward the end of the project. I wanted the project to emerge over time, throughout the semester, in order to develop depth of thought and reflection. Each week students selected an item to bring to class that they felt represented themselves and their culture.

Table 1. Elements of the Project Development

Element	Description
Brainstorming	Broad interpretations of "culture" for students to make personal connections
Evolving over time	Weekly assignments over the course of the semester to allow for depth of thought
Self-selecting	Personal choice of focused materials to support ownership of the process
Peer Sharing	In-class, small and large group sharing with a responsive and inquisitive audience
Writing	Personal, reflective writing to describe and consider relevance of memoir items
Synthesizing	Putting it altogether in visual display and letter writing for final presentation

To frame our thinking about our work with media, we took a critical look at photography and poetry. We read Rita Dove's (1991) poem "Fifth Grade Autobiography" and Ted Kooser's (1980) "An Old Photograph" and discussed the layers of story a photo can offer. We considered what to ask about a photo to further learn about the setting, circumstances, and people in the photograph. What happened before and after the photo was taken? Who took it? Why was it taken? What does it represent? What has occurred since it was taken? As a community of learners, students then worked in small groups, shared photos they selected to bring to class, elaborated on their stories, and responded to peers' questions. This peer share added to the ideas for what would be the next step in the process: for each student to write about his or her photograph. Critical consideration of the meaning of a variety of material continued throughout the project, as did the sequence of self-selection, peer share, and reflective and descriptive writing.

Students produced a variety of writing and visuals as part of their journey. Writing was both formal and informal as students developed free writes, poems, essays, letters, lists, and word collages. They created visual arrays with shape poems and collages. Synthesizing products took form in presentations as a tri-fold poster, electronic slide show, or collection of materials. As part of the synthesizing process, students recalled their cultural memoir journey and its significance to them through a final personal letter to someone of their choice. Lastly, students considered their future role as teacher, discussed and wrote about culturally responsive teaching and the usefulness of the cultural memoir project in their curriculum.

Learning from Multiple Sources

We utilized sources of information for our cultural stories that included photographs, artifacts, documents, videos, audiotapes, newspaper, and other media items as described in Table 2. These related to family traditions, heritage, celebrations, and events, as well as personal accomplishments and activities, travel, and relationships with loved ones. My look at students' reflective writing revealed issues, topics, and patterns of what they were learning using the various media shared. One student told of questioning the value of a photograph as a source of information. "As I reminisce back to the first assignment we were given, I was totally baffled as how viewing a picture would help me to determine my culture. But as the assignment was explained in further detail, my mental questions were answered. I realized that photographs do say more than words." Another remarked, "But wait! Is this type of wedding traditional to everyone or just to our family? As I considered my question, I realized that I was beginning to depict my culture, even if it was this very minute concept."

Table 2. Sources for Learning about Self and Culture

Source	Example
Photographs	Vacations, events, family at home, special settings, children, and self at work and play
Artifacts	Jewelry, bibles, household items, and specialty items (music boxes, whistles, and radio tubes)
Documents	Diplomas, awards, birth certificates, passports, deeds, prayers, licenses, and maps
Media	Videotapes, audiotapes, newspaper articles, magazines of family events, accomplishments, and personal achievements
Literature	Known and new poems, short stories, religious passages, books, traditional tales, and songs connecting to family and ethnicity
Internet	Geographic websites, historical information, traditions, migration, and ethnic–traditional foods and celebrations

Some students realized there could be a powerful story behind the seemingly simplest of objects or artifacts. Terry brought in a wooden hanger as his artifact. We were all puzzled and the questions started to flow, as did the story. Terry's grandfather was a tailor in Poland who came to America through Ellis Island. It was his desire to assimilate into the American culture and thus when he settled into his Midwest community he changed his name to Smith. Terry's father was raised as a Smith and Terry was raised as a Smith. As Terry was to marry and start a chapter of his own in the family history, he explored his roots and found the one artifact that was evidence of his grandfather's origin—a wooden coat hanger his grandfather brought with him from Poland with his original name burned into the wood. Terry married, had his own children, decided to legally reclaim his name, and now raises his two daughters as great-grandchildren of the tailor from Poland. All of this from a wooden coat hanger!

Some students began to see values represented by artifacts. One connected a favorite object with values she realized came from her family: "You instilled in me a work ethic for which has carried over to me earning a college scholarship, which ultimately led me to earn this NCAA ring." Another was surprised about artifacts concluding: "One thing that really dawned on me throughout the course of this semester is how much a little piece of paper or a coin kept in my wallet can mean."

Many documents brought to class represented special moments and achievements, family events, memberships, travel, and religion. Some students specifically connected to ethnic heritages. One stated, "What better document than the Irish blessing, which we say often in our house. Being Catholic and religious, this blessing is special to me." They realized how much could be learned from a document. In her final letter to her grandfather one student wrote:

> My birth certificate has masses of information about our family. This particular document has many stories about where you lived, where you have gone, how old you were, and when you had my dad. And they connected their present experiences with family traditions, values and history.

Comments included:

> My program plan was a huge deal when I finally got it. It symbolized a dream of teaching, accomplishment and victory. My great-grandmother is the only other teacher in my family and she taught until she was in her late 80's. My program plan symbolized a continuing family tradition and a dream.

Media shared came in the form of newspaper articles, videotapes, and audiotapes. *Sister to Sister* was the magazine an African-American student shared telling of the importance of unity among African-American women in light of historical separations in slavery. Another student celebrated an ethnic, and deeply personal media from her deceased father and stated:

> …it was a tape of Cajun music. Not only did it remind me of how much I loved music but why I loved music, my father. The writing helped me to realize that music is a huge part of my life and has been since I was very young. My father used to play the guitar for me.

She concluded with a brief descriptive poem:

> 120 minutes the whole thing
> A life time really
> The voice, the laugh, the smile, the song
> The memory
> A dad's voice survives his death

Genres of literature shared varied. One student brought in a popular novel his sister suggested he read to learn about life in Ireland and immigration to the United States. While this student preferred to watch the film version of the novel, he became curious about the dialect used in the novel and read the entire work. Poems found in collections and those passed down in families including a few written by ancestors were shared and read aloud in class. A close look at traditional German folktales by one student sparked discussion that compared these to commercial versions of *Cinderella* and *Snow White*. This student wondered if her love of theater was related to this rich heritage of literature and concluded, "I want to know that I have more of the German culture in me than just my love for *Beauty and the Beast!*"

Internet searches were structured to challenge students to find something they did not know about their culture. Many went to sites for ethnic traditions and geographic information. One student went to an Ellis Island website (Morse, 2002) and was fascinated with what could be found.

> All I had to do was type in my Grandfather's last and first name and wait for matches . . . it gave me a wealth of information, date of arrival, age, marital status, port of departure and what I thought was the coolest bit of information, the name of the actual ship he was on and a picture of the ship!

Creating Multiple Products

Writing and creating visuals added to the development of cultural memoir as outlined in Table 3. Some were formative: draft writing and brainstorming; others were summative: collages, presentations, and final letters. A student tells of the value of these:

> By creating a word collage, a shape poem, and an 'I Am' poem, I found new ways to represent myself symbolically and in words. I was very interested in capturing the essence of who I have become, of what makes me special and unique.

Table 3. Products Created about Self and Culture

Product	Description
Word Collages	Self selected, brainstormed words in 5 categories; added drawings, graphics, and photos
"I Am" Poems	Lyrical, free form, list poems about roles, goals, daily activities, and ethnicity
Second Thought Writing	Affirming, discovering, and connecting to culture and early draft writing
Personal Letter	Written to audience of choice and summarizing cultural memoir journey
Visual Presentation	Tri-fold displays, trunks and suitcases, and electronic slide shows

Students played with language as they created word collages. Students quickly jotted down series of words on post-it notes in categories and worked at home to create a collage with this collection, arranging words and concepts, and illustrating connections. They added visuals, photographs, drawings, and graphics. Several students created digital versions using graphic organizing software to map their words and import visuals. One student reflected on traditions revealed through the collage as she reached back to her ancestors:

> We had to think of five sets of five words that described our family, our heritage, our memories, us and any five words of our choosing. Many of my words were from you [grandma]. I shared . . . Christmas Eve dinner at your house, the Easter bread that you taught me to make, canola, and patelli.

Her words reappeared in her "I Am" poem.

I am a Heinz 57:

Italian

German

English

Scottish

Native American Sioux

I am Catholic:

Midnight Mass on Christmas Eve

Confession

Communion

Confirmation

Marriage

The Nicene Creed

I am female:
A daughter
A sister
A wife
A mother
A student
An athlete
I am a product of tradition:
Spaghetti and Meatballs every Sunday
Christmas Eve dinner at my Grandmother's house
Easter Bread
Pattelli
Canoli
Pizzelli

Several examples of "I Am" poems (Allen & Labbo, 2001) were read aloud in class toward the end of the project development; then students created their own as part of the process to clarify culture and identity. These came in many forms but all connected to culture personally and, as this second example shows, to history, literature, and a variety of experiences.

I am my culture, images of Africa, memories of slavery,
Civil Rights struggle with Dr. King
I am my people's dream
I am Maya Angelou, "Phenomenal Woman,"
with my mother's reflection, my grandmother's smile.
I am every woman's determined spirit.
I am weak and strong, self-sufficient and liberated,
our struggle has not ended it is growing steadily.
I am five feet-one inches tall,
my heart speaking the loudest of all.
I am the sister of two brothers.
I am a dreamer and a learner,
Composed in all I am, myself.

Revisiting draft writing we had developed early in the semester where students described their "culture," they created second thought writing (Allen & Labbo, 2001). These compositions reflected their increasing awareness of self and culture. One student commented:

As I wrote out the '2nd Thoughts' paper, I realized that I have grown over the semester. I see culture in broader spectrum. It is not just in a few places and does not just constitute a few aspects; it is everywhere and a part of everything. Thank you for giving me the opportunity to find myself this semester.

Synthesizing the journey took form in both a visual compilation and a personal letter. While most decided to create compilations as trifold displays, a few collected and displayed material and story in trunks, hatboxes, and suitcases. Several students created electronic slide presentations that integrated visuals, music, and writing. These were presented during a class celebration and in the spirit of the project, included food students brought that connected to their "cultural story."

Nearly half of the students chose to write their final letters to grandparents, while a fifth wrote to children born and yet to be born. Several wrote to siblings or parents, and a few wrote to a friend or to me, their professor. The content recounted the journey over the semester and importantly what it meant to them personally. One told how "there have been many stories that I have written about dealing with our ancestors during this journey. From this journey I have become more informed about our culture and what it means to be Irish." While another described, "Throughout this journey I have had an uplifting of feelings about our family history." And another acknowledged to her parents,

> The other thing that I believe to be a huge part of my culture is my ethnicity. You have always been so proud of being Lebanese and this has rubbed off on me. I take great pride in what I am and the history of our family. Our traditions are something that I will always carry on.

Sarah sums it up below:

> Dear Grandma: Hi! It's [Sarah]. I haven't spoken with you in such a long time. I miss talking with you. I am writing to tell you about a journey I went on recently. It was a cultural memoir journey. It was fascinating! I hope you enjoy hearing about my journey as much as I enjoyed taking it. Each part of the journey involved a memory.

What Was Learned

Students told how they learned about themselves as result of the cultural memoir project. One student revealed:

> I have learned so much about myself from doing that project. Since I am older than most of my classmates, I approached the project from a different perspective. I used it as an opportunity to look back at my family and its' culture while examining myself because of all the changes that I have recently made in my life.

In contrast, a younger, more traditional student wrote the following reflection. Before I did this project I didn't really know what my nationality was. When I asked my parents they seemed really happy to talk about it, it was almost like they had been waiting for me to ask.

One young man compared himself to others:

During this assignment I have considered who I am and what my culture means to me. At times it was very hard, as it did not appear that I was as 'cultured' as others were in my class. Our family has never really celebrated our German and Irish heritage or taken spirituality very seriously. Many in my group would talk about religious, ethnic, or life-altering experiences that have occurred during their life span. I did not share many of these experiences and would sometimes feel left out. But then I realize the type of 'sports culture' that exists in our family and I realize how lucky that I am to have experienced the many great sporting events over the span of my lifetime.

Another student began her journey declaring that she had little "culture" and was a "Heinz 57" with no particular influences. Her dissonance about this took her down many paths and in the end she narrowed the "57" to five cultures that were reflected by flags in her final display. Her final letter told of this and revealed its importance in sharing this new perspective with her three growing children.

Students appreciated and learned about their families and what was part of their heritage. One noted:

This memoir made me remember and appreciate the values that my mother has instilled in me. The concept that I am taking away from this memoir is that, my ancestors dealt with the cruelties of slavery and immense discrimination but they worked over their shortcomings and so can I.

In her final letter to her yet to be born child another student wrote, "Did you know that Grandma Rosie's father was a Native American? Mom's father was an actual blacksmith?"

They learned about culture, expanding on their initial brainstorming about what it is generally and how it influences them. One admitted, "I came to realize that culture is not just the past, but also the present, what is happening in my life now. I also came to realize that culture is all around me." Another commented on ways of learning about culture. "The record of our family and many African Americans has not been well documented. The next best thing is oral history and objects." Other realizations occurred as one student remarked:

I thought from the beginning that our family was not very cultural. I guess that just depends on how you define the word. To me culture meant ethnicity, very old things and traditions passed down through time. But culture can also be your family's way of life. Behaviors, morals and beliefs are all included in my culture. That is where I took my journey.

Conclusions

Experiences such as the cultural memoir project place diversity front and center (Nieto, 2000). This is one approach to the important work Nieto urges teacher-educators to do. Students developed the project with depth as they learned about themselves, about others and the power of culture. A journey presupposes that the traveler will change along the way (Nieto, 2000) and thus the cultural memoir project has potential to become a cultural journey. It is imperative that teacher educators create a forum to explore these important issues and perspectives. Reflection and discussion were paramount to making connections and developing the "why and what else" that moves one toward new knowledge, new understanding. And the use of multiple literacies, print and non-print media, facilitated broader access to perspectives and experiences, created more vehicles for constructing meaning and story of culture.

Developing culturally engaged teaching (Allen & Labbo, 2001) and multiple literacies (Kellner, 1998) will empower teachers to continue their work in the 21st century. Preservice teachers can learn to draw on cultural "funds of knowledge" (Moll et al., 1992) as resources in creating supportive classroom environments for the diverse student populations they may have the opportunity to teach. The preservice teachers in my course who participated in the cultural memoir project considered it as one approach to raising issues of diversity and culture in their classrooms, or as Nieto (2000) describes, placing these issues "front and center," thus creating the potential for meaningful relationships with students. One preservice student remarked, "Interestingly enough, when people research their roots, I think they find they have more in common than they would have believed." And lastly, one nontraditional student summarized the ideas of culturally responsive teaching consistent with Delpit's (1995) work. This student captured and reflected the goals of this cultural memoir project in connecting her experience to teaching by stating:

> There are so many ways to utilize a student's culture in activities that meet learning needs. By looking at the curriculum through a "cultural lens" I can structure projects, activities and lessons that tap into a student's own cultural differences. . . . Now that my own cultural lens has been widened and adjusted, my teaching can only improve if I let it.

References

Allen, J., & Labbo, L. (2001). Giving it a second thought: Making culturally engaged teaching culturally engaging. *Language Arts, 79,* 40-52.

Bussert-Webb, K. (2001). I won't tell you about myself, but I will draw my story. *Language Arts, 78,* 511-519.

Daisey, P., & Jose-Kampfner, C. (2002). The power of story to expand possible selves for Lantina middle school students. *Journal of Adolescent & Adult Literacy, 45,* 578-587.

Delpit, L. (1995). *Other people's children.* New York: The New Press.

Dove, R. (1991). Fifth grade autobiography. In *Grace notes: Poems* (p. 8). New York: Norton Roth Publishing Company.

Gallego, M., & Hollingworth, S. (1992). Research directions: Multiple literacies: Teacher's evolving perceptions. *Language Arts, 69,* 206-213.

Kellner, D. (1998). Multiple literacies and critical pedagogy in a multicultural society. *Educational Theory, 48,* 103-122.

Kooser, T. (1980). An old photograph. In *Sure signs: New and selected poems* (p. 5). Pittsburgh, PA: University of Pittsburgh Press.

Ladson-Billings, G. (1995). Multicultural teacher education: Research, practice and policy. In J. Banks & C. Banks (Eds.), *Handbook of research in multicultural education* (pp.747-759). New York: Macmillan.

Moll, L., Amanti, D., Neff, D., & Gonzalez, N. (1992). Funds of knowledge for teaching. *Theory into Practice, 32,* 132-141.

Morse, S. P. (2002). *Searching the Ellis Island database in one step.* Retrieved November 20, 2002, from http://www.jewishgen.org/databases/EIDB/ellis.html

National Center for Educational Statistics. (2002). *State nonfiscal survey of public elementary/secondary education, 2000–01.* Retrieved November 22, 2002, from http://nces.ed.gov/pubs2002/snf_report/

National Council for Accreditation of Teacher Education (2002). *Professional standards for the accreditation of schools, colleges, and departments of education.* Washington DC.: National Council for the Accreditation of Teacher Education.

Nieto, S. (2000). Placing equity front and center: Some thoughts on transforming teacher education for a new century. *Journal of Teacher Education, 51,* 180-187.

Sheridan, S. R. (2000). A theory of multiple literacies. *Multiple literacies: Drawing/writing,* 1-3. Retrieved January 13, 2003, from http://www.drawingwriting.com/multlit.html

Short, K., & Pierce, K. (1995). Exploring the world through multiple literacies. *The Reading Teacher, 48,* 600-608.

FAMILY LITERACY, 1983-PRESENT

Laurie Elish-Piper

Northern Illinois University

Abstract

This paper reviews research, theory, and practice related to family literacy from 1983 to the present. It examines how families contribute to children's literacy development by reviewing studies of home and community contexts and family characteristics that influence education in diverse families. Studies of family storybook reading and family literacy intervention programs are also reviewed. Important conclusions from this review include: (a) all families contribute to children's literacy development in unique ways that may be influenced by but are not dictated by SES; (b) mismatches between home and school literacy are problematic for learners; (c) storybook reading supports children's literacy development but is more common in middle-income than low-income homes; and (d) family literacy programs are increasing in popularity, and those that operate from a strengths' perspective offer promise for diverse families. The paper concludes with a brief discussion of the future of family literacy in the current political climate.

Background and Definition

Family literacy is a relatively new concept in the field of education. Denny Taylor's 1983 book, *Family Literacy: Young Children Learning to Read and Write,* and Shirley Brice Heath's 1983 book, *Ways with Words,* were the first two publications that brought the concept of family literacy into the forefront of education. An ERIC search for the years prior to 1981 results in no entries; the earliest entry appears in 1982; and in the year 1991 there were 435 entries for that year alone. By 2002, a simple ERIC search resulted in 1,020 entries containing the key word "family literacy." Clearly the interest in family literacy has grown since the early 1980s to the present.

According to the International Reading Association, family literacy is a complex concept; therefore, they offer the following multidimensional definition of family literacy:

1. Family literacy encompasses the ways parents, children, and extended family members use literacy at home and in their community.

2. Family literacy occurs naturally during the routines of daily living and helps adults and children "get things done."

3. Examples of family literacy could include using drawing or writing to share ideas, composing notes or letters to communicate messages; keeping records; making lists; reading and following directions; or sharing stories and ideas through conversation, reading, and writing.

4. Family literacy may be initiated purposefully by a parent, or it may occur spontaneously as parents and children go about the business of their daily lives.

5. Family literacy activities may also reflect the ethnic, racial, or cultural heritage of the families involved.

6. Family literacy activities may be initiated by outside institutions or agencies. These activities are often intended to support the acquisition and development of school-like literacy behaviors of parents, children, and families.

7. Family literacy activities initiated by outside agencies may include family storybook reading, completing homework assignments, or writing essays or reports (Morrow, Paratore, & Tracey, 1994).

The definition and concept of family literacy have continued to evolve over the years as researchers and practitioners have come to realize that "no single narrow definition of family literacy can do justice to the richness and complexity of families, and the multiple literacies, including often unrecognized local literacies that are part of their everyday lives" (Taylor, 1997, p. 4). While the lack of a unified definition of family literacy has been problematic for researchers and theorists, "the lack of a clear definition has not, however, stopped family literacy programs from emerging all over the world" (DeBruin-Parecki & Krol-Sinclair, 2003, p. 2).

How Do Families Contribute to Children's Literacy Development?

Families contribute to children's literacy development in many meaningful ways. Nickse, Speicher, and Buchek (1988) identified four main ways parents and other family members influence their children's literacy development and achievement: (a) providing a positive home environment that supports literate behaviors, (b) sharing literacy activities with children, (c) providing literate role models, and (d) nurturing and encouraging positive attitudes and goals about education.

During the past two decades, research has been conducted to examine family influence on children's literacy development. Such research has focused on the following contexts: (a) research in homes and communities, (b) family characteristics related to education, (c) storybook reading, and (d) intervention programs in family literacy. Each of these areas is discussed in the remainder of this paper.

Studies of Literacy in Homes and Communities

In the 1980s researchers began to study and document the ways that families use literacy and support literacy development in the context of their homes and communities. As the field of family literacy was just emerging, most of these studies used qualitative methodologies and focused on description.

One of the earliest studies focusing on literacy in the family context was Taylor's (1983) study of six middle-income families, each with a first-grade child who was learning to read and write successfully. She examined interactions among all family members, including mothers, fathers, and siblings. She concluded that "in each of the families, literacy facilitates the accomplishment of many essential daily tasks and is a critical factor in the continuation of present lifestyles" (p. 26). Taylor also argued that "it seems reasonable to assume that if literacy becomes socially significant in the lives of the parents, it is likely to become socially significant in the lives of the children" (p. 88).

Shirley Brice Heath's (1983) ethnographic study of literacy development within the context of family and community focused on documenting literacy and language in three culturally different communities in the Piedmont Carolinas. Heath concluded that oral and literate traditions existed in the three communities she studied, but the forms and functions of language differed in each community. These differences influenced how the children performed in the schools they attended. Those children from nonmainstream backgrounds did not succeed in schools that held mainstream definitions of and expectations for literacy. Heath went on to argue that teachers and schools must explore ways to build on the home literacy experiences that children bring to school so bridges could be built between home and school.

To examine how low-income families influence children's literacy development, Taylor and Dorsey-Gaines (1988) studied low income, inner city families with children who were successfully learning to read and write in first grade. While these families struggled to meet their basic needs, they still used literacy for many purposes. These purposes included instrumental, social-interactional, news-related, recreational, confirmational, sociohistorical, and critical/educational. Taylor and Dorsey-Gaines concluded that a mismatch existed between the rich literacy environments provided in the homes and the schools the children attended. To address this mismatch, they suggested "family and community involvement in school programs would be essential, and our children would surely benefit from the connections that were being made to their everyday lives" (p. 210).

While Taylor and Dorsey-Gaines (1988) argued that low-income families could support literacy development, it is important not to over-generalize and assume that all low-income families provide the same types of literacy experiences and support to their young children. Such a caution is supported by Teale's (1986) longitudinal, naturalistic study of home literacy environments of low-income families with preschool children. The families included "Anglo, Black, and Mexican American" (p. 175). The frequency of literacy interactions among parents, children, siblings, and other family members in the home ranged from a high of 4.06 per hour to a low of .34 per hour. This translated into the children in the study being involved with reading and writing from 5 to 53 times per day, spending between 40 minutes to 7.5 hours on these activities per day. This wide range indicates that while all of these low-income families did engage children in literacy activities, the quantity and quality differed significantly.

Consistent with the findings of Teale's (1986) study, Purcell-Gates (1996) found that in her sample of 20 low-income families, great variability existed in the type and frequency of literacy acts. She concluded that in homes where adults read and wrote for a variety of purposes and exposed children to these literacy practices, children had a greater understanding of the alphabetic principle. In addition, these parents tended to be more involved and supportive of their children's literacy development once the children began formal literacy instruction in school.

To understand the influence of family on low-income children's literacy development and school success, Snow, Barnes, Chandler, Goodman, and Hemphill (1991) conducted a longitudinal study of low-income families in the northeast United States. The researchers found that literacy environment in the home, mother's educational level, and mother's educational expectations for the child were "the most powerful predictors of both word recognition and of vocabulary" (p. 66) achievement. In addition, the "organization in the home, participation in activities, the presence of TV rules, and the parent-child relationship scale showed substantial correlations with writing production" (p. 94). Snow et al. (1991) concluded that

> Excellent classrooms can compensate for less than ideal home conditions, but ideal home conditions (at least within the range sampled in this study) cannot always compensate for very poor classrooms. However, for the majority of children in intermediate classrooms, home and school appear to have a complementary relationship—home experiences seem adequately to provide what schools cannot. In the absence of excellence in the classroom, the role of the home becomes much more important (p. 61).

While Snow et al. (1991) examined family influence on education, many of their findings focused on the mother's role. To examine specifically the role of fathers in children's academic achievement and literacy development, Nord, Brimhall, and West (1997) studied paternal involvement in school. They concluded that fathers in two-parent homes were more involved in their children's schooling than fathers who did not live in the home. Furthermore children with involved fathers tended to receive higher grades, enjoyed school more, and passed on to the next grade more than their peers with less involved fathers. Specifically in the area of literacy, Ortiz, Stile, and Brown (1999) studied literacy activities between fathers and children in New Mexico. They concluded that the fathers engaged in literacy activities such as book reading, reading environmental print, writing, and teaching letters with their children. The National Center on Fathers and Families is also conducting research to examine critical issues related to father's contributions to education and literacy development within the family context (Gadsden, 2003).

Another area that has received limited attention in the family literacy research literature is teen parents. Studies by Neuman and Gallagher (1994) and Neuman (1995) indicate that teen parents often lack knowledge of how to support their young children's literacy development and the relationship of such support on future performance in school. These studies also concluded that with appropriate modeling, mentoring, and support, teen parents can effectively nurture the literacy development of their young children.

This brief review of key studies examining the influence of families on children's literacy development indicates that families do make significant contributions to their children's literacy development, regardless of socioeconomic status (SES). It is important to note, however, that all families from a SES group do not interact with their children around literacy in a predetermined manner. To examine this issue further, the next section of this paper will review research on characteristics of diverse families that support children's literacy and school success.

Family Characteristics Related to Education in Diverse Families

Clark's (1983) naturalistic study of low-income, African-American families with high achieving children and families with low achieving children indicated that parental behaviors and expectations contributed to the children's performance in school more than just socioeconomic status. Parental behaviors in the homes of high achieving children included: (a) frequent, parent-initiated school contact; (b) parental calmness when dealing with the child; (c) the presence of explicit achievement-centered rules and norms; and (d) "clear, specific role boundaries and status structures with parents as dominant authority" (p. 200).

In her ethnographic study of Latino families, Delgado-Gaitan (1990) concluded that the parents were committed to and involved in supporting their children's success in school. The connections between preschool and home were stronger than those between elementary school and home. Once the children reached second grade and beyond, parents reported confusion about school procedures and expectations as a result of the mismatch with their own educational experiences outside the United States.

Valdes (1996) studied Mexican American families to learn about "how bilingual language and literacy skills developed in newly arrived immigrant children outside the school setting" (p. xv). Valdes found that these parents perceived their children's behavior as their responsibility and academic matters were the responsibility of the teacher. Parents reported that to cross this boundary would be disrespectful and inappropriate.

Considering the Delgado-Gaitan (1990) and Valdes (1996) studies in tandem, it appears that these families had significantly different viewpoints regarding their roles in their children's education and schooling from middle-income parents from the dominant culture. Teachers in both studies appeared to expect parent involvement to be consistent across groups and to manifest itself in ways such as communicating directly with the school and teacher, helping with homework, and attending school events even though these expectations were not explained explicitly to the parents. When the Latino families did not respond in the manner the teachers expected, teachers tended to conclude that families were not interested or supportive of the school and their children's education. Such a mismatch between school and home is consistent with the findings of studies by Taylor and Dorsey-Gaines (1988) and Heath (1983).

To examine family characteristics that nurture literacy development, Baker, Scher, and Mackler (1997) researched home factors that supported reading engagement. These factors included availability of reading materials and literacy technology (e.g., computers and televisions), adults reading in the home, adults reading to children regularly, conversation and language play, adults' valuing reading, and connections between home and school literacy. In many low-income homes, literacy is used for functional and survival purposes (Elish-Piper, 1996, 1997; Purcell-Gates, 1996) whereas, literacy in school tends to focus on academic purposes, such as reading narrative texts and responding to comprehension questions. Again, the issue of a mismatch between school expectations and home practices appears to be an important finding in these studies.

Storybook Reading in Families

Reading aloud to young children is typically viewed as the most important thing parents can do to foster their children's literacy development. Dickinson (1989) concluded, "while all families in literate cultures make use of print in varied ways, lower income families...are less likely than middle-class parents to read books with their children" (pp. 125-126).

Most studies of parent-child storybook reading have focused on middle-income mothers and their children (e.g., Neuman, 1997; Ninio, 1980; Pellegrini, Brody, & Sigel, 1985). Such studies concluded that parent-child storybook reading fostered vocabulary development, concepts about print, alphabetic knowledge, and interest in reading. Concerned that storybook reading did not appear to take place as often in low-income, minority homes as it did in middle-income homes, Patricia Edwards (1989, 1993, 1995) studied how low-income, African-American mothers interacted with their children while reading storybooks. Edwards concluded that simply telling low-income parents to read to their children was not sufficient; teachers must also show them how to do so in productive ways. This finding supported the development of workshops, family literacy programs, and other interventions to help parents learn how to read with their children (Edwards, 1995).

Intervention Programs in Family Literacy

Family literacy programs began to emerge in the 1980s as a method of intervening to assist low-income, low-literate families. Initially, family literacy programs tended to be short-term programs and workshops that aimed to help parents learn to read storybooks with their children (Morrow & Paratore, 1993). More recent programs have moved toward longer-term programs that provide direct educational services to both parents and their young children.

In 1986, six pilot sites of the Parent and Child Education (PACE) program in Kentucky were started, and by 1990, 33 sites were in operation in 30 counties in Kentucky (Heberle, 1992). Research on the PACE program documented improved parental attitudes toward education (Hibpshaman, 1989) and increased expectations about their children's likelihood of graduating from high school and pursuing postsecondary education (Kim, 1989). In addition, 70% of the parents in PACE programs either obtained their GED or raised their Test of Adult Basic Education (TABE) scores by two grade levels or more (Kim, 1987). In addition, children in the PACE programs exhibited positive gains on the developmental checklist, *The Child Observation Record* (Schweinhart & Storerin, 1992), in the following areas: "Using Language, Representing Experiences, Classification, Seriation, Number Concepts, Spatial Relations, Temporal Relations, Movement, and Social and Emotional Development" (Heberle, 1992, p. 144).

In 1988, the William R. Kenan, Jr. Charitable Trust provided grant monies to fund several family literacy programs in Kentucky and North Carolina. The PACE program model was modified to create the Kenan Trust model. In 1989, the National Center for Family Literacy was founded using funds from the Kenan Trust (Brizius & Foster, 1993). The Kenan Trust model included the following components: (a) early childhood education, (b) adult education, (c) parent support group, and (d) parent and child together time (PACT). These programs were designed for parents who had not graduated from high school and their 3- to 4-year-old children. By 1993, the National Center for Family Literacy (NCFL) had helped to start over 900 family literacy programs across the United States (Brizius & Foster, 1993). At present, NCFL identifies 2064 family literacy programs in the U.S. (NCFL, 2002).

The first Even Start programs began operation during the 1989-1990 school year. Even Start programs are federally funded family literacy programs that target under-educated parents and their children, ages 0-8. Even Start programs have three goals: (a) "to help parents become full participants in the education of their children", (b) "to assist children in reaching their full potential as learners", and (c) "to provide literacy training for participating parents" (St. Pierre, 1993, p. 2).

Although family literacy programs are rapidly increasing in number and popularity (NCFL, 2002), concern exists regarding the appropriateness of such family interventions programs. Auerbach (1989), Gadsden (1994), and Taylor (1994) cautioned family literacy educators to the dangers of deficit based programs that operate from the belief that families have many liabilities that programs must fix. Auerbach (1989) argued that family literacy programs must operate from a social-contextual model wherein home and community uses of literacy form the foundation for any family literacy program. The work of Luis Moll and his colleagues in the area of "funds of knowledge" has been an important foundation for this view of family literacy (Moll, Amanti, Neff, & Gonzalez, 1992). Using this perspective, all families are viewed as having important knowledge, skills, and experiences that support and enhance learning. These funds of knowledge are then used as the basis for instruction to allow all families to contribute to their children's literacy in meaningful ways.

Paratore (2001) studied a family literacy program in an urban community in an attempt to determine how a program could operate from a strengths or social-contextual model of family literacy wherein family strengths, needs, and goals form the core of the program. The Intergenerational Literacy Project (ILP) was a collaborative effort between a school district and university. The main goal of the ILP was to help children come to school ready to learn by providing parents with literacy and English language support and instruction. The families represented a large number or cultural and linguistic groups. Over the ten year period of the program's operation, adult attendance and retention in the program exceeded traditional adult education and in many family literacy programs. Parents used reading and writing outside class to achieve personal goals, making literacy part of their daily lives. In addition, parents increased the literacy interactions with their children. Eighty percent of parents reported engaging in storybook reading with their children at least one time per week. Important features of the ILP included a bilingual and bicultural approach that embraced various languages and cultures as part of the curriculum. In addition, the ILP operated from a sociocultural view of learning and incorporated cooperative grouping, strategic reading, shared storybook reading, and on-going authentic assessment into the program. Handel (1999) also examined the issue of how family literacy in school contexts can operate from a strengths model. Her findings were consistent with Paratore (2001) in terms of the need to honor and respect the unique contributions of each family and to make meaningful connections between home and school literacy practices and experiences.

Discussion and Conclusions

While this review has not been exhaustive, important conclusions can be drawn from the studies reviewed. These findings focus on the following areas:

1. All families contribute to their children's literacy development in unique ways that may be influenced by, but are not dictated by socio-economic status. While variation exists even among low-income families, literacy use and support does appear to be present in low-income homes. Family characteristics and beliefs about school and schooling are also important contributors to children's literacy development. Unfortunately, in many diverse families expectations for school involvement differ greatly from what teachers expect. As a result, this mismatch of expectations often leads teachers to conclude that diverse families are not interested in supporting children's schooling.

2. Mismatches between home and school literacy uses and practices can cause confusion, frustration, and limited progress for learners. As Heath (1983) and Taylor and Dorsey-Gaines (1988) argued, teachers must identify ways to connect home and school literacy so all children can learn and succeed in school.

3. Storybook reading is a useful way to support children's literacy development; however, this practice is not as common in low-income homes as it is in middle-income homes. As Edwards (1989) concluded, it is critical for educators to teach parents how to read with their children rather than just assuming they know how to do so in productive ways.

4. While family literacy programs are increasing in popularity and availability, some educators have voiced concerns that such programs may operate from a deficit perspective that functions to blame families for their differences. Research on family literacy programs that operate from a strengths or social-contextual perspective offer promise for supporting diverse families.

Recent Developments and Future Directions

Family literacy is now a concept that has found its way into many schools, libraries, community colleges, community centers, places of worship, and workplaces. In addition, high profile attention has been placed on family literacy through the efforts of "first ladies" such as Barbara Bush and Laura Bush. The passage of the Literacy Involves Families Together (LIFT) Act in December 2000 has also pushed schools to become directly involved with family literacy. With the increasing attention on family literacy comes additional scrutiny. For example, the Federal Government has stated in its recent Request for Proposals (Funded by NICHD and NIH) for research in family literacy that little to no empirical evidence exists to show the positive impact of family literacy. Purcell-Gates' (2000) review of research on family literacy also concluded that additional research is needed to document outcomes of family literacy programs on literacy practices and skills. These calls for additional research bring into question the nature of outcomes often sought in family literacy programs and the research methods most suited to answer related questions. Furthermore, funding for Even Start has been cut at the federal level due to the lack of "scientifically-based research." It is anticipated that this funding cut will result in a decrease in the number and availability of family literacy programs in the coming years. Clearly, the field of family literacy is at a critical juncture where researchers and practitioners must make known the outcomes and impact of such programs on the families they serve.

As demographics continue to change and family structures take on multiple forms, it is imperative that family literacy researchers study various types of families, including single parent families, teen parents, and families with grandparents or other members raising children. In addition, the research base will be strengthened if studies include families from various racial, cultural, linguistic, and socioeconomic backgrounds. By expanding the research base, it will be possible to define, understand, and support family literacy for all families.

Other recent changes in family literacy include a broadening of the curriculum to address areas such as health and financial literacy. In addition, some educators have started to argue that all teachers need to be knowledgeable about and support the development of family literacy for their students (McIntyre, Kyle, Moore, Sweazy, & Greer, 2001; Smith & Elish-Piper, 2002). As family literacy has grown from a novel idea to a well established concept and approach to enhancing literacy, such challenges will need to be met with solid research, theory, practice, and advocacy (Purcell-Gates, 2000) so educators can support literacy development for all.

References

Auerbach, E. R. (1989). Toward a social-contextual approach to family literacy. *Harvard Educational Review, 59,* 165-181.

Baker, L., Scher, D., & Mackler, K. (1997). Home and family influences on motivations for reading. *Educational Psychologist, 32,* 69-82

Brizius, J. A., & Foster, S. A. (1993). *Generation to generation: Realizing the promise of family literacy.* Ypsilanti, MI: High/Score Press.

Clark, R. M. (1983). *Family life and school achievement.* Chicago, IL: The University of Chicago Press.

DeBruin-Peracki, A., & Krol-Sinclair, B. (2003). Introduction. In A. DeBruin-Peracki & B. Krol-Sinclair (Eds.), *Family literacy: From theory to practice* (pp. 1-6). Newark, DE: International Reading Association.

Delgado-Gaitan, C. (1990). *Literacy for empowerment: The role of parents in children's education.* New York: Falmer.

Dickinson, D. K. (1989). Effects of a shared reading program on one Head Start language and literacy environment. In J. B. Allen & J. M. Mason (Eds.), *Risk makers, risk takers, risk beakers: Reducing the risks for young literacy learners* (pp. 125-153). Portsmouth, NH: Heinemann.

Edwards, P. A. (1989). Supporting lower SES mothers' attempts to provide scaffolding for bookreading. In J. B. Allen & J. M. Mason (Eds.), *Risk makers, risk takers, risk breakers: Reducing the risks for young literacy learners* (pp. 222-250). Portsmouth, NH: Heinemann.

Edwards, P. A. (1993). Connecting African-American parents and youth to the school's reading curriculum. In V. L. Gadsden & D. A. Wagner (Eds.), *Literacy and African American youth: Issues in learning, teaching, and schooling.* Norwood, NJ: Ablex.

Edwards, P. A. (1995). Empowering low-income mothers and fathers to share books with young children. *The Reading Teacher, 48,* 558-564.

Elish-Piper, L. (1996/7). Literacy and their lives: Four low-income families enrolled in a summer family literacy program. *Journal of Adolescent and Adult Literacy, 40,* 256-268.

Gadsden, V. L. (1994). *Understanding family literacy: Conceptual issues facing the field* (Tech. Rep. No. 94-02). Philadelphia, PA: University of Pennsylvania, National Center on Adult Literacy.

Gadsden, V. L. (2003). Expanding the concept of "family" in family literacy: Integrating a focus on fathers. In A. DeBruin-Parecki & B. Krol-Sinclair (Eds.), *Family literacy: From theory to practice* (pp. 86-125). Newark, DE: International Reading Association.

Handel, R. (1999). *Building family literacy in an urban community.* New York: Teachers College Press.

Heath, S. B. (1983). *Ways with words: Language, life and work in communities and classrooms.* Cambridge, UK: Cambridge University Press.

Heberle, J. (1992). Pace: Parent and child education in Kentucky. In T. S. Sticht, M. J. Beeler, & B. A. McDonald (Eds.), *The intergenerational transfer of cognitive skills: Volume I: Programs, policy, and research issues* (pp. 136-148). Norwood, NJ: Ablex.

Hibpshman, T. P. (1989). *An explanatory model for family literacy programs.* Frankfort, KY: Kentucky Department of Education, Office of Research and Planning.

Kim, Y. K. (1987). *Parent and child program evaluation report.* Lexington, KY: University of Kentucky, Human Development Institute.

Kim, Y. K. (1989). *Evaluation study of Kentucky's pilot adult basic education program.* Lexington, KY: University of Kentucky, Human Development Institute.

Literacy Involves Families Together (LIFT) Act. 106th Cong. (2000). Retrieved April 11, 2002, from HtmlResAnchor http://www.famlit.org/policy/congress106.html

McIntyre, E., Kyle, D., Moore, G., Sweazy, R. A., & Greer, S. (2001). Linking home and school through family visits. *Language Arts, 78,* 264-272.

Moll, L., Amanti, C., Neff, D., & Gonzalez, N. (1992). Funds of knowledge for teaching: Using a qualitative approach to connect homes and classrooms. *Theory Into Practice, 31,* 132-141.

Morrow, L. M., & Paratore, J. R. (1993). Family literacy: Perspectives and practices. *The Reading Teacher, 47,* 194-200.

Morrow, L. M., Paratore, J. R., & Tracey, D. H. (1994). *Family literacy: New perspectives, new opportunities.* Newark, DE: International Reading Association.

National Center for Family Literacy. (2002). Retrieved December 29, 2002, from http://www.famlit.org/media/pfacts.html

Neuman, S. B. (1995). Toward a collaborative approach to parent involvement in early education: A study of teenage mothers in an African-American community. *American Educational Research Journal, 32,* 801-827.

Neuman, S. B. (1997). Children engaging in storybook reading: The influence of access to print resources, opportunity, and parental interaction. *Early Childhood Research Quarterly, 11,* 495-514.

Neuman, S. B., & Gallagher, P. (1994). Joining together in literacy learning: Teenage mothers and children. *Reading Research Quarterly, 29,* 382-401.

Nickse, R. S., Speicher, A. M., & Buchek, P. C. (1988). An intergenerational adult literacy project: A family intervention/prevention model. *Journal of Reading, 31,* 634-642.

Ninio, A. (1980). Picture-book reading in mother infant dyads belonging to two subgroups in Israel. *Child Development, 51,* 587-590.

Nord, C. W., Brinhall, D., & West, J. (1997). *Father's involvement in their children's schools.* Washington, DC: U.S. Department of Education.

Ortiz, R. W., Stiles, S., & Brown, C. (1999). Early literacy activities of fathers: Reading and writing with young children. *Young Children, 54*(5), 16-18.

Paratore, J. R. (2001). *Opening doors, opening opportunities: Family literacy in an urban community.* Needham Heights, MA: Allyn & Bacon.

Pellegrini, A. D., Brody, G. H., & Sigel, I. E. (1985). Parents' bookreading habits with their children. *Journal of Educational Psychology, 77,* 332-340.

Purcell-Gates, V. (1996). Stories, coupons, and the "TV Guide": Relationships between home literacy experiences and emergent literacy knowledge. *Reading Research Quarterly, 31,* 406-428.

Purcell-Gates, V. (2000). Family literacy. In M. L. Kamil, P. B. Mosenthal, P. D. Pearson, & R. Barr (Eds.), *Handbook of reading research, volume III* (pp. 853-870). Mahwah, NJ: Erlbaum.

Schweinhart, L., & Storer, E. (1992). *Child observation record.* Ypsalanti, MI: High Scope.

Smith, M. C., & Elish-Piper, L. (2002). Primary-grade educators and adult literacy: Some strategies for assisting low-literate parents. *The Reading Teacher, 56,* 156-165.

Snow, C. E., Barnes, W. S., Chandler, J., Goodman, I. F., & Hemphill, L. (1991). *Unfulfilled expectations: Home and school influences on literacy.* Cambridge, MA: Harvard University Press.

St. Pierre, R. (1993). National evaluation of the Even Start Family Literacy Program. Report on effectiveness. (Report No. ED OUS 93 47). Washington, DC: U. S.

Department of Education. (ERIC Document Reproduction Services No ED 365476).

Taylor, D. (1983). *Family literacy: Children learning to read and write.* Exeter, NH: Heinemann.

Taylor, D. (1997). *Many families, many literacies: An international declaration of principles.* Portsmouth, NH: Heinemann.

Taylor, D. (1994, May). The ideologies and ethics of family literacy pedagogies: A postformal perspective. In L. M. Morrow (Moderator), *Perspectives on intergenerational/family literacy.* Forum conducted at the 39th annual convention of the International Reading Association, Toronto, Ontario, Canada.

Taylor, D., & Dorsey-Gaines, C. (1988). *Growing up literate: Learning from inner-city families.* Portsmouth, NH: Heinemann.

Teale, W. (1986). Home background and young children's literacy development. In W. Teale & E. Sulzby (Eds.), *Emergent literacy: Writing and research* (pp. 173-206). Norwood, NJ: Ablex.

Valdes, G. (1996). *Con respeto: Bridging the distances between culturally diverse families and schools.* New York: Teachers College Press.

CELEBRATING PRESERVICE AND INSERVICE TEACHER EDUCATION

A View of the Literacy Beliefs and Growth Processes of Undergraduate Preservice Teachers with a Concentration in Reading: Interns, Paraprofessionals, and Interns Serving as Teachers of Record

I. LaVerne Raine
Ceretha Levingston
Wayne M. Linek
Mary Beth Sampson
Patricia E. Linder

Texas A&M University-Commerce

Abstract

Prior studies that describe change in the beliefs about literacy develop-ment of preservice teachers serve as a foundation for this current qualitative study. In this study the beliefs of three different groups of undergraduate stu-dents enrolled in the internship level of their teacher certification program are described and compared. The influencing factors affecting those beliefs are also examined. The internship level is the first of two semesters complet-ing the field-based program. One group consisted of students completing the program traditionally. A second group was composed of students who had been hired as non-certified teachers of record during their internship. The third group was classified as paraprofessionals because they were completing teacher certification while retaining their full-time job in the schools as edu-cational aides.

Introduction

On January 8, 2002, President Bush signed into law the No Child Left Behind Act of 2001. The Act is the most sweeping reform of the Elementary and Secondary Education Act (ESEA) since ESEA was enacted in 1965. It redefines the federal role in K-12 education and will help close the achievement gap between disadvantaged and minority students and their peers. It is based on four basic principles: stronger accountability for results, increased flexibility and local control, expanded options for parents, and an emphasis on teaching methods that have been proven to work (United States Department of Education [USDOE], 2002).

It is critical that we understand the development of teacher beliefs related to teaching, learning, and best practice as current research indicates (Cunningham & Allington, 1999; Fazio, 2001; Fazio, in press; USDOE, 1987) and recent federal directives require (USDOE, 2002) that teachers use research based strategies for students to reach their full potential in reading. But federal mandates do not ensure that best practice will be consistently implemented in classrooms. This is because teachers' beliefs about teaching method and best practice impact their classroom behavior (Fazio, 2001; Fazio, in press; Wuthrick, 1995). Since teachers' beliefs are mainly based on their prior experience (Wells, 1994), it is critical to understand how beliefs develop about best practice and teaching methods that work.

Previous research indicates a variety of factors lead to the development and change of beliefs. For example, Risko, Roskos, and Veukelich (1999) indicate that reflection is necessary for the development of beliefs. Several researchers (Dressman, Graves, & Webster, 1999; Wolf, Hill, & Ballentine, 1999) say that some type of disequilibrium must be created, while other researchers believe that dissonance must be introduced for change to occur (Azjen, 1988; Festinger, 1957). Still other researchers indicate that it is helpful, if not necessary, to have someone serve as a reflective mirror to stimulate growth, change beliefs, and align teaching behavior with best practice (Fazio, 2001; Fazio, in press; Wuthrick, 1995).

Recent research (Linek et al., 1999; Smith, Sampson, Linek, & Raine, 2001; Zeek & Wickstrom, 1999) has described how preservice teachers' beliefs about literacy develop in a variety of teacher education program designs. These program designs include: a reading methods course on a university campus, a university reading methods course with unsupervised field experience, and a field-based reading methods course. Although preservice teachers in each program experienced change, factors contributing to development of and changes in beliefs varied by program design. Factors common to all programs were course assignments/readings, instructor modeling, cognitive dissonance, and reflection. Students participating in a field-based program described several unique types of dissonance that impacted their developing beliefs about literacy instruction. These factors included experiential, cultural, emotional, and political dissonance. Findings of this research indicate that a field-based model of teacher education helps students develop a more insightful and complex view of the process of literacy teaching and learning.

Recent research (Darling-Hammond, 1999, 2000; Pearson, 2000) also indicates that certified teachers have better results with their students and that students of certified teachers do better on a number of reading measures than students of non-certified teachers. However, even though field-based teacher education programs appear to provide the best preparation and certified teachers provide the best instruction, the growing teacher shortage is putting more and more non-certified teachers into our classrooms. The shortage is so severe in some places that even people who do not possess an undergraduate degree are now permitted to teach. For example, the state of Texas allows preservice teachers within 36 hours of certification to be hired as the teacher of record (Texas Education Agency, 2001). These non-certified teachers may be teaching reading before they complete any reading methods courses. Due to this shift in policy, more research is needed to determine what effect the practice of hiring non-certified teachers is having on the development of teacher beliefs.

Research on the development of preservice teachers' beliefs has described what occurs in early childhood programs (Martin, Martin, & Martin, 1999), initial literacy methods courses (Linek et al., 1999), traditional student teaching programs (Linek et al., 1999), and field-based teacher education programs (Smith et al., 2001). However, little is known about how paraprofessionals' beliefs develop since they worked as educational aides before entering their teacher education program. There is also a dearth of information on how undergraduate students who are acting as teachers of record before completing their degree and teacher certification courses develop their beliefs about best practice. If states are going to continue to permit untrained and non-certified teachers to teach children, we must find out what helps to shape their beliefs about reading and whether these beliefs differ from preservice teachers who complete teacher education programs before becoming teachers of record.

This qualitative study builds on previous studies that described shifts in beliefs experienced by preservice teachers enrolled in their campus and field-based literacy courses. The purpose of the study is to compare the beliefs, practices, and change processes of three groups of university students completing their teacher preparation coursework. One group consists of preservice teachers completing the traditional field-based program. The second group is composed of undergraduate university students who have been hired as non-certified teachers of record. The third group is composed of paraprofessionals who have worked for at least three years prior to entering the teacher certification program and who continue to work as educational aides. With attention to the range of conditions that governed the experiences of this group, questions that guided this study were:

- Can the development of literacy beliefs and related growth processes of undergraduate teacher preparation students with a concentration in reading be observed and constructed through their written comments on literacy?
- Can the factors influencing the growth process be ascertained at the end of the internship?
- Are there discernable differences in the development of literacy beliefs and growth processes in the three groups?

Background and Procedures
Participants

The twenty-two participants for the present study were all students in the 2001 Fall internship semester of the pre-service teacher certification preparation program at a Texas University. They were seeking an undergraduate degree with teacher certification and a concentration in reading. The field-based teacher preparation program involves two semesters in which students take coursework in seminar settings on campus while serving as student teachers in selected area schools. The first semester is known as internship and the second and final semester of the program is called residency. The current study focuses on the internship semester.

Historically, students would complete both semesters leading to teacher certification and graduation from the university prior to being employed in the public schools. But with the occurrence of a shortage of certified teachers, public school administrators have begun to hire pre-service teachers near the completion of the teacher preparation program. With this shortage in some of the area schools, three of the twenty-two participants were the teacher of record for their particular situation. The traditional manner to complete internship and residency is in the classroom of an experienced, certified teacher who serves as a mentor for the preservice teacher/student. But, three of the participants were hired as teachers of record, during the early part of the semester and thus were not under the direct mentorship of another teacher. Special administrative considerations were extended to them to make it possible for them to meet and complete the requirements of the university program while performing the duties of a "regular" teacher.

Further uniqueness of the twenty-two participants was noted with two of them working as paraprofessionals in their respective public school. The paraprofessional program allows certain individuals who have been serving as teacher aids to complete a certification program with a university while retaining their full-time job as an educational aide in a public school. Thus these two individuals would go through different types of experiences and alignment of mentorship than the other two groups.

Data Collection

The twenty-two participants for this study completed a pre- and post-questionnaire (Smith et al., 2001) during regular sessions of a reading methods course in which they were all enrolled and attended together. This semi-structured, open-ended questionnaire developed by two of the researchers probes for beliefs and views on literacy and literacy instruction. The pre-questionnaire was completed the first session of the course and the post-questionnaire was completed during the last session of the course near the end of the semester.

The written responses were collected for analysis for this study from the following prompts:

- Prompt one: What is a good reader? Why do you say that?
- Prompt two: As you are working through this semester, have your thoughts and feelings about teaching reading and writing to elementary students changed from the beginning of this semester? If so: (a) Explain how your thoughts and feelings have changed. (b) What particular aspects of your teacher preparation do you believe are making the biggest difference for you? Why do you say that?

Data Analysis

To control for biases that might enter during the reading of the responses, the names of the participants were replaced with numbers and the questionnaires were randomly stacked without identity to which group the papers belonged. Using constant comparative analysis (Strauss & Corbin, 1990) the data from the pre- and post-questionnaires were read by one of the independent researchers. Independent researcher is defined here as someone who was not involved in any way with the instructional exposure of the subjects. As this analysis proceeded codes were devised for the emerging categories (Bogdan & Biklen, 1992) from the participants' responses to two of the selected prompts: (a) beliefs about good readers, and (b) factors influencing literacy beliefs and change processes. The categories that emerged were grouped and themes were identified. Two additional independent researchers then read and categorized all of the data using the scheme developed by the first researcher. All disagreements were then discussed until consensus was reached by all three of the independent researchers. Categories and themes were then corroborated by the two seminar instructors who were members of the research team. A frequency count was then used to tally each response. Some of the responses fell into more than one category so that the total of the responses to each prompt is greater than the number of participants. It was only after this analysis that the assigned numbers belonging to the students making up the three groups were revealed so that the responses for each group could be read to discover any commonalities that would be unique to a particular group and to discern if there were differences between the groups.

Results

The analysis of the responses of the pre- and post-questionnaires to each of two prompts was coded into descriptive categories and a frequency tabulation of the number of times each category was included in the written responses. A total of eleven categories were developed from the pre-questionnaire concerning the first prompt: 1) Beliefs about good readers (see Table 1). Each of the categories are listed with an example from responses that created the category. The number following the quote indicates the code number of the participant who gave that response.

- Comprehends/Understands Text: "A good reader is someone who understands and comprehends the material they are reading. A good reader does not mean someone who gets all the words correct. I say this because if the reader does not understand/comprehend the material then they are not benefiting from the material." (#10)
- Fluency: "A good reader is someone who reads fluently and comprehends the text. I say this because someone who has trouble pronouncing words usually does not comprehend what they are reading." (#15)
- Accuracy: "A good reader can read with accuracy and fluency. If they come to a word they don't know they look for context clues, picture clues, or use some strategy to comprehend the word." (#13)
- Letter/Sound Relationships: "A good reader is a child who has fluency throughout a page and when given a word that is unfamiliar the child will push each sound through to be able to learn a new word. I have seen good readers read." (#1)
- Reads for Enjoyment: "A good reader is someone that enjoys reading. The more a person reads, the better they become at reading." (#21)
- Use Context/Picture Clues: "To me a good reader is a student who catches his/her mistakes and uses context clues and pictures to figure things out. I don't think speedy readers are necessarily good readers. If a student can speed through without comprehending then they are not good readers." (#6)

Table 1. Beliefs About Good Readers

	Pre			Post		
Category	Intern N=17	Teacher of Record N=3	Para-Professional N=2	Intern N=17	Teacher of Record N=3	Para-Professional N=2
Comprehends/ Understands Text	2,3,4,6,8, 10,15,16, 18,19,20 f=11	7,12 f=2	21 f=1	2,3,4,5,6, 8,10,15, 17,19,20 f=11	7,12 f=2	22 f=1
Fluency	1,5,8,11, 13,15 f=6			1,10,13 f=3	7,12 f=2	
Accuracy	5,11,13,20 f=4			5,11,13 f=3		
Letter/Sound Relationships	1,2,8,20 f=4			1,8,16,20 f=4		
Reads for Enjoyment	9,11 f=2			9 f=1		21 f=1
Use Context/ Picture Clues	11,13 f=2			6,11,18,20 f=4		
Reads for Learning	9 f=1			9 f=1		
Not Afraid to Read Aloud	11 f=1	14	f=1			
Self-Monitoring	8 f=1			2,6,8,11 f=4	7 f=1	
Actively Engaged in Text	8 f=1			3,4 f=2		
Understands that the Words Printed on the Page Convey Meaning & Represent Language	8 f=1					
Makes Connections-Text to Text		22	f=1			
Develops a Purpose for Reading				8,9 f=2		
Reads on Level				5,11 f=2		
Uses Cueing Systems				8 f=1		
Makes Connections-Self to Text/Text to Self				3 f=1		22 f=1
Reads Independently/ Silently/Efficiently					14 f=1	
Summarize/ Explain What is Read					14 f=1	22 f=1

Note: The individual numbers that appear first in each section of the chart refer to a specific participant.
Note: f refers to frequency.

- Reads for Learning: "A good reader is someone who is interested in reading for learning and enjoyment. The more interested a person is in reading, the more time they will spend reading. The more the person reads the better he/she will become." (#9)
- Not Afraid to Read Aloud: ". . . They tend not to be afraid of reading aloud . . ." (#11)
- Self-Monitoring: "A good reader is one that reads fluently, understands what they are reading and as a result self corrects when something they read doesn't make sense." (#7)
- Actively Engaged in Text: "A good reader is someone who reflects on what they have read. They think deeper into the context rather than simply reading the words off the page. They have a clear comprehension of the material they read. I think these are all characteristics of a good reader because they are actively engaging in the text." (#4)
- Understands that the Words Printed on the Page Convey Meaning & Represent Language: "A good reader is someone who reads fluently, engages in decoding and self-checking, and reads for meaning (comprehension). A good reader is actively engaged in the text and understands that the words printed on the page convey meaning and represent language." (#8)
- Makes Connections- Text to Text: "A good reader is someone who can read a book and then explain what it is that they read. They should also be able to relate part of parts of it to something they have previously read or encountered if they are going to truly become an 'owner' of this information." (#22)

The greatest frequency of responses occurred in the category: Comprehends/Understands Text. Looking at the responses revealed that even when students did not mention specifically the term comprehension, the implications that good reading encompasses comprehension was evident. See participant #11 with entries in five categories. In her own words, "A good reader is one who reads with accuracy and fluency. They tend not to be afraid of reading aloud and often read for enjoyment. Also, they use context clues whenever possible to figure out a word they may have difficulty with. My reasoning for these assumptions is what I believe because every time I have encountered someone who I feel is a good reader, they always have one or more of these characteristics." It is thought that participant #11 was not omitting the need for comprehension, but was being descriptive as to the components that make up or involve comprehension. The post-responses of the same individual could be described similarly. "A good reader is one who can successfully read a text with at least 90% accuracy, missing no more than

5 (10) words per 100 that they encounter. A good reader uses context clues when necessary to decode words and also re-reads a text when they miss a word to make the text make sense." At the end of the semester the participants again responded to the same prompt. Their responses revealed six additional categories and three of the categories from the pre- were not included in the post-. The majority maintained their belief that comprehension is the central factor, but were now more elaborate and expansive in their descriptions of the skills that good readers posses. Examples of the post-responses that produced the additional categories follow:

- Develops a Purpose for Reading: "A good reader is someone that reads for learning and for fun. A good reader always tries to make challenges and goals in their reading. A good reader will pick out a more challenging book to try to read." (#9)
- Reads on Level: "A good reader is a child who can read at their level and . . ." (#5)
- Uses Cueing Systems: "A good reader is someone who makes use of the cueing system when reading. A good reader develops a purpose for reading and checks him/herself for understanding. A good reader has decoding skills and sometimes reads text more than once to understand." (#8)
- Makes Connections- Self to Text/Text to Self: "A good reader is someone who makes meaning from printed text by activating prior schema and making connections and then also interact with text. It is important to make meaning and have some background knowledge to bring to text." (#3)
- Reads Independently/Silently/Efficiently: "A good reader is able to read independently, silently, and efficiently. If a child is ready to read alone, he has the confidence & skills needed to tackle an unknown text. If a child reads silently, he has internalized the reading process & it is second nature to him. An efficient reader is a good reader because he is able to skim, summarize, interpret, and read between the lines. This makes reading faster and more enjoyable." (#14)
- Summarize/Explain What is Read: "A good reader is someone who understands what they have read well enough to be able to apply it to their life or themselves and is able to summarize what it is that they read. If you cannot explain what you have read then you obviously did not understand or get anything out of it. If you cannot apply it then you will likely let it go in one ear & right back out the other." (#22)

The analysis of the written comments revealed a total of ten categories in response to the second prompt: 2) factors influencing literacy beliefs and change processes (see Table 2). Five categories were identified from the pre-questionnaire and eight categories were identified on the post-questionnaire. Of these categories three were identified both at the beginning of the semester on the pre- and again at the end of the semester on the post-. Those categories also had the highest number of frequency responses. The categories with an example from the responses that depict that category follow:

Table 2. Factors Influencing Literacy Beliefs and Change Processes

Category	PRE			POST		
	Intern N=17	Teacher of Record N=3	Para-professional N=2	Intern N=17	Teacher of Record N=3	Para-professional N=2
Classroom Experience/ Practical Application	3,5,6,8, 9,13,15, 16,17, 18,19 f=11	14 f=1	21,22 f=2	1,2,3,4,5, 8,10,13, 15,16,17, 20 f=12	14	f=1
Gaining Reading Strategies/Techniques	2,4,10, 20 f=4	12 f=1	9,18 f=2			21,22 f=2
University Seminars and Reading Classes	9,20 f=2	7 f=1		3,4,5,9,15,19 f=6	14 f=1	
How To Evaluate Students	10 f=1					
Time Management	11 f=1					
Planning				1,13 f=2	12 f=1	
Substitute Teaching				1 f=1		
Mentors				1 f=1		
University Liaison					7 f=1	
Grading Papers				10 f=1		

Note: *The individual numbers that appear first in each section of the chart refer to a specific participant.*
Note: *f refers to frequency.*

- Classroom Experience/Practical Application: "Being out in the classroom and getting to experience it hands-on. I learn more when I am actually doing something. You get to see what goes on and I have really learned how not to do things, but also how to do things. I have also gotten some good ideas to use." (#17 post-)
- Gaining Reading Strategies/Techniques: "Learning the different learning styles. Finding strategies to use to teach to a diverse group of students." (#18 post-)

- University Seminars and Reading Classes: "I feel that being able to learn new strategies and then go out in the field and try them is a great help." (#15 post-)
- How to Evaluate Students: "How to evaluate students and what to do while I am teaching to work reading skills into all aspects of the curriculum. I feel so empty when it comes to planning lessons and knowing what to do in front of the classrooms! I really need all the strategies I can get so that I will feel more comfortable when it is my turn to teach." (#10 pre-)
- Time Management: "Probably the time management required to get all the assignments completed will make the biggest difference for me. As a teacher, I think it is important to be organized and this class will get me to thinking about order, time, and organization." (#11 pre-)
- Planning: "Planning lessons, and practicing teaching are making the biggest difference for me. There is no substitute for making my own lesson cycle, teaching it to students, and seeing how well it does in actual practice, and making adjustments to make it work better." (#13 post-)
- Substitute Teaching: "My teacher preparation is being enhanced by substitute teaching and practicing strategies on my classes . . ." (#1 post-)
- Mentors: " . . . I also had to prepare a two week teach for my class and that really prepared me for that scary 'P' word, Planning! So I feel that my mentors have guided and prepared me the most for this new experience of teaching that I will be so ready for." (#1 post-)
- University Liaison: "My liaison – she has been my savior when I run into trials! (Name) is wonderful." (#7 post-)
- Grading Papers: "Observation. Being out there & seeing how students really learn. Also grading papers . . ." (#10 post-)

Across most of the responses both pre- and post- was a common theme of the importance of being in an experience that required the application of what was being learned. The importance of classroom experience in a teacher preparation program was commonly agreed upon. Of interest to the researchers was a subtle shift in the view of this experience. While the frequency count for the category of Classroom Experience/Practical Application actually decreased by one (total f=14 on pre- and total f=13 on post-), the category of University Seminars and Reading Classes frequency count changed from f=3 on pre- to f=7 on the post-. It was in the university setting that the participants were learning about the reading strategies and techniques that were being utilized in the practical situations of the public schools. This realization gained importance as they put to use and practice what they were being taught. This belief or understanding of the need for coordinated university seminars and preservice practice is foundational to the construct of teacher education and field-based programs. And even in this small number of participants that understanding was recognized by the end of one semester.

Discussion

This descriptive study has investigated the literacy beliefs of teacher preparation students in a variety of assignments in the public schools. The participants were asked to give reflective written responses to two prompts that would yield insight to the make up of their views. Teacher preparation students may be taught best practices in teaching literacy and the various components of a literacy program, but is the individual teacher's implementation of these practices governed by personal beliefs? If so, then it is important to study the development of the beliefs of preservice teachers. As practices are put to the test in the actual teaching of children, cognitive dissonance (Kagan, 1992) occurs and beliefs are crafted and changed in the process. In investigation of the development of the beliefs the researchers posed three questions, which are addressed below.

Question 1: Can the development of literacy beliefs and related growth processes of undergraduate teacher preparation students with a concentration in reading be observed and constructed through their written comments on literacy?

Expansion and elaboration of responses relating to literacy beliefs at the end of the first semester of the field-based teaching experience gave evidence that the beliefs about literacy do develop over a span of time in which the participant is directly involved with performing literacy instruction while receiving literacy coursework. A total of eleven categories were developed from the pre-questionnaire concerning beliefs about good readers (see Table 1). This was expanded with six additional categories added on the post-questionnaire. The beliefs of the participants were forged out of their unique experiences as they implemented course requirements and developed their teaching practices. It is important to note that to eliminate bias the instructors involved in teaching seminars and the methods courses that the participants were taking did not view the questionnaires and responses until after the analysis was completed by three co-researchers.

Question 2: Can the factors influencing the growth process be ascertained at the end of the internship?

The written responses of the participants revealed a common appreciation for their experiences. The practical experiences of teaching, as with anything that requires experience to gain ability and confidence in performing, were a major reporting both at the beginning of the semester and again at the end of the semester. As a whole they felt that their experiences, which provided the practicing of instructional strategies they were learning in university seminars, were of benefit to them. The combination of learning in university seminars and practice in the field provided a synergistic effect stronger than each would have had if provided in sequence rather than simultaneously.

Question 3: Are there discernable differences in the development of literacy beliefs and growth processes in the three groups?

Of the participants in this study seventeen were completing internship in the traditional preservice field-based program and were acting as student teachers two days per week and were in university seminars one day per week. Two of the participants were serving as paraprofessionals and were in their respective public schools five days per week. The remaining three participants were hired as the teacher of record for their respective schools and were in their own classrooms five days per week. Both the teachers of record and the paraprofessionals attended alternative certification program courses, which met in the evenings, and all twenty-two of the participants had a common literacy course that they attended in the evenings for a total of fifteen contact hours. From the written responses of the participants there were no discernable differences among the three groups. What they did report was how they were putting to use the techniques and strategies that they were learning. Some participants said that they had not changed in their beliefs for example participant # 22 stated, "I don't feel my thoughts or feelings have changed that much. I have learned some great strategies that I have really enjoyed trying with my students. This has taught me how to look back and reflect and modify as needed. These activities have made me a better teacher and listener" (post-). Others indicated that they had changed in their beliefs for example participant #4 commented, "My thoughts and feelings about teaching reading and writing have changed. I used to think it would be a breeze to teach these areas, and I now know that is not the case. It is a great challenge and one that I will take very seriously" (post-). In either view all comments indicated professional growth.

It is evident that these students were developing their beliefs and identifying factors that helped them in their development. However, as noted in previous research (Sampson & Linek, 1994), there was some resistance to admitting that they had changed. All participants stated in one form or another that they had grown professionally, but several specifically stated that they had not changed. The only group in which all participants consistently stated that they had not changed was the paraprofessionals. This group had worked in the schools as educational aides for at least three years before entering the teacher certification program. It is possible that working in schools for extended periods of time prior to beginning the teacher certification coursework which provides information about research based teaching strategies, requires practice in context, and requires reflection, may not be enough to break through a belief system that is rooted in extended experience teaching without formal knowledge about best practices.

The current study was limited to one semester so the question remains whether the short time frame is why there is still resistance or whether extended exposure to teacher certification coursework will impact this perception. The current study was also limited to the analysis of written responses. Although this provides insight into the development of beliefs, it does not provide insight into whether or not teaching behavior reflects best practices. The next phase of this study will attempt to answer these questions.

References

Azjen, I. (1988). *Attitudes, personality, and behavior.* Chicago: Dorsey.

Bogdan, R. C., & Biklen, S. K. (1992). *Qualitative research for education: An introduction to theory and methods.* Boston: Allyn and Bacon.

Cunningham, P., & Allington, R. (1999). *Classrooms that work: They can all read and write.* New York: Longman.

Darling-Hammond, L. (1999). *Solving the dilemmas of teacher supply, demand, and standards: How we can ensure a competent, caring, and qualified teacher for every child.* New York: National Commission on Teaching and America's Future.

Darling-Hammond, L. (2000). How Teacher Education Matters. *Journal of Teacher Education, 51,* 166-173.

Dressman, M., Graves, C., & Webster, J. (1999). Learning to read the research: How preservice teachers come to terms with cognitive versus holistic model of reading. In T. Shanahan & F. Rodriguez Brown (Eds.), *National Reading Conference yearbook 48* (pp. 437-450). Chicago: NRC.

Fazio, M. (2001). *Constructive comprehension and metacognitive strategy instruction in a field-based teacher education program: Effecting change in preservice and inservice teachers.* Unpublished doctoral dissertation, Texas A & M University-Commerce, Texas.

Fazio, M. (in press). Effecting change in preservice and inservice teachers. In M. B. Sampson, P. E. Linder, J. Dugan, & B. Brancato (Eds.), *College Reading Association yearbook.* Readyville, TN: College Reading Association.

Festinger, L. (1957). *A theory of cognitive dissonance.* Stanford, CA: Stanford University Press.

Kagan, D. M. (1992). Professional growth among pre-service and beginning teachers. *Journal of Educational Research, 62*(2), 129-169.

Linek, W. M., Nelson, O. G., Sampson, M. B., Zeek, C. K., Mohr, K. A. J., & Hughes, L. (1999). Developing beliefs about literacy instruction: A cross-case analysis of preservice teachers in traditional and field based settings. *Reading Research and Instruction, 38*(4), 371-386.

Martin, M., Martin, S., & Martin, C. (1999). Pre-service teachers constructing their meanings of literacy in a field-based program. In J. Dugan, P. Linder, W. Linek, & E. Sturtevant (Eds.), *Advancing the world of literacy: Moving into the 21st century.* Carrollton, GA: CRA.

Pearson, P. D. (2000, May). Learning to teach reading: Setting the research agenda. Paper presented at the meeting of the International Reading Association, Indianapolis, IN.

Risko, V., Roskos, K., & Veukelich, C. (1999). Making connections: Preservice teachers' reflection processes and strategies. In T. Shanahan & F. Rodriguez-Brown (Eds.) *National Reading Conference yearbook 48* (pp. 412-422). Chicago: NRC.

Sampson, M. B., & Linek, W. M. (1994). Change as a process: A view of an instructor and her students. In E. G. Sturtevant & W. M. Linek (Eds.), *Pathways for literacy: Learners teach and teachers learn* (pp. 47-58). Pittsburg, KS: College Reading Association.

Smith, B., Sampson, M. B., Linek, W. M., & Raine, I. L. (2001). Examining the literacy beliefs and change processes of reading specialists in a field-based teacher education program: Critical dissonance factors. In W. M. Linek, E. G. Sturtevant, J. R. Dugan, & P. E. Linder (Eds.), *Celebrating the voices of literacy* (pp. 235-250). Readyville, TN: CRA.

Strauss, A., & Corbin, J. (1990). *Basics of qualitative research: Grounded theory procedures and techniques.* Newbury Park, CA: Sage Publications, Inc.

Texas Education Agency (TEA). (2001). *Texas Administrative Code.* Retrieved September 25, 2003, from http://info.sos.state.tx.us/pls/pub/readtac$ext.ViewTAC?tac_view=2&ti=19

United States Department of Education (USDOE). (1987). *What works: Research about teaching and learning.* Washington, DC: Author.

United States Department of Education (USDOE). (2002). *Office of elementary and secondary education (OESE).* Retrieved September 15, 2003, from http://www.ed.gov/about/offices/list/oese/index.html?src=mr

Wells, G. (1994). *Changing schools from within: Creating communities of inquiry.* Toronto: OISE.

Wolf, S., Hill, L., & Ballentine, D. (1999). Teaching on fissured ground: Preparing preservice teachers for culturally conscious pedagogy. In T. Shanahan & F. Rodriguez-Brown (Eds.), *National Reading Conference yearbook 48* (pp. 423-436). Chicago: NRC.

Wuthrick, M. (1995). Case studies of teacher change from conventional to holistic literacy instruction. In W. M. Linek & E. G. Sturtevant (Eds.), *Generations of literacy.* Harrisonburg, VA: CRA.

Zeek, C., & Wickstrom, C. (1999). The making of a teacher: The influence of personal literacy development on preservice teachers' current teaching practices. In T. Shanahan & F. Rodriguez-Brown (Eds.), *National Reading Conference yearbook 48* (pp. 479-490). Chicago: NRC.

Effective Professional Development: Tell Me and I Will Hear, Show Me and I Will See, Support Me and I Will Evolve

Allison L. Swan

West Virginia University

Abstract

This study describes the experiences of four elementary teachers as they participated in LEADERS, a professional development initiative in primary reading instruction. The study examined closely which project resources teachers believed were most beneficial in facilitating the implementation of newly learned classroom strategies. The main sources of data included field notes, classroom observations, and teacher self-reporting. The teachers identified the support provided from the university site project's design. The yearlong duration was also noted as a significant factor in its success.

In *Making a Difference Means Making It Different: Honoring Children's Right to Excellent Reading Instruction* (2000), the International Reading Association (IRA) stated that "children have a right to well-prepared teachers who keep their skills up to date through effective professional development" (p. 5). The National Commission on Teaching and America's Future (1996) recognizes that the most important element in successful student learning is high-quality teaching and therefore calls for professional development that is long-term, stable, and systematic. The National Reading Panel (2000) found that participation in high-quality professional development does produce higher student achievement.

Historically, attempts to raise the bar on teacher knowledge through professional development have been carried out in one-day teacher training sessions with outsiders presenting a variety of unconnected strategies and methods. "What everyone appears to want for students—a wide array of learning opportunities that engage students in experiencing, creating, and solving real problems, using their own experiences and working with others—is for some reason denied to teachers when they are the learners" (Leiberman, 1995, p. 591). Current literature informs us that the traditional one-day, isolated, transfer models of professional development are not effective (Birman, Desimone, Porter, & Garet, 2000; Darling-Hammond & Ball, 1999; Lieberman, 1995; Snow, Burns, & Griffin, 1998). In the *Handbook of Reading Research*, Anders, Hoffman, and Duffy (2000) synthesized current research and presented six features for high-quality professional development: (a) intensive/extensive commitment; (b) coaching/clinical model; (c) teacher reflection; (d) deliberation, dialogue, and negotiation; (e) voluntary participation; and (f) collaboration.

Effective professional development requires a great deal of planning, resources, and commitment on part of the developers and stakeholders (Anders et al., 2000; National Reading Panel, 2000; Snow et al., 1998). A project's design should reflect a coherent connection between national, state, and district goals; standards; mandates; and the activities proposed for professional development. The focus of professional development efforts should be grounded in the knowledge base of teachers and questions derived from observations and work with students (Darling-Hammond & McLaughlin, 1995). Opportunities for self-reflection and analysis are also critical for learning to teach (Darling-Hammond & Ball, 1999). Snow et al. (1998) acknowledged that a mentoring coaching clinical approach is essential for effective professional development. Project planners must create opportunities for teachers to work together with colleagues to enhance collaboration and establish a community of learners (Anders et al., 2000; Birman et al., 2000; Darling-Hammond, 1998; Joyce & Showers, 1995; Snow et al., 1998).

Research has been conducted to characterize the specific types of resources teachers consider most beneficial. Teberg's (1999) study reported that teachers believed the two most important variables for implementation were time and money. Time is needed to plan for new classroom practices. The teachers surveyed were quite adamant that these times not take the place of or be combined with their existing planning and preparation period. The research also disclosed that novice teachers wanted financial reimbursement for attending conferences and workshops whereas seasoned teachers preferred their financial contributions be used to provide built in release time to work with other teachers. The results from Klingner, Vaughn, Hughes, and Arguelles' (1999) study indicated that teachers felt that the supportive teaching network, administrative support, response of the students, and their own increased knowledge of the strategies helped them both implement and sustain newly learned strategies. Barriers to the continued use of the strategies included time (preparation for high stakes achievement testing, demands of content coverage or reading block time), mismatch between teaching style and strategy, not having an in depth understanding of the practice, and competing strategies implemented by the school district.

In their blueprint for staff development, the National Staff Development Council (1995) focused their standards on content, context, and process features. The professional development project described in the below study addressed primary reading instruction, took place in a large urban district, and was designed to include process features reflecting best practice as presented in current literature such as coaching/feedback, reflection, balanced reading instruction, and data driven instructional decision making. The purpose of this study was to determine which factors (e.g., site liaison, peer cohort group, administration, change in students' literacy achievement, electronic listserv, website) the teachers believed were most helpful in facilitating the implementation of newly learned classroom practices.

Methods
Professional Development Project

The Literacy Educators Assessing and Developing Early Reading Success (LEADERS) project is a three-year, multi-site, Eisenhower-funded grant project that involved three universities and nine school districts representing 19 elementary schools across the state of Pennsylvania. The schools targeted for participation were schools with large numbers of students from high-poverty backgrounds and/or a large percentage of low performing students. Primary grade teachers volunteered to participate in the yearlong professional development activities. The activities included a weeklong summer institute (30 hours), Saturday workshops (42 hours), and site visits (60 hours). The LEADERS project endorsed a balanced approach for reading. This was defined as a combination of instruction that emphasized sound-letter relationships (phonics skills-based), and immersed students in language and literature (meaning-based) using a variety of instructional techniques, materials, assessments, strategies, and methods beneficial to students' learning styles.

Throughout the year of the project, the participants were supported in a variety of ways. First, both the district and school-level administration supported the project by assisting with recruitment efforts, contributing to the teachers' stipend, and donating teacher in-service days. Second, each school was provided a coach/site liaison. This role was fulfilled by University faculty, doctoral and master's students with teaching experience, and seasoned classroom teachers on special assignment. At the schools, the liaisons visited the classrooms at least twice a month to demonstrate lessons, observe teachers trying new strategies, assist with assessments, work with students, provide resources, and plan lessons with teachers. The third way in which teachers were supported was through peer collaboration. At minimum, the project required a commitment of at least two and not more than five teachers per school for each year of the three-year project. The project established a secure list serve and encouraged teacher communication and idea-sharing. Collaboration between teachers was also facilitated by providing time for discussion and idea-sharing.

The project emphasized the importance of authentic assessment and instructional planning based on students' strengths and weaknesses. Each teacher administered the LEADERS Literacy Assessment Battery, an assessment which included measures to assess phonemic awareness, sight words, pseudowords, fluency, comprehension, writing, and student attitude toward reading and writing. The assessments were given to all students during the fall. Using these results, each teacher and site liaison created a data-driven instructional plan for the class. Additionally, each teacher agreed to conduct an instructional action research project based on the analysis of these results.

Participants

Greene Elementary (pseudonym), a Title 1 School with 79% poverty was situated within a large urban school district located in the Southwestern region of the state. The K-5 school served 338 students, of which 38% were African American and 62% Caucasian. During the year of this study, the school was participating in the LEADERS project for a second year. Further, intensive data collection was carried out during the year at this school. In addition to data presented in this paper on the importance of the project's process features, data were also collected and analyzed which looked at teacher change in practice and beliefs and student growth. The later findings are presented in a larger, in-depth case study monograph (Swan, 2002).

The four teachers who took part in this research study were all Caucasian females. The teachers had a mean of 12.5 years of teaching experience with range from 6 to 20 years. All four teachers held some type of credential or credits toward a Master's degree in addition to undergraduate teaching degrees in either Elementary Education or Early Childhood Development. Three of the four teachers had been employed at the school building from five to eight years; one teacher, through a district transfer, was new to the building. All four teachers voluntarily agreed to participate in both the LEADERS project and this qualitative research study. A fifth teacher participated in the LEADERS project but was excluded from this research study due to a maternity leave of absence.

Data Sources and Analysis

As a participant observer, it is the job of a researcher to become immersed in the scene in order to combine his/her own *etic*, or outsider's perspective, of the setting while gaining (through a trusting relationship) knowledge of the group's *emic*, or insider perspective (Fetterman, 1989). During the year of this study, I served as the LEADERS site liaison/coach for Greene Elementary. I met the teachers for the first time during the August workshop. Over the course of the year, I saw each teacher almost every week. In addition to visiting their classrooms during the reading and language arts blocks, I was also at the school for special events (e.g., Halloween parade, chorus concert). Some of my classroom visits were lengthy—I stayed in a particular classroom for multiple periods. Other visits were brief, lasting just a few minutes. I worked with the teachers in the classroom by planning for new instruction, discussing student achievement, demonstrating, or team teaching. At Greene, I also worked directly with students in all four classrooms. I conducted assessments, worked in small groups, and sometimes read with individual students. LeCompte and Preissle (1993) refer to these repeated observations as "living among participants" (p. 342).

Data collection took place on an ongoing basis during the course of the project's duration (a complete school year) as the events unfolded naturally in the classroom. Data for this case study were collected from two main informant sources: teacher self-report and researcher documentation and field notes. Instruments included: field notes, classroom observations, interviews, self-report literacy practice logs, focus group transcripts, and LEADERS project documentation.

Analysis involved iterative cycles of closely examining documents, field notes, interviews and artifacts; searching for themes; and verifying results. The goals were to (a) search for a global theme or pattern, (b) identify categories of the global theme, (c) develop and assign a coding hierarchy, and (d) cite evidence or details to then support the categories.

The question Merriam (1998) poses regarding validity is, if the "research findings match reality and capture what is really there?" (p. 201). As mentioned, my LEADERS site liaison/coach role afforded me entrance into each classroom. The regularities of the classroom experiences allowed me to observe what normally occurred over the course of the whole school year. Lincoln and Guba (1985) suggest thinking about reliability in qualitative research more as "dependability and consistency" (p. 288). The ongoing collection and recursive analysis aided in the reliability of the findings. Further, during the final interviews, each teacher and I discussed this study's findings and each of the four teachers agreed with the overall outcomes.

Results

The purpose of this study was to determine which features teachers believed were most useful in facilitating the implementation of newly learned classroom practices. The teachers' self reported data indicated that it was the

(a) support from the university, (b) support and collaboration with peers, (c) ability to make decisions about what to implement in their classrooms, and (d) yearlong duration which facilitated their implementation and understanding of the LEADERS project's goals.

University Support

The teachers all identified, as a critical and significant dimension of LEADERS, the support, coaching, and mentorship of the project from the university's site liaison. The project used a coaching/clinical model (Anders et al., 2000; Joyce & Showers, 1995; Snow et al., 1998) as a framework for the relationship between the teachers and the site liaison. The fourth grade teacher said:

> I think the site liaison presence here adds to the project. The fact that there is a connection. You are in our classrooms and we go back and talk about what we are doing. Oh, if we want to try something, you're here to help us. It is the resources you are providing us with—not just the ideas. (Lilly, Final Interview)

By participating in the project, teachers were also given opportunities and access to the teaching resources they needed for instructional purposes and for this the teachers were grateful. Using project funds, each teacher was able to order student materials (e.g. big books, classroom libraries) for her classroom. The teachers also had access to both children's books and professional resources from the University's Reading Center. Additionally, each teacher received membership in the International Reading Association; this included a journal subscription to *The Reading Teacher*, a primary reading resource. One teacher said:

> Between the site liaison's presence, the presence of the books, the presence of the things we need to purchase—there is a lot of support. That is what I'm feeling more than anything else—supported. And I think that is really important. Without the support, the project is just another in-service. (Susan, Focus Group Transcript)

Collaboration

Collaboration among colleagues has been identified as an important component of effective professional development (Anders et al., 2000; Birman et al., 2000; Darling-Hammond, 1998; Joyce & Showers, 1995; Newman, 1994; Snow et al., 1998). The LEADERS project encouraged collaboration among colleagues in each individual school, within the school district, and across the state. At Greene, all four teachers also cited the importance of working together with other professionals as a considerably important part of their experience. The teachers at Greene Elementary created and developed a strong in-house support system for themselves and established a strong community of learners. At the school, the teachers supported each other's instructional efforts, team teaching, and often discussed and compared notes of their action research projects. They participated in activities in and out of school with a common goal of improving practice in order to increase student achievement. Because of the commitments the teachers made to the project, they interacted more and formed their own support network at the school. Three of the teachers decided to continue this professional relationship and expanded it to include new opportunities during the next school year, including a primary book study group and a home and school, parent and teacher involvement project. The kindergarten and second grade teachers commented:

> Kelly, the other kindergarten teacher, was involved in the project last year, and that is nice because she understands the project and we can talk about it. I was thrilled to see she was going to be involved with us this year. We always go into each other's class and take notes. (Nancy, Focus Group Transcript)

> I went to observe someone in the project doing literature circles, and that was very helpful. When I saw Jess (LEADERS teacher at a different school), she had a lot of good ideas on how to do literature circles. I want to try out some things Jess showed me. I think a lot of those things she picked up from LEADERS, too. And then in my building, Lilly and I have been working with the poetry reading with her kids coming down to my class. And I still want to go observe Beth (learning support teacher) and Lilly because they have done that partner reading, and I want to see it in action. (Susan, Focus Group Transcript)

Ownership

The teachers from Greene felt ownership in this project, particularly through the self-selected action research projects they completed. They engaged in what has been identified as instructional decision-making based on student needs (Anders et al., 2000; Guskey, 2000; Joyce & Calhoun, 1999) which provided the teachers a venue for reflective teaching. The teachers used the results from the informal assessment battery to create flexible groups and plan for instruction. Unlike other mandated activities, the action research project was decided, created, and completed by each individual teacher. Completing the focus project successfully required much teacher reflection (Anders et al., 2000; Darling-Hammond, 1998; Grisham, 2000; Olsen & Singer, 1994; Richardson, 1994; Snow et al., 1998). Through decision-making, reflection, and increased collaboration, the teachers took ownership of this professional development project. This ownership was empowering and served to strengthen teachers' beliefs in their own efficacy and professionalism. The fourth grade teacher reflected:

The LEADERS project is relaxed enough; it's not all about demands. I honestly think, it is a cooperative thing. We are treated like professionals. No one is telling you, this is what you have to do. It's more like what do you think about trying this. The assumption is there that we are already doing a good job. And it's not like your kids' test scores are bad so you *will* go to this workshop, which is our alternative for professional development. (Lilly, Phone Interview)

Duration

The teachers involved in LEADERS made a voluntary yearlong commitment to the project which began two weeks before the school year and ended shortly after their school year was over. All four teachers at Greene Elementary attended every workshop and site based meeting and acknowledged the project's ongoing duration as another important aspect for its success. The fourth grade teacher said:

I think another specific difference is that is ongoing. Its not like it is *A* workshop. I think that it is a big difference between an in-service where you have to go sit in (district in-service site name) for two hours. You may try something from those meetings, but there is nothing there to keep you moving in that direction and this program did. I mean we were going to meet with each other again, so we were vested in trying things so we could talk about it when we got together. The ongoing part was the biggest difference. (Susan, Focus Group Transcript)

All four teachers at Greene Elementary agreed that the most prevalent barrier to planning and implementing new practices in the classroom was time (and lack of it). Since the project was not a district-wide initiative, the teachers were never mandated or required to include the new techniques into their lesson plans and classroom instruction. And this made a big difference in how the project was perceived. Implementation occurred only when teachers could find the time to plan for the new instruction within their reading block. Due to the overwhelming demands on the teachers' time during the school day, finding time was the number one barrier to planning and implementing new practices at Greene Elementary.

In summary, the factors that facilitated understanding and implementation of the goals were deeply rooted in the design of the professional development (support, materials, feedback, ongoing nature, reflection, and ownership). The factors that were barriers were rooted in the nature of the school and classrooms (time).

Discussion

The design of the LEADERS project was aligned with research on best practices for professional development. The duration of the project was long-term, and the teachers were supported in a variety of ways. The teachers were encouraged to apply newly learned strategies and were provided coaching and feedback when they did. They made instructional decisions based on the needs of the students in their classrooms. The teachers were provided opportunities to work with other professionals (e.g., teachers and site liaisons) and were expected to reflect on their practices both formally and informally.

Although the teachers in this study did not cite the school's administration as a factor directly related to the project's success, this notion does merit discussion. On two occasions, the school district's central administration and school principal excused the teachers from their district-wide inservice program to attend LEADERS workshops at the university. Further, the school principal was an active, vocal supporter of the LEADERS project. He organized half-day releases for the teachers in the LEADERS cohort to visit another LEADERS school in the district. He also extended an invitation to another school to spend time at Greene. In fact, when the visitors arrived, he asked his LEADERS teachers to demonstrate lessons focusing on their action research projects (e.g., literature circles). The school principal also agreed to fund small purchases for the LEADERS teachers (e.g., multiple copies of books for literature circles, colored baskets and stickers for leveled book libraries). He supported the research being conducted in his school and engaged in informal dialogue with the site liaison during almost all visits. He inquired about the teachers, their students, and observations of the school. His support of his teachers and this professional development effort was evident. The principal was a positive, accommodating leader of a variety of endeavors at Greene aimed at enhancing the students academic experiences and therefore the teachers may have seen his support as a given.

Again, the LEADERS project was not an internal school district initiative, but it was supported by the school district's administration. The National Academy of Education (1999) stated that we are "politically and economically poised to invest in teacher development in ways unlike previous reforms" (p. 59). And schools are investing. However, due to outside pressure and attention to low test scores, some districts may be advocating or mandating one curricular approach for teaching and providing professional development around this one approach or teaching method. This type of model for school-based reform is not always in alignment with the daily work of teachers and their students. By focusing strictly on the curricular level, schools are leaving a vital factor, the classroom teacher, out of the decision-making process. This teacher proof curricula (Stigler & Hiebert, 1999) approach has become somewhat accepted within standards-based reform. Instead of handing teachers a script to follow, reformers need to increase teachers' content knowledge, improve their skills and practices, and develop their abilities to plan effective instruction. Helping teachers to evolve professionally into better teachers will require a great deal of commitment and support.

Currently, the literature stresses the importance of ongoing teacher support and coaching as a variable in successful project implementation. What is not forthcoming in the literature are detailed descriptions of what kind and how much support is needed. Research questions such as the following address this issue. Is the type of support and who provides this support factors to be considered? Do varying levels of clock hours play a role in what or how teachers respond? Do the students of teachers who receive more support from a more experienced coach do better than those who do not? Should the mentoring responsibilities be provided by an outside partner (e.g., University) or by an experienced teacher housed within the school?

Conclusion

Given the emphasis on professional development as a means of improving student achievement, we need models that demonstrate how to promote "best practices" in schools. Popular "sit and get," "hit and run," and "spray and pray" training sessions must be replaced with effective research-based practices for professional development which include factors such as support, feedback, duration, planning, and teacher reflection. The LEADERS project presents one model, based on current research in the areas of reading and professional development that can provide opportunities for study. It is important to understand how best to design professional development so that its implementation is understood (e.g., barriers and facilitators), transferred into the classroom, and reflected in students' academic performance.

References

Anders, P., Hoffman, J., & Duffy, G. (2000). Teaching teachers to teach reading: Paradigm shifts, persistent problems, and challenges. In M. Kamil, P. Mosenthal, P. D. Pearson, & R. Barr (Eds.), *Handbook of reading research* (pp. 719-742). Mahwah, NJ: Lawrence Erlbaum Associates.

Birman, B., Desimone, L., Porter, A., & Garet, M. (2000). Designing professional development that works. *Educational Leadership, 57*(8), 28-33.

Darling-Hammond, L. (1998). Teacher learning that supports student learning. *Educational Leadership, 55*(5), 6-12.

Darling-Hammond, L., & Ball, D. L. (1999). *Teaching for high standards: What policymakers need to know and be able to do.* Philadelphia: National Commission on Teaching and America's Future Consortium For Policy Research In Education.

Darling-Hammond, L., & McLaughlin, M. (1995). Policies that support professional development in an era of reform. *Phi Delta Kappan, 76*(8), 597-604.

Fetterman, D. M. (1989). *Ethnography step by step.* Newbury Park, CA: SAGE Publications, Inc.

Grisham, D. (2000). Connecting theoretical conceptions of reading to practice: A longitudinal study of elementary school teachers. *Reading Psychology, 21*(2), 145-170.

Gusky, T. (2000). *Evaluating professional development.* Thousand Oaks, CA: Corwin Press.

International Reading Association. (2000). *Making a difference means making it different: Honoring children's right to excellent reading instruction.* Newark, DE: International Reading Association.

Joyce, B., & Calhoun, E. (1999). Strengthening teachers: Stetting a standard for professional development and school renewal. *American School Board Journal, 186*(3), 35-37.

Joyce, B., & Showers, B. (1995). *Student achievement through staff development: Fundamentals of school renewal.* White Plains, NY: Longman.

Klingner, J., Vaughn, S., Hughes, M. T., & Arguelles, M. (1999). Sustaining research-based practices in reading: A three year follow up. *Remedial and Special Education, 20*(5), 263-275.

LeCompte, M. D., & Preissle, J. (1993). *Ethnography and qualitative design in educational research.* San Diego, CA: Academic Press.

Lieberman, A. (1995). Practices that support teacher development. *Phi Delta Kappan, 76*(8), 591-596.

Lincoln, Y. S., & Guba, E. G. (1985) *Naturalistic inquiry.* Thousand Oaks, CA: Sage Publications.

Merriam, S. (1998). *Qualitative research and case study in education.* San Francisco, CA: Jossey-Bass Inc.

National Academy of Education. (1999). *Recommendations regarding research priorities. An advisory report to the National Educational Research Policy and Priorities Board.* New York: National Academy of Education.

National Commission on Teaching and America's Future. (1996). *What matters most: Teaching for America's future.* New York: Teachers College Press.

National Reading Panel. (2000). *Teaching children to read: An evidence-based assessment of the scientific research literature on reading and its implications for reading instruction.* Washington, DC: National Institute of Child Health and Human Development.

National Staff Development Council. (1995). *Standards for staff development: Elementary school edition.* Oxford, OH: National Staff Development Council.

Newman, F. (1994, Spring). School-wide professional community. *Issues in Restructuring Schools* (pp. 1-2). Madison, WI: National Center on Organization and Restructuring of Schools.

Olsen, J., & Singer, M. (1994). Examining teacher beliefs, reflective change, and the teaching of reading. *Reading Research and Instruction, 34*(2), 97-110.

Richardson, V. (Ed.). (1994). T*eacher change and the staff development process: A case in reading instruction.* New York: Teachers College Press.

Snow, C., Burns, M. S., & Griffin, P. (Eds.). (1998). *Preventing reading difficulties in young children.* Washington, DC: National Academy Press.

Stigler, J. W., & Hiebert, J. (1999). *The teaching gap. Best ideas from the world's teachers for improving education in the classroom.* New York: The Free Press.

Swan, A. L. (2002). *A case study on the effects of a professional development project in early reading instruction.* Dissertation Abstracts International, 63(05), 1770A. (UMI No. 3054342).

Teberg, A. (1999). *Identified professional development needs of teachers in curriculum reform.* Paper presented at the American Educational Research Association, Montreal, Quebec.

How Well Can Teachers Determine Reading Levels from an Informal Reading Inventory?

Jerry L. Johns
Susan K. L'Allier

Northern Illinois University

Abstract

This study examined how reliably practicing teachers completed summary sheets and interpreted data regarding three students' performances on an informal reading inventory. Participants (N=31) enrolled in a graduate course in reading received instruction in the administration, scoring, and interpretation of the Basic Reading Inventory. After instruction, participants completed summary sheets and interpreted those results to determine the independent, instructional, and frustration reading levels for each student. Their responses were compared to the consensus responses of three experts. Results indicated that the participants were able to reliably complete the summary sheets, showing a 98% average agreement rate with the experts. Participants' reliability for determining the three reading levels was an 89% average agreement rate. Focusing on the errors made by the participants, the investigators provide suggestions as to how instruction provided by teacher trainers and schools district personnel can lead to similar, or even better, reliability results.

Once an informal reading inventory is given, the data are usually entered on a summary sheet, and the student's three reading levels (independent, instructional, and frustration) are determined. This study was undertaken to determine how reliably teachers entered data and determined three students' reading levels on the *Basic Reading Inventory* (Johns, 2001).

Framework for the Study

Informal reading inventories "are excellent tools for combining both diagnostic and summative assessments in an authentic format" (Paris & Carpenter, 2003, p. 580). Most informal reading inventories include a set of common components: (a) graded word lists to help determine the starting point for passage reading, (b) one or more sets of graded passages for students to read orally and/or silently, and (c) questions for each passage. Analysis of the oral miscues (deviations from the printed text) and responses to the questions help to determine a student's reading strengths and weaknesses and also provide some of the basic information with which to determine a student's independent, instructional, and frustration levels.

While discussion of the value and types of informal assessments occurred in the early decades of the 20th century (Durrell, 1937; Gray, 1920; Waldo, 1915; Wheat, 1923), the use of an informal reading inventory that included the determination of the three reading levels was refined through the work of Betts (1946). Since that time, many informal reading inventories have been published (Jongsma & Jongsma, 1981; Pikulski, 1990), and guidelines for developing one's own inventory have also been established (Johnson, Kress, & Pikulski, 1987).

As the number and use of published informal reading inventories grew, so too did the research about various aspects of those inventories. Much of this research has contributed to determining the components and scoring guidelines of current inventories. One of the early controversies concerned whether a 95% criterion level for the word recognition score is the most valid criterion for the instructional level (Anderson & Joels, 1986; Betts, 1946; Davis & Ekwall, 1976; Homan & Klesius, 1985; Johns & Magliari, 1989). There continues to be a lack of agreement regarding this criterion.

Research that focused on what should be counted as a reading miscue (Anderson & Joels, 1986; Ekwall, 1974) has also influenced today's informal reading inventories. Most notably, Goodman's (1973) work about significant miscues led to many of today's informal reading inventories including some method of analyzing whether or not each miscue is a meaning-changing one.

The passages and comprehension questions also received much attention. Concerns arose over whether passages in informal reading inventories were representative of their specified grade levels and whether they were consistent across the sets of passages within the same reading inventory. In their reliability study, Helgren-Lempesis and Mangrum (1986) found that the same-level passages across forms of a single inventory were more consistent than critics suggested. Research has also had an impact on the comprehension dimension of many currently published inventories. Caldwell's (1985) work led to many inventories incorporating a prior knowledge assessment of passage topics. In addition, criticism surrounding the validity of questions as the sole measure of comprehension (Allen & Swearingen, 1991) has led to some inventories now recommending that students be asked to retell the passage before answering the questions. To address the criticism that students had to rely on memory alone to answer the questions (Cardarelli, 1988; Kender & Rubenstein, 1977), at least one inventory (Leslie & Caldwell, 2001) now recommends that students be asked to refer back to the text (look-backs or reinspection) to make a second attempt at questions not answered by initial recall.

While discussion about the critical components and procedures continue, there has been and continues to be widespread use of published informal reading inventories in schools today (Ackland, 1994; Harris & Lalik, 1987; Margolis & McCabe, 1988; Searles, 1988). Classroom teachers are using them for a variety of purposes: (a) to match a student to appropriate instructional materials (Harris & Lalik, 1987; Searles, 1988), (b) to determine a student's strengths and weaknesses (Ackland, 1994), and (c) to document progress (Edger, 2000; VanLeirsburg & Johns, 1995). In this age where standards developed by state agencies and professional organizations call for the use of multiple indicators to demonstrate progress, the informal reading inventory is often used as one of those indicators.

If teachers are using informal reading inventories, it is important to know how reliably they are scoring and interpreting the results. Reliability of administration and scoring has been a frequently-cited concern (Harris & Lalik, 1987; Kelly, 1970; Klesius & Homan, 1985; Paris, Paris, & Carpenter, 2001) but an area of relatively little research. Windell (1975) developed a module to teach about the informal reading inventory and found that preservice special education teachers who went through the module could effectively determine a student's instructional level. Traynelis-Yurek and Strong (2000) examined preservice teachers' actual scoring of a simulated informal reading inventory. Even though they had received instruction about the administration and scoring prior to the simulation activity, these preservice teachers, who came from three different teacher-training programs, still had difficulty accurately scoring miscues and comprehension.

Two studies compared the effectiveness of two different types of instruction. In his work with graduate students, Roberts (1974) examined students' ability to identify oral reading errors and reading level. The results indicated that participants in the experimental group who received basic instruction about the procedures and scoring plus practice sessions with instructor feedback were significantly better at identifying oral reading errors than participants in the control group who only received the basic instruction. However, the experimental group was not significantly better at determining the reading level. Wedman, Hughes, and Robinson's (1993) study focused on preservice teachers. The control group received lectures about and examples of how to score an informal reading inventory. The experimental group received the lectures and examples but also scored informal inventory responses in group and individual settings, receiving feedback about their scoring from the instructor. On a multiple-choice test related to the administration and scoring of informal reading inventories, the experimental group scored significantly better than the control group.

The small amount of research about reliability of teacher scoring and instructional effectiveness has mostly been conducted with preservice teachers. This study examines the reliability of scoring by practicing teachers who received approximately two hours of instruction. In addition to the information about the reliability of scoring, this study will also contribute to the field by delineating a methodology that could be used in future studies.

Method
Sample

Thirty-one students enrolled in a graduate reading course titled "Diagnosis and Treatment of Reading Difficulties" were asked to complete three summary sheets from the *Basic Reading Inventory* (Johns, 2001). All the students were majoring in reading and they were all teachers—mostly elementary teachers—with classroom experience ranging from 2 to 26 years. Information concerning the amount of actual experience the teachers had with informal reading inventories in their classrooms was not collected as a part of this study, but informal reports from the course instructor revealed that such experience was not extensive.

This reading course was their second or third graduate course in reading. In an earlier course that focused on formal and informal assessments, these graduate students had learned about informal reading inventories, administered at least one informal reading inventory, and prepared a written summary report of the results. As part of the "Diagnosis and Treatment of Reading Difficulties" course, the students reviewed the administration and scoring procedures for a variety of assessments, including the *Basic Reading Inventory*. In addition, attention was given to the interpretation of assessment results. Approximately two hours of class time was spent on the *Basic Reading Inventory*, including a discussion of scoring procedures and determining reading levels.

Materials for the Study

The teachers involved in the study did not actually administer the *Basic Reading Inventory*. Instead, they were asked to complete and score the data given on each summary sheet. This procedure, while limiting in some respects, permitted a standard set of exercises to be presented to the teachers.

One investigator prepared partial summary sheets reflecting performances for three different elementary students who might have taken the *Basic Reading Inventory*. The students' summary sheets were based on the performances of actual students from three different grades (i.e., second, fourth, and sixth). For each student's summary sheet, various bits of information were missing.

The graduate students did simple addition and used various scoring guides to fill in the missing information prior to estimating each student's reading levels. The summary sheets presented to the graduate students in this study are shown in Appendices A, B, and C.

The summary sheets, scoring guides, and a one-page summary of the *Basic Reading Inventory* administration and scoring procedures were then sent to three experts who had considerable experience using and teaching informal reading inventories. They independently filled in the missing information and determined each student's three reading levels (e.g., independent, instructional, and frustration). One of the experts was a reading consultant/specialist with a master's degree in reading who had been in her current position for two years. Another expert was a Title I reading teacher with 21 years of total teaching experience. The final expert had 34 years of experience in various positions: classroom teacher, reading specialist, reading coordinator, and reading consultant.

The experts' sheets were compared to the investigator's completed "master" sheets. Only one expert's summaries did not match the master sheets in 2 of the 39 areas completed, so the initial agreement among the experts and the investigator was 98%. Where there was not initial agreement, a discussion of the differences resulted in total agreement among the three experts and the principal investigator.

Procedure

The instructor of the "Diagnosis and Treatment of Reading Difficulties" course was sent the master copies of the materials that had been previously sent to the experts. She then duplicated the materials and, following the class lectures and sample exercises, had her students complete the summary sheets during a portion of one of the class sessions. The materials were then returned to the investigators for analysis.

Each completed summary sheet was compared to the master sheet that represented the consensus responses of the experts. On the summary sheet for the first student (Appendix A), seven pieces of information needed to be completed: the total score for words in isolation for grade two and the reading level associated with this total (two items); the reading level associated with a specific number of miscues for grade three (1 item); the reading level associated with a specific comprehension score for grade two (1 item); and the overall reading levels (3 items). For the summary sheet on the second student (Appendix B), 11 pieces of information needed to be completed: the totals for words in isolation for grades two and four and the reading level associated with each total (four items); the reading level associated with the miscues for grades two and four (two items); the reading level associated with the comprehension questions in grades two and four (two items); and the overall reading levels (three items). On the third student's summary sheet (Appendix C), 21 pieces of information were required. Completing this summary sheet required teachers to make the most decisions and judgments as only the subtotals of words identified, the number of miscues made, and the number of questions missed were provided.

Each subject's summary sheet was then compared to that of the experts. Three percentages of agreement were determined for each summary sheet. The first was an agreement percentage based on the total number of decisions that were made. The second was a percentage based on all items except those related to the three reading levels. The third percentage was based on how well the subjects agreed with the experts' determination of the three reading levels. It was expected that subjects would have a high degree of agreement with experts in totaling numbers and using scoring guides to map specific numbers to their corresponding levels for individual passage miscues and comprehension responses. However, the most difficult and important task was to estimate each student's independent, instructional, and frustration levels based on all the available data. Such decisions require the synthesis of data and professional judgments and, thus, it was expected that the most critical reliability issue in this study—the percentage of agreement about the reading levels—might be somewhat lower than that of the simpler tasks.

Results

Based on the above procedures, reliability percentages with expert consensus were determined. Table 1 displays the findings.

Table 1. Percentages of Agreement with Experts in *Basic Reading Inventory* Scoring

STUDENT	OVERALL AGREEMENT	NON-READING LEVEL INFORMATION AGREEMENT	READING LEVEL AGREEMENT
1	94%	100%	85%
2	96%	98%	94%
3	97%	98%	89%
Average	96%	98%	89%

The total overall agreement with the experts was extremely high. For each of the summary sheets, the percentage was 94 or better. Total agreement was 96% when the data for the three summary sheets were combined. When all data except the information on the three reading levels were considered, the percentage of agreement was slightly higher for each of the summary sheets. The overall agreement with the experts was 98%. When the subjects' determination of the reading levels was compared to that of the experts, the percentage of agreement ranged from 85 to 94 with an average agreement percentage of 89. The average percentage of agreement was very high considering that the determination of reading levels requires data synthesis and judgments. Determining the reading levels for the first student did not appear to involve more synthesis or judgments than were required for the latter two students. It is hypothesized that the lower agreement percentage for the first student may be due to the fact that the subjects were required to complete less information and, thus, may have spent less time thinking about all of the data. One might also hypothesize that the first student provided the subjects with the necessary practice so that their abilities to synthesize and make appropriate judgments improved as they worked with the data for the second and third students.

Conclusions, Discussion, and Limitations

The question posed in the title of this study was "How well can teachers determine reading levels from an informal reading inventory?" A reasonable answer, based on the data reported in this study, is that teachers can achieve extremely high levels of agreement with experts in completing three different summary sheets. When the task involves entering data and using scoring guides, the agreement with experts is 98%. When the task becomes more complex and requires professional judgment, overall agreement with experts still remains very high (89%).

Determining a student's three reading levels (i.e., independent, instructional, and frustration) is one of the major reasons for giving an informal reading inventory. As can be seen by the agreement percentages for the three summary charts, there is a range of agreements (85%-94%) with experts. Students' reading performances rarely match the standards commonly used for assigning reading levels (Johns, 2001). The result is that the teacher is faced with making judgments in "gray" areas. For example, the summary sheet for the first student (Appendix A) presented at least two areas where judgments needed to be made in determining the student's three reading levels. Grade 1 is not clearly independent because of the number of miscues, and grade 2 is not clearly instructional because of the number of comprehension questions missed. The subjects needed to resolve these items by considering the data within a particular grade as well as among the various grades. One subject's thinking *may* have been something like the following:

> Grade 1 is not clearly at the independent level, but the pre-primer and primer levels are clearly independent. The miscue score for grade 1 is between independent and instructional. Because the other two levels (word list recognition and comprehension) are independent, I will

tentatively call grade 1 independent. Although pre-primer, primer, and grade 1 are all independent, I will tentatively record on the summary sheet that grade 1 is the student's independent level, since I should use the highest level at which the student is independent.

For grade 2, the comprehension score is between independent and instructional. The word list recognition and miscue scores for grade 2 are clearly instructional, so I estimate grade 2 to be instructional. The data for grade 3 is frustration in each area, so that grade is the student's frustration level.

When synthesizing all of these decisions, it seems that the data support grade 1 as the highest independent level, grade 2 as the instructional level, and grade 3 as the frustration level.

It is encouraging to see that teachers, when given some basic instruction about and examples of the scoring and interpretation of an informal reading inventory, agree with experts in assigning reading levels nearly 90% of the time.

This study is limited to one informal reading inventory and a single group of teachers enrolled in a graduate reading course. The implications of the results should be restricted to the types of teachers who enroll in such courses. Teachers in this particular course taught a variety of grade levels and all of them were pursuing a master's degree in reading. As a group, they were interested in reading and were expected to become proficient in administering, scoring, and interpreting a variety of assessment instruments.

Another limitation is that the teachers did not actually administer the informal reading inventory; they were only required to complete the summary sheets. While their collective judgments were highly consistent with expert scoring, this finding should not be generalized as representing the reliability of the complete administration and scoring of an informal reading inventory. A future study that examines how reliably graduate students score miscues and comprehension responses from a standard videoed administration of an informal reading inventory would provide additional information about the qualitative and quantitative judgments required during those steps of the process. However, the results of this study do indicate that teachers, given data about miscues and comprehension responses, could make the critical decisions needed to appropriately determine a student's independent, instructional, and frustration reading levels.

Finally, the three summary sheets that served as the basis for this study were developed to represent a range of decisions that teachers are expected to make when compiling the results from the *Basic Reading Inventory*. These sheets cannot represent the full range of data teachers will encounter, but they offer some variety for determining reading levels. Because three different summary sheets were completed, greater confidence can be placed in the agreement percentages. The range of percentages for reading level agreement reported in Table 1 makes it clear that some data posed greater challenges for making decisions about reading levels. Overall, the results from this study offer compelling evidence that teachers can achieve a high percentage of agreement in completing summary sheets and determining students' three reading levels on the *Basic Reading Inventory*.

Future Directions: Helping Teachers Achieve Higher Levels of Scoring Expertise

As the data were being compiled and analyzed, several observations were made. These observations led to the following recommendations that teacher trainers and professionals in school districts may want to incorporate into their training sessions in order for the teacher participants to achieve higher levels of scoring expertise with the *Basic Reading Inventory*. The investigators believe these recommendations are applicable for instruction about other informal reading inventories as well.

It is recommended that teachers review and follow the prescribed administration and scoring procedures for the informal reading inventory. Provide teachers with copies for easy reference when they are summarizing results. For example, a one-page summary of the administration and scoring procedures for the *Basic Reading Inventory* can be found on page 48 of the manual (Johns, 2001).

Encourage teachers to recheck their work. In this investigation, twenty errors were the result of using the scoring guides incorrectly or failing to supply the data requested. This number represented 2% of the total decisions teachers had to make when completing the summary charts. The consequence of these errors, while seemingly small, appeared to impact the determination of the students' reading levels in several instances.

Review the general guidelines for determining a student's three reading levels. Demonstrate by thinking aloud how data are considered for a particular grade level and how to make a judgment for that level as well as the levels before and after the level in question. For the *Basic Reading Inventory,* Section Three of the manual (Johns, 2001, pp. 49-56) would be a helpful resource.

Give teachers guided practice in determining reading levels. The summary sheets included in Appendices A, B, and C may be used for training purposes. Table 2 provides the reading levels as determined by the three experts. In addition, provide other examples of summary sheets based on students' reading. Take time to discuss the results and answer questions to achieve greater consensus.

**Table 2. Experts' Consensus of the Reading Levels
for the Three Summary Sheets**

SUMMARY SHEET	INDEPENDENT LEVEL	INSTRUCTIONAL LEVEL	FRUSTRATION LEVEL
A	1	2	3
B	2	3	4
C	3	4	5

Gaining confidence and expertise with the *Basic Reading Inventory* or any informal reading inventory requires experience with the assessment instrument. Time and quality training programs will help teachers use informal reading inventories to make more informed decisions about the levels at which students are reading and to place them in materials that will support them as they become better readers.

References

Ackland, R. T. (1994). Let's look at reading: Interactive professional development using informal reading inventories. *Dissertation Abstracts International, 55*(11), 3477.

Allen, D. D., & Swearingen, R. A. (1991, May). *Informal reading inventories: What are they really asking?* Paper presented at the Annual Meeting of the International Reading Association, Las Vegas, NV.

Anderson, B., & Joels, R. W. (1986). Informal reading inventories. *Reading Improvement, 23*, 299-302.

Betts, E. A. (1946). *Foundations of reading instruction.* New York: American Book Company.

Caldwell, J. (1985). A new look at the old informal reading inventory. *The Reading Teacher, 39*, 168-173.

Cardarelli, A. F. (1988). The influence of reinspection on students' IRI results. *The Reading Teacher, 41*, 664-667.

Davis, E. E., & Ekwall, E. E. (1976). Mode of perception and frustration in reading. *Journal of Learning Disabilities, 9*, 53-59.

Durrell, D. (1937). Individual differences and their implications with respect to instruction in reading. In G. M. Whipple (Ed.), *The teaching of reading: The 36th yearbook of the National Society for the Study of Education* (Part 1, pp. 325-356). Bloomington, IL: Pubic School Publishing Co.

Edgar, M. (2000). *Appraising reading achievment.* (ERIC Document Reproduction Service No. ED441217)

Ekwall, E. E. (1974). Should repetitions be counted as errors? *The Reading Teacher, 27*, 365-367.

Goodman, K. S. (1973). Analysis of oral reading miscues: Applied psycholinguistics. In F. Smith (Ed.), *Psycholinguistics and reading* (pp. 158-176). New York: Holt, Rinehart and Winston.

Gray, W. S. (1920). The value of informal tests of reading achievement. *Journal of Educational Research, 1*, 103-111.

Harris, L. A., & Lalik, R. M. (1987). Teacher's use of informal reading inventories: An example of school constraints. *The Reading Teacher, 40,* 624-630.

Helgren-Lempesis, V. A., & Mangrum, C. T., II. (1986). An analysis of alternate-form reliability of three commercially-prepared informal reading inventories. *Reading Research Quarterly, 21,* 209-215.

Homan, S. P., & Klesius, J. P. (1985). A re-examination of the IRI: Word recognition criteria. *Reading Horizons, 26,* 54-61.

Johns, J. L. (2001). *Basic reading inventory* (8th ed.). Dubuque, IA: Kendall/Hunt.

Johns, J. L., & Magliari, A. M. (1989). Informal reading inventories: Are the Betts criteria the best criteria? *Reading Improvement, 26,* 124-132.

Johnson, M. S., Kress, R. A., & Pikulski, J. J. (1987). *Informal reading inventories* (2nd ed.). Newark, DE: International Reading Association.

Jongsma, K. S., & Jongsma, E. A. (1981). Test review: Commercial informal reading inventories. *The Reading Teacher, 34,* 697-705.

Kelly, D. (1970). Using an informal reading inventory to place children in instructional materials. In W. K. Durr (Ed.), *Reading difficulties: Diagnosis, correction, and remediation* (pp. 111-119). Newark, DE: International Reading Association.

Kender, J. P., & Rubenstein, H. (1977). Recall versus reinspection in IRI comprehension tests. *The Reading Teacher, 30,* 776-779.

Klesius, J. P., & Homan, S. P. (1985). A validity and reliability update on the informal reading inventory with suggestions for improvement. *Journal of Learning Disabilities, 18,* 71-76.

Leslie, L., & Caldwell, J. (2001). *Qualitative reading inventory-3.* New York: Longman.

Margolis, H., & McCabe, P. (1988). The use of test results by elementary school teachers to place students in basal and content materials. *Ohio Reading Teacher, 22,* 6-14.

Paris, S. G., & Carpenter, R. D. (2003). FAQs about IRIs. *The Reading Teacher, 56,* 578-580.

Paris, S. G., Paris, A. H., & Carpenter, R. D. (2001). *Effective practices for assessing young readers.* (Report No. CIERA-3-013). Ann Arbor, MI: Center for the Improvement of Early Reading Achievement.

Pikulski, J. J. (1990). Informal reading inventories. *The Reading Teacher, 43,* 514-516.

Roberts, J. D. (1974). Identification of oral reading errors and functional reading levels on informal reading inventories. *Dissertation Abstracts International, 35*(9), 5994.

Searles, E. F. (1988). What's the value of an IRI? Is it being used? *Reading Horizons, 28,* 92-101.

Traynelis-Yurek, E., & Strong, M. W. (2000). Preservice teachers' ability to determine miscues and comprehension response errors of elementary students. *Journal of Reading Education, 26*(1), 15-22.

VanLeirsburg, P., & Johns, J. L. (1995). Portfolios: Teachers' perceptions and practices. *Michigan Reading Journal, 29,* 14-23.

Waldo, K. D. (1915). Tests in reading in Sycamore schools. *The Elementary School Journal, 15,* 251-268.

Wedman, J. M., Hughes, J. A., & Robinson, R. R. (1993). The effect of using a systematic cooperative learning approach to help preservice teachers learn informal reading inventory procedures. *Innovative Higher Education, 17,* 231-241.

Wheat, H. G. (1923). *The teaching of reading.* Boston: Ginn and Company.

Windell, I. (1975). Development and evaluation of a module to train special education teacher trainees to determine a pupil's instructional reading level. (ERIC Document Reproduction Service No. ED111142)

Appendix A Summary Sheet of Reading Performance for a Second-Grade Student

Eighth Edition	BASIC READING INVENTORY PERFORMANCE BOOKLET	A Oral Reading

Jerry L. Johns, Ph.D.

Student _____   Grade _____ Sex M F   Date of Test _____
School _____   Examiner _____   Date of Birth _____
Address _____   Current Book/Level _____   Age _____

SUMMARY OF STUDENT'S READING PERFORMANCE

| Grade | Word Recognition | | | | | | Comprehension | | | |
| | Isolation (Word Lists) | | | | Context (Passages) | | Oral Reading Form A | | Silent Reading Form D | |
	Sight	Analysis	Total	Level	Miscues	Level	Questions Missed	Level	Questions Missed	Level
PP	16	3	19	Ind.	0	Ind.	0	Ind.		
P	15	3	18	Inst.	1	Ind.	1/2	Ind.		
1'	16	4	20	Ind.	2	Ind./Inst.	1	Ind.		
2	14	2			5	Inst.	1 1/2			
3	9	2	11	Frus.	10		5	Frus.		
4										
5										
6										
7										
8										
9										
10										
11										
12										

◄——— Fill in.

ESTIMATE OF READING LEVELS

◄—— Fill in.

Independent _____   Instructional _____   Frustration _____

| Word Recognition Scoring Guide | | | Comprehension Scoring Guide | |
Total Miscues	Level	Significant Miscues	Questions Missed	Level
0–1	Independent	0–1	0–1	Independent
2–4	Ind./Inst.	2	1½–2	Ind./Inst.
5	Instructional	3	2½	Instructional
6–9	Inst./Frust.	4	3–4½	Inst./Frust.
10 +	Frustration	5 +	5 +	Frustration

Scoring Guide for Graded Word Lists

Independent	Instructional	Frustration
20 19	18 17 16 15 14	13 or less

1. Complete the summary where necessary.
2. Study the overall results.
3. Estimate reading levels. Fill in the chart. Remember:
   •Reading levels generally go in order.
   •Only the instructional level can have a range of two or more levels.

Appendix B. Summary Sheet of Reading Performance for a Fourth-Grade Student

Eighth Edition

BASIC READING INVENTORY PERFORMANCE BOOKLET
Jerry L. Johns, Ph.D.

A Oral Reading

Student _____ Grade _____ Sex M F Date of Test _____

School _____ Examiner _____ Date of Birth _____

Address _____ Current Book/Level _____ Age _____

SUMMARY OF STUDENT'S READING PERFORMANCE

Grade	Word Recognition						Comprehension			
	Isolation (Word Lists)				Context (Passages)		Oral Reading Form A		Silent Reading Form D	
	Sight	Analysis	Total	Level	Miscues	Level	Questions Missed	Level	Questions Missed	Level
PP										
P										
1	20	0	20	Ind.	1	Ind.	2	Ind./Inst.		
2	19	1			4		1			
3	13	2	15	Inst.	5	Inst.	2½	Inst.		
4	9	4			8		5½			
5	6	2	8	Frus.						
6										
7										
8										
9					ESTIMATE OF READING LEVELS					
10										
11										
12					Independent _____ Instructional _____ Frustration _____					

← Fill in.

← Fill in.

Word Recognition Scoring Guide

Total Miscues	Level	Significant Miscues
0–1	Independent	0–1
2–4	Ind./Inst.	2
5	Instructional	3
6–9	Inst./Frust.	4
10 +	Frustration	5 +

Comprehension Scoring Guide

Questions Missed	Level
0–1	Independent
1½–2	Ind./Inst.
2½	Instructional
3–4½	Inst./Frust.
5 +	Frustration

Scoring Guide for Graded Word Lists

Independent	Instructional	Frustration
20 19	18 17 16 15 14	13 or less

1. Complete the summary where necessary.
2. Study the overall results.
3. Estimate reading levels. Fill in the chart. Remember:
   •Reading levels generally go in order.
   •Only the instructional level can have a range of two or more levels.

Appendix C. Summary Sheet of Reading Performance for a Sixth-Grade Student.

| Eighth Edition | **BASIC READING INVENTORY PERFORMANCE BOOKLET** Jerry L. Johns, Ph.D. | | A Oral Reading |

Student _____ Grade _____ Sex M F Date of Test _____
School _____ Examiner _____ Date of Birth _____
Address _____ Current Book/Level _____ Age _____

SUMMARY OF STUDENT'S READING PERFORMANCE

Grade	Word Recognition						Comprehension				
	Isolation (Word Lists)				Context (Passages)		Oral Reading Form A Questions		Silent Reading Form D Questions	
	Sight	Analysis	Total	Level	Miscues	Level	Missed	Level	Missed	Level
PP										
P										
1										
2	18	1			2					
3	18	2			6		1			
4	15	3			10		2			
5	11	2			12		4			
6	9	1					6			
7										
8										
9				ESTIMATE OF READING LEVELS						
10										
11										
12				Independent _____ Instructional _____ Frustration _____						

← Fill in.

← Fill in.

Word Recognition Scoring Guide			Comprehension Scoring Guide	
Total Miscues	Level	Significant Miscues	Questions Missed	Level
0–1	Independent	0–1	0–1	Independent
2–4	Ind./Inst.	2	1½–2	Ind./Inst.
5	Instructional	3	2½	Instructional
6–9	Inst./Frust.	4	3–4½	Inst./Frust.
10 +	Frustration	5 +	5 +	Frustration

Scoring Guide for Graded Word Lists

Independent	Instructional	Frustration
20 19	18 17 16 15 14	13 or less

1. Complete the summary where necessary.
2. Study the overall results.
3. Estimate reading levels. Fill in the chart. Remember:
   •Reading levels generally go in order.
   •Only the instructional level can have a range of two or more levels.

CELEBRATING
TECHNOLOGY

Teachers' Evaluations of Word Identification Software: Implications for Literacy Methods Courses

Barbara J. Fox

North Carolina State University

Abstract

Reports two studies of teachers' and parents' evaluations of word identification software for beginning readers, and explores five implications for including software in literacy methods courses. No significant differences were found in word identification preferences among reading and special education teachers, and among teachers with different theoretical orientations. Significant differences were found for teachers' and parents' evaluations, and for software identified as consistent with teachers' theoretical orientations. Open-ended questions provided insight into teachers' rationale for software evaluations.

Evidence-based teaching practices became federal education policy when the No Child Left Behind Act was signed into law on January 8, 2001. The U.S. Department of Education cites systematic phonics as an effective evidence-based practice, and recommends that phonics be taught early, before the second grade (Armbruster, Lehr, & Osborn, 2001). Convinced that technology-enhanced learning is a means of improving achievement, policy makers included in the No Child Left Behind Act provisions for schools to purchase technology resources (The Facts About 21st Century Technology, 2002). The benefits of technology-enhanced learning, however, may not depend so much on access to technology, but rather on the quality of the technology teachers select.

Word identification software can improve the phonological awareness and word identification of school age (MacArthur, Ferretti, Okolo, & Cavalier, 2001) and preschool children (Mioduser, Tur-Kaspa, & Leitner, 2000). Children as young as three and four are developmentally ready to interact with computers, and kindergartners successfully use computer software individually or in small groups (Haugland, 1995). With the new federal emphasis on evidence-based practice, some teachers may use word identification software to give beginning readers extra practice with phonics and phonics-related skills. Word identification software might provide a way to adjust phonics practice to meet individual needs and, potentially, conserve class time. By using word identification software for a portion of phonics practice, teachers increase the class time available for exploring new information and applying phonics when reading and writing. In light of the national emphasis on early reading achievement, parents may purchase word identification software in the belief that it stimulates their children's interest in reading, and at the same time helps children learn letter names, letter-sounds and written words.

While there is a plethora of word identification software from which to choose, relatively little is known about teachers' and parents' software preferences. Insight into teachers' preferences may provide teacher educators with a basis for selecting software to highlight in literacy methods courses, and may also provide guidance in planning experiences that better equip preservice and inservice teachers to teach in technology-enhanced, evidence-based learning environments. In addition, insight into parents' preferences may help literacy teacher educators guide preservice and inservice teachers in their interactions with parents who wish to purchase software for their young children.

Study 1

The purpose of this study was to conduct a preliminary investigation of the software evaluations of reading teachers, special education teachers and the parents of young children. If reading and special education teachers differ in their evaluations, then literacy teacher educators may wish to select examples of software preferred by each teacher group. Conversely, if there are no differences in teachers' preferences, then teacher educators may select software solely based on its potential to support word learning. Literacy methods courses usually include a component on interacting with parents. With easy access to word identification software, some parents purchase word identification software for their children to use at home. Insights into parents' software evaluations may help teacher educators structure experiences so as to guide preservice and inservice teachers in responding to parents' software questions. The two research questions were:

Question 1. Do reading and special education teachers differ in their evaluations of word identification software for supporting the class-room instruction of beginning readers?

Question 2. Do teachers and parents differ in their evaluations of word identification software for supporting the learning of beginning readers?

Method

Participants

The participants were 24 teachers in a graduate literacy methods course in a university in a southeastern state, 12 reading and 12 special education teachers, and 24 parents of children ages four through seven. The mean number of years teaching was 2.9 (SD = 1.4) for reading teachers and 2.8 (SD = 1.5) for special education teachers. T-tests revealed no significant difference in teaching experience between the two groups. All the parents completed high school, and over half of mothers (62%) and fathers (82%) had a four-year college degree. Seventy percent reported that they purchased educational software for their children, 83% reported that their children used the family computer for playing non-educational games, and 37% indicated that the school encouraged them to purchase educational software.

Materials

Teachers evaluated seven word identification programs for beginning readers, while parents evaluated three of the seven programs. The software was appropriate for beginning readers who have not yet learned the alphabet, phonics letter-sound associations and often-used whole words. Programs included activities to develop rhyme and sound awareness, and some experience spelling and writing often-used words. Programs A, B and C, rated by teachers and parents, were appropriate for children ranging in age from three to seven. The age range designated by the manufacturers of programs D through G, rated by only teachers, was ages four to six for programs D and E, four to seven for program F, and five to eight for program G. The software programs provided drill and practice for the purpose of bringing to fluency skills the teacher had already taught. Hence, the programs were appropriate for students who did not need teacher guidance to be successful completing activities. Consistent with drill and practice, the word identification software did not present new information, as would be expected by tutorial programs, nor did it present simulated situations or emphasize competition as is characterized by education games (Grabe & Grabe, 2001). Although the word identification software was similar in the skills presented and in its focus on phonics, the software did vary in the themes around which drill and practice were delivered, the on-screen hosts and practice activities.

A questionnaire was used to evaluate the programs (Fox, 2003). The questionnaire focused on the six design components of: (a) Speech and Language; (b) Print, Pictures and Animation; (c) Content; (d) Navigation; (e) Practice; and (f) Management. For a copy of the software evaluation questionnaire, see Fox (2003). Speech and Language dealt with the clarity of voices and the appropriateness of the vocabulary for young children. Print, Pictures and Animation included the use of pictures of familiar objects, upper and lower case letters, and animation that supports learning. Content focused on letter names, letter-sounds and phonemic awareness knowledge in the program. Navigation dealt with the ease with which children can access the software content. Practice focused on opportunities to cement learning, use knowledge in different ways, and receive feedback on responses. Management dealt with the availability of printable reports on children's performance, and provisions for teachers or parents to designate activities for individual children. Each component was further divided into four characteristics and an overall component rating, for a total of five questions for each of the six components. The questions were specifically tailored for word identification software, since generic questions may not focus on the important characteristics of this type of software (Bitter & Pierson, 1999). Each component was rated concerning the support it provided word identification learning utilizing the following five-point scale: (1) Extremely Effective, (2) Very Effective, (3) Effective, (4) Somewhat Effective, and (5) Not Effective.

Procedure

Teachers and parents completed a questionnaire to evaluate software programs. Teachers reviewed software in a MacIntosh G8 computer laboratory on a university campus. The programs were randomly loaded on computers by a technician before the teachers entered the laboratory. Teachers completed the questionnaires in three hours, were free to rate the software in any order, and turned in each questionnaire as it was completed. Parents completed the evaluations of programs A, B and C in three weeks.

Results

A oneway ANOVA revealed no significant difference in the evaluation of word identification software by reading and special education teachers. Reading and special education teachers were combined in further analyses. A significant difference was found among composite scores, $F(6,159) = 15.77$, $p<.01$. A post hoc analysis using Tukey-Kramer's Honestly Significant Difference revealed that program A differed significantly from all other programs, and that program B differed from programs C and G. Programs A, B and C were selected for parents to review, as these programs differed significantly from one another.

A oneway ANOVA showed significant differences in parents' evaluations of software programs, F (2,69) = 9.78, p<.01. Tukey-Kramer post hoc analysis showed that programs A and B differed significantly from program C. Analyses of teachers' and parents' evaluations of design components revealed significant differences in Navigation for program A, F (1,47) = 4.46, p<.03. For program B, significant differences were found for Practice, F (1,47) = 13.86, p<.01), and Management, F (1,46) = 16.35, p<.001. For program C, significant differences were found for Content, F (1,47) = 4.41, p<.05, Practice, F (1.47) = 8.31, p<.01 and Management, F (1,47) = 7.46, p<.01. Parents rated the design components significantly higher, or more favorably, than the teachers. Table 1 shows the means and standard deviations for ratings of the design components.

Table 1. Means and Standard Deviations for Ratings of Software Design Components

DESIGN COMPONENT	PROGRAM A		PROGRAM B		PROGRAM C	
	M	SD	M	SD	M	SD
			TEACHERS			
Speech and Language	1.65	.71	1.83	.91	3.16	.91
Print, Pictures and Animation	1.87	.79	2.20	.88	2.87	.99
Content	2.00	.93	2.58	1.44	3.62**	.92
Navigation	1.70**	.90	2.25	1.07	3.29	.95
Practice	1.95	.99	3.33**	.86	3.37*	.76
Management	2.25	.89	4.66**	.76	4.66*	.63
			PARENTS			
Speech and Language	1.84	.94	2.00	.86	2.70	.85
Print, Pictures and Animation	2.00	.91	2.32	.85	2.68	.94
Content	1.96	1.09	2.32	1.88	3.04**	1.01
Navigation	2.36**	1.22	2.50	1.06	3.04	1.24
Practice	1.88	.83	2.20*	1.22	2.64*	.99
Management	2.36	.99	3.45*	1.25	4.04*	.93

Differences between pairs of means *p<.05, **p<.01.
Low scores indicate favorable evaluations

Discussion

The finding that teachers differentiated among programs is consistent with previous research showing that the teachers discriminate among word identification software (Fox, 2003). Failure to find a significant difference in the evaluations of reading and special education teachers suggests that these experienced teachers may have shared a common set of values or principles upon which they based software evaluations. Another explanation is that teachers' evaluations were an artifact of the emphasis on phonics, as mandated by the No Child Left Behind Act. Taken from this perspective, evaluations may reflect teachers' views of phonics as a component of good teaching in their school cultures, which is a variable that has been shown to affect how teachers use software (Windschitl & Sahl, 2002). Parents were more likely than the teachers to favorably evaluate software. One interpretation of differences is that the parents did not have the same in-depth knowledge of classroom curricula as the teachers, and hence may have had greater expectations for the benefits of exposure to software, particularly for programs B and C. Another explanation is that evaluations reflected the different ways in which parents and teachers may use software. Teachers who wish to use software to support classroom learning may have evaluated the management component for its potential to inform instructional decisions, and the content for compatibility with classroom learning expectations. Parents may have viewed software as serving the dual purposes of providing education and entertainment, and hence were less critical of the software. Further research would clarify reasons for differences in teacher's and parents' evaluations.

The study is limited by the small number of participants and by the characteristics of the teacher and parent groups. Only experienced teachers participated, hence the data cannot be generalized to preservice teachers. The parents had computers at home and were well educated. Therefore, generalizations are limited to parents with similar computer access and education. The study was further limited by using a questionnaire that did not include open-ended questions, and did not provide information on the linkage between teachers' theoretical orientation to reading and software evaluations.

Study 2

Preservice and inservice teachers in literacy methods courses may hold a variety of theoretical beliefs about reading and learning to read, ranging from bottom-up phonics to top-down whole language (Vacca, et al., 2003). Belief systems are important because they affect teaching practice (Richardson, Anders, Tidwell, & Lloyd, 1991) and how teachers use technology (Windschitl & Sahl, 2002). In a study of appropriate practice in kindergarten through third grade classrooms, teachers' beliefs made a significant contribution to teaching practice even when the effects of teacher education (highest degree and years of experience) and grade taught were controlled (Maxwell, McWilliam, Hemmeter, Ult, & Schuster, 2001). However, the connection between theoretical beliefs and teaching practice is complex and subject to a variety of influences including the increasing pressure for accountability, teacher education programs, the culture of the school, and teachers' perceptions of students' needs (Grisham, 2000; Harlin, 1999).

In making software selections, teachers consider a variety of factors, including their instructional goals (Baker, 2003) and their willingness to use software by integrating it into their classrooms (Grabe & Grabe, 2001). Valmont (2003) suggests that teachers consider three variables when selecting word recognition software: (a) the scope and sequence of the software, (b) age-appropriate activities, and (c) how well the software matches classroom learning objectives. According to Valmont, word identification software can support teaching phonics from a part-to-whole (synthetic), whole-to-part (analytic) or word family (analogy) approach. Software can be successfully used to teach word identification from any of these approaches, provided that software is flexible in the way it can be used (Valmont, 2003) and teachers use only those parts of programs that meet students' needs (Fox & Mitchell, 2000).

The purpose of the second study was to carry out a preliminary investigation of the relationships among teachers' theoretical orientations and software evaluations, and to gain insight into teachers' rationale for their software preferences. Research questions were:

Question 1. Do teachers with different theoretical orientations to reading differ in their evaluations of word identification software?

Question 2. Do teachers with different theoretical orientations differ in their perceptions of how consistent word identification software is with their own theoretical views?

Method
Participants

Participants consisted of 16 teachers enrolled in a graduate literacy methods course in a university in a southeastern state. The mean number of years teaching was 3.2 (SD = 1.2). Participants, all experienced teachers, completed the Theoretical Orientation to Reading Profile (TORP) (De Ford, 1985). Students answered questions and tallied scores to derive an indication of a phonics, skills or whole language orientation to reading instruction. The results revealed that five participants held a whole language orientation toward reading, seven a skills orientation and four a phonics orientation.

Materials

Materials consisted of the same three software programs (A, B, and C), and the same software design component questionnaire as was used in the previous study. Materials also included a software reflection questionnaire (see Appendix A) and a questionnaire on perspectives toward word identification software (see Appendix B).

Procedure

The second week of a sixteen week semester teachers completed the TORP to indicate their theoretical beliefs about reading (De Ford, 1985). Four weeks after determining beliefs, or six weeks after the course began, teachers reviewed software. This study used the same procedure for evaluating software as the first study, except that participants had 90 minutes to complete the design component questionnaire. One week after evaluating the software, the seventh week, participants completed a software reflection questionnaire for each program (Appendix B) and a software perspectives questionnaire (Appendix B).

Results

A oneway ANOVA revealed no significant differences in the overall evaluation of word identification software among teachers with different theoretical orientations. Teachers were grouped together for further analyses. Significant differences were found for the perceived effectiveness of activities, $F_{(2,45)} = 22.94$, p<.01, for overall program effectiveness, $F_{(2,45)} = 30.72$, p<.01, for effectiveness in meeting classroom learning objectives, $F_{(2,45)} = 15.02$, p<.01, and for effectiveness in supporting classroom instruction in phonemic awareness, $F_{(2,45)} = 22.94$, p<.01, letter-sound learning, $F_{(2,45)} = 18.48$, p<.01, letter name learning, $F_{(2,45)} = 7.98$, p<.01, and spelling, $F_{(2,45)} = 14.30$, p<.01. Tukey-Kramer post hoc analyses showed that program A differed significantly from programs B and C for all comparisons. A significant difference was found for software the teachers perceived to be consistent with their own theoretical orientation, $F_{(2,45)} = 17.18$, p<.01. Tukey-Kramer post hoc analysis revealed that program A was significantly different from programs B and C. All teachers, regardless of their theoretical orientation, judged the most preferred program, program A, to be more consistent with their own theoretical views.

Table 2 shows teachers' responses to software reflection questions (Appendix A) that asked if teachers would use the software in their own classrooms(Question 2), recommend it to parents (Question 7), and liked or disliked the software (Question 8). When asked to explain their reasons for liking or disliking particular software programs (Question 8, Appendix A), teachers who liked programs cited: (a) a clear word identification focus with a variety of skills and strategies; (b) leveled activities; (c) effective practice with letter-sounds, letter names and phonemic awareness; (d) easy-to-understand management; and (e) the likelihood that children would find the software engaging. Teachers who disliked programs noted that: (a) the software was confusing, (b) it was difficult to move around in the program (poor navigation), (c) activities were inconsistent and educationally irrelevant,

(d) there was too much play and too much wait time, (e) the vocabulary was inappropriate for young children, (f) the graphics were poor, and (g) children did not have enough opportunities to interact with the program.

Table 2. Teachers' Willingness to Use and Recommend Software

Judgments	Program A		Program B		Program C	
	Yes	No	Yes	No	Yes	No
Would Use Software in the Classroom	16	0	7	9	6	10
Recommend Software to Parents	16	0	6	10	3	13
Like This Software Program	16	0	7	9	2	14

N = 16

Teachers who indicated they would use the software (Question 2, Appendix A) and recommend it to parents (Question 7, Appendix A) mentioned that: (a) the software was easy for the children and the teacher to use; (b) the practice was valuable; (c) the program had good depth and breadth of skills; (d) there were multiple, leveled opportunities for children to practice; (e) the software effectively structured letter-sound and blending activities; (f) the activities were educationally relevant; and (g) the software was fun and engaging. Teachers comments on software they would not recommend to parents included: (a) the program was so confusing that children would get lost and frustrated, (b) children would need adult help, (c) there was insufficient focus on skills and knowledge, (d) there were not enough activities and not enough practice, (e) the content of activities was inappropriate, (f) the graphics were distracting, and (g) the software was more entertaining than educational.

Navigation and management were the two most frequently cited characteristics of good word identification software (Question 1, Appendix B). Seventy-five percent of teachers cited clear and easy navigation, and a management component that allows teachers to select tasks, access reports of children's performance, and track children's progress. Easy to recognize pictures that correspond to the sounds associated with letters, and explanations of why answers are incorrect were each cited by 37% of the teachers. Multiple, sequenced levels of difficulty, and words and concepts that are familiar to children each were cited by 31% of teachers. Twenty-five percent mentioned appealing graphics.

In explaining the role of word identification software in today's classroom (Question 3, Appendix B), 81% responded that software is a supplemental tool for practicing and reinforcing skills the teacher has already taught. Only 12% believed that word identification software is useful for interesting children in learning to read. No teacher mentioned using software to teach new word identification information to beginning readers. Teachers' responses included the following comments: "It should be used as a tool to reinforce curricular and instructional objectives, not as a replacement for authentic instruction;" "It can never replace direct instruction, modeling or feedback of the classroom teacher;" "It can be a fun way to supplement or review previously taught skills;" and "It appeals to children and is helpful for extra support; it is not a main form of instruction."

In responding to a question that asked teachers to rate the effectiveness of word identification software for supporting classroom instruction (Question 3, Appendix B), one teacher rated software as extremely effective, one teacher rated software as very effective, nine as effective, and five as somewhat effective. No teacher indicated that word identification software is not effective in supporting classroom learning. Teachers who thought that software was effective or somewhat effective mentioned that: (a) children are motivated to use the computer, (b) software is interactive, and (c) children can work at their own pace. Teachers who indicated that software is somewhat effective observed that software must be closely monitored by the teacher and that there is not enough good software available.

Discussion

These teachers held a relatively positive view of word identification software. All teachers responded that software is a legitimate part of the elementary school reading program, and that its purpose is to reinforce the word identification information, skills and strategies that the teacher has already taught. These teachers judged program A to be most consistent with their own personal theoretical orientation, regardless of how they viewed reading, according to the TORP. In responding to open-ended questions, the teachers indicated that they would not use software that lacked a word identification focus, had limited activities or was perceived to primarily be for entertainment. One interpretation is that these teachers did not differ in the value they placed on word identification and, therefore, theoretical orientation did not significantly affect how they evaluated different programs. Another interpretation is that the programs differed significantly in quality, and hence teachers' evaluations were more a reflection of software quality than theoretical orientation.

This study is limited by the relatively small number of programs evaluated, the use of only drill-and-practice software, the small number of participants, and the fact that all teachers had classroom experience. Therefore, results cannot be generalized to preservice teachers. Further research might investigate the perspectives of preservice teachers, and include an oral interview so as to further examine teachers' perceptions. Future research might compare and contrast drill-and-practice software with tutorial software, and examine the manner in which practicing teachers use word identification software in their classrooms.

Discussion of Implications for Literacy Methods Courses

In light of the current emphasis on phonics and technology-enhanced learning, it is important that teachers and parents select software for beginning readers that is the most likely to support word learning. Taken together, the findings of these two studies have five implications for literacy teacher educators who wish to include word identification software in their methods courses. The first implication is that using a questionnaire to guide word identification software evaluations may help teachers focus on important components of software design. Regardless of teachers' theoretical orientation or teaching focus, these experienced teachers considered the overall quality of the software, including navigation and management, when evaluating programs.

Preservice and inservice teachers might begin by evaluating the six design components so as to identify the most preferred programs, and then examine in detail the specific content and activities of software that teachers believe to be the most supportive of classroom literacy instruction. There should be a close connection between the content of word identification software, classroom instructional content and classroom learning objectives. In other words, what the children practice with software should also be the same content, skills and strategies that the children are learning in their classroom literacy programs. In evaluating content, preservice and inservice teachers might consider the research evidence in support of content, and also the match between content and classroom learning expectations. In so doing, teachers have opportunities to consider a range of software, and to identify how the content of preferred software corresponds to state, district or classroom learning expectations.

The second implication is that software evaluations should consider the features of child-friendly software. Child-friendly software allows beginning readers to easily access and understand program content. Beginning readers may not be skilled at using a mouse, have incompletely developed fine motor skills, and may not know how to interact with software programs. Child-friendly features include, but are not limited to, a clear program structure depicted by an easy-to-identify site map or easy-to-understand buttons, the buttons children click on should be large, and arrows, when they are used to draw children's attention to objects on the screen, should be large and point directly to the desired location on the screen (Segers & Verhoeven, 2002). Beginning readers may have difficulty with a click-and-drag procedure. For this reason, double clicking on objects, which then move into position, is more appropriate for children whose fine motor development is incomplete (Segers & Verhoeven, 2002). Added to this, young children must be able to use the program independently, without adult help. In practical terms, this means that children must be able to enter and exit individual activities, as well as begin and leave the program on their own.

Child-friendly software also includes content that young children understand. Pictures should be easy to recognize and depict objects that are likely to be familiar to most young children. The software should use words children already know in spoken language, and the voices should be clear and free of unusual accents. To help preservice and inservice teachers appreciate the critical aspects of child-friendly word identification software, literacy teacher educators might ask their students to identify concepts, pictures and vocabulary that are likely to be familiar or unfamiliar to young children, and to document how navigation allows children to easily access the program content.

The third implication is that preservice and inservice teachers need hands-on experiences with software. Software reviews on the Internet and in journals may be helpful, but actually using the software gives teachers opportunities to develop insight into the effectiveness of navigation and management, the appropriateness of pictures and words, and the match between content and classroom learning expectations (Abbott & Faris, 2000). Literacy teacher educators might ask preservice and inservice teachers to design lessons that include specific software programs, to observe children using the software and to reflect on children's reactions.

Fourth, it is important that preservice and inservice teachers are aware of the characteristics of word identification software that parents find appealing. These results suggest that parents may have higher expectations for the effects of the practice in word identification software and may be more concerned with entertainment than teachers. Parents also may place more value on word identification software with familiar media characters, cartoon-like graphics, and time-consuming transitions or on-screen rewards. One third of the parents reported that the school encouraged them to purchase educational software. We might infer, then, that many of these parents were purchasing software on their own, without guidance from their children's teachers, and with the expectation that the software provides beneficial practice. It is important, therefore, for preservice and inservice teachers to learn how to decide which software programs are useful for home practice, and then to learn how to advise parents in software selection.

The fifth and last implication is that literacy teacher educators should consider aspects of word identification software that make it teacher-friendly. Just as good navigation contributes to making software child-friendly, so too does it contribute to making software teacher-friendly. Good navigation provides for easy access to program content, which is essential if children are to interact with software independently. When some children use software independently, teachers are free to work with other children, either individually or in small groups. Teacher-friendly software also has a management component that allows teachers to track children's progress, designate activities for individual children, view the results of children's performance on activities, and select specific skills or knowledge for children to practice. Reports should be printable, easy to read, and include an option to view the entire class or the performance of individuals. Teacher educators might ask preservice and inservice teachers to critique printable reports, and to demonstrate how reports might be used to inform classroom instruction.

Technology in general, and word identification software in particular, are among the tools teachers use when teaching beginning reading. Experienced teachers not only indicated that word identification software has a place in the classroom, but also were willing to use the most preferred program and to recommend it to parents. Research shows that giving teachers opportunities to evaluate software in methods courses results in more confidence reviewing software and more awareness of issues related to technology-enhanced learning (Clark, Martin, & Hall, 2000). Literacy teacher educators, through the literacy methods courses they teach, have opportunities to structure learning experiences so as to help preservice and inservice teachers make informed and educationally sound decisions when using word identification software in their classrooms and when recommending software to parents. This, in turn, may help teachers select the most instructionally relevant, child-friendly and teacher-friendly word identification software for beginning readers.

References

Abbot, J. A., & Faris, S. E. (2000). Integrating technology into preservice literacy instruction: A survey of elementary education students' attitudes toward computers. *Journal of Research on Computing in Education, 33*, 149-161.

Armbruster, B. B., Lehr, F., & Osborn, J. (2001). *Put reading first: The research building blocks for teaching children to read kindergarten through grade 3.* Washington, D.C.: Partnership for Reading.

Baker, E. A. (2003). Integrating literacy and technology: Making a match between software and classroom. *Reading and Writing Quarterly, 19*, 193-107.

Bitter, G. G., & Pierson, M. E. (1999). *Using technology in the classroom* (4th ed.). Boston: Allyn and Bacon.

Clark, P., Martin, L., & Hall, V. (2000). Preparing preservice teachers to use computers effectively in elementary schools. *The Teacher Educator, 36*, 102-114.

De Ford, D. E. (1985). Validating the construct of theoretical orientation in reading. *Reading Research Quarterly, 20*, 351-367.

Fox, B. J. (2003). Apples and oranges: Teachers' judgments of word identification software. In P. E. Linder, M. B. Sampson, J. A. R. Dugan, & B. Brancato (Eds.), *Celebrating the faces of literacy* (pp. 133-149). Commerce, TX: The College Reading Association.

Fox, B. J., & Mitchell, M. J. (2000). Using technology to support word recognition, spelling, and vocabulary acquisition. In S. B. Wepner, W. J. Valmont, & R. Thurlow (Eds.), *Linking literacy and technology: A guide for K-8 classrooms* (pp. 42-75). Newark, DE: International Reading Association.

Grabe, M., & Grabe, C. (2001). *Integrating technology for meaningful learning* (3rd ed.) Boston: Houghton Mifflin.

Grisham, D. L. (2000). Connecting theoretical conceptions of reading to practice: Longitudinal study of elementary school teachers. *Reading Psychology, 21,* 145-170.

Harlin, R. P. (1999). Developing future professionals: Influences of literacy coursework and field experiences. *Reading Research and Instruction, 38,* 351-370.

Haugland, S.W. (1995). Computers and young children. *Early Childhood Education Journal, 23,* 99-100.

MacArthur, C. A., Ferretti. R. P., Okolo, C. M., & Cavalier, A. R. (2001). Technology Applications for students with literacy problems: A critical review. *The Elementary School Journal, 101,* 273-301.

Maxwell, K. L., McWilliam, R. A., Hemmeter, M. L., Ult, M. J., & Schuster, J. W. (2001). Predictors of developmentally appropriate classroom practices in kindergarten through third grade. *Early Childhood Research Quarterly, 16,* 431-452.

Mioduser, D., Tur-Kaspa, H., & Leitner, I. (2000). The learning value of computer-based instruction of early reading skills. *Journal of Computer Assisted Learning, 16,* 54-63.

Richardson, V., Anders, P., Tidwell, D., & Lloyd, C. (1991). The relationship between teachers' beliefs and practices in reading comprehension. *American Educational Research Journal, 28,* 558-586.

Segers, E., & Verhoeven, L. (2002). Multimedia support for early literacy learning. *Computers & Education, 39,* 207-221.

The Facts About 21st Century Technology. (2002). Retrieved January 8, 2002, from http://www.nclb.gov/start/facts/21centtech.html

Vacca, J. L., Vacca, R. T., Gove, M. K., Burkey, L, C., Lenhart, L. A., & McKeon, C. A. (2003). *Reading and Learning to Read* (5th ed.). Boston: Allyn and Bacon.

Valmont, W. J. (2003). *Technology for literacy teaching and learning.* Boston: Houghton Mifflin.

Windschitl, M., & Sahl, K. (2002). Tracing teachers' use of technology in a laptop computer school: The interplay of teacher beliefs, social dynamics, and institutional culture. *American Educational Research Journal, 39,* 165-205.

Appendix A. Software Reflection: *Name of Software*

Directions:
Please complete the following items for *Name of Software*. The answers to these questions reflect your own personal opinion; there is not right or wrong way to respond.

1. Is this software consistent with your own theoretical view of reading and learning to read?
   Circle one: YES   NO   SOMEWHAT

2. Would you use this software to support classroom instruction in word identification for beginning readers?
   Circle one: YES   NO   Why or why not?

   _____

   _____

3. In your personal opinion, how effective is this software in supporting classroom instruction in:
   A. *Phonemic awareness*
      1. extremely effective   2. very effective   3. effective
      4. somewhat effective   5. not effective
   B. *The letter-sounds of phonics*
      1. extremely effective   2. very effective   3. effective
      4. somewhat effective   5. not effective
   C. *Letter names*
      1. extremely effective   2. very effective   3. effective
      4. somewhat effective   5. not effective
   D. *Spelling*
      1. extremely effective   2. very effective   3. effective
      4. somewhat effective   5. not effective

4. How do you rate the overall effectiveness of the activities in this software program?
      1. extremely effective   2. very effective   3. effective
      4. somewhat effective   5. not effective

5. How do you rate this software in terms of meeting your own classroom learning objectives for beginning readers in word identification?
      1. extremely effective   2. very effective   3. effective
      4. somewhat effective   5. not effective

6. In general, how effective do you think is this software for helping children become better at word identification?
      1. extremely effective   2. very effective   3. effective
      4. somewhat effective   5. not effective

7. Assuming that children have a computer at home, would you encourage parents to purchase and use this software at home?
   YES   NO   Why or why not?

   _____

   _____

8. Did you like this software?
   YES   NO   Why or why not?

   _____

   _____

Appendix B. Software Perspectives

Directions:

Please complete the following six questions. The answers to these questions reflect your own personal perspective; there is no right or wrong way to respond.

1. In your opinion, what are the top five characteristic of effective word identification software for beginning readers?

    1. _____   2. _____
    3. _____   4. _____
    5. _____

2. What is the role of word identification software in today's classroom reading programs?

    _____
    _____
    _____
    _____

3. Generally speaking, how effective do you think word identification software is for supporting word identification instruction in your own classroom reading program?

    1. extremely effective   2. very effective   3. effective
    4. somewhat effective   5. not effective

    Please explain your reasoning:

    _____
    _____
    _____
    _____
    _____
    _____
    _____
    _____

Think and Link:
Technological Applications
for Literacy Development
Within a Thematic Unit

Francine Falk-Ross

Northern Illinois University

Richard Scott

Kaneland Middle School

Abstract

An action research project introducing new technology to fifth grade students and preservice teachers during the same semester in an overlapping format was initiated to develop new understandings in concept development for both groups. Two topics are reviewed. First, the need for integration of technology into literacy programs is explained as an important area for program development. Second, the specifics of one thematic unit development in a fifth-grade classroom provides a model for integrating reading education and technology in class lessons. Self-evaluations from a survey for preservice teachers and final test scores for students reveal progress in new learning.

The development of strategies for integrating visual literacies, i.e., computer technology and online research investigations, into classroom content reading instruction has been gaining momentum in recent years (Leu, 2000; Luke, 2002; Miller, 1998; Pailliotet, 1998). Researchers and teachers have found that the use of technology in literacy instruction has been shown to be an enriching component for young students in content area reading comprehension (Vacca et al., 2003) and linked with increased levels of achievement (McCorduck, 1992). However, knowing the advantages of including technology in classroom literacy programs, increasing familiarity with the use of online applications for literacy education becomes a necessary competency for preservice and practicing teachers (Leu, 2000). This need for integration of technology into the courses of preservice teacher's education is well-documented (Baumgartner, 1999; Falba et al., 1999); however, teachers' perceptions and preservice teachers' familiarity with technological approaches to literacy instruction remains a determining factor in how often and how well the applications are used (Hardy, 1998). The mandate for teacher educators to familiarize preservice teachers with new technological applications for the classroom has been set (Leu, 2000; O'Bannon, Matthew, & Thomas, 1998) and new programs need to developed for teachers and their students, alike.

With these current pedagogical issues in mind, an action research project was initiated in the context of a Midwestern suburban middle school to develop stronger connections between technology and literacy lessons, and to support and prepare preservice teachers in these methods. More specifically, the purposes of this project focused on the introduction of new literacy approaches using technology to both preservice teachers and middle school students in one semester, in the context of a fun and challenging series of activities. A second purpose was to compare the new understandings of students who used additional technological tools and applications with the understandings of students who used more traditional methods of instruction. The questions that guided this action research project were: How can preservice teachers with access to new technology tools and knowledge develop and implement technology-rich classroom literacy lessons? In what specific ways can the addition of technology enrich students' literacy experiences and achievement? In what specific ways can the infusion of new technology experiences prepare preservice teachers for 'smarter' (i.e., increased access to technology) classrooms?

Theoretical Framework

Two areas of research inform the development of this action research project which focuses on the enrichment of knowledge in the use of technology for literacy learning for students and preservice teachers. These include studies relating to the intersection of technology and literacy education, and theories of social constructivist approaches to teaching and learning. Each year new research indicates the transformative nature of technology on literacy development (Reinking, Labbo, & McKenna, 1997) and the transactional relationship (Bruce, 1997) between the two. Both areas frame current investigations and new understandings of classroom instruction in reading.

Standards documents for reading program development set technology integration as a goal (International Reading Association [IRA], 1998; National Council for Accreditation of Teacher Education [NCATE], 2002; National Council of Teachers of English [NCTE], 1996), and researchers are providing models for educational programming for classrooms (e.g., Karchmer, 2000; Leu, Karchmer, & Leu, 1999) and preservice teacher education (Kinzer & Risko, 1998). In short, it is important that the preservice teachers be familiar enough with technology to be able to identify, synthesize and evaluate information literacy problems (Spitzer, Eisenberg, & Lowe, 1998). Although many pre-service teachers may have technology knowledge in areas of basic communication (i.e., email), information access (i.e., purchasing, news), and word processing, they still require specific instruction to integrate the use of technology into literacy instruction to use these more frequently (Leu & Leu, 2000). Preparation and experiences offered in teacher education classes are needed to develop and support this new and still developing area of expertise.

Second, successful approaches to teaching/learning activities connecting technology and literacy may become dependent upon social learning contexts due to the nature of the interactions (Leu, 2000). Collaborative experiences, such as small group work in classrooms (for students) and peers/pairs associations in practicum assignments (for preservice teachers), are guided by theories of social construction of knowledge (Wertsch, 1997). In the case of this project, the theories support and translate into the hypothesis that through working together to access, question, clarify, and apply online and software-based information, students and preservice teachers can internalize useful new knowledge. Information that is applied and used as it is taught is more easily internalized because students (and preservice teachers) learn best when they can make timely and meaningful connections between what they already know and new learning in the classroom, based on schema theory (Anderson, 1984).

Methodology for Development and Analysis of the Project
Participants and Context

The action research project included 50 students in two fifth-grade classrooms in a Midwestern suburban elementary school district, and 4 preservice teachers in their second professional semester in elementary education classes at a local 4-year university. Two preservice teachers were assigned to each classroom, so they could collaboratively develop lessons for the thematic unit. Two other fifth-grade classes, serving as the control or comparison group, were taught the content material using the same thematic unit without the technological enrichments. These classes were compared at the end of the semester by the scores and quality of responses on the final test.

Classroom Preparation and Technology Readiness

The two school classrooms and one university classroom were electronically re-wired to accommodate several computer hookups for technological tools. A whiteboard was purchased for computer projections during class lectures and presentations. The researcher and teacher became familiar with the use of computer applications and developed the main activities for a thematic unit on the Revolutionary War prior to the beginning of the semester, allowing for additions by the preservice teachers during the three-week practicum experiences.

In order to integrate the software applications and online access into the lessons, a newer tool was introduced to broaden the uses for whole class viewing, i.e., the Mimio Board. The Mimio consists of a short elongated bar that acts as a technological device to replicate a Smart Board but it is a smaller and less expensive for the district to purchase. The more comprehensive Smart Board responds to the user's touch to point and select computer options. Using the Mimio apparatus, a whiteboard in the classroom serves as a computer screen while an electronic writing device that resembles a large pen serves as a 'mouse' in choosing options. The Mimio Board is a form of technology with which most preservice and practicing teachers are not currently familiar, but which promises to become more popular in coming years due to its inexpensive price and its ease of use. The presentation of a new project (through a grant by the Verizon Corporation) would allow for classroom research and Internet browsing to become a whole class activity, and would expand reading opportunities.

University and School Class Projects

The introduction to new technology tools occurred during the first weeks of the fall semester in both the school classrooms and university reading methods classes. This included guided instruction in use of the Mimio Mouse and Board, regulations for Internet access and use, and setups for software installation and use. Preservice teachers were supported in their construction of knowledge of technological applications for literacy instruction through lectured explanations, modeling demonstrations, and initial practice in computer laboratories. Topics in lectures focused on evaluation of technology activities in reading programs and development of lesson plans for integration of these applications into balanced classroom instruction. For the fifth-grade students, the classroom teacher introduced the new technology tools individually and students practiced using these for the first month of classes periodically in other lessons to become familiar with setup and rules for use. In the school classrooms research investigations, performance-based activities, and WebQuest projects had been used by classroom members, but always at computers in corners of the room with little teacher monitoring or whole class discussion. These activities would be introduced and used in whole class forums in the context of the focal thematic unit. Assessment tasks for monitoring progress included artifacts of online learning (i.e., projects such as letters to King George and notes from online research/browsing), writing samples, and final tests for the students. Preservice teachers completed journals and technology (pre- and post-) surveys to assess if there were positive changes in technology competencies and lesson planning understandings, both of which were general end goals for this project for the semester.

Project and Progress Analysis

Several forms of assessment were used to evaluate progress in new learning in the two overlapping projects of the students and the preservice teachers. At the beginning and end of the semester, the preservice teachers were asked to complete a survey of technological knowledge such as how well they were able to manipulate text within a document, download files from the Internet, and setup software programs. This was used as a basis for comparing individual progress at the end of the semester. A series of lesson plans were required to assess how well the preservice teachers were able to organize instruction and align goals and activities with reading and learning standards.

Students' achievement was evaluated mostly through comparison of the essay completions on the final test, which was the same for all the fifth-grade classes. Progress in understandings was also accomplished through analysis of artifacts from classroom assignments. These included written summaries of reading material, accuracy of role playing activities, and a war facts competition between all fifth grade classes consisting of those students who had experienced the technological additions and those who used the more traditional resources (i.e., texts without WebQuest, software, or Internet browsing) for learning.

Technology Applications Within the Thematic Unit

Use of a thematic unit was the most appropriate context for combining several small group introductions and use of technological approaches to build literacy learning, and fit in the middle school approach that guided curriculum approaches for this fifth-grade class. This thematic unit involved the typical integrated methods of instruction, including research investigation to build background knowledge, shared teacher and student choice of reading materials, small group development of mini-projects, and authentic activities to apply new learning. The individual activities were all based on the theme, each set of activities amplifying a different aspect of the central concept and often reflecting topics from several disciplines.

In this set of two class studies, the Revolutionary War was chosen as a main theme, consistent with the curriculum set by the district for the grade. The main stages of development of the thematic unit using the new technological tools included literacy learning through activation of background knowledge, graphic organizers, reading assignments, online activities and software applications, and assessment tasks. Almost all of these lessons were presented using the Mimio Board in some part.

Activation And Building Of Background Knowledge

In order to build a common foundation of information for a varied population of students, the preservice teachers projected onto the large whiteboard a few online sites with general facts and photos related to the Revolutionary War. The advantages of using the Mimio Board for this purpose were first, that the presentation of Internet material was available to the class to read and share as a whole and second, that the process of accessing the information was modeled for those students who might be unfamiliar with the specific steps. There were many sites that served as resources for this purpose. Internet sites often change frequently, however one exemplary site was the online companion to the Public Broadcasting Service's documentary, *Liberty! The American Revolution* (PBS Online and Twin Cities Public Television, 1997). Students were able to return to this site in smaller groups at computer nooks at other times during the semester to review information or just for their own enjoyment.

Timelines and Graphic Organizers

In content area reading, it is helpful for students to document and track significant information using graphic organizers in some form. The first organizer that was used was a KWL-Plus (Carr & Ogle, 1987) chart that was projected onto the whiteboard to be completed by the class as the unit continued for three weeks. Students were also introduced to a software product appropriately named *Timeliner 5.0* (Snyder, 2003) that ordered the important dates for historical events and critical lawmaking. Preservice teachers, assisted by the cooperating teachers, were able to explain and visually organize the causes and effects of specific famous incidents using this software.

Reading Materials

All Internet investigations and software products provided reading material for literacy instruction and new learning. Important vocabulary was explained to students in the context of ongoing reading during whole class viewing of Internet sites and was reviewed during smaller heterogeneous groupings of students. Some of the new literacy learning was in the introduction to new terms on the Internet and software programs just to use these resources. The Mimio Board was used to project the process of finding and reading about the Revolutionary War for activities such as read alouds and strategies such as 'think alouds' to be shared by all students as models or review, depending on each student's individual level of achievement. A complementary investigation involved a novel study of *George Washington's Socks* (Woodruff, 1993), which served to balance the visual literacies introduced and integrated throughout this unit of instruction.

Online And Computer Assignments

One of the most significant online assignments developed by the preservice teachers was the WebQuest they developed for the students to provide an interactive forum for reading and learning about the causes and effects of the war, the dress and habits of people of that time period, the perspectives and dispositions of patriots and loyalists, and about problem solving, in general. Following models from other Internet sites and assisting one another, the preservice teachers learned to collaborate with peers for instruction, how to organize the progression of lessons, and how to integrate the processes of reading, writing, listening, talking, viewing, and representing visually into meaningful lessons. Internet sites for content area knowledge came from the preservice teachers' own investigations, but exemplary sites included: *Teach-nology* by Technology, Inc. (2003); *Funbrain* from the Family Education Network, Inc. (2000); *Techtrekers* (Rollins, 2003); and *Teacher Tools* (2002). The preservice teachers browsed the Internet for additional sites to share, providing practice with this literacy and expertise in specific areas of knowledge about the Revolutionary War, and to extend their investigations at home.

Additional assignments based on performance-based activities were also a part of this teaching/learning unit. Guided by the preservice teachers, the students expressed their new knowledge in written and dramatic modes. Powerpoint presentations to share small group and individual learning, and software games to assist in problem solving, i.e., *Decisions, Decisions 5.0* (Snyder, 2003), were interspersed between lessons. From the information learned online and from tradebooks, students developed persuasive letters in 'old-fashioned handwriting' with yellowed paper to replicate materials used in the Revolutionary War time-frame in order to argue and defend the perspectives of patriots and loyalists, actively role playing and taking specific stances typical of the times.

Observable Changes in Teaching and Learning

As set forward in the purposes and inquiry questions developed for this action research project, the thematic unit as developed and implemented above created opportunities for positive changes in the learning for classroom students and preservice teachers. That is, the first purpose of the action research project was realized in that stronger connections between technology and literacy lessons were constructed through a series of fun and challenging technology-based literacy activities. The second purpose was accomplished in that students and preservice teachers (and researchers) gained new understandings of thinking and linking on the Internet for literacy learning, and new insights and ideas for enriching lessons were implemented. As these connections and new lessons emerged, the nature of the classroom instruction expanded beyond that of the curricular activities presented the previous year, as experienced by the students in the classrooms with the traditional approach. These changes provided additional opportunities for student choice, interactive learning, and individual mentoring beyond what most students in the traditional classrooms were offered. Although the technological activities can not be shown to be directly responsible for changes in students' performance, the added dimension of a new literacy and new format to lesson delivery contributed to each students' personal development. Responses to the inquiry questions documenting changes in students' achievement and preservice teachers' self-evaluated preparation follow.

Changes In Teaching/Learning: Classroom Students

Expanded responses. In general, the students in the two fifth-grade classes that used new technological resources and, as a result, participated in more interactive class discussions and instruction, responded to questions and assignments in greater length and depth than those in receiving the more traditional instruction, as judged by the cooperating teachers and preservice teachers through interviews and journals, and by test scores. The same basic information had been covered by all classes in order to meet the grade requirements; however, the technology presented mostly through use of the Mimio Board, provided a visual support and amplification of most concepts. Students and preservice teachers often referred back to online sources when making connections in learning.

Final test scores. Specifically, the test scores on the final short-answer test given to fifth-graders in the technology-rich and traditional classrooms following the thematic unit showed an average gain of the scores of students using the new technological approaches over the control group of 11 points out of a total of 64 points. Using the first question in the test, "What do you believe to be the one biggest event that led to the Revolutionary War?" a question worth 12 points, the point distribution illustrates the differences in how adequately students responded, seen in Table 1.

Table 1. Differences in Question 1 responses on Final Test.

Classes	Students' Scores		
	10-12 points	7-9 points	0-6 points
Mr. S's Technology-rich Classroom	18	5	2
Mr. C's Traditional Classroom	8	6	13

The reason for these differences in grades, according to the teachers, was reflected in the quality and length of the responses. The answers from students in the technology-rich classrooms were richer in content detail with more critical analysis, revealed students' better understanding of cause and effect in the unit, and were lengthier and more focused than those of the students receiving traditional (non-technological) instruction. Examples that follow provide a comparison between the responses written by students in the enriched and traditional classrooms. These examples were chosen as typical representatives of the length and quality of the written responses from the four fifth-grade class members. The first question prompt on the final test is used for comparisons (See Appendix).

Changes In Teaching/Learning: Preservice and Cooperating Teachers

New technology skills. The most obvious change in all teachers' practice according to their responses on the pre- and post-survey was the increased knowledge of specific skills required to use computers for software applications and online investigation, such as installing programs, moving windows, formatting text, and locating saved downloaded information. Most teachers were familiar with general strategies for word processing, emailing, and some online purchasing; however, the language and process of applications were not well understood prior to the semester of the project. They articulated that they would use feel more relaxed about using computer applications in the future for instructional purposes. Learning to setup and use the Mimio Board introduced many new skills in the use of technology such as hooking up cables to provide communication between projectors, computers, and technology tools. Although the comfort level of all the teachers for use of these tools was still not high, they noted in their surveys that their problem-solving strategies, such as how to return to previous screens and move between applications on the computer, were increased as they used the computer more often and more efficiently.

Opportunities for interaction with students. Several teachers expressed in class discussions that they felt there was an increased amount of preservice teacher-student interaction as they needed to mentor and mediate the students' choices and navigation on the Internet, and that this allowed them to become more aware of students' individual needs. There were more opportunities to air opinions and to revise misunderstandings. All preservice and cooperating teachers noted that the new experiences were transforming to them in providing a new view of how technology and the visual literacies can be integrated into lesson plans and classroom instruction.

Implications

In review, this action research project introducing new technology to fifth grade students and preservice teachers during the same semester in an overlapping format was initiated to develop new understandings in concept development for both groups. Using a series of new and familiar technological tools, including the Mimio Board, computer software, and Internet access, literacy lessons in two fifth-grade classes were expanded beyond those traditionally used in a thematic unit on the Revolutionary War. Two other fifth-grade classes, receiving instruction without the technological enrichment served as controls for comparison of final test responses. The preservice teachers were becoming familiar with these same technology tools as they were integrating their use into lesson plans and implementations. Observations of the progress in both groups' understandings about the intersection of technology and literacy development to inform future approaches was the main purpose of this action research project.

Past research indicates that the explosive use of computer technology for communication and organization in schools and workplaces mandates that teachers and students in educational settings become familiar with the new literacy required to navigate the Web (Kinzer & Risko, 1998; Leu, 2000). Teachers have become familiar with new activities for building literacy strategies in students, but may still be using traditional presentation methods and resources. In order to use and model the educational uses of technology in classrooms, teacher educators must prepare preservice teachers for these opportunities by integrating technology into their own classes, such as described in this project, and by educating cooperating teachers through involvement in research projects or professional development workshops. The Mimio Board was chosen due to its ease of use, mobility, and affordable price for school budgets. It was an effective tool to teach preservice and practicing teachers how to integrate technology into literacy lessons. For some classrooms, however, the use of the Mimio will be limited due to the nature of technology on off-campus school-based teaching sites, the expertise of the preservice and practicing teachers, and the expertise of the cooperating teachers in practicum sites.

Projects for infusion of the use of new literacy through computer technology such as these may include use of new tools (such as the Mimio Board) or expansion of the use of known and familiar forms of technology (such as software programs or Internet browsing) for authentic classroom units of instruction. As the Internet and software programs become the resources of choice for home and business work, technological applications in the classroom need to become more frequent and meaningful for students and teachers, also. Discussions of access and availability for use in classrooms by teachers will be a necessary topic for school and practicum site personnel. Further research in the area of technological innovations in school classrooms will provide stronger data, illustrative models, and statistical support for the nature of new learning attributable to technology advances.

References

Anderson, S. L. (1984). Teacher Training Technologies from Four Observational Perspectives. *Journal of Classroom Interaction, 20*(1), 16-28.

Baumgartner, P. (1999). Information technologies and the training of teachers. *Educational Media International, 36*(1), 3-9.

Bruce, B. C. (1997). Current issues and future directions. In J. Flood, S. B. Heath, & D. Lapp (Eds.), *Handbook of research on teaching literacy through the communicative and visual arts* (pp. 875-884). New York: Simon & Schuster Macmillan.

Carr, E., & Ogle, D. (1987). K-W-L plus: A strategy for comprehension and summarization. *Journal of Reading, 30*(7), 626-631.

Falba, C. J., Strudler, N., Bean, T. W., Dixon, J. K., Markos, P. A., McKinney, M., et al. (1999). Choreographing change one step at a time: Reflections on integrating technology into teacher education courses. *Action in Teacher Education, 21*(1), 61-76.

Family Education Network, Inc. (2000). *Funbrain*. Retrieved August 15, 2003, from http://www.funbrain.com/

Hardy, J. V. (1998). Teacher attitudes toward and knowledge of computer technology. *Computers in the Schools, 14*(3-4), 119-136.

International Reading Association (IRA). (1998). *Standards for reading professionals*. Newark, DE: Author.

Karchmer, R. (2000). Using the Internet and children's literature to support interdisciplinary instruction. *The Reading Teacher, 54*(1), 100-104.

Kinzer, C. K., & Risko, V. J. (1998). Multimedia and enhanced learning: Transforming preservice education. In D. Reinking, M. C. McKenna, L. D. Labbo, & R. D. Kieffer (Eds.), *Handbook of literacy and technology: Transformations in a post-typographic world* (pp. 185-201). Mawah, NJ: Lawrence Erlbaum.

Leu, D. J. (2000). Literacy and technology: Deictic consequences for literacy eduction in an information age. In M. Kamil, P. Mosenthal, P. D. Pearson, & R. Barr (Eds.), *Handbook of reading research* (Vol. 3, pp. 743-777). Mahweh, NJ: Lawrence Erlbaum Associates.

Leu, D. J., Jr., Karchmer, R., & Leu, D. D. (1999). The Miss Rumphius effect: envisionments that transform literacy and learning on the Internet. *Reading Teacher, 52,* 636-642.

Leu, D. J., & Leu, D. D. (2000). *Teaching with the Internet: Lessons from the classroom* (3rd ed.). Norwood, MA: Christopher-Gordon Publishers, Inc.

Luke, C., (2002). New literacies in teacher education, *Journal of Adolescent and Adult Literacy, 43*(5), 424-435.

McCorduck, P. (1992). How we knew, how we know, how we will know. In M. C. Tuman (Ed.), *Literacy online: The promise (and peril) of reading and writing with computers*. Pittsburgh, PA: University of Pittsburgh Press.

Miller, J. W. (1998). Literacy in the 21st Century: Emergent themes. *Peabody Journal of Education, 73*(3-4), 1-14.

National Council for Accreditation of Teacher Education (NCATE). (2002). *Professional standards for the accreditation of schools, colleges, and departments of education*. Washington, DC: Author.

National Council of Teachers of English (NCTE). (1996). *IRA/NCTE standards for the English language arts*. Urbana, IL: Author.

O'Bannon, B., Matthew, K. I., & Thomas, L. (1998). Faculty development: Key to the integration of technology in teacher preparation. *Journal of Computing in Teacher Education, 14*(4), 7-11.

Pailliotet, A. W. (1998). Reading and writing across the media: Using diverse educational technologies for literacy learning. *Educational Media and Technology Yearbook, 23,* 76-93.

PBS Online and Twin Cities Public Television. (1997). *Liberty! The American Revolution.* Retrieved August 15, 2003, from http://www.pbs.org/ktca/liberty/index.html

Reinking, D., Labbo, L., & McKenna, M. (1997). Navigating the changing landscape of literacy: Current theory and research in computer-based reading and writing. In J. Flood, S. B. Heath, & D. Lapp (Eds.), *Handbook of research on teaching literacy through the communicative and visual arts* (pp. 77-92). New York: Simon & Schuster Macmillan.

Rollins, D. (2003, August 7). *Webquests.* Retrieved August 15, 2003, from http://www.techtrekers.com/webquests/

Snyder, T. (2003). *Decisions, Decisions 5.0* [Computer software]. Watertown, MA: Tom Snyder Productions.

Snyder, T. (2003). *Timeliner 5.0.* [Computer software]. Watertown, MA: Tom Snyder Productions.

Spitzer, K. L., Eisenberg, M. B., & Lowe, C. A. (1998). *Information literacy: Essential skills for the information age.* New York: ERIC Clearinghouse on Information & Technology.

Teacher Tools (2002, May 30). Retrieved August 15, 2003, from http://www.teachertools.org/index.html

Teachnology, Inc. (2003). *Teach-nology.* Retrieved August 15, 2003, from http://www.teach-nology.com/

Vacca, J. A., Vacca, R. T., Gove, M. K., Burkey, L., Lenhart, L. A., & McKeon, C. (2003). *Reading and learning to read* (5th ed.). Boston: Allyn, Bacon and Longman.

Wertsch, J. V. (1997). *Mind as action.* Oxford: Oxford University Press.

Woodruff, E. (1993). *George Washington Socks.* New York: Apple Paperbacks.

Acknowledgement

The authors would like to acknowledge the special help of Marilyn Dalton for her contributions to this article.

Appendix. Writing Samples from Question 1 on Final Test

Question 1. What do you believe to be the one biggest events that led to the Revoultutionary War? Explain your answer.

From the technology-rich classrooms:

I think it was the Battle of Lexington and Concord. My first reason is that the British found out where colonists were hiding weapons. The reason colonists got so mad was that the colonists did not have a lot of money so they could not buy much more. My second reason is that the colonists just had enough and wanted to break away from the motherland. (LS)

I think that the French and Indian War was the one biggest event that led to the Revolutionary War because after the colonists just fought to be able to move west-ward to have more land, King George III established the Intolerable Acts. The Intolerable Acts were taxes on sugar and having the colonists pay taxes on goods that were bought into the 13 colonies. The taxes were called the Intolerable Acts because the colonists could not put up with how the king was taxing them for the French and Indian War and how they had no decision on how to pay the money back to the king. (AS)

I think the Declaration of Independence was one of the biggest events leading up to the Revolutionary War. I think it was that because it was telling the British that they are not part of Great Britain and what they would do once they were not part of Britain. So that was the final writing; they told Britain that they are not part of it. Then King George the Third agreed to their writing and said there would be a battle. If the British won they would own the colonies; if the colonists won this would be their own nation. Yet, the colonies were competing against the strongest country in the whole world then. (DZ)

From the traditional classroom:

The Stamp Act and taxes because it made the colonists pay too much money (J0)

They raised taxes and when the Second Continental Congress sent the Olive Branch Petition the British king did not accept it. (EH)

I believe that it was how the colonists wanted to be free and not go by the King's laws. They were so far away from there, there was no reason to go by his rules. It was like if there was no killing this animal. That animal might not be in the colony. (JF)

I think that the biggest event was when the British just gave up and let the Patriots win. That was the last battle and it was at Yorktown. (SD).

I think it was the soldiers walking the streets of America because the colonists were uncomfortable. I also think it was the Boston Massacre that triggered the problem. I think if soldiers came to my house to sleep, I'd be uncomfortable, too.

CELEBRATING THE
PROCESS OF CHANGE

Quality Assurance: Assessing the Candidate and the Program Through Portfolio Review

Barbara Combs

University of North Dakota

Ellen Jampole

SUNY at Cortland

Ruth Oswald

The University of Akron

Abstract

Teacher education institutions are faced with the task of changing the way they provide training for their candidates in order to comply with new state standards as well as rigorous accreditation requirements. Designing and implementing new programs brings forward new ways of assessing candidate performance, one of which is portfolio review. This paper provides a description of the development and implementation of the portfolio assessment project at the undergraduate level at one institution of higher learning and at the graduate level at another. The authors will describe each of their portfolio assessment systems, discuss issues of concern and actions taken, and present candidates' responses.

Introduction

Diaz (2002) reminds us that today's educational reform agenda in our nation includes a renewed emphasis on standards and assessment in order to strengthen candidate learning and teacher development. Undergraduate and graduate teacher education programs are undergoing revision all across the country as they attempt to address new demands from state education departments for program re-registration and National Council for Accreditation of Teacher Education (NCATE) accreditation (or re-accreditation). Many teacher education institutions are faced with the task of changing the ways they provide training for their candidates to comply with new, more rigorous requirements focusing on the identification of outcomes, the design of learning and assessment experiences, and the development of strong connections with P-12 schools. In addition, NCATE's (2002) newly revised standards demand performance-based assessments emphasizing the need for demonstrated expertise in subject matter knowledge and pedagogical skills thus assuring that high quality teachers enter the field. Designing and implementing new programs to meet these demands often require the reconsideration of existing assessments and development of new ones, one of which is a portfolio review. The primary purpose of this article is to offer a description of the portfolio as performance assessment in an undergraduate and graduate program at two different institutions. Before doing so, it is important to set our description within a theoretical framework

Portfolios and Teacher Education

Although the use of the portfolio in teacher development emerged in the late 1980's (Delandshere & Arens, 2003), Grade Point Average (GPA) derived from individual coursework, comprehensive exams, and state mandated teacher tests remained the primary means of determining whether or not an individual met requirements for licensure. Such assessments, summative in form, did little to guide candidate learning or promote program improvement. In addition, Mokhtari, Yellin, Bull, and Montgomery (1996) have noted that education reform advocates declared that standardized testing practices have been a major deterrent to school improvement. More and more, teacher preparation institutions are looking for alternative means for teacher candidates to demonstrate what they know and can do. In contrast to standardized tests, portfolios provide opportunities for authentic assessment of achievement.

A Descriptive Definition of Portfolios

As candidates develop and maintain a portfolio, they learn to reflect and assess their own learning (Airasian, 2001; Cohen & Wiener, 2003; Stiggins, 2001). The portfolio serves as a tool and process by which pre-service and in-service teachers might clarify and further grow their ideas, teaching philosophies and instructional strategies (Lyons, 1998). Campbell, Cignetti, Melenyzer, Nettles, and Wyman (2001) discussed three kinds of portfolios: (a) the working portfolio, (b) the presentation portfolio, and (c) the professional portfolio. The working portfolio is used with preservice teachers as a professional growth tool. It is usually organized around professional standards such as Interstate New Teacher Assessment and Support Consortium (INTASC) (1992), National Association for the Education of Young Children (NAEYC) (2001), International Reading Association (IRA) (1998), or Professional Assessments for Beginning Teachers (Praxis) (Educational Testing Service [ETS], 2003). Working portfolios might contain complete collections of work and samples in unabridged form. They might require a file drawer or box and contain entire units, teacher-made materials, and even uncompleted projects.

The presentation portfolio is used when interviewing for a job and provides tangible evidence of what the candidate can do in practice. It is comprised of carefully selected artifacts that are streamlined and organized to display samples that are evidence of exemplary teaching.

The professional portfolio is used to document a teacher's ongoing professional development. Teachers in the twenty-first century need to provide evidence of their skills and expertise. This documentation can be used for teacher evaluation, licensure, professional advancement, and for consideration for National Teaching Certification. The portfolio development and review process at each of these different levels support the concept of the teacher as a reflective practitioner (Lyons, 1998) and lifelong learner as portfolios evolve from "working" to "presentation" to "professional." In addition, a review of candidates' portfolios can reveal much about the strength and weakness within the teacher preparation program.

Portfolios for Teacher Candidate Assessment and Growth

NCATE Standard 1 (NCATE, 2002) calls for candidates who "know and demonstrate the content, pedagogical and professional knowledge, skills, and dispositions necessary to help all students" (p. 1) gleaned through multiple assessments that demonstrate that candidates meet professional, state, and institutional standards. The working portfolio, as described by Campbell et al. (2001) can address both of these demands. For example, at the University of Southern Maine, portfolios are designed using a standard-based model (Lyons, 1996) where evidence in the form of portfolio artifacts is linked to locally developed teacher performance standards. In a study conducted by Delandshere and Arens (2003), portfolio use at three teacher preparation institutions required candidates to organize their portfolios around the INTASC (1992) standards. Both programs described in this article use a professional standards-based model (INTASC, 1992; IRA, 1998) as the foundation for candidates' portfolio preparation.

Portfolios for Program Assessment and Change

Lott-Adams (1995) suggests that portfolios should be aligned not only with professional standards, but also with the goals of the particular institution and the individual teacher educators who serve as faculty there. In this way, portfolio use can reveal the effectiveness of the education program and guide faculty in making appropriate program changes. This is in keeping with NCATE Standard 2 (NCATE, 2002) relating to the unit (teacher education program) assessment system indicating that the unit "employ an assessment system that collects, summarizes, and analyzes data to improve candidate performance as well as program quality" (¶. 2). The systematic collection and review of candidates' portfolios and presentations can yield information that makes it a valuable one for all involved be highlighting areas of strength and need.

Benefits and Concerns

There are three key benefits of portfolio development for teacher education candidates. First, the use of portfolios in the teacher education program provides candidates with a model that mirrors an authentic assessment technique (Lott-Adams, 1995). They come to understand what it means to collect multiple artifacts and reflect on what the artifacts reveal about the learner firsthand. Such understanding can help them develop their own assessment practices with students. Second, candidates learn to talk confidently with others about what they know as well as set goals to enhance areas in which they might not be as strong (Painter, 2001). Third, a wealth of information can be gathered about individuals and groups of candidates that can then be used to improve the teacher preparation program (Lott-Adams, 1995; Lyons, 1996).

As with most things in life, benefits have a flip side. At the forefront of concerns, is the dual nature of the portfolio development system within the teacher preparation program. While portfolios are used formatively as reflective tools to engage and guide candidates in a process of learning and reflection, they are also use summatively to evaluate candidates' abilities (Snyder, Lippincott, & Bower, 1998). Such a dual role is problematic and often leads candidates to perceive the portfolio process as merely a hurdle to be jumped over (Reis & Kidd, 2002). Another area of concern relates to the labor-intensive processes involved in the development and review of portfolios. Faculty support is critical in order to prevent a superficial response to the teacher candidate's portfolio. Without consensus as to the purpose and procedure for review, issues of the validity and reliability cloud the use of portfolios as assessment (Delandshere & Arens, 2003; Reis & Kidd, 2002; Smith et al., 2001). Candidates must also clearly understand the purposes and procedures for portfolio development in order to avoid frustration and confusion (Lyons, 1996) which results in presentations lacking deep reflection and well articulated explanations of the evidence provided (Delandshere & Arens, 2003).

Portfolios are not a panacea and tensions in their use are clearly evident; still, they have much to recommend as a means of performance assessment and teacher development. The heart of this article concerns the development and implementation of a portfolio review process that strives to prepare candidates to be reflective and effective teachers of quality. One is part of an undergraduate level program at The University of Akron and the other is the culminating performance for a graduate level reading program at the State

University of New York at Cortland. Programs will be described, issues of concern as well as actions taken will be presented, and candidate responses to the newly implemented requirements will be offered as well.

The Undergraduate Education Portfolio at the University of Akron

The Birth of the Portfolio Review Process

The implementation of the Education Portfolio as an undergraduate program requirement was an important part of the University of Akron's initiative demonstrating that our teacher preparation program is in compliance with current requirements to retain accreditation and prepare our candidates for licensure.

Diaz (2002) says:

> NCATE requires both a link between conceptual framework and assessment and the use of performance-based assessment over time in the teacher education program . . . The standards or outcomes for a program need to be examined so that they guide what happens in coursework and fieldwork in order that the demonstrations of knowledge, skill, and disposition implicit in the meaning of the standards meet those standards. (p. 76)

In addition, the Education Portfolio was instituted to align with Ohio's new licensure requirements that are a performance-based approach to assessment (Ohio Department of Education, 1998). Darling-Hammond and Cobb (1996) noted that portfolio assessment should clarify the criteria for assessment and licensing because it places greater emphasis on the abilities that teachers develop rather than on the titles of classes they must take. It is no longer enough to take candidates through a sequence of courses with the outcome being a grade point average and a required score on a licensure/certification examination.

As we began the process of developing our portfolio requirement in the College of Education, we soon realized it was not a simple add-on. All of the specialized programs such as Early Childhood, Physical Education, and Secondary Mathematics realized they would need to help candidates link possible portfolio artifacts to national standards, thus ensuring candidates meet specified criteria in those areas. Some of the departments chose to begin with existing class assignments, link them to their own national program standards, and designate appropriate assignments, the products of which would become portfolio artifacts. Other departments chose to begin with the standards, placing the responsibility on the teacher candidates to choose appropriate artifacts from their coursework to demonstrate their mastery of each standard. The following are some of the important issues we faced:

- How will we ensure that artifacts connect clearly to professional standards for excellence?
- Will artifacts be candidate or instructor selected or both?
- Who will evaluate portfolios? (advisors, instructors?)
- When will portfolios be evaluated?
- How will we be sure that the process helps candidates learn to be reflective about their work?
- How will we provide possibilities for candidates making their portfolios unique and creative?

Elements of the Portfolio Review Process

Many lengthy discussions concerning the portfolio requirement occurred at department meetings and among the faculty and administration. Sub-committees worked toward consensus during a portfolio retreat. The process continued for the greater part of a semester and finally, after numerous revisions, the following elements were implemented:

- Candidates were required to connect all artifacts to professional standards for excellence.
- Each department determined the appropriate artifacts that reflect their teacher-candidates' learning.
- Instructors evaluated portfolio artifacts that are course specific.
- Evaluation check points were established: sophomore year, junior year, pre-student teaching, post-student teaching (advisors involved in this evaluation). Students became familiar with performance standards and gained an in-depth understanding of portfolio requirement. In addition, we recognized that this was a process. We were learning as we went and adaptations were made along the way. An orientation course was offered twice a semester; and candidates were required to sign up at the same time they were taking *Characteristics of Learners/Teaching* and *Learning Strategies* courses. The purpose of the course was to orient candidates to the portfolio requirement.

Responses to the Portfolio Review Process

We have completed one semester with the education portfolio requirement. Disappointingly, based on personal communications as well as course teacher evaluations, many of our teacher-candidates see it as simply "one more thing" to do . . ."a BIG thing." These results are similar to those of Delandshere and Arens' (2003) study. Still, we are only beginning. Campbell, Melenyzea, Nettles, and Wyman (2000) wrote that they were hopeful that their students would come to understand that a portfolio was not a scrapbook of college course assignments and memorabilia designed to impress someone; we hope for the same thing. We want our candidates to view the portfolio as an organized documentation of growth and achievement providing tangible evidence of the attainment of professional knowledge, skills, and dispositions. We want to instill in our candidates an understanding of portfolios as part of a process of monitoring ongoing professional growth.

Mokhtari et al. (1996) conducted a study of a group of pre-service teachers' attitudes toward portfolio assessment. They found that even though there were initial concerns about the time and effort involved in using portfolios, the subjects agreed that portfolio assessment helped them reflect on their own work, assess their own learning and growth, and provided multiple ways of assessing their learning over time. We are hopeful that teacher candidates at our institution will come to a similar realization as we continue this process. Our College of Education recently passed the new NCATE evaluation with excellent reviews. We feel confident that the implementation of this education portfolio requirement supports our conceptual framework and our goal to prepare our candidates to be teachers who are capable of making decisions as they reflect on their practice.

The Graduate Literacy Educator's Portfolio at SUNY Cortland
The Birth of the Portfolio Review Process

The development of the Graduate Literacy Education Program Portfolio Review System at the State University of New York at Cortland was born out of frustration. Both faculty and candidates were unhappy with the culminating requirements leading to the Master's Degree in Reading Education. Once all coursework with the exception of electives was completed, candidates could elect to complete a traditional thesis, enroll in an independent master's project, or apply to take a three hour comprehensive exam. In the vast majority of cases, candidates elected to take the exam. In the semester prior to exam, a brief workshop was offered to those planning to take the exam. All preparation for this final test was done without the guidance of faculty advisors. Instead, candidates prepared individually or in study groups. Once the exam results were in, they were informed by mail, and if they received a passing score they would send a request for the diploma to the graduate school and subsequently apply to the state for certification as a reading specialist. Many candidates complained of the cold disconnection from program and faculty as well as their inability to truly demonstrate all that they had learned.

For three key reasons, faculty were even less happy than candidates. First, while most candidates could comfortably discuss what they would do to assess and instruct their students, they were unable to successfully connect these actions to the literature and research in the field. This exam did not help faculty know what the candidates understood about the scholarship that we hoped would provide the foundation for their teaching. Second, candidates' on-demand writing evidenced a lack of voice, and a limited development of ideas as these writers rushed to "dump" their knowledge on the page. With the exception of a few papers each semester, the exam responses were difficult and frustrating to read. Finally, the review and scoring of exams was an add-on to the 12 hour semester faculty workload. Two times per year, in Fall and Spring, each of the six Reading Education faculty were required to review and score 200 or more exam responses. Each exam question was reviewed by two faculty. Additionally, adjunct faculty who were often unfamiliar with the full scope of the program were "begged" to be part of the review process so that candidates could be apprised of the results in a timely fashion. To complicate matters, no common scoring framework or rubric existed and little was known about the individual faculty rationales for scores.

Candidate and faculty complaints made the time ripe for change, but the road to the current culminating portfolio project was neither straight nor easily traveled. In the Fall semester of 1998, the Provost asked Combs and Jampole to study the feasibility of implementing a portfolio review system for the undergraduate Elementary Education program. New State Education mandates were emerging that would require colleges of education to revise programs substantially. They were to include ways to monitor and assess undergraduate candidates, throughout their program, to ensure that state standards for student learning as well as professional teaching standards were being met. We had both been using portfolio review in our courses for a number of years and believed strongly in the power of this assessment process, since it gave students voice and was seen as a best practice in assessment (McLaughlin & Vogt, 1996). Thus, we were happy to have the opportunity to work on the development of such an assessment and evaluation system. During the fall and spring semesters, we studied existing programs and devised a plan and budget for the implementation of a program portfolio process that we believed would meet the needs of our undergraduates and faculty as well as address standards and mandates. We presented the plan to the Provost with the expectation that we would spend the Fall of 1999 and Spring of 2000 laying the groundwork for the implementation of the Undergraduate Portfolio Assessment System to begin its pilot year in the Fall of 2000. Weeks and then months passed with no word, and when we finally pressed to find out the status of our plan, we were told that resources were not available and the plan had been "shelved."

While our goals for the undergraduate program were not to be realized, we were still convinced that portfolio assessment was a powerful means of assessing candidate performance. In addition, we remained disappointed and frustrated with the culminating activities in the graduate Reading Education program. We began to talk about the possibility of developing a portfolio assessment and evaluation system for the graduate program. We wanted an authentic assessment using multiple measures of candidate progress. In addition, we wanted candidates to be active and engaged in demonstrating their knowledge. Finally, we knew that there would need to be a shared language between faculty and candidates so that they could understand the criteria by which they were to be evaluated (Stiggins, 2001). Through many afternoon tea and coffee discussions, our possibilities evolved into a culminating course designed to mentor candidates through the development and presentation of a Literacy Educator's Portfolio. We garnered education faculty support through discussions at Education Department faculty meetings and through smaller reading faculty discussion groups. With faculty agreement, we offered two sections of the course as a pilot. It served as a substitute for the comprehensive exam in the Spring of 2000. Although not every reading faculty member agreed with the use of portfolios, there was consensus that this process was superior to the previous use of one-time exams and no major objections were voiced. When the new Literacy Education Program was approved by the State of New York's Education Department, The Master's Portfolio became a permanent culminating course requirement and the comprehensive exams were phased out.

Elements of the Portfolio Review Process

The preparation and presentation of the Literacy Educator's Portfolio is completed in a culminating course: *EDU 653: The Master's Project in Literacy Education.* It is a three credit hour course offered each Fall and Spring semester as well as during the summer session. During the summer session, the number of class sessions meetings is severely curtailed, although the time per session is greater. Due to this time crunch, we encourage summer session enrollment of only those candidates who are fully aware of course and rubric requirements ahead of time and need little assistance or those who may have additional time to finish in the following semester. An enrollment cap of 15 per section per semester has been set. As described in the syllabus, the Master's Project is the culminating experience in the Literacy Education Program and results in the development of a Literacy Professional Portfolio. Through portfolio preparation and presentation, candidates must demonstrate a comprehensive understanding of the scholarship in the teaching of literacy as well as an ability to apply this understanding in a variety of instructional settings in ways that result in positive student learning. The International Reading Association has determined the major understandings and skills that literacy specialists must have to become specialized literacy professionals. Therefore, this course is designed to allow candidates to demonstrate that they have met, at an acceptable level, all of the standards of IRA as outlined in *Standards for Reading. Professionals Revised* (International Reading Association, 1998).

Over the course of a semester, candidates attend class sessions to guide them in the development of the portfolio. Workshops are conducted during weeks 1-7. They are designed to address portfolio content requirements and provide in-class work and share time to support candidates during the preparation process. Workshop topic sessions include synthesis paper preparation, artifact selection, entry slip development, and a review and critique of model portfolios.

In the synthesis paper, candidates demonstrate their understandings and beliefs about literacy development, instruction, and assessment and tie these to the scholarship in the field. Candidates must follow American Psychological Association (2001) guidelines in the preparation of this 15-25 page paper. The paper is reviewed by the instructor at least once during the semester, and it is not unusual for candidates, with feedback from the instructor and/or peers, to complete three to five revisions. When successfully finished, the paper may serve as the primary artifact satisfying the criteria for Category 1: Theory and Knowledge Base, in the scoring rubric (see Appendix).

Workshops focusing on the selection of appropriate artifacts are also held. Candidates are expected to select artifacts primarily from class and project work as well as field and practicum experiences to demonstrate their knowledge and abilities across the following broad categories: (a) Theory and Knowledge Base, (b) Literacy Instruction, (c) Literacy Assessment, (d) Organizing and Enhancing Literacy Programs, and (e) Professional Development. They may also draw from their own experiences as classroom teachers (Since all teachers in the graduate literacy education program hold teaching licenses, many are practicing teachers.). In addition, they are informed early in the process that they may be required to study and develop additional artifacts if they lack proficiency in any of the category areas. Workshop sessions dealing with artifact selection and reflection generally begin with an analysis of the rubric requirements for each category, followed by candidates listing possible artifacts for inclusion and sharing rationales for their choices.

Once candidates have had time to reflect on, discuss and consider the reasons for selecting particular artifacts, they prepare entry slips for each. Generally a paragraph to a page in length, the entry names the artifact and details how it demonstrates the candidate's knowledge or ability in a given category. For example, a candidate may include as an artifact a graphic organizer detailing the differences between norm-referenced and criterion-referenced tests. In the entry slip the candidate would label the artifact, present a summary of understandings of each type of test and include a brief statement noting how each would be utilized in the literacy specialist's program. This might satisfy one criterion for the broad category "Assessment of Literacy Development."

Early in the course, model portfolios are displayed and candidates are encouraged to review and critique these, often in paired or small group discussions. While they are expected to prepare a portfolio that is a unique display of their knowledge and abilities, models often provide a much needed jumping off point and serve to allay fears. In addition, the Literacy Professional Portfolio Scoring Rubric (see Appendix) is reviewed so that candidates understand the elements of a target, acceptable, and unacceptable portfolio. As noted by Smith et al. (2001), the rubric is useful to faculty as well by providing a common ground decreasing subjectivity and increasing reliability. Both target and acceptable level portfolios are available for candidates' perusal during workshop and conference time.

Individual conferences are held during weeks 8-10. Candidates meet one-on-one with the instructor. They bring examples of their work completed thus far and share any questions or concerns they have. The purpose of the conference is to ensure the candidate (and the instructor) that he/she is moving in the right direction to meet rubric requirements.

Originally, candidates were given the choice to sign-up for and attend these 20-30 minute conferences with the course instructor. However, after facilitating the course for two semesters, we found that a small number of candidates, whom we believed should have taken advantage of this opportunity, too often chose not to attend. We did not discover weaknesses in a candidate's knowledge and or skills until the time of the presentation. This was too late to ameliorate concerns and finish the course and program by the end of the semester. Thus, candidates were given an incomplete for the course often leaving them frustrated and dismayed since many were on a deadline to meet program requirements and state mandates in order to keep their teaching positions. The stakes to finish on time are high. With these realities in mind, we decided to make the conferences a requirement, so that candidates understand by mid-semester the likelihood of completing the course and program successfully. If not, they are able to take action to seek appropriate extensions.

The culminating activity of this course and the graduate program is the presentation of the Literacy Professional Portfolio. During the final four weeks in the semester, each candidate presents her portfolio to three evaluators: the course instructor, a literacy education faculty member, and an external evaluator who holds a literacy specialist's certificate and is selected by the candidate. The candidate is allowed 30 minutes and following the presentation steps out of the room, leaving the portfolio behind. Evaluators, using the scoring rubric (see Appendix) as a guide, discuss the strengths and weaknesses of the candidate's presentation and the portfolio. If any areas are determined to fall below the "acceptable" level on the rubric, evaluators propose a learning plan for the candidate.

The candidate is invited back into the room. If the portfolio and presentation meet criteria at the target or acceptable level as described in the rubric, the candidate is congratulated and told that the course instructor will review the portfolio in-depth over the next week to be sure everything is in order. Generally, a candidate has been able to present only a portion of the artifacts; therefore, a complete portfolio review is needed to be sure that all requirements in all categories have been adequately addressed. At the end of one week, the candidate is apprised of the results of this second review. If all requirements are met, the candidate turns a mini-folio (the synthesis paper, copies of transcripts and teaching certification, entry slips, completed rubrics, and the completed evaluator sign-off sheet). These elements may be in hard copy, on compact disk (CD) or floppy disc. Once we have received these, a grade of S (satisfactory) is given and the candidate, having successfully and happily completed the program, may file for graduation and certification.

If the portfolio and presentation or the subsequent more thorough review by the course instructor, reveal any weaknesses, a learning plan addressing perceived weaknesses is proposed for the candidate. The proposed learning plan typically takes one of two forms. First, the candidate may be asked to read from the literature in a particular area. This process would involve specific readings of articles, longer texts or literature reviews to increase the candidate's knowledge base. Once the readings are complete, the candidate prepares a written review of the information learned. The instructor determines whether the candidate has successfully addressed the requirements in this area and has finished the course or needs to read more material and prepare an additional review. The second type of learning plan involves observation and or participation in an authentic learning environment. Candidates may be required to spend a certain amount of time observing a teacher and under her or his guidance, practice the assessment or instructional techniques that are designated as weak. In this case, the mentor teacher indicates to the course instructor whether or not the candidate has redressed the concern. In addition, the candidate collects data in the setting as additional artifacts for the portfolio. To date no candidates have been asked to retake courses, although we do reserve this option for any graduate candidates who exhibit extreme weakness in the knowledge base or practices of the field.

We are extremely pleased with this course and find the process a powerful one for candidate reflection on and demonstration of their understandings and abilities across the entire program. We also find the products, the portfolios themselves, useful as tools for program review.

The National Council for Accreditation of Teacher Education (NCATE) requires routine assessment and revision of graduate level programs to maintain high levels of quality (NCATE, 2002, ¶. 2). Although the development of *EDU 653: The Master's Project in Literacy Education* was conceived and implemented prior to our accreditation seeking, the course and portfolios serve us well to determine the level at which our candidates collectively meet professional standards and how well we meet the needs of our candidates. The scoring rubric is at the heart of this part of program assessment. Over the course of several semesters, we developed and revised the rubric. Initially, we included all 92 original competencies in IRA's Standards for Reading Professionals (1998) matrix. We found that candidates looked at these 92 and were immediately seized with high levels of anxiety. So, we revised the document by synthesizing the competencies under five core categories and offered bulleted sub-categories to help further direct our candidates' thinking. This has proven to produce less anxiety while still addressing all of the elements necessary to meet IRA's standards.

Because we have purposefully designed the rubric to address IRA standards, we are able to use the portfolios to conduct an annual program review. The departmental review procedures have been developed in the past year; however, circumstances have made it difficult to put these procedures in place. Within the last two years, the Literacy Education Program has revised its entire program to meet new state certification requirements, has sought and received IRA program accreditation, and has evolved into a Literacy Education Department. We therefore look forward to implementation of the program review plan in the near future. In order to complete the review, a sample of Literacy Professional Portfolios, inclusive of artifacts, is collected each semester. For each section offered, the instructor is asked to gather one "target," one "acceptable" and one "unacceptable" level portfolio. Since 3 or more sections of the course are offered each semester, this provides an opportunity for faculty to review at least 18 portfolios each summer. Although all faculty in the Literacy Education Program are invited to a day long session; at least one instructor from each course and the practicum director is expected to attend. Over the course of the day, each of the portfolios will be reviewed by each faculty member and a list of strengths and weaknesses made. Each faculty member will share her or his list and a master list of recurring patterns related to program strength or need will be created. Strengths and weaknesses will be discussed with special attention to weaknesses. A series of action plans will be generated to address the most significant weaknesses. Finally, a report will be prepared noting strengths, detailing weaknesses and laying out action plans which will then be used to direct program changes.

Responses to the Portfolio Review Process

Over the last three years, we have moved from the expectation that candidates take a pass/fail, one day comprehensive exam to the preparation and presentation of the Literacy Professional Portfolio. Our candidate responses are similar to other reports of programs implementing portfolio evaluation (Lyons, 1996; Reis & Kidd, 2002; Snyder et al., 1998). The majority of candidates have embraced the opportunity to display their expertise in a format that gives them power and voice. Instructors and candidates note that the semester long course allows candidates to determine for themselves strengths and weaknesses as well as display the best of what they have learned in a unique, colorful and creative way. There are very few surprises by the time of the presentation. Candidates also appreciate the opportunity to reflect and are usually surprised at the amount of information to which they have been exposed in coursework, field experiences and practicum. They are even more surprised and pleased at the information they recall and indeed have begun to implement in their daily teaching lives.

Each semester, candidates evaluate the course in two ways. First, they complete department required course Likert Scale evaluations. Second, a small sample of candidates respond orally and in writing to one or more of the following questions: What do you think of this course? What was the hardest thing for you to do? What was the easiest? What would you change?

Candidates consistently give high ratings for the course, an average of 4.5 or above on a 5 point scale. They especially enjoy the close contact and supportive atmosphere as they work with peers and instructors to prepare their portfolios. In addition, their comments support our notion that the culminating project is an extremely worthwhile:

> Thank you for giving me the opportunity to really show you what I know. I was in charge; I was the decision maker. This [portfolio] let me gather my thoughts, organize them, and present them in such a way that my principal, colleagues, and you understand the depth and breadth of my knowledge.

> I can't believe everything I know and what I still need to know. This really helped me pull it together. I hated you from the end of the first night of class because I thought this is too much. But it's not really. It just takes time and patience.

Finally, unsolicited comments from external evaluators including former program candidates and school administrators provide further evidence of the power of the portfolio process to demonstrate candidate knowledge and ability as literacy specialists. Former candidates commonly express a belated wish to have had the opportunity to display their learning in this authentic way. They view the portfolio as ongoing documentation of their ability and speak of the possibility of using it as a tool for annual professional evaluation. Administrators are sometimes external evaluators and sometimes invited visitors to the portfolio presentations. All to date have been impressed by the candidate's demonstrated expertise as well as the education program's attention to coursework and practical experiences. When an administrator is present, there are usually kudos given to both the candidate and the program.

The discussion thus far may lead one to believe that the portfolio and program review process are nearly perfect. We can easily argue that point. Although we are pleased with our progress to date, there are several continuing problems that need immediate as well as long term attention. As a group, the Literacy Education Department faculty can easily agree that the culminating course should be led by full-time faculty only. Making that agreement into reality, however, is not always a possibility and in some semesters, adjunct faculty have been hired as course instructors. For the short term we have too many candidates for too few available faculty. Capping admissions may help us address this concern.

A second problem is directly related to the variety of faculty who are assigned as instructors. Since three or more sections of *EDU 653* are offered each semester, and each course is facilitated by a different faculty member, congruency is a concern. In addition, because faculty also teach other sections of both graduate and undergraduate theory and methods courses, it is difficult for us to meet to discuss course expectations. Still, the rubric and syllabus common to all sections does help to maintain some consistency. Major differences occur in the attention given to the products with some instructors giving more weight to the development of the synthesis paper while others attend more to the collection of and rationale provided for selected artifacts. We hope that future program review discussions will help to bring instructors closer to matching expectations for candidate work.

In addition, a paired course section design, while having the positive benefit of enhancing congruency, has been difficult to implement. As originally devised, two faculty members would facilitate course sections at the same classroom site, but on different nights. One faculty member would become the "program faculty evaluator" of candidates in the second section during candidate portfolio presentations. Since the scheduling of courses was not the responsibility of Literacy Education Program faculty, sections of courses were frequently offered on the same night at the same time and at different campus sites (2 hours apart) making it impossible for faculty to pair for presentations. The emergence of the Literacy Education Department should help us to address this concern.

A third area posing problems among full-time faculty concerns the selection of external evaluators for the presentations. We are torn as to the purpose and expectation for these volunteers. All faculty agree that evaluators of the portfolio, should have literacy certification, since the graduate program leads to certifications in literacy. Some believe that not only should they be certified literacy specialists, they should also be practicing as specialists in the schools. Some believe that candidates may and should select the outside evaluator themselves. Thus, the candidate may have a knowledgeable cheerleader who can support as well as evaluate. Others feel that the outside evaluator must be a neutral observer and should be selected from a list of voluntary evaluators who have been solicited by faculty. We are still in discussion concerning this issue and have not come to a final decision. Currently, candidates may select the outside evaluator with two caveats. The evaluator must have literacy certification and cannot be related to the candidate.

The current rhetoric surrounding teacher preparation and professional development require that schools of education prepare "quality" elementary and secondary school teachers who demonstrate a high level of competence in subject matter knowledge and teaching skills (National Science Teachers Association, 2002, ¶ 5). While candidate testing may be a quick, easy way to determine some level of quality, the authors believe that the portfolio development and review process of our graduate and undergraduate candidates offers quality assurance to our institutions, P-12 schools and the candidates themselves that they will make a positive difference in their students' learning.

References

Airasian, P. W. (2001). *Classroom assessment: Concepts & applications* (4th ed.). Boston: McGraw Hill.

American Psychological Association (APA). (2001). *The publication manual of the American Psychological Association* (5th ed.). Washington, DC: APA.

Campbell, D. M., Cignetti, P. B., Melenyzer, B. J., Nettles, D. H., & Wyman, R. M. (2001). *How to develop a professional portfolio.* (2nd ed.). Boston: Allyn and Bacon.

Campbell, D. M., Melenyzer, B. J., Nettles, D. H., & Wyman, Jr., R. M. (2000). *Portfolio and performance assessment in teacher education.* Boston: Allyn and Bacon.

Cohen, J. H., & Wiener, R. B. (2003). *Literacy portfolios: Improving assessment, teaching, and learning* (2nd ed.). Upper Saddle River, NJ: Merrill.

Darling-Hammond, L., & Cobb, V. L. (1996). The changing context of teacher education. In F. B. Murray (Ed.), *The teacher educator's handbook* (pp. 14-62). San Francisco: Jossey-Bass Publishers.

Delandshere, G., & Arens, S. (2003). Examining the quality of evidence in preservice teacher portfolios. *Journal of Teacher Education, 54*(1), 57-73.

Diaz, M. E. (2002). How will teacher education use assessments? In R. W. Lissitz, & W. D. Schafer (Eds.), *Assessment in educational reform both means and ends* (pp. 66-79). Boston: Allyn and Bacon.

Educational Testing Service (ETS). (2003). *The Praxis series: Professional assessments for beginning teachers.* Retrieved August 21, 2003, from http://www.ets.org/praxis/

International Reading Association. (1998). *Standards for reading professionals.* Newark, DE: IRA.

Interstate New Teacher Assessment and Support Consortium (INTASC). (1992). *Model standards for beginning teacher licensing, assessment, and development: A resource for state dialogue.* Retrieved September 10, 2002, from http://www.ccsso.org/content/pdfs/corestrd.pdf

Lott-Adams, T. (1995). A paradigm for portfolio assessment in teacher education. *Education, 115*(4), 568-661.

Lyons, N. (1996). A grassroots experiment in performance assessment. *Educational Leadership, 53*(6), 66-68.

Lyons, N. (1998). Portfolio possibilities: Validating a new teacher professionalism. In N. Lyons (Ed.), *With portfolio in hand: Validating the new teacher professionalism* (pp. 11-22). NY: Teachers College Press.

McLaughlin, M., & Vogt, M. E. (1996). *Portfolios in teacher education.* Newark, DE: International Reading Association.

Mokhtari, K., Yellin, D., Bull, K., & Montgomery, D. (1996). Portfolio assessment in teacher education: Impact on preservice teachers' knowledge and attitudes. *Journal of Teacher Education, 47*(4), 245-252.

National Association for the Education of Young Children (NAEYC). (2001). *NAEYC standards for early childhood professional preparation: Baccalaureate or initial licensure level.* Retrieved December 15, 2002, from http://www.ncate.org/standard/new%20program%20standards/naeyc%202001.pdf

National Council for Accreditation of Teacher Education (NCATE). (2002). *NCATE unit standards.* Retrieved November 29, 2002 from http//www.ncate.org/standard/unit_stnds_ch2.htm#stnd2

National Science Teachers Association. (2002). *Questions and answers about teacher quality.* Retrieved January 2, 2003, from http://www.nsta.org/nclbqanda

Ohio Departmnet of Education. (1998). *Teacher education and licensure standards.* Retrived November 29, 2002, from http://www.ode.state.oh.us/teaching-profession/teacher/certification_licensure/standards/standards.asp

Painter, B. (2001). Using teaching portfolios. *Educational Leadership 58*(5), 31-34.

Reis, N., & Kidd, V. S. (2002). The benefits, tensions, and visions of portfolios as a wide scale assessment for teacher candidates. *Action in Teacher Education, 23*(4), 10-17.

Smith, P., Harris, C., Sammons, L., Waters, J., Jordan, D., Martha, D., et al. (2001). Using multimedia portfolios to assess preservice teacher and P-12 learning. *Action in Teacher Education, 22*(4), 28-39.

Snyder, J., Lippincott, A., & Bower, D. (1998). Portfolios in teacher education: Technical or transformational? In N. Lyons (Ed.), *With portfolio in hand: Validating the new teacher professionalism* (pp. 123-142). NY: Teachers College Press.

Stiggins, R. (2001). *Student-involved classroom assessment* (3rd ed.). Upper Saddle River, NJ: Merrill.

Appendix. Scoring Rubric for Literacy Professional Portfolio

Candidate's Name: _____	Overall Evaluation
Date of Presentation: _____	Passing Score: 15
Reviewer's Name & Position: _____	Candidate's Score: _____

Directions to the Reviewer:

The course instructor will complete the first two areas. For all other categories, circle either T for Target; A for Acceptable or U for Unacceptable. Write comments indicating candidate's strengths or needs. It is important that for any area you believe to be unacceptable, you provide specific suggestions as to what the candidate must do to reach the acceptable or target level.

Overall Appearance (all portfolios must meet the following criteria)

- The portfolio is clearly organized either by page number, tabs, and/or colored dividers.
- The portfolio is reader friendly with artifacts and entry slips or guides presented in a neat and conventionally correct form.
- All required elements are included:
  - Table of Contents
  - Copy of Certificate of Qualification or Provisional Certification
  - Informal transcript from Cortland (photocopies will be permissible)
  - Synthesis paper that addresses the candidate's beliefs and understandings in relation to the theory and knowledge base standards; draws upon appropriate research and scholarship in the field and appropriately uses APA style
  - Portfolio Guides for each artifact (The portfolio guides provide a satisfactory rationale for artifacts in the portfolio
  - Guides may occur as one long piece at the beginning of a major category (Guided Reflections) or they may be shorter pieces attached to each artifact (entry slips). In either case, they provide a brief description of each artifact as well as an appropriate explanation as to why a particular artifact meets the criteria as described in the IRA Standards)
  - Multiple artifacts of evidence to support each category describe in this rubric

Circle one: Y   N   If no, indicate what must be added:

Category 1: Theory and Knowledge Base

The Master's candidate must demonstrate comprehensive knowledge grounded in theory and research in each of the following areas:

- The acquisition and development of literacy
- Individual differences in literacy learners and learning including but not limited to cultural, linguistic, and ethnic diversity
- Reading and writing processes
- Difficulties in literacy acquisition and development
- Principles and practices of literacy instruction
- Principles and practices of literacy assessment

Target (5)	Acceptable (3)	Unacceptable (1)
•Synthesis paper demonstrates a comprehensive understanding of the theory and knowledge in all areas listed, draws upon broad research and scholarship in the field, is clear, well organized, mechanically correct, and uses APA style correctly. AND IF INCLUDED IN THIS CATEGORY •Other designated artifacts and entry slips/ guided reflections demonstrate comprehensive knowledge of the theory and research and all areas listed above are addressed.	•Synthesis paper demonstrates a fairly complete understanding of the theory and knowledge in all areas listed (although it may demonstrate greater depth of understanding in some areas than others), draws upon appropriate research and scholarship in the field, is written in a manner that is easily read and understood with few mechanical problems, and uses APA style correctly. AND IF INCLUDED IN THIS CATEGORY •Other designated artifacts and entry slips/guided reflections demonstrate comprehensive knowledge of the theory and research and all areas listed above are addressed (although may demonstrate greater depth of understanding in some areas than others).	•Synthesis paper demonstrates a limited or incorrect understanding of the theory and knowledge in one or more areas, may be difficult to read due to lack of organization and the presence of mechanical problems, and may use APA style incorrectly. AND IF INCLUDED IN THIS CATEGORY •Other designated artifacts and entry slips/ guided reflections demonstrate limited or incorrect understanding of the knowledge and theory in one or more areas listed.

Comments/Suggested Additions:

Category 2: Instruction

The Master's candidate must demonstrate proficiency in providing instruction including, but not limited to:
- Teaching all aspects of literacy development
- Creating appropriate instructional environments
- Aiding students who are having difficulty in developing or acquiring literacy through the regular classroom program as well as in compensatory or special education programs. (This instruction may occur in individual, small group, or whole class settings.)

Target (5)	Acceptable (3)	Unacceptable (1)
• Artifacts and entry slips/ guided reflections demonstrate comprehensive proficiency in providing instruction in all areas listed above. The candidate's artifacts provide evidence that he/she has implemented and reflected upon a broad variety of instructional approaches and tools indicating in-depth knowledge and a strong ability to provide for the instructional needs of all learners K-12.	• Artifacts and entry slips/ guided reflections demonstrate proficiency in providing instruction in all areas listed above although some may be represented in more depth than others. The candidate's artifacts provide evidence that he/she has implemented and reflected upon a variety of instructional approaches and tools indicating basic knowledge and some ability to provide for the instructional needs of all learners K-12.	• Artifacts and entry slips/ guided reflections demonstrate limited proficiency in providing instruction in all areas listed above. The candidate's artifacts provide weak evidence that he/she has implemented and reflected upon a variety of instructional approaches and tools indicating limited knowledge and limited ability to provide for the instructional needs of all learners K-12

Comments/Suggested Additions:

Category 3: Assessment of Literacy Development

The Master's candidate must demonstrate knowledge of and proficiency in the area of literacy assessment for all learners including but not limited to:

- Norm-referenced and criterion-referenced tests
- Formal and informal inventories
- Portfolio based assessment
- Student self-evaluations and work/performance samples
- Observations, anecdotal records, journals
- Other formal and informal indicators of student progress that may used to inform instruction and student learning

Target (5)	Acceptable (3)	Unacceptable (1)
• Artifacts and entry slips/ guided reflections demonstrate comprehensive proficiency in assessment in all areas listed above. The candidate's artifacts provide evidence that he/ she has implemented and reflected upon a broad variety of assessment methods and tools indicating in-depth knowledge and a strong ability to assess and design appropriate and effective instruction for all learners K-12.	• Artifacts and entry slips/ guided reflections demonstrate proficiency in assessment in all areas listed above although some may be represented in more depth than others may. The candidate's artifacts provide evidence that he/she has implemented and reflected upon a variety of assessment methods and tools indicating basic knowledge and some ability to assess and design appropriate and effective instruction for all learners K-12.	• Artifacts and entry slips/ guided reflections demonstrate limited proficiency in assessment in one or more areas listed above. The candidate's artifacts provide weak evidence that he/she has implemented and reflected upon a variety of assessment methods and tools indicating limited knowledge and a limited ability to assess and design appropriate and effective instruction for all learners K-12

Comments/Suggested Additions:

Category 4: Organizing and Enhancing Literacy Programs

The Master's candidate must demonstrate knowledge and proficiency in the following areas:

- Collaborating and communicating effectively with faculty, staff, administration, parents/caregivers, and students in order to develop, organize, implement, and enhance literacy programs
- Developing and organizing literacy programs in regular classroom, compensatory program and special education program settings
- Providing guidance, instruction, and support for paraprofessionals

Target (5)	Acceptable (3)	Unacceptable (1)
•Artifacts and entry slips/guided reflections demonstrate comprehensive proficiency in all areas listed above. The candidate's artifacts provide evidence that he/she has knowledge of and/or has implemented and reflected upon program development and enhancement such that he/she can readily assume the administrative responsibilities of a reading specialist in any K-12 setting.	•Artifacts and entry slips/guided reflections demonstrate proficiency in all areas listed above although some may be represented in more depth than others may. The candidate's artifacts provide evidence that he/she has knowledge of and/or has implemented and reflected upon program development and enhancement such that he/she can with some initial experience and feedback assume the administrative responsibilities of a reading specialist in any K-12 setting.	•Artifacts and entry slips/guided reflections demonstrate limited proficiency in one or more all areas listed above. The candidate's artifacts provide weak evidence that he/she has knowledge of and/or has implemented and reflected upon program development and enhancement such that he/she has limited ability to assume the administrative responsibilities of a reading specialist in any K-12 setting.

Comments/Suggested Additions:

Category 5: Professional Development

The Master's candidate must demonstrate a commitment to the literacy profession by providing evidence of on-going study and inquiry in literacy areas and a willingness to share their knowledge and learn from others. Included artifacts may provide evidence in the following:

- Attendance or participation in professional conferences
- Roles on decision-making teams in district or professional organizations
- Memberships in professional organizations related to literacy instruction
- Publishing literacy related material
- Providing literacy related professional development

Target (5)	Acceptable (3)	Unacceptable (1)
• Artifacts and entry slips/guided reflections demonstrate strong and on-going commitment to the professional development of the self others.	• Artifacts and entry slips/guided reflections demonstrate some on-going commitment to the professional development of the self and others.	• Artifacts and entry slips/guided reflections demonstrate limited commitment to the professional development of the self and others.

Comments/Suggested Additions:

Required revisions to meet criteria for a passing score (List on back if more space is needed):

A Tale of Two Cities (or Universities): Developing a Joint Doctoral Reading Program

Mary W. Strong
Shelley B. Wepner
Nancy M. Ziomek
Beth Herbine
Julie Foley

Widener University

Abstract

This paper (or tale) describes a joint reading doctoral program developed by two universities (one public and one private) that has been in existence for two and a half years. Topics covered include: history and rationale for the program; program development/outcomes; administrative concerns; and faculty and student concerns and issues.

The perspectives of the key participants—administration, faculty and students—provide a multifaceted overview of the development and progress of the program. The paper also discusses insights about the program gained through trial and error, and suggests a list of guidelines that other institutions can use to begin a similar program.

"It was the best of times, it was the worst of times, it was the age of wisdom, it was the age of foolishness, it was the epoch of belief, it was the epoch of incredulity, it was the season of Light, it was the season of Darkness, it was the spring of hope, it was the winter of despair, we had everything before us, we had nothing before us, we were all going direct to Heaven, we were all going direct the other way . . ." (Dickens, 1859, p.13)

Our tale of two universities is not as tumultuous or heroic as Charles Dicken's *Tale of Two Cities*. It does, though, demonstrate how two institutions with dramatically different structures (private versus public, nonunionized versus unionized, doctoral research intensive versus master's comprehensive) could come together as partners in the educational enterprise. Our story provides evidence of the potential for two institutions to modify their ideals and past practices, both on an individual and institutional level, for the sake of providing a better opportunity for students. Although there were some stormy moments in the process, it did give way to a new and better program.

Our story also demonstrates the necessity of collaboration and leadership in developing such a partnership (Kadel & Routh, 1994; Mattessich & Monsey, 1992; Melaville & Blank, 1991; Winer & Ray, 1994). As Kerka (1997) writes, collaboration is an intense, long-term effort that results in a formal and sustained commitment to accomplish a shared, clearly defined mission. It requires the ability of the collaborators to see the "big picture" so that allowance is made for the alteration of structures and policies. For collaboration to occur, one or two persons need to serve as leaders to accomplish the mission (Combs, Miser & Whitaker, 1999; English, 1992). Those in leadership positions (whether self-appointed or appointed by others) need to believe in others, and at the same time help them to appreciate the need to change and compromise. These leaders need to understand that collaboration involves working with key stakeholders, inspiring and effectively involving key shareholders in planning for the change, and learning about and establishing a comfortable and compatible culture for the key stakeholders. While collaborative models are prevalent in business and industry, they appear to occur less frequently in higher education, thus, the rationale for the following description of our experience.

Background
How and Why the Partnership Began
Our tale began with a discovery by the coordinator of the graduate reading program at Kutztown University that many of her master's degree students needed access to a doctoral program in reading/language arts to prepare them for the supervisory and administrative positions they were seeking in neighboring school districts. However, Kutztown University is part of a state university system; therefore, it was not permitted to offer doctoral programs. Kutztown University is located in a rural town in the eastern part of Pennsylvania and the coordinator of the graduate reading program had formed a partnership 15 years ago with another university to offer a doctorate. This partnership, which lasted approximately 6 years, was a "shared program"

with a large doctoral research extensive, urban institution for students interested in doctoral work in Psychology of Reading. The twenty students who successfully completed the program were actively involved in the Graduate Reading Alumni Association. They were filling leadership positions in school districts in the tri-county service area of Kutztown University, or providing instruction for teacher candidates at several universities.

As graduates of an earlier program, members of the Kutztown's Graduate Reading Alumni Association knew of the institutional history of a shared doctoral program, and requested that a doctoral program be reactivated. The coordinator of the graduate reading program, who was also the advisor to the Graduate Reading Alumni Association at Kutztown University, decided to once again, find a way to offer a doctoral program to her students. She studied four universities that offered doctoral programs related to reading. The criteria for evaluation included travel distance from Kutztown University, degree requirements, residency demands, and focus of the content of the program (e.g., Teaching English as a Second Language, psychology, research).

She found that Widener University, located two hours away, appeared to be the most philosophically aligned with her master's degree program and seemed to offer advanced courses that she wanted her students to take in a doctoral program. Widener's doctoral program stressed reading as a psychological process rather than as a curricular process. The Widener program also appeared to be a natural extension of the approach that was the core of the master's program at Kutztown University; thus, enabling students to be able to anticipate success with their doctoral work.

The coordinator of the graduate reading program shared the results of her search with Kutztown graduates by sending a letter to all students who had graduated from the university within the last 10 years (See Appendix A). About 40 percent of the graduates of the Kutztown University's reading master's program expressed an interest in a doctoral program and requested more information. She was pleased to be able to communicate this interest in the program to Widener University as part of her effort to establish an alliance.

The coordinator of the graduate reading program at Kutztown then used her own professional contacts with a Widner faculty member to move forward with the idea. Through these connections, the Kutztown coordinator called the Widener faculty member to see if her institution would be open to the idea of a partnership with Kuztown University. The response that she received was, "Let's talk."

While intrigued with the idea and always interested in bringing new students into the doctoral program, the Widener University faculty member knew that a decision about the partnership was beyond her realm of responsibility. She quickly approached the director of the education program, who then presented the idea to her supervisor for the initial approval. Widener University, while not experienced with this type of partnership, had a history of offering off-campus programs and was known for its entrepreneurial and collaborative spirit.

Faculty and Administrative Negotiations

From the outset, the faculty from each institution initiated this partnership and drove the process. This was a critical factor in the success of this partnership. The administrators were involved to assess its feasibility, negotiate the financial and structural details, and record both informally and formally the nature of the agreement between the two universities. The coordinator of the graduate reading program from Kutztown and the Widener reading/language arts faculty member actually brought their administrators (Kutztown Provost, Kutztown dean, and Kutztown education department chair and Widener dean and Widener associate dean) together to determine whether the needs of both institutions could be met while still satisfying the student needs. The program initiators also brought together their faculty colleagues from both institutions to determine how the program would be shaped.

When the administrators from both institutions met, they each decided that the overall good of the program was worth the compromises that had to be made. Kutztown University made concessions concerning faculty salary and student tuition. Both full-time and adjunct faculty from Kutztown University would accept the lower adjunct salary scale of Widener University. The Kutztown cohort students who would enroll in the Widener doctoral reading program would have to pay Widener's tuition, which was considerably higher than Kutztown's tuition.

Widener University would allow the Kutztown students to transfer in their entire master's degree program from Kutztown. This allowed the Kutztown cohort to take 12 fewer credits than the students in the regular reading doctoral program at Widener. Widener also agreed to study the curriculum to determine which previously required doctoral courses could be eliminated from the Kutztown cohort program. The coordinator of the graduate reading program at Kutztown then arranged an informational meeting with the Kutztown students and sent out a letter to those students who had expressed initial interest in the program (See Appendix B).

When the reading/language arts faculty from both institutions met voluntarily at Widener for two one-half day luncheon sessions during the summer, they collaborated and compromised on the coursework, the faculty responsible for teaching the courses, admissions criteria, and the policies and procedures for the comprehensive examination and dissertation. Kutztown cohort students would be able to take courses from both the reading/language arts and educational leadership doctoral programs to better prepare them for PK-12 administrative posts. The faculty knew from the university administrators that a minimum of 12 students from the Kutztown cohort needed to be enrolled each semester so that the courses could be taught. This would help to offset the added expense of paying Widener faculty for their travel to Kutztown to teach courses. Kutztown also agreed to require students to travel to Widener for a specific research course and possibly a second course that could only be offered on Widener's campus by a particular faculty member. Otherwise, all courses would be offered at Kutztown University. In addition, the Kutztown cohort would have to subscribe to Widener's criteria for admissions as well as the policies and procedures for the comprehensive examination and dissertation.

The coordinator of the graduate reading program at Kutztown and the original Widener faculty contact then wrote and presented proposals to their respective curriculum committees for approval. At the same time, the director of the education program from Widener University wrote an articulation agreement that delineated each institution's commitment concerning class size expectations, faculty compensation, and tuition rate differentials that eventually was given to each institution's legal counsel for editing and the necessary disclaimers.

The process of working out the details spanned many months and required meetings with interested parties from the two universities at both sites. For example, Widener's program does not have a specific sequence in which courses must be taken. However, the new Kutztown program would have a specific sequence because of the cohort paradigm. The faculty-administrative teams of both universities were driven by the idea of providing a unique opportunity for these students. Even though each university group had to protect its own program, faculty and finances, it did so collegially. To facilitate collaboration and communication, a faculty liaison was assigned to each site. The coordinator of the graduate reading program at Kutztown served as the Kutztown liaison. Widener agreed to pay her the equivalent of a total of three credits each year because she served as the first contact for all students, evaluated their transcripts, completed the recommendation form, identified the courses that needed to be offered, and worked with her registrar to identify classrooms for the courses. The key advisor for the Widener reading/language arts program served as the Widener liaison. Given that the original Widener contact retired a year after the program began, the director of the education program appointed the next faculty member in line to assume this responsibility. The Widener liaison did not receive compensation, but did receive service credit for her annual merit review. The Widener liaison served as the advisor for the Kutztown students, and as the contact person for program issues and concerns.

Administrative Issues Concerning the Partnership

When two universities are brought together, there are many issues that need to be resolved: administrative oversight of the program; faculty responsibility for travel and off-campus teaching; territorial concerns with coursework, online instruction, and dissertations; financial responsibilities for marketing, physical facilities for classrooms (e.g., lighting and heating), travel, lodging, and meals; and the notion of long-distance relationships. With any new initiative, there are the usual differences in perspectives from both faculty and staff.

For example, one Widener faculty member thought that her course was to be taught at Widener. However, the Kutztown cohort students thought that the course was going to be taught at Kutztown. It took about four months, a dozen calls, a few very uncomfortable conversations, and scores of e-mail between the liaisons of the programs and two administrators to resolve where the course was to be taught and who would teach it. On another occasion, Widener's Admissions Committee had not accepted students that the coordinator of graduate reading programs at Kutztown thought should be accepted. Again, with the same intense level of intra- and inter-university communication, the issue was finally resolved when the Widener's Admission Committee agreed to accept the students because of previously agreed-upon criteria.

What seemed inconsequential to one university could be monumental for another. We found that in order for this type of partnership to work, administrators must be able to help themselves and their faculty *negotiate* for coursework, credits, students, and instruction; *compromise* for coursework, credits, students, and instruction; *apologize* for all of the above; and exhibit *patience* with everything from determining if meals for faculty are covered to getting two lawyers from two different academic cities to agree on the language of a formal agreement.

Scheduling and Other Issues

The coordinator of scheduling at Widener University was assigned the task of scheduling the Kutztown cohort classes after the program had been in operation for a while. She had to quickly learn Kutztown's structure and intricacies and how they differed from the scheduling of classes at the Widener Campus.

When the Widener coordinator of scheduling began working with the Kutztown cohort program, there were two cohorts in operation. Both Kutztown cohort groups had been promised a sequence of courses that would insure that their program would be completed in a timely fashion. It then became Widener's coordinator of scheduling task to make sure these promises were met. The Widener faculty members were approached to see if they were interested in and available to teach the courses expected that semester. A schedule that would allow the faculty the extra time needed to teach an off-campus course had to be developed. If there were no Widener faculty available, the coordinator of the graduate reading program at Kutztown University then had to check with Kutztown faculty to arrange course coverage.

This scheduling practice was further complicated by professors who were understandably territorial about their courses and very much wanted to insure the quality of the program. Not every Widener faculty member was happy to hear that, even though they were not available to teach one of their courses off campus that semester, it "needed" to be taught by someone from Kutztown University.

Widener's liaison worked closely with the coordinator of scheduling and the instructors to assist with scheduling and other issues. Yet, even with these efforts to communicate, there were rumors, worries, and concerns among program administrators, faculties and students. For example, one rumor was that the Kutztown cohort students were not welcome on the Widener campus. The Widener liaison made a trip to the Kutztown campus to dispel this rumor. Another issue was an expressed concern by some faculty and administrators that the Kutztown cohort program would negatively impact the enrollment on the Widener campus (which it didn't). At one point, there was even concern expressed to the Kutztown liaison that the contract was not being implemented as initially approved. A meeting was held between the liaisons to ensure that the intent and purpose of the contract was being honored.

On the other hand, because of their geographical proximity to Kutztown University, some Widener students wanted to take courses at the Kutztown campus rather than Widener. After one semester of allowing this to happen and finding an oversized enrollment in a course, the Widener faculty and the Kutztown liaisons decided to deny future similar requests. This decision was made in order to preserve the integrity and identity of the Widener-Kutztown partnership.

Kutztown cohort students had to grapple with the issues of driving two hours to the Widener campus to take their comprehensive exams, meet with their dissertation advisors, defend their dissertation proposals, and defend their dissertations. This travel requirement obviously added even more complexity and stress to the process of finishing a degree.

Roles and Issues of the Faculty Liaison

The Widener faculty liaison found that her usual duties as an academic advisor became even more demanding with this partnership. Since the program was prescribed, many Kutztown cohort students did not see the need for meeting with a Widener advisor in the initial stage of the program. Students often would sign their own registration forms for a scheduled course as the "Kutztown Cohort" on the advisor line. Of course, the Widener University Registrar's office did not recognize this signature. The registration form was forwarded to the Widener faculty liaison who would then be obliged to cross out "Kutztown Cohort" and sign her name above.

Some Kutztown cohort applicants were confused as to where to interview for admission to the program. Originally, the prospective students were to interview with the graduate reading coordinator at Kutztown University, but some of them decided to travel to Widener to interview because they believed the Widener faculty liaison to be the senior faculty member in the reading/language arts program and program advisor. She had to send them back to the Kutztown liaison to complete the admissions process.

Since there were two Kutztown cohort groups matriculating one year behind each other, it was challenging to remember which cohort group needed which course, and when the course was needed. What further complicated the matter was the fact that there were approximately five to six students in each cohort group who had missed the sequence of courses (This was due to ordinary life circumstances such as the birth of a child, serious illness, or new job assignment). Therefore, it became the Widener faculty liaison's responsibility to arrange for faculty to teach independent studies or to schedule additional sections of a course out of sequence.

The Widener faculty liaison also inherited additional responsibilities with comprehensive examinations and dissertations. After the comprehensive examinations were passed by the Kutztown students, dissertation advisors and committees had to be selected. The chair of each dissertation committee had to be a professor from Widener University. A second committee member was to be selected from Widener University and a third member was to be selected from Kutztown University. Widener and Kutztown faculty had to collaborate on developing the Kutztown faculty dissertation committee list. Because so few Widener faculty were available to chair dissertations, the Widener faculty liaison had to chair several Kutztown dissertations in addition to her main campus group. It should be noted though, as with all Widener dissertation chairs, she was paid one-fourth of each student's tuition.

The Widener faculty liaison had to work with the Widener library staff to insure that the Kutztown cohort students would have access to the library resources necessary for preparing for the comprehensive exams. Again, many of the library staff had to be educated about the program.

The Widener faculty liaison began to be perceived as the "lightening rod" for faculty anxiety about the program. Some of the Widener faculty presumed that she was "in charge" of the Widener doctoral reading program offered at Kutztown. The Widener faculty brought all of their concerns about the reading courses that were being offered in the cohort program to her. Some of them thought that either there were not enough reading/language arts classes required in the program or that some other courses that were offered on the main campus should be offered for the Kutztown cohort. Thankfully, the Widener faculty liaison could say that she was not solely responsible for the program of courses, but rather that the originators of the program (the coordinator of the graduate reading program at Kutztown University, the deans and the reading faculty of both universities) had made that decision.

Issues of the Traveling Professors

To date, there have been six Widener professors, from the eight who teach in the reading program, who have chosen to teach the Kutztown co-hort program courses at the Kutztown campus. Two professors from Kutztown have been hired as adjuncts. One Widener professor has declined to teach long distance. In the meantime, two of the Widener professors involved in the program have recently retired which may necessitate hiring two new adjuncts or having two more Widener faculty travel in the future.

As with any new role, there were pre-stage jitters. The long distance relationship added to the usual faculty concerns about teaching a new course. Since they had never been to Kutztown University before, the faculty had initial worries about the facilities on that campus. For example, would they be able to make PowerPoint presentations or just have a chalkboard and chalk in their classrooms? Would the room configurations lend themselves to the way they liked to run their classes?

Another area of concern for the Widener professors was insuring that required texts and journal articles were available and easily accessible to the students. Could the same assignments and presumptions of access to materials be made for off-campus courses? What assumptions, if any, could be made about student background knowledge? Did the Kutztown cohort students know the Widener grading policy and grievance procedures? If they did not, whose responsibility was it to inform them about these policies and procedures?

Ordinary issues such as classroom supplies, parking spaces, and inclement weather became more significant in this collaborative relationship. Time and ingenuity have helped the Widener faculty deal with these issues. Email has served as one of the most important tools to assist communication among the travelling faculty and the students in the program.

A continuing major issue for a traveling professor has been the increased difficulty of being accessible to students. Travel time limits faculty availability at the Widener campus. An even more difficult issue is accessibility to

Kutztown cohort students before or after class. A two-hour ride home at the end of an evening class severely limits after-class conferencing.

The faculty have had to learn, sometimes through trial and error, about their new roles and responsibilities and about those of program advisors and schedulers on both campuses.

Issues of Student Cohort Members

A cohort is defined in The American Heritage Dictionary (1981, p.259) as "a group or band united in some struggle." That definition easily fits the feelings many of the members of the first Kutztown cohort group, as they made the decision to return to post-graduate school. The members of the original Kutztown cohort group consisted of 22 females, spanning from 30 to 60 years in age.

The cohort members varied in marital status and included members who were single, married, divorced, and widowed. As with all students, life events continued to arise as they struggled to complete coursework and prepare for comprehensive examinations. Among those events were one marriage, three childbirths, the loss of several parents, and two individual battles with cancer. The Kutztown cohort students credit the kinship established within the group as a way to handle these events.

Students united in the initial cohort group held various educational positions and included classroom teachers (K-8), reading specialists, a special education supervisor, resource teachers, a regional educational agency consultant, and a stay-at-home mother. The school districts represented in the cohort were rural, urban and suburban.

Cohort members gradually coalesced into a tightly knit, mutually supportive group. This cohesiveness was aided by the obvious desire for cooperation between Kutztown University and Widener University. Although issues arose periodically (as were previously mentioned), all were resolved through frequent and repeated communication. While cohort members were initially more familiar and at ease with the coordinator of the graduate reading program at Kutztown University, relationships quickly developed between the various cohort members and Widener faculty members.

An important benefit of participation in the program was the ability for students to work on research interests with each other and with members of both faculties. Among the topics explored by the cohort group were kindergarten literacy, vocabulary development, bilingual education, the connection between technology and literacy instruction, and the role of the reading specialist in state testing preparation. Widener faculty members connected members of the cohort group with individuals at their university who shared similar interests. At the same time, cohort students were encouraged to maintain a connection with Kutztown faculty who could also help contribute to the educational process. According to one cohort student, the experiences of the initial cohort group were so successful that a second cohort group was formed to "band together in a united struggle" (J. Foley, personal communication, September 28, 2002).

Recommendations from Lessons Learned

Even with the best of intentions in the best of times, it is not easy to bring together two different university cultures. Depending on the person you talk to, this partnership has been good and bad, has been filled with great deeds and bad mistakes. We have experienced dedication and unreliability as we encountered frustration and forgiveness. There are some recommendations that grew out of this story, which, while specific to our experience, reflect what the literature says about collaborative partnerships (Karasoff, Blonsky, Perry, & Schear, 1996; Kerka, 1997; Mattessich & Monsey, 1992; Weifand, 1999). The recommendations can be listed under these three categories: (a) putting characters or players in the right roles, (b) plotting for a successful partnership, and (c) setting the stage for a collaborative culture.

Putting Characters or Players in the Right Roles

Multiple persons from the faculty and administration need to be involved in a collaborative partnership. We found that, similar to other collaborative partnerships (Karasoff et al., 1996; Kerka, 1997; Melaville, Blank & Asayesh, 1993; Robinson & Mastny, 1989), a grassroots movement is always better than a top down act. Roles and responsibilities of the principal persons need to be clearly defined. There also needs to be a clear understanding of the issues to be addressed (Kerka, 1997; View & Amos, 1994).

Figure 1 identifies the roles, responsibilities and issues that surfaced during the Widener-Kutztown partnership. As Figure 1 depicts, there are three major types of stakeholders; faculty liaisons, administrators, and key faculty. Each university should appoint a faculty liaison who will coordinate administrative functions (e.g., scheduling, recruiting, admissions, comprehensive exams) with the other liaison and work with their own faculty to accommodate the students. For example, the Faculty Liaison from the degree-granting institution should be a member of the Admissions Committee to help clarify and implement the agreed-upon admissions requirements for the cohort group (Penney, 2001).

Administrators need to be involved (either to initiate or endorse such a program) to determine the academic, structural, and financial value of the program in relation to the institution's mission.

Key faculty, the instructional mainstay of the program, must be involved to ensure their willingness to participate as "long distance" instructors and

Figure 1. Roles, Responsibilities and Issues Related to Program Partnership

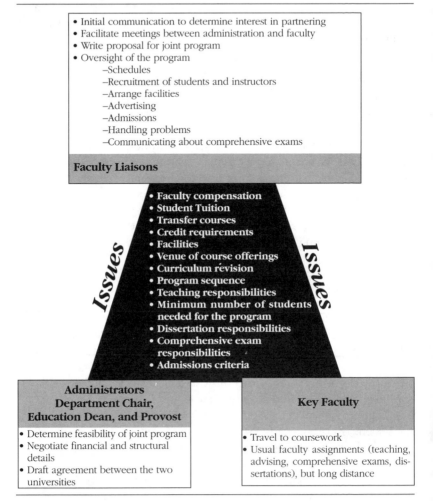

- Initial communication to determine interest in partnering
- Facilitate meetings between administration and faculty
- Write proposal for joint program
- Oversight of the program
  - –Schedules
  - –Recruitment of students and instructors
  - –Arrange facilities
  - –Advertising
  - –Admissions
  - –Handling problems
  - –Communicating about comprehensive exams

Faculty Liaisons

Issues

- **Faculty compensation**
- **Student Tuition**
- **Transfer courses**
- **Credit requirements**
- **Facilities**
- **Venue of course offerings**
- **Curriculum revision**
- **Program sequence**
- **Teaching responsibilities**
- **Minimum number of students needed for the program**
- **Dissertation responsibilities**
- **Comprehensive exam responsibilities**
- **Admissions criteria**

Issues

Administrators Department Chair, Education Dean, and Provost

- Determine feasibility of joint program
- Negotiate financial and structural details
- Draft agreement between the two universities

Key Faculty

- Travel to coursework
- Usual faculty assignments (teaching, advising, comprehensive exams, dissertations), but long distance

advisors. The multiple issues that emerge from the implementation of any new program model (e.g., faculty compensation, credit requirements, student tuition, program sequence, venue of course offerings, dissertation responsibilities) should be addressed and agreed upon from the outset with the understanding that new issues will surface. All stakeholders from both universities need to be involved in resolving both obvious and newly emerging issues.

At least two people, one from each institution, need to shepherd the program. Provision needs to be made for these point people to learn the culture of the other institution. The importance of the key players learning each other's culture is frequently cited in the literature. (Karasoff et al., 1996; Mattessich & Monsey, 1992; National Assembly of National Voluntary Health and Social Organizations, 1991; Nichols, Baird & Kayongo-Male, 2001). As with any good partnership, those involved need to be collegial and patient with one another (Karasoff et al., 1996; Mattessich & Monsey, 1992; Solomon, Boud, Leonitis, & Staron, 2001).

Plotting for a Successful Partnership

A survey of potential students interested in the program and the need for the program should be included early in the planning process (Kerka, 1997; Melaville et al., 1993). We found that the informal survey conducted by Kutztown University motivated the principal persons to move forward with the idea of a partnership. A formal agreement then needs to be written, reviewed by each university's legal counsel, and approved at all levels. The agreement needs to be reviewed periodically to allow for amendments that account for unforeseen circumstances (Mullen & Kochan, 2000).

The curriculum should be subject to review by faculty from both universities to adjust for changes in the field and accommodate student needs. We discovered, after several administrations of the comprehensive exams, that one Widener doctoral course should have been included in the original course sequence for Kutztown students. The liaisons and faculty are currently discussing the possibility of requiring this course for the third student cohort.

Setting the Stage for a Collaborative Culture

Face-to-face and electronic meetings between liaisons, administrators, and key faculty should be periodically conducted to address issues related to the program (Kadel, 1991; Nichols et al., 2001). Frequent communication between liaisons, administrators, and key faculty is a critical factor to success. Faculty who teach at the site should take the initiative to schedule meetings with students. Faculty liaisons also should schedule a meeting at least once a year at the cohort site to help alleviate students' anxiety about the geographical distance between their home base and the degree-granting institution (Simpson, Mercier, Streit, & Hill, 2002). Faculty liaisons need to make sure that information about such things as course schedules and the comprehensive examinations are shared with cohort students well in advance of the event (Weifand, 1999).

Policies need to be established and clearly articulated from the outset about such issues as faculty travel, the teaching of online courses, and student travel to avoid confusion and complaints. Policies and procedures for students should be established cooperatively by both institutions to insure that students know how to get answers to their questions and assistance with their problems. A policy handbook should be written that is specifically tailored to this program.

Conclusion (The End of the Tale)

A Tale of Two Cities (Dickens, 1859) ends with the character, Sydney Carton, sacrificing his life to save the woman he loves and her family. He travels to the guillotine, strengthened by the knowledge of what his sacrifice will accomplish. His final words are, "It is a far better thing that I do than I have ever done; it is a far, far better rest that I go to than I have ever known" (p. 368).

While our "Tale" wraps up on a less dramatic note, we have come away from it strengthened by the knowledge that our small sacrifices have served to accomplish our mission of creating a joint doctoral program. And, while unlike Sydney Carton, we cannot fully "rest" because our tale or joint program continues to unfold, we close in hoping our program continues to become even a "far better thing."

References

Combs, A., Miser, A. B., & Whitaker, K. S. (1999). *On becoming a school leader: Person centered challenge.* Alexandria, VA: Association of Curriculum Development.

Dickens, C. (1859). *A tale of two cities.* London: Waller J. Black .

English, F. W. (1992). *Educational administration: The human science.* New York: Harper Collins.

Kadel, S. (1991). *Interagency collaboration: Improving the delivery of services to children and families.* SERVE, Southeastern Regional Vision for Education. (ERIC Document Reproduction Service No:ED 349 511).

Kadel, S., & Routh, D. (1994). Implementing collaborative services: New challenges for practitioners and experts in reform. In L. Adler & S. Gardner (Eds.), *The politics of linking schools and social services: The 1993 Yearbook of the politics of education association* (pp. 24-36). Washington, DC: Falmer Press.

Karasoff, P., Blonsky, H., Perry, K., & Schear, T. (1996). *Integrated and collaborative services: A technical assistance planning guide.* San Francisco: San Francisco State University, California Research Institute.

Kerka, S. (1997). *Developing collaborative partnerships: Practice application brief.* Washington, DC: Office of Educational Research and Improvement, U.S. Departmentof Education.

Mattessich, P., & Monsey, B. (1992). *Collaboration: What makes it work: A review of research literature on factors influencing successful collaboration.* St. Paul, MN: Amherst Wilder Foundation.

Melaville, A., & Blank, M. (1991). *What it takes: Structuring interagency partnerships to connect children and families with comprehensive services.* Washington, DC: Education and Human Services Consortium.

Melaville, A., Blank, M., & Asayesh, G. (1993). Realizing the vision: A five-stage process. In A. Melaville, M. Blank, & G. Asayesh (Eds.), *Together we can* (pp. 19-21). Washington, DC: U.S. Department of Education & U.S. Department of Health and Human Services.

Mullen, C., & Kochan, F. (2000). Creating a collaborative leadership network: An organic view of change. *International Journal of Leadership in Education, 3*(3), 183-200.

National Assembly of National Voluntary Health and Social Welfare Organizations. (1991). *The community collaboration manual.* Washington, DC: Author.

Nichols, T., Baird, P., & Kayongo-Male, D. (2001). Partnerships offer promise and perils: A study of collaborations with state universities. *Tribal College Journal, 13*(2), 20-23.

Penney, S. (2001). Change and collaboration: The urban collaborative. *Metropolitan Universities: An International Forum, 12*(2), 44-48.

Robinson, E., & Mastny, A. (1989). *Linking school and community services.* Rutgers, NJ: Center for Community Education, School of Social Work.

Simpson, J., Mercier, G., Streit, T., & Hill, L. (2002). Trust building: The secret to highly collaborative partnerships. *Metropolitan Universities: An International Forum, 13,* 41-48.

Solomon, N., Boud, D., Leonitis, M., & Staron, M. (2001). Tale of two institutions: Exploring collaboration in research partnerships. *Studies in the Education of Adults, 33*(2), 135-42.

The American Heritage Dictionary of the English Language. (1981). Boston: Houghton Mifflin Company, p. 259.

View, V. A., & Amos, K. J. (1994). *Living and testing the collaborative process: A case study of community-based services integration.* Arlington, VA: National Center for Clinical Programs.

Weifand, M. (1999). *Improving the effectiveness of higher education institutions through inter- university co-operation: The case of Peking University.* (ERIC Document Reproduction Service No. ED 454793).

Winer, M., & Ray, K. (1994). *Collaboration handbook: Creating, sustaining, and enjoying the journey.* St. Paul, MN: Amherst H. Wilder Foundation.

Appendix A

Kutztown University

of the Pennsylvania State System of Higher Education
Kutztown, PA 19530
(610) 683-4000
TDD (610) 683-4499

DEPARTMENT OF ELEMENTARY EDUCATION

May 17, 1999

Dear Graduate Reading Alumnus,

The Graduate Reading Faculty are in the process of trying to establish an alliance with Widener University. The goal of developing this alliance is to offer the Widener doctoral program in Reading/Language Arts at Kutztown University.

Your work at Kutztown appears to be an excellent foundation for the Widener program. This effort is motivated by our wish to be a vehicle that continues providing leaders for communities we serve and to contributes to your continued growth. Enclosed please find a brief description.

The purpose of this letter is to get a general sense of the interest of our alumni. This is not asking for a commitment or an application. Would you please let us know your level of interest in pursuing a doctoral program (i.e. somewhat, very, absolutely).

It is hoped that you deem this request worthy of your consideration. I look forward to hearing from you. Please contact me at any of the following alternatives:
home: (610) 385-
         office: (610) 683-
         fax: (610) 683-

Sincerely,

Appendix B

 Kutztown University
of the Pennsylvania State System of Higher Education
Kutztown, PA 19530
(610) 683-4000
TDD (610) 683-4499

DEPARTMENT OF ELEMENTARY EDUCATION

November 15, 1999

Dear Graduate Reading Program Alumnus:

Enclosed please find summary information about the Widener Doctoral Program in Reading and Language Arts that has been established in alliance with Kutztown University. The program is to start in January 2000 by offering the first course (ED 712) in the sequence of required courses.

Please be advised that all interested parties are invited to a meeting on Thursday, December 9th at 6:00 in room 209 in the Beekey Building. Dr.   of Widener University and faculty from the Graduate Reading Program at Kutztown will be available at that time to answer questions. Dr.   will be the instructor of ED 712: History and Philosophy of Reading Education.

Please feel free to share information about this meeting with colleagues who may be interested in the program, but who have not been graduated from our reading program.

This is an exciting opportunity. It is hoped that you deem it worth your consideration if you are interested in further study. Please let me know if you plan to attend (RSVP   ).

Sincerely,